READERS AND DOERS OF THE WORD

THE FUN WAY

365 Days of Bible-Related Activities
for Families to read through the Bible in one year
and for use in the classroom.

by
Fern A. Ritchey

"Doers of the Word and Not Hearers Only"
--James 1:22

EDEN PUBLISHING
8635 West Sahara Ave., Ste. 459, The Lakes, NV 89117

PRINTING HISTORY OF THIS BOOK

First Edition © Copyright 1988 by Fern A. Ritchey and published May 1988 by Minute Man Press, Corning, NY.
Revised Second Edition © Copyright 1994 by Fern A. Ritchey and published March 1994 by Eden Publishing, 8635 West Sahara Avenue, Ste. 459, The Lakes, NV 89117.
New Cover Design by Don Manarina. Text Design and Technical Assistance provided by Norine V. Grzesik-Rathbone.

Library of Congress Catalog Card Number 94-70392
Library of Congress Cataloging in Publication Data
    Ritchey, Fern A. READERS AND DOERS OF THE WORD
      1. Educational Activities for Children and Adults.
      2. Bible-Related Crafts, Puzzles, Activities.
      3. Supplemental Educational Materials for Christian Ministry.
ISBN 1-884898-02-5

ACKNOWLEDGMENTS

    First, thank you loving Heavenly Father for the ideas in this book, for always quickly answering my plea as to how to make Bible study interesting, praying dynamic and witnessing fun.
    Second, thanks Donald, Joyce, Dale and grandchildren for supporting me through the years, cheering me on and for being willing to try out any new ideas.
    Third, thanks to all of you children, teens and others who rolled up your sleeves to earn money for mission trips, supporting a child overseas, giving a play, making marionettes for a Queen Esther show, memorizing Scripture or whatever the project. Thanks for zestfully carrying out the activities in this book. God will bless each one of you eternally, and in this present pilgrimage with Jesus our Companion who is the Way, the Truth and the Life.

Thanks also for permission to quote from:
(NKJ) The New King James Version, copyright 1984, Thomas Nelson, Inc., Publishers.
    This translation is used primarily throughout READERS AND DOERS OF THE WORD unless otherwise noted.
(GNB) The Good News Bible (Today's English Version), Old Testament copyright, American Bible Society, 1976; New Testament copyright, American Bible Society, 1966, 1972, 1976.
(TLB) The Living Bible, paraphrase, copyright 1971 by Tyndale House .

TABLE OF CONTENTS

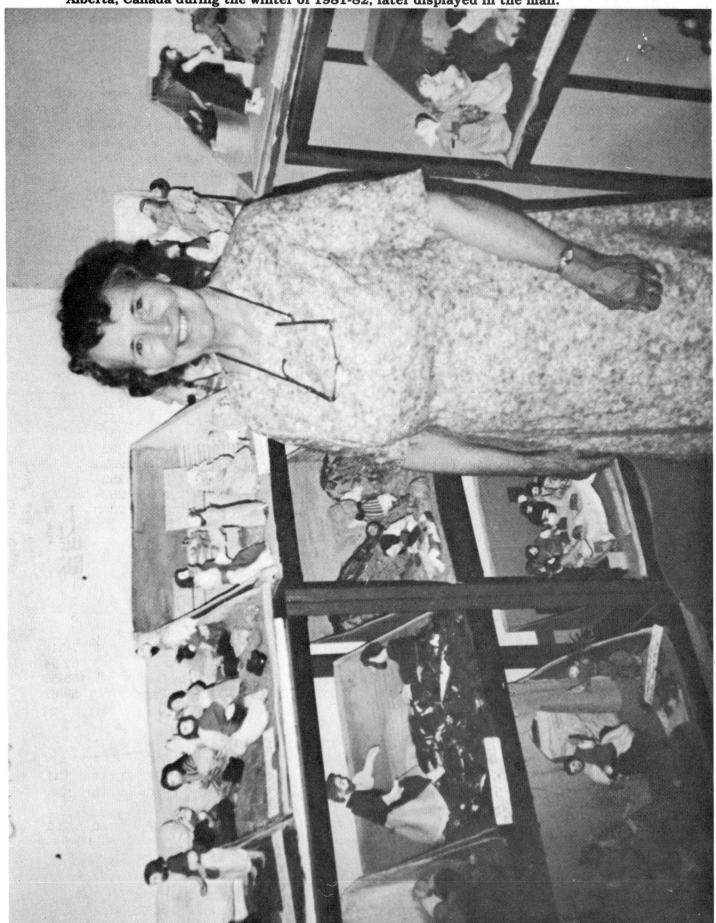

Author Fern Ritchey standing by scenes made by children at Rocky Mountain House, Alberta, Canada during the winter of 1981-82, later displayed in the mall.

BEFORE YOU START!

A TRUE STORY

The idea for putting together this book began to form many years ago at a little Baptist Church in Las Vegas. Nevada. I was asked to teach a class of 15 nine- and ten-year olds, mostly boys. I love children, so replied, "Sure!"

But they were a little more tricky to control than other classes I had worked with. In fact, all my special puppets, flannelgraphs, object lessons, and games didn't keep them quiet or orderly.

On Easter Sunday they were friskier than usual, so I decided to take them outside so as not to disturb the other classes. They sat along the low bank that is, all but two boys who ran to the rest room and two who climbed the tree behind us.

With a quick prayer for the Spirit's guidance, I started showing them lovely pictures of the life of Jesus, as I think it is so important to get the whole story at once, not just His birth at Christmas and His resurrection at Easter. We must grasp the whole magnificence of Jesus coming to earth, to grow up like us, overcome Satan, show God's love, healing, miracles, how to live His Life, and then His triumphant death on the Cross in our place and resurrection to give us eternal life with Him!

A few listened intently, two girls explored the fascinating articles in their Easter purses, and one boy tied his shoestring. The pictures of the storm at sea, walking on the water, healing the lepers, His transfiguration, and bringing Lazarus back to life were catching their interest. We were up to the Crucifixion.

"He has done so much for us," I explained. "We should do all we can for Him to thank Him for dying in our place, for paying the price for our sins. We should give Him our hearts and our lives."

One little boy boldly proclaimed, "I want to give my heart to Jesus!" The next one said, "I do, too." Then the first added, looking up into the tree, "Hey, you guys, come down here. This is the thing to do!"

The boys slid down, the others returned from the rest room; all listened quietly to the rest of the story.

I invited those who wanted to accept Jesus as their Savior to stand with me. Nine came! I had fleeting thoughts that someone in the church had witnessed my predicament and was praying for me. But, no! It was Jesus Himself drawing those dear little children into His arms. Jesus touched their hearts and they loved Him!

At the church service I described what had happened and urged prayer that these children would truly be transformed, born again. Tears of joy in many eyes promised support.

Next Sunday the class was at complete, eager attention, Bibles open, chairs still. They were changed! We took turns praying for definite needs, discussed the Bible story as it applied to us, they worked the flannelgraph presentation. Oh, the Spirit was doing a tremendous job!

The following Saturday we drove fifty miles to the mountains. Not minding the heat as I did, they climbed a hill while I watched from the car. When they returned, they told me they had prayed at the top. I was touched by how lovingly they responded to our Lord's presence.

As Mother's Day approached, I suggested we invite their mothers for a special program with every class member taking part. Eagerly they volunteered, one to read a Bible portion, another to pray, a girl to tell the flannelgraph story, a boy to report on the mountain trip. I volunteered to bring refreshments. As they made invitations, one little prince drew hearts and kisses all over his.

Mother's Day was as triumphant as Easter. The boys, like little gentlemen, stood while introducing their mothers. The program ran like clockwork without a word from me. The mothers and I sat there entranced. I didn't even have the fun of serving the goodies; they did it all, with finesse.

Each Sunday the children ecstatically told me of little victories in their homes. One boy said he and his father now talked together, that he had told his Dad about Jesus. A girl with several stepbrothers and sisters explained how well they were getting along. Some of the parents started attending the church services. Truly, these boys and girls have been born again; they were new creations in Christ Jesus. God was alive to them, and life was exciting and rich.

God can work in our lives like that, too. We can really know Him; He can be our greatest Friend; He can make life exciting and rich in Him. Let's do that as a part of God's family: Study the Bible together. Pray over problems. Thank the Lord for answers. Have fun working the puzzles and games. Invite friends to know Him, too.

SUGGESTIONS

WHEN? The best time for your family to be together may be just before bedtime, or right after supper; when you have at least a half-hour free together. Inevitably outside activities will interfere, but on such occasions at least pray together in a little circle so that each one feels God's presence and blessing going with him.

It may work bet to meet only two or three times on week nights, but spend more time on the weekends after chores are done and there is time to do craft projects. The goal is to make it so meaningful to the family as a union that no one will want to miss it.

BIBLE READING. Use modern language translations. There are a number to select from: New King James, New International Version, Good News, Living Bible, or use several to compare the stories.

If the children are too young to read, or their attention span is short, one of the older ones should study the Scripture ahead of time and tell the story. If the Bible verse is especially helpful, memorize it. Discuss the lessons learned and how they apply to daily living. We want to be "doers of the Word and not hearers only" (James 1:22). The younger children can be coloring as the Bible is read, or working on the project of the day. Keep the Bible reading time from becoming drawn out or boring.

PRAYER TIME. Feel free as a family unit to pray at all times: when difficulties arise, when decisions have to be made, or when thanks for answered prayer is timely. Let prayer be spontaneous, for God is with us all the time and everywhere. We can talk to Him in the car, at school, while working or playing, together or individually. What a privilege we have to be in His presence and His interest.

It is good to learn to pray aloud, sometimes in a circle holding hands, or kneeling when especially in earnest, or to clap for answered prayer! "To pray without ceasing" is to feel His presence and talk to Him silently or aloud at all times--to sense His companionship like a shining halo around us. I have experienced this since I was born again at age twelve, and I am now in my late seventies. What a glorious way to live! He truly wants to be "one with us."

Amazing examples of answered prayer in my own family are too numerous to relate them all, but we have always had a sense of God's leading, in His ability to meet our needs, both great and small. When our son Dale received a telegram to accept a full tuition scholarship to Carnegie Institute of Technology by the next day, he hesitated, because his dream was to attend Massachusetts Institute of Technology, but he didn't know whether they would offer him a scholarship. "God knows," I encouraged. "But how will we know?" he asked. "Let's ask Him," I replied. So we prayed, then opened the Bible, and there was the story of Peter's vision on the housetop to eat unclean food that all good is clean to God. That answer from God proved true: MIT didn't offer him tuition, but Dale had four years at CIT and went on for his Ph.D. at Cornell, God supplying the means every step of the way.

ACTIVITIES. This is the fun part. Our motto is: "Families for pray, play and display [witness] together, stay together!" The activities are arranged for all ages: preschool, children, teens, and adults. Infants and toddlers may be in bed, but if not, put them in a playpen with toys they enjoy, so that they will feel part of the group.

Don't feel obligated to do all the activities in this book. You may have others better suited to your family. The purpose is to grow in Christ together with enjoyment. The longer projects may be worked on at odd moments, Saturdays, when bored with the usual things. It's good to have something the children will enjoy doing after school. You may choose to do some of the projects another year. Invite initiative, creativity, singing, writing, painting, debating an issue. Encourage family "council meeting" for family outings, parties, witnessing, privileges, chores, allowances, supporting a child overseas, vacations. Each member should have a part. When witnessing, even the youngest child can hand out little gifts and say, "We love you." How that sweetness will linger in the heart of the recipient."

While a copy machine is ideal, many of us may have to rely on carbon paper or tracing pictures to make enough copies for everyone in the family. For word puzzles, take turns circling a word.

Keep a notebook of special subjects you are interested in, so that you will have references handy when needed, such as Angels, Numbers, Prophecies, How God Communicates with Us, Healings, Miracles, How God Uses Children, the Ordinary People, etc. Mark your Bibles for outstanding verses, with dates and lessons learned.

Keep a well lighted work area it doesn't need to be spotless--with storage shelves for supplies, and a table to work on.

SUPPLIES. Most of the activities are made with things around the house, so start gathering boxes of all sizes and other items listed below:

Sunday School pictures, stories	beads, jewelry, sequins, glitter
Christmas and greeting cars	cords, nylon hose, fabrics, trims
pictures from magazines, calendars	scissors, knife, punch, pointed pliers
backs of calendars for posters	crayons, paints, brushes, felt pens
construction paper, newspapers	masking tape, scotch tape, glue
popsicle sticks, chenille cleaners	shells, cones, bark, dried flowers
scrap wallboard, tiles, glass, plastic	eraser, ruler, florist wire, 3X5" cards

APPENDIX. Detailed helps and answers to the puzzles, word blocks, quizzes, and additional information are listed by the Day in the Appendix. Special holiday projects are included. Following the Appendix is the INDEX listing activities by title with the Day the activity is presented.

INTRODUCTION TO BIBLE STUDY, NEW TESTAMENT

The Bible is divided into two large sections: the Old Testament beginning with the creation and history of God's people until the coming of Jesus as Savior; and the New Testament telling of Jesus' ministry on earth, the start of the Church [all Christians] and instructions to the Church. Each Testament ends with prophecies.

Since it is of the utmost importance that we know Jesus as our Savior and Lord and be filled with the Spirit, we will study the New Testament first. In a later year you will find it fascinating to read from Genesis to Revelation and see, from God's viewpoint for this is his Book how intricately He works through the ages to bring about His plans, how the thread of salvation through faith in Jesus is woven from Genesis 3:15 to the end of the Bible, how prophecies are fulfilled, how true the Bible is, how inspired by the Spirit.

THE GOSPELS. The first four books in the New Testament are called the gospels as they tell about the life of Christ, the good news.

Matthew, a Hebrew and one of Jesus' disciples, wrote to the _Jews_ about Jesus the _King,_ the promised Messiah.

Mark, follower to Jesus and later missionary aide to Paul, wrote to the _Romans_ about Jesus as the _Servant._

Luke, a doctor and _Greek_ who traveled with Paul, presented Jesus as the _Son of Man,_ meeting man's requirements as the _Gentiles_ need Him also.

John, the apostle closest to Jesus in love and understanding, presented Jesus as the _Son of God_ (the Word, Light, Shepherd, Vine), bringing union between God and all _Christians,_ both Jews and Gentiles, the Church.

The first three gospels are termed Synoptic, as they present the ministry of Jesus historically; the gospel of John presents Jesus Himself, in a close, loving relationship to us.

THE BOOK. The Holy Spirit inspired about 40 authors to write 66 books [39 in the Old Testament, 27 in the New] over a period of 1500 years, yet there is God's finger from beginning to end, no contradictions, His loving instructions to us.

GOD LOVED THE WORLD SO VERY MUCH

(One Christmas season, as I was trying to write a poem on all that God has given us in Christ, the Spirit said put it to the tune of "Danny Boy," so it becomes a beautiful carol!)

God loved the world so much He gave His only Son,
To bridge the gap that God and man be one;
In starlit night He brought Him forth to dwell on earth;
With angels bright He heralded His birth.
    God loved so much, He gave to us His precious child,
    So pure and sweet, so holy and so mild,
    That we in Christ may see the righteous way to live
    With love so deep, our hearts to Him we gladly give.
The gift God gave is greater far than words can say,
For Jesus is the Light, the Truth, the Way,
The Bread of Life, the Water ne'er to thirst again,
Abundant Life, with whom to die is gain;
    The Prince of Peace who never will from us depart,
    The Morning Star who rises in our heart,
    The mighty Rock who keeps us firm unto the end,
    The open Door, Good Shepherd, and unfailing Friend.
'Twould be enough, if this were all our Father gave,
But greater yet God's plan our souls to save:
'Twas on the cross our Lord, our Savior died for man!
He suffered loss; He was the spotless Lamb.
    He gave His life that we might free and sinless be;
    He rose from death to share eternity!
    Oh, how our souls cry out, We love You, love You so!
    Oh, fill us now that we like You may truly grow!
Oh, precious Lord, as Intercessor now You pray
We feel Your presence in us day by day;
Your yoke is light--our burdens You so quickly bear;
As Word of Life, You guide with wisdom rare.
    Oh, Son of God, in faith we pray that we may be
    So one in thought, so one in harmony,
    That through our lives Your loving care may others touch
    'Till they will know *God loved the world so very much!*

PUBLISHER'S NOTE TO READERS:
    After much deliberation, the publishers finally opted to keep the 365 days of Bible-related activities in the author's own typewritten format. When several typesetters failed to capture and preserve the unique qualities and spiritual impact of this book, the publishers decided any other method of presentation detracted from the author's spontaneous "hands on," Spirit-led approach.
    May you and your family derive great benefit from Mrs. Ritchey's homey, practical methods and rich knowledge of the Bible.

GOD'S COMMAND!

"LOVE THE LORD YOUR GOD WITH ALL YOUR HEART,
    WITH ALL YOUR SOUL, AND WITH ALL YOUR STRENGTH.
NEVER FORGET THESE COMMANDS THAT I AM GIVING YOU TODAY.
    TEACH THEM TO YOUR CHILDREN.
REPEAT THEM WHEN YOU ARE AT HOME AND WHEN YOU ARE AWAY,
    WHEN YOU ARE RESTING AND WHEN YOU ARE WORKING.
TIE THEM ON YOUR ARMS AND WEAR THEM ON YOUR FOREHEADS AS A REMINDER.
    WRITE THEM ON THE DOORPOSTS OF YOUR HOUSES AND ON YOUR GATES."
--DEUTERONOMY 6:5-9 (GNB)

       These are commands from God! We are to love Him with everything within us. We are to put reminders around us to remember Him and His Word. **READERS AND DOERS OF THE WORD** will help us do that with fun. Since we will live with God eternally, now is the time to know Him as our Best Friend and He is! Now is the time to hide His Word in our hearts. Now is the time to find His plan for our lives! Now is the time to tell others of His extravagant gift of salvation, for He is the Way, the Truth and the Life!

DAY 1.   Matthew 1, 2
          A Son is Born

Matthew 1:23 Behold a virgin shall
be with child, and bear a Son, and
they shall call His name Immanuel,
which is translated, "God with us."

Prayer: Thank You for sending Jesus
          as our Savior and Lord.

COMMENTS: So that the Jews would know that Jesus was the true promised Messiah, Matthew lists His genealogy, including Abraham to whom the promise was given, David the God-chosen King, and Solomon the wisest king.

ACTIVITY: As we read the Gospels, there will be two main activities:

A.   Younger children will make PICTURES of the Life of Christ for books. They will have moving parts to help tell the stories.

B.   For older children and teens, a Diorama of SCENES of the Life of Christ will be made using half-boxes, 12 x 12 x 15" (approximately), with paper mache backgrounds and people made of popsicle sticks, clay heads, and dressed from scrap materials. The scenes may be shown at malls, fairs, churches, institutions, wherever God leads you to tell the story of Jesus. You will require space such as a basement, garage, or a neighborhood club room, church basement, or shop. This is a good project to invite other children to help. Keep it available to work on at odd times as it will take months to complete. (See Appendix, Day 1), for detailed lists of Jesus' Ministry, maps of locations of the scenes, and detailed instructions.

Today, our story is of the visit of the wise men to the "child" in the home in Bethlehem. First, we give instructions for the A-Picture scene; then the B-Picture scene.

A.   PICTURE. The first picture in the book is of the wise men (astrologers) presenting their gifts to the child Jesus in His home (note they did not present the gifts in the stable when Jesus was an infant, verse 2:11).

Use carbon
paper to trace
the wise man
on heavy paper.

1. Trace the moving part - wise men. Cut out.
Put scotch tape on the back of the man and the picture where the brad will go through to make the wise man bow in worship. The tape will reinforce the paper. Punch a hole in the two black spots. Insert a brad. Then open the wings of the brad. Color the picture.
Scotch-tape a patch over the wings of the brad so that it will not catch on another picture.

2. Punch holes and put the picture in a binder.
Find a picture of Jesus to paste on the front of your notebook. Print a title such as, "My Friend Jesus" above the picture and your name at the bottom.

NOTE: Each child makes his or her own book.

brad

B.   HOW TO MAKE FIGURES FOR THE DIORAMA SCENES

Pray that God will give you the
ability to do a super job.

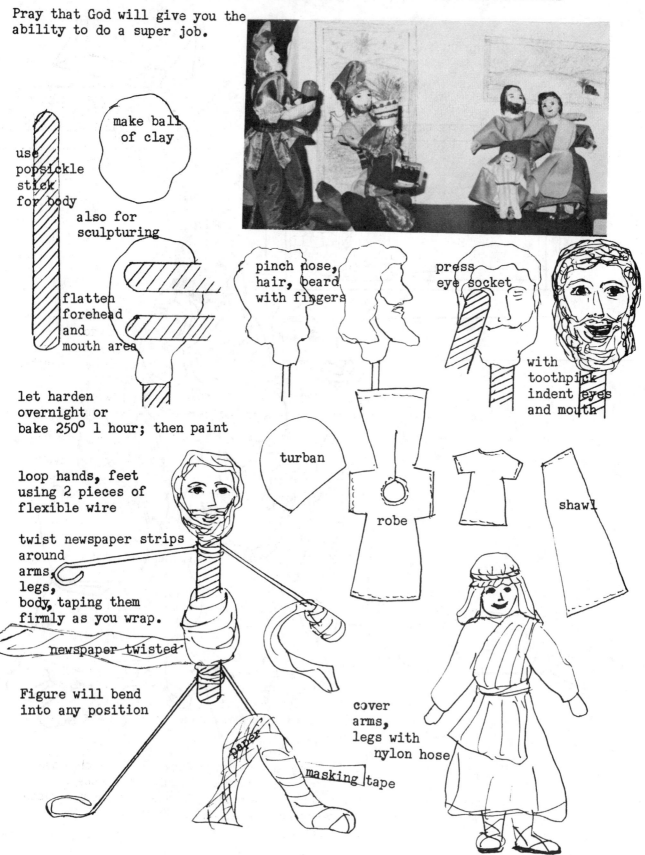

make ball
of clay

use
popsickle
stick
for body

also for
sculpturing

flatten
forehead
and
mouth area

pinch nose,
hair, beard
with fingers

press
eye socket

with
toothpick
indent eyes
and mouth

let harden
overnight or
bake 250° 1 hour; then paint

loop hands, feet
using 2 pieces of
flexible wire

twist newspaper strips
around
arms,
legs,
body, taping them
firmly as you wrap.

newspaper twisted

Figure will bend
into any position

paper

masking tape

turban

robe

shawl

cover
arms,
legs with
nylon hose

B.   SCENE. For the diorama scene, use a cardboard box about 15 x 12 x 12". Cut diagonally along the sides as shown. You may be able to use the box for 2 backgrounds.

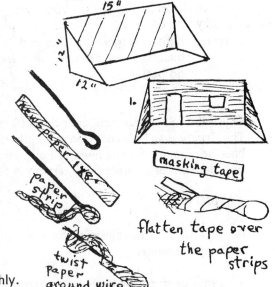

1. Paint the inside to represent the home with wooden door and window. Paint the sides also, continuing around.

2. Use blocks of wood for seat and a table.

3. People. Follow the instructions, using a popsickle stick for the backbone. Twist two pieces of wire to form arms and legs. Tear strips of newspaper about 1" x 8" to twist around the arms, legs, and body to give shape. As you do an arm or leg, cover it with masking tape to hold in place. It is tricky to accomplish, but if you hold the arm in your left hand with the newspaper twisted about 4", then with a 6" strip of masking tape in your right hand, flatten the hand portion, then turn the tape over-hand on to arm continuing up arm smoothly.

4. Clay Heads. Use cornstarch, baking powder clay (recipe in Appendix). Knead a ball larger than the size head, so as to bring clay down around the neck holding on to the shoulder wire so that it won't pull off. Another popsickle stick makes a handy sculpturing tool. Follow the pictured instructions. Stand the figures in a narrow bowl to dry overnight.

Paint the heads, hands and legs, using tempera colors. The Israelites were tanned, had black or brown hair and eyes. The men wore beards. Felt pens are best for shaping eyebrows, eyes, and mouth.

5. Clothes. If the legs are going to show, as with fishermen, take small patches of nylon hose, tan color, and stitch up the backs of the legs, pulling the hose tightly over foot and leg. Add felt sandals and stitch across like laces. Roman soldiers will wear leather boots. Use felt or scrapes of gloves.

Be sure to use plain or striped materials for the robes, shawls, turbans (not flowered prints). If you sew the hems and cuffs on a machine, leave the robe flat. Sew around the hems. Then sew the side seams. It's much simpler to handle.

For the wise men, add bright colors, silks, and fancy trims. Find small objects for the gifts. Paint them gold or glue on sequins, etc.

6. Bend the wire to have the figures seated or kneeling. Attach the family to the back of the background box with a piece of wire encircling their waists, and fitted through two punched holes in the box behind them. Twist to hold in place. Flatten the wire ends, and put masking tape over them so as not to scratch anything. Attach wire similarly to the kneeling legs of the wise men. Insert the wire through two punched holes in the bottom of the box. Twist, flatten wire ends, and tape flat.

7. Make only one scene for each story. (The pictures can be copied and each child can color and have his or her own book.) All the family can work together on the scenes, deciding or volunteering who will paint, sculpture, sew, etc. Or, select a scene per person so each member of the family will be making an entire scene by himself.

✝✝✝✝✝

DAY 2.   Matthew 3, 4
Baptism

Prayer: Father, forgive our sins and
mistakes; we are sorry and will
do better.

Matthew 3:16-17 Then Jesus, when He had
baptized, came up immediately from the
water; and behold, the heavens were open to
Him, and He saw the Spirit of God descending
like a dove and slighting upon Him. And
suddenly a voice came from heaven, saying,
"This is My beloved Son, in whom I am well
pleased."

COMMENTS: Jesus was conceived by the Spirit and also anointed by the Spirit at His baptism.
The Trinity was present: God the Father spoke, the Spirit descended like a dove, and Jesus was
blessed. Jesus did not need to be baptized as He had never sinned, but He did it as an example for
us. Baptism is a symbol: immersion is cleansing from sin, rising is entering the new life in the Spirit.

ACTIVITY:

A. PICTURE. The animation for the baptism picture is the dove descending
to Jesus' shoulder.

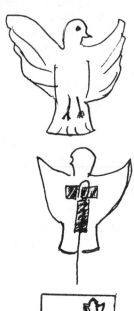

1. Draw or trace the dove on to cardboard. Cut out. Use florist wire or
lightweight household wire about 8" long to pull the dove down. To attach
the wire to the back of the dove, bend the top of the wire like a hook.
Place flat against the dove. Insert scotch tape in and out of it, then put
another piece of tape above the taped wire to keep the wire from slipping out.

2. Trace and color the picture. Locate the two little lines at shoulder and
water's edge. The wire will go in at the shoulder and out at water. On the
back of the picture, reinforce the slits with scotch tape. Then cut a small
opening with knife or razor blade.

3. As you tell the story, pull the wire down, showing the dove descending
on Jesus' shoulder.

B. SCENE. Color the back and sides of the cardboard box with blue sky, distant
hills, and low trees close by the bank of the river. Show the river coming from
a distance, gradually getting a darker blue as it merges with the painted river
in the bottom of the box. For perspective, the colors are brighter and sunnier
in the foreground, and lighter and more bluish in the distance.

1. To make the riverbank, crumple newspaper into balls and tape down with masking tape. Then
cover it with strips of newspaper dipped into flour-water paste (1 cup of flour to 3 or 4 cups of
water). Dip the strips into the water. Slip off the excess with two fingers. Then smooth the strip
over the crumpled "bank" until it is entirely covered. Let dry overnight. Apply tan or brown latex
paint. Stick in weed "trees" by punching holes in the paper mache.

2. The figures of Jesus and John the Baptist are from the waist up.
John wore a camel's hair robe, so use rough brown material. Jesus'
clothing will be similar in all the scenes - white robe, blue shawl.
Keep Him the center of attention. He will have a glowing
countenance. Try to sculpture and paint character into all the faces.
Jesus was a joyful person, loving and kind.

3. Use blue enamel paint for the river. Make reflections in the
water with short white, wavy lines.

4. For a light from heaven, use a triangular piece of plastic painted light yellow to come down from top of background box to behind Jesus. Make a clay dove and attach its wire feet to Jesus' shoulder.

Scenes pictured in this book were made by children in two groups. One was a Baptist youth group, ages 7 - 15, in Homesite Baptist Church in Las Vegas, Nevada, who displayed 30 scenes in the Las Vegas Mall during Easter, 1971. The other was a Junior High Sunday School class in Church of the Nazarene, Rocky Mountain House, Alberta, Canada. This second group earned their way for two trips to teach others to make the scenes. In 1984, we spent Easter at Tijuana, Mexico, teaching 60 little Mexican children to make the scenes, neither group knowing the other's language. In December, 1985, another trip was make to Los Angeles, teaching Bangladesh immigrants to make the scenes. Both times, we flew to California, rented a van, and visited Disneyland and other sights. (You will find projects in this book of ways we earned the money for these trips.)

✝✝✝✝✝

DAY 3.   Matthew 5
             Sermon

Matthew 5:16 Let your light so shine before men, that they may see your good works and glorify your Father in heaven.

Prayer: Help us to be a light to the world.

COMMENTS: The Sermon on the Mount (chapters 5 - 7) contains vital messages from Jesus for each one of us. He illustrated them with everyday objects or activities so that they would constantly remind us of His words. Memorize the outstanding verses for they will come to your mind many times in the future when you have decisions to make or are going through trials. Jesus said some astounding things: to love your enemies, do good to them. Do you think loving people who hurt you, forgiving them, and keeping friends with them would help? Let's test it and see if it works the next time a quarrel comes up.

ACTIVITY: For this lesson, we'll make use of Jesus' illustrations, like an object lesson. For verses 5:14-16, use a flashlight or candle. In a dark room, put out all the lights except the candle or flashlight. Does it help to see your way around? Now put a bowl over the light. Suppose you were lost in the woods. How much would a flashlight help? Now imagine you are adrift in a rowboat far from shore. It is too dark to see the shore. Would a light in a house help? It would be a guide, just as our lights from our living like Jesus is a help to those who are lost, having trouble, or are seeking a better way to live. If we don't tell others who need our encouragement and guidance, it is like putting a bowl over our influence for good.

How would you demonstrate salt as an object lesson?

✝✝✝✝✝

DAY 4. Matthew 6
Don't Worry

Prayer: Forgive us for worrying;
we trust You.

Matthew 6:26 Look at the birds of the air, for they neither sow nor reap nor gather into barns; yet your heavenly Father feeds them. Are you not of more value than they?

COMMENTS: Worry is wasted time and energy. Let's form the habit of putting our cares into the capable hands of our Heavenly Father. List things we worry over. How might God take care of them? He does the impossible!

ACTIVITY: Pre-schoolers - Look through old magazines, catalogs, and Sunday School papers for pictures of birds, insects, animals, and pictures of people. With help, cut them out and put them in folders - one for birds, people, etc.

The rest of you work the Word Block containing the names of 33 birds, fowl, and insects mentioned in the New King James version (other translations may have other names). Find the names using the Scripture references. Circle them. They may appear forward, backward, up, down, or diagonally. All names in the Scripture verses are not in the word block. (Answers are in the Appendix, Day 4).

	1	2	3	4	5	6	7	8	9	10	11	12	13
1	G	R	A	S	S	H	O	P	P	E	R	F	H
2	A	E	S	P	R	A	X	I	E	A	G	L	E
3	N	D	W	A	O	W	X	G	V	M	F	I	N
4	T	I	A	R	O	K	N	E	R	X	A	E	X
5	O	P	N	R	S	A	N	O	X	X	L	S	X
6	S	S	M	O	T	H	W	N	W	C	C	L	S
7	T	E	D	W	E	X	L	H	R	L	O	I	W
8	R	A	O	X	R	X	O	I	I	X	N	C	A
9	I	G	V	A	X	R	C	A	K	I	T	E	L
10	C	U	E	X	N	K	U	C	R	A	N	E	L
11	H	L	B	E	E	Q	S	T	O	R	K	X	O
12	F	L	T	T	B	A	T	H	E	R	O	N	W

Deuteronomy 14:12-18   Matthew 23:37   Exodus 23:28   Acts 12:23

Genesis 15:9   Matthew 26:34   Exodus 8:21   1 Samuel 24:14

Matthew 10:29   Leviticus 11:22   Matthew 23:24   Exodus 8:16

Isaiah 38:14   Proverbs 6:6   Matthew 6:19   Leviticus 11:18 KJ

Numbers 11:32   Judges 14.8   Job 8:14

✝✝✝✝✝

DAY 5.   Matthew 7
            Ask, See, Knock

Matthew 7:7 Ask, and it will be given to you; seek, and you will find; knock, and it will be opened to you.

Prayer: Father, we present these special needs for Your help.

COMMENTS: Memorize Matthew 7:7. It tells us to put action into our prayers. It also tells us not to give up, to keep trying in many ways.

ACTIVITY: To teach the verse to pre-schoolers, use 3 drawings: mouth, eyes, and door with hand knocking. Have them repeat the parts with the pictures. For older ones, use cardboard blockouts to fill in parts of the verse.

You probably noticed that this verse is an acrostic (a word formed with the first letters of several words):

A sk
   S eek
      K nock

Here's another one:

F oresaking
A ll
I
   T ake
  H im

Make others using love, peace, power, service, etc. Use a concordance (there may be one in the back of your Bible) to look up the word you choose, and read the word relating to it, then make an acrostic.

✝✝✝✝✝

DAY 6.   Matthew 8, 9
            Healing

Matthew 8:16-17a When evening had come, they brought to Him many who were demon-possessed. And He cast out the spirits with a word, and healed all who were sick, that Scripture might be fulfilled.

Prayer: Thank You, Lord, for Your healing power, which is effective today, too.

COMMENTS: Jesus healed <u>all</u> who came to Him. That was part of His prophesied mission. In a notebook, have a page for prophesies and list these:
Matthew 1:22-23 fulfilled the prophesy in Isaiah 7:14
Matthew 2:5-6 - Micah 5:2   Matthew 2:16-18 - Jeremiah 31:15
Matthew 2:14-15 - Hosea 11:1   Matthew 8:16-17 - Isaiah 53:4-5
There are many other prophecies fulfilled in the New Testament which are proof of the authenticity of God's Word and that He is in charge of the world.

ACTIVITY: A. PICTURE. This is a picture of Jesus healing people. Trace the girl. Color and cut her out. Reinforce the brad hole with scotch tape on the reverse sides of the girl and the picture. Punch holes and insert the brad. When telling the story of Jesus healing the girl, lift her to stand up.

B. SCENE. This is a joyful scene. Use bright colors in sky and background. People are dancing and clapping with job. Dress the beggar in tattered clothes.

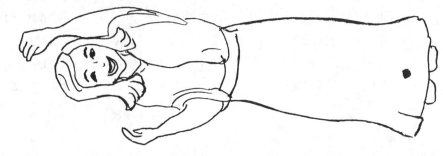

DAY 7.   Matthew 10, 11
            Come to Me

Matthew 11:28 Come to Me, all you who labor and are heavy laden, and I will give you rest.

Prayer: Thank Jesus for carrying our burdens.

COMMENTS: Jesus not only knows our names, our personalities, but every heartache, every trial we bear. He yearns to carry them for us, to fold us in His arms of love. The yoke was a wooden frame for a team of animals to pull the load together. That's what Jesus means - He wants to share our load, to pull with us. He makes it easy and companionable. Imagine! Traveling the highway of life with our Creator, our Savior and Lord as our Friend and Companion; seeing life with Him, getting His viewpoint, growling like Him. Tough times become heaven on earth as we are yoked with Him.

ACTIVITY: Make a poster on Jesus Cares. From a Sunday School paper, put a picture of Jesus in the center. Surround Him with pictures of all types of people, some working, some crying, blind poor, sick, paperboy in a blizzard, street people hunting for food, etc. Consider how we can help them.

✝✝✝✝✝

DAY 8.   Matthew 12
            Accounting

Matthew 12:36. But I say to you that for every idle word men may speak, they will give account of it in the day of judgment.

Prayer: Seek God's forgiveness for our wrong-speaking.

COMMENTS: How sobering! We will eventually be judged by our own words. A huge computer (perhaps in our own minds) keeps accurate account. Let's watch what we say, be honest, kindly, encouraging, uplifting, witnessing of Jesus' love and caring. "Finally, brethren, whatever things are true, whatever things are noble, whatever things are just, whatever things are pure, whatever things are lovely, whatever things are of good report, if there is any virtue and if there is anything praiseworthy - meditate on these things." (Philippians 4:8)

ACTIVITY: Use an old dart game (or make one with a board and suction cups). With chalk, designate areas: good words, gossip, lies, back-biting, complaining, ridiculing, anger, compliments, praise, encouragement, etc. Keep score of good words (+ 5 pts.) and bad words (- 3 pts.). Top score wins.

✝✝✝✝✝

DAY 9.   Matthew 13
            Kingdom

Matthew 13:44 Again, the kingdom of heaven is like treasure hidden in a field, which a man found and hid; and for joy over it he goes and sells all that he has and buys that field.

Prayer: Help us to treasure heavenly things.

COMMENTS: Jesus said the Kingdom is within us, now. We are children of the King of kings. Let's walk tall, speak wisely, and take on the role of a prince or princess in God's Kingdom.

ACTIVITY: Using the Parable of the Sower as an object lesson, put sections in a long window box for stony, thorny, trampled or good soil. Plant seeds. Watch them grow or die. Compare the soil with our own response to God's Word sown in our hearts.

✝✝✝✝✝

DAY 10. Matthew 14
Walk on Water

Prayer: Help us to do the mighty
things, the miraculous things
that You want to accomplish in us.

Matthew 14:29 So He said, "Come." And when Peter had come down out of the boat, he walked on the water to go to Jesus. But when he saw the wind was boisterous, he was afraid; and beginning to sink he cried out, saying, "Lord, save me!"

COMMENTS: What unprecedented faith to step into the sea and walk on the water! Had it been a calm morning, Peter may have walked the entire way to Jesus, but frightening waves seized his faith and his feet. To accomplish the impossible, we must keep our eyes on Jesus, listen to His words, and trust Him to keep our faith strong. Jesus never fails us! He lifts us to victory; and with Him, we conquer; even if we stub our toe or fall along the way, He lifts us!

ACTIVITY:

A. Picture. Color sky dark with dawn light at horizon; waves dark with white tips. Cut out Peter. Fold tab sides to make it firmer to pull him down into the water, then raise him. If tab isn't strong enough, use wire.

Note the two straight lines in the water. Put scotch tape along the lines on back side. Slit the lines and insert Peter, pulling his feet down as shown.

B. Scene. This is a windy scene with high waves. Paint background sky dark with dawn light. Crumple paper and tape down to make waves. Cover with paper mache' flour-water paste. Use navy-colored enamel paint for the tossing waves and add white tips.

Make Jesus' head and arms and legs of clay. Peter's head and arms are made the same way with both reaching for each other. Put starch or Elmer's glue on the clothing to make them windswept (in the same direction). Add a small cardboard boat in distance.

✝✝✝✝✝

DAY 11. Matthew 15, 16
Our Cross

Prayer: Let us dedicate our lives to
the Lord, to give our all to Him.

Matthew 16:24-25 Then Jesus said to His disciples, "If anyone desires to come after Me, let him deny himself, and take up his cross, and follow Me. For whoever desires to save his life will lose it, and whoever loses his life for My sake will find it."

COMMENTS: When we give all to Christ, we gain everything. If we give nothing of ourselves, eventually we lose all. Never hesitate to trust God with the important things in life: education, friends, activities, work, marriage, children, future, vacation, money, and death. He has the master plan for our lives. He will never forsake us.

ACTIVITY: In "saving our lives," let's look around to see in what ways we can help others bear their crosses. An elderly couple may like a picnic with a younger family. A working mother may appreciate a volunteer (without pay) baby sitter. We might help a sick child by giving him a box with a toy, balloon, crayons and coloring book, scissors, glue, pictures from magazines for a scrapbook, raisins, or dried fruit. What about a flower for Mom; a note of thanks in Dad's lunchbox; helping your brother or sister with a chore; a note on the bulletin board - "You did well on that test!;" volunteering to keep the yard mowed; or assisting teacher in cleaning the schoolroom, or helping the boss after work? What about filling the gas tank or washing the car after using it? Or, unasked, wash the dishes, take out the trash, or clean your room?

✝✝✝✝✝

DAY 12. Matthew 17, 18
       Agree

Prayer: Take God at His Word; believe
           He always answers.

Matthew 18:19 And I tell you more: whenever two of you on earth agree about anything you pray for, it will be done for you by My Father in heaven (GNB)

COMMENTS: What a promise! As a family discusses prayer needs of members of the family; goals; needs of relatives and neighbors, of the nation, the world. Make a prayer list, definite prayers with a date when the prayer was asked and the date when God answered it. Include needs of missionaries. Pray the natives will understand and respond to the leading of the Spirit. Uphold leaders, people in authority, pastors, teachers, governors, presidents, kings, prisoners, the ill, the starving children, and orphans overseas.

ACTIVITY: The Transfiguration of Jesus is astounding. Here He was praying, then all of a sudden Peter, James and John witnessed Him in His heavenly glory, with Elijah and Moses talking to Him about His soon trial, death and resurrection. Let's pray particularly that in the picture and scene He may appear glorious.

A. PICTURE. The animation for this scene is to pull the figures out with a wire. Color them. Cut out the transformed people. Color and cut the slit in the picture, reinforcing the back of the slit with scotch tape.

Be sure the upright block on the 3 men is longer than the slit. The pull-out should cover Jesus kneeling.

B. SCENE. Dress Jesus in silky, white cloth with glitter in his hair and on his arms, hands and feet. Dress Moses and Elijah in white robes, the disciples normal attire.

The scene is a mountaintop. Use taped-down paper mache, with boulders, bits of plastic greenery, and a few plastic flowers.

✝✝✝✝✝

DAY 13. Matthew 19, 20
           Possible

Matthew 19:26 But Jesus looked at them and said to them, "With men this is impossible, but with God all things are possible."

Prayer: Help us to pray with the faith that You can do the impossible.

COMMENTS: The disciples were surprised that rich men would have trouble getting to heaven, that riches distract us from depending upon God. But, Jesus said that all things are possible with God!

ACTIVITY: We learn to be tricky on occasions - not to let money trick us into greediness; but to twist it around to use money for God.

Here is a tricky message. Can you read it? Let everyone try, then check the answer (Appendix, Day 13). Make some tricky verses or slogans as a witness, such as - Jesus Never Fails; Give God Prime Time; God Does the Impossible; or Try God.

DAY 14. Matthew 21, 22
           Believe

Matthew 21:22 And all things, whatever you ask in prayer, believing, you will receive.

Prayer: Help us to truly believe!

COMMENTS: It is important to believe that God will answer our prayers. We must envision it as answered and act as though it already was - take steps to help achieve it. Jesus praised those who believed, who stood firm that God would answer, particularly for healing. But, we must remember that we are to do everything to God's glory, to further His work, to think as He would. We must not ask amiss - for our greediness, or self-glory, or laziness.

ACTIVITY: Jesus used a fig tree as an object lesson. The Bible names other trees, plants, and flowers. See how many you can find in the word block. These references might help you find some of them - 41 are in the New King James, and Luke 6:1 and Isaiah 44:14 are in some other versions:

Mark 15:17	Isaiah 35:1	Ezekiel 27:15	Luke 12:27
Exodus 25:33	Luke 19:4	Hosea 4:13	Ezekiel 4:9
Song of Solomon 2:3	Psalm 137:2	Hosea 10:4	Judges 9:14
Isaiah 44:14	Luke 21:29	Joshua 2:6	Ezekiel 23:24
Ezekiel 27:17	Isaiah 41:19	2 Samuel 6:5	Exodus 30:23
Numbers 11:5	Exodus 12:8	Exodus 2:3	Judges 15:5
Genesis 40:10	Matthew 13:31	Ezekiel 41:18	1 Samuel 14:2
Matthew 13:25	Luke 11:42		

The younger children can look through magazines for trees, plants, and flowers. Use old garden catalogs. Let them sort and put them in folders. Use them later for bookmarks, scrapbooks, or gifts to others.

✝✝✝✝✝

41 Plants and Trees of the Bible

	1	2	3	4	5	6	7	8	9	10	11	12	13	14	15
1	O	L	I	V	E	B	O	N	Y	E	K	H	X	M	B
2	A	N	B	A	R	L	E	Y	L	C	H	S	T	U	U
3	K	Q	I	X	R	A	L	P	O	P	E	A	G	S	L
4	X	N	R	O	H	T	P	L	K	E	R	D	R	T	R
5	X	C	I	N	N	A	M	O	N	E	B	X	A	A	U
6	B	O	U	X	X	E	L	I	L	I	E	S	P	R	S
7	R	R	F	C	H	H	P	M	Y	R	T	L	E	D	H
8	A	N	I	L	E	W	X	W	O	L	L	I	W	X	C
9	M	X	R	E	A	M	E	L	O	N	R	O	S	E	A
10	B	A	L	M	R	X	B	E	A	N	D	F	I	G	N
11	L	M	L	A	P	O	M	E	G	R	A	N	A	T	E
12	E	R	O	M	A	C	Y	S	R	X	M	I	N	T	X

†††††

Day 15. Matthew 23, 24
Signs

Prayer: Help us to be alert to Your signs
to keep busy winning souls.

Matthew 24:7 For nation will rise against nation, and kingdom against kingdom. And there will be famines, pestilences, and earthquakes in various places.

COMMENTS: Although we will not know the time our Lord will return, we are told to watch and pray. Many signs have already come to pass. Reading our newspapers and listening to the news on TV and radio warns us that Jesus will return soon. That will be a time of rejoicing for us. But, if friends or loved ones do not know Jesus as Savior, it will be sad.

ACTIVITY: Make a poster of current signs of the times: earthquakes; famines; various evils; crimes; war; drugs; abortion; and seekers of pleasures more than of God. Put these on one side under Satan's Works. On the other side, past God's Works: missionaries world-wide; radio-TV world-wide telling the Gospel; Bible translated into thousands of languages; large churches; programs to feed the starving; housing the homeless; sponsoring orphans and street children; work with prisoners; movies of Jesus; Bible study groups, Christian athletic groups; Christian Policemen; Teen Missions; Work Missions; modern-language Bible versions; rehabilitation programs; summits for peace and disarmament; groups to overcome alcoholism; drugs; and child abuse. Satan is working overtime, but not as triumphantly as God!

DAY 16. Matthew 25
Compassion

Matthew 25:40 The King will reply, "I tell you, whenever you did this for one of the least important of these brothers of Mine, you did it for Me!" (GNB)

Prayer: Show us what You want us to do to minister, clothe, feed others.

COMMENTS: We will be judged for how we help the suffering, needy, and lost. List ways we can help. What about sponsoring a child overseas through World Vision or other organizations? Each member can contribute from his or her allowance and earnings. It's a true blessing to a child and to the family. Put the child's picture on the prayer list or bulletin board. Write to the child. Remember birthday and Christmas gifts. What about writing to prisoners, teenagers in institutions; visiting the elderly, retarded, deaf or blind in homes or institutions; street people and destitute families of the unemployed? Boxes of food, clothing, books, toys, Sunday School story papers, New Testaments, Bible story books all can be passed on to those who have none.

ACTIVITY: Jesus trained 12 men to carry on His work. Who were they? Put their names in the word block below as they are recorded in Matthew 10:2-4.

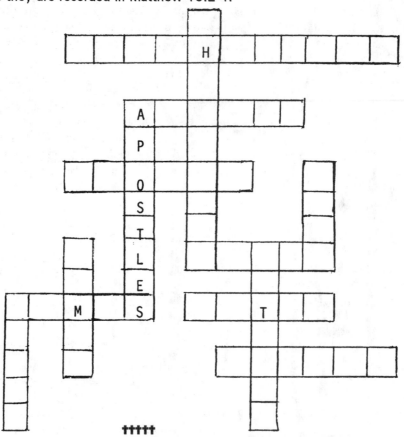

DAY 17. Matthew 26
The Cup

Prayer: Thank Jesus for going to the cross for us, for suffering alone for us.

Matthew 26:26-28. While they were eating Jesus took a piece of bread, gave a prayer of thanks, broke it, and gave it to His disciples. "Take and eat it," He said. "This is My body." Then He took a cup, gave thanks to God, and gave it to them. "Drink it, all of you." He said, "This is My blood, which seals God's Covenant. My blood poured out for many for the forgiveness of sins." (GNB)

COMMENTS: The cup which Jesus referred to was the suffering on the cross, bearing all our sins, and crying out, "My God, My God, why have You forsaken Me?" When taking communion at church, remember His suffering in our place. Thank Him for His magnificent, exorbitant love for us that cost His life, but which He gave willingly. Thank Him for the blessings He pours on us, for answering prayers, and for His Friendship.

ACTIVITY: A. PICTURE. For the added part to the picture, attach with a staple, a cord with knots in it to the soldier's hand.

B. SCENE. Dress Jesus in a purple robe, crown of thorns made by twisting florist's wire leaving clipped ends for the thorns, and a reed in his hand. The soldier wears a tunic and skirt of leather, carries a shield and a spear made of heavy silver cardboard or foil pie pan, and a headpiece of aluminum foil. Pilate wears a cloth tunic with a Roman design at the collar and hem drawn on with felt pen. The throne can be made of cardboard with heavy cloth or velvet glued on as cushions.

✝✝✝✝✝

DAY 18. Matthew 27, 28
Resurrection

Prayer: Praise the Lord for His victory over Satan and death.

COMMENTS: Glory and praise to God! Jesus rose from the grave! That first prophecy in Genesis 3:15 was fulfilled. We no longer need to fear death for as believers in Him, we spend eternity with our Lord. We are no longer Satan's for we were brought by Jesus.

ACTIVITY: A. PICTURE. Paint this a joyful, bright scene with morning sun. The cutout of soldiers before the stone will roll left by placing brad at bottom, thus opening the tomb door and making the guards fall, revealing the angel.

B. SCENE. For the diorama scene, the angel will sit at the tomb opening, the women at left holding spice jars. Use glitter on angel's hair and shoulders. Add flowers to make a joyful Easter scene. The cave, of course, will be made of crumpled paper tapped down with an opening to form a cave. Strips of paper are dipped in water-flour paste, dried, then painted, making the hillside.

Matthew 28:5, 6. But the angel answered and said to the women, "Do not be afraid, for I know that you seek Jesus who was crucified. He is not here; for He is risen, as He said. Come, see the place where the Lord lay."

✝✝✝✝✝

DAY 19. Mark 1, 2
        Paralytic Healed

Prayer: Help us to be such good friends
           to take them to Jesus.

Mark 2:10, 11 "But that you may
know that the Son of Man has power
on earth to forgive sins." He said to
the paralytic, "I say to you, arise, take
up your bed, and go your way to your
house."

COMMENTS: Mark is the shortest of the Gospels, striking right out with the ministry of
Jesus, just as the Romans would like the story of a hero - his work, drive, and force. Mark
uses terms such as centurion, legion, and includes remarks by Roman solders such as, "Truly
this man was the Son of God." Mark presents Jesus as the Servant, the lively, zealous
helper.

ACTIVITY: A. PICTURE. Trace and cut out the cot being lowered,
but leave the paper inside the hanging ropes. Pull down
with wire between slits in the picture. Strengthen the wire
behind cot by bending it like a hook, putting scotch tape in
and out of the hooks. Cover it all with tape.

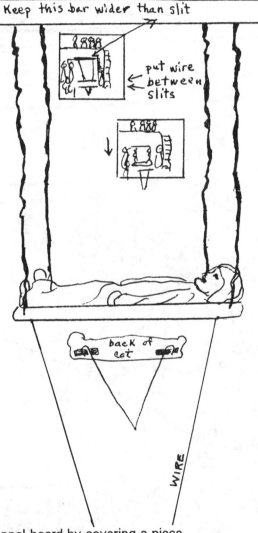

Keep this bar wider than slit

put wire between slits

back of cot

WIRE

B. SCENE. Make a cardboard house with steps outside.
Have an opening in the roof with the 4 friends holding the
ends of the cot ropes. The paralytic man will be standing
with arms outstretched toward Jesus, praising Him.
                                                    †††††

DAY 20. Mark 3, 4
        Chosen

Mark 3:14, 15 He chose twelve, whom He
named apostles. "I have chosen you to be with
Me," He told them. "I will also send you out
to preach, and you will have authority to drive
out demons." (GNB)

Prayer: Help us to be true disciples, ready
           to do your will.

COMMENTS: Jesus boldly cast out demons and charged
His disciples to do the same. Resist the devil. Don't listen
to him in rock music, crime movies, violence, pornographic
literature; fight drugs, alcohol, perversion, immorality, and
murders! Satan slips in his subtle sins in minor ways then
builds them up into fear, hatred, revenge, and cruelty. But,
praise God. He can cast out such attitudes. He transforms
us by His Holy Spirit. He overcomes the enemy within us
and in the world!

ACTIVITY: This will be a flannelgraph lesson. Make a little flannel board by covering a piece
of heavy cardboard with plain flannel, taping it on the back. Place it on an easel or prop it
against something so that it sits at an angle. The pictures will slip off if placed on an upright
board. Each picture or card to be used on the board needs flannel pieces glued on the back
so they will stick to the flannelboard. Children love to work with flannelgraph stories.
Backgrounds can be sketched, colored with crayons or watercolors, and placed over the
board. Trees, hillsides, etc., can be cut separately and placed on the board as the change of
scenery requires. Words or sentences can be printed on cardboard strips. There are
numerous uses for flannelboards.

Today's lesson will be not a story with people and scenery, but the simple use of words. For the four parables in today's reading in Mark 4: (1) Sower; (2) Light: (3) Growing Seed; and (4) Mustard Seed, print the words on separate cards (with strips of flannel glued on the back). Under (1) put card - We plant the Word. Under (2) We witness; under (3) God makes the Word grow; and under (4) Small beginning makes large growth. The lesson to be explained is that God uses us to tell others about Jesus, planting the Word. As His Light, we help them to grow like Jesus, studying the Word. The Holy Spirit makes them grow in knowledge and grace, and God's Kingdom expands.

✝✝✝✝✝

DAY 21. Mark 5
          Don't be Afraid

Prayer: Strengthen our faith.

Mark 5:36 Jesus paid no attention to what they said, but told him, "Don't be afraid, only believe." (GNB)

COMMENTS: Throughout His ministry, you can feel Jesus lifting, urging, yearning for people to believe, to be healed, to be saved, and not to doubt. He praised those who put faith into action, as the woman who touched the hem of His garment. He called attention to their faith to help others believe.

ACTIVITY: For an object lesson, use a magnet with pins or small nails. Show how the Lord draws us to Himself. In our natural state, we are like the opposing pole of a magnet, resisting. When we "turn around" in conversation and repentance when we accept Jesus as Savior, we turn from our old ways and we find we are magnetically drawn to Jesus. We find that we are joined to other believers, and so become "one" in God's family.

✝✝✝✝✝

DAY 22. Mark 6
          Unbelief

Prayer: Help us to believe firmly in You!

Mark 6:5, 6 He was not able to perform any miracles there, except that He placed His hands on a few sick people and healed them. He was greatly surprised, because the people did not have faith. (GNB)

COMMENTS: Jesus truly expects us to believe in Him, to act on our faith. He is acutely disappointed when we don't. After all, God's love sent Him to us. Jesus gave His all to save us. He conquered Satan and will conquer him through us in our daily living - why do we hesitate to trust Him? Our unbelief blocks His miracles! Our unbelief keeps others from following Him! If we could only get the vision of the multitudes heading for eternal death because we don't cry out, "Stop! Here's the Savior! Here's the Way - you're lost! Come to Jesus, He wants to help you." God's depending upon us to spread His message of salvation. Oh, empower us by Your spirit to reach the lost!

ACTIVITY: Even a child can be used by God to help Him do miracles, as in the story today.

A.   PICTURE. Pull the row of baskets Jesus is filling by the wire through the slit.

B.   SCENE. Make baskets, fish and bread from clay. Have the boy watching Jesus perform the miracle of multiplying the food.

✝✝✝✝✝

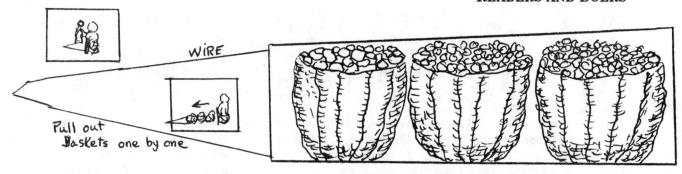

WIRE

Pull out baskets one by one

DAY 23. Mark 7, 8
Ashamed

Prayer: Help us, Lord, to boldly stand
up for You.

Mark 8:38 If a person is ashamed of
Me and of My teaching in this godless
and wicked day, then the Son of Man
will be ashamed of him when He comes
in the glory of His Father with the holy
angels. (GNB)

COMMENTS: Without thinking, many people use the Lord's name as a slang or curse word,
or just as an exclamation, which shows they do not realize He is real. When the time is ripe,
we should tell them about our experience in knowing He is real and how He loves us. Also,
there may be times at school, work, or in the neighborhood gatherings when God is being
discussed as just a myth. Then we should boldly say He Lives!

ACTIVITY: Jesus used many illustrations in His parables. See how many you can find in the
word block. The words are across and down.

The younger children can add pictures to their files such as birds, rocks, trees, scenery,
children, calendar pictures, Sunday School pictures, pictures from ads about children's books,
and catalogs. We will use them later in making gifts and songbooks. Large envelopes from
the mail make good files.

ACROSS

1. Matthew 13:3-9, 18-23
3. Matthew 13:31, 32
8. Matthew 21:28-32
13. Matthew 13:24-30, 36-43
19. Luke 19:11-27 (KJ)
20. Matthew 25:14-30
21. Matthew 13:44
22. Matthew 22:1-14
23. Luke 15:11-32
24. Luke 15:3-7
25. John 10:1-16
26. Luke 16:19-31
27. Luke 18:9-14

DOWN

1. Luke 16:1-9
2. Matthew 7:24-27
4. Luke 12:16-21
5. Luke 7:41-47
6. Luke 14:15-24
7. Matthew 18:23-35
9. Luke 15:8-10
10. Mark 4:26-29
11. Luke 13:6-9
12. Luke 11:5-8
14. Luke 10:30-37
15. Luke 18:1-8
16. Matthew 25:1-13
17. Matthew 13:33
18. Matthew 20:1-16

✝✝✝✝✝

Word Block on the Parables and Sayings of Jesus

DAY 24. Mark 9
Possible

Mark 9:23 "Yes," Jesus said, "If you yourself can" Everything is possible for the person who has faith." (GNB)

Prayer: Thanks for possibility thinking!

COMMENTS: Jesus dares us to step out in faith; like hanging on a cliff and jumping into the arms of Jesus! He catches us. He won't fail us! We have to let go for God to deliver us.

ACTIVITY: At least once a month, we should have an outing or party. Why not have one for handicapped children. They always need extra attention from outsiders. Talk with their mothers. Arrange for them to bring the children to the picnic area (a place safe from cars or strangers) and provide special foods or attention they need. Prepare funny little hats with their names in big letters (for all to get acquainted). Give each an envelope of slips with his name on each one (stickup on the back) to exchange as they meet others. They will have these new names to take home to call or write.

Play simple games depending upon their capabilities. See that each wins a prize such as a picture of Jesus with children pasted on cardboard that they can hang in their rooms. Assign a member of your family to each guest to assist them. Balloons on strings are fun. Have them line up for the colors in God's rainbow. Tell about God's rainbow promise to Noah. Each child can name a flower the color of his rainbow. Have plastic flowers (old ones can be used if washed and perked up) for them to make into corsages to wear.

For snack time, give each a banana. Arrange the chairs (wheelchairs) in a circle with several prizes in the center. The children throw their banana peel toward the center and receive the prize for the closest to their banana peel. (Each child receives a prize.)

Use the story of the "Little Train that Could," lining up the wheelchairs. (Provide wagon, skateboard or steno chair with wheels for those who don't have wheelchairs), like a train. The family members assist by pushing his or her guest so that they can form the train climbing the hill. As the story ends with "I thought I could, I thought I could!," they all cheer and clap. Then leave them with the lesson that we can all work together to overcome difficulties and win the victory. Give each a bookmark with a rainbow, a flower pasted on it, and the verse, "All things are possible with God." These can be prepared ahead with the flowers the children have accumulated in their files.

ttttt

DAY 25. Mark 10
Children

Prayer: Thanks for loving children and caring.

Mark 10:14 But when Jesus saw it, He was greatly displeased and said to them, "Let the little children come to Me, and do not forbid them; for such is the kingdom of God."

COMMENTS: Oh, how Jesus loves children. And don't we all? Even toddlers love other little children and smile across a congregation at them.

ACTIVITY: A. PICTURE. Put a picture of Jesus in the center of your page. Then find pictures of children to paste around Him - all races and sizes.

B. SCENE. Make this a Palestine street scene with cardboard houses in the background. Use salt boxes or small cereal boxes. Paint them white. Add felt-pen lines to imitate stones, doors, and windows. For a well, cover a yogurt box with flour-salt clay and press pebbles into it. Jesus can be sitting by the well on a large stone with the children gathered close to Him.

ttttt

DAY 26. Mark 11, 12
Say it

Prayer: We believe and will say so.

Mark 11:23 For assuredly I say to you, whoever says to this mountain, "Be removed and be cast into the sea," and does not doubt in his heart, but believes that those things he says will come to pass, he will have whatever he says.

COMMENTS: It is a command to believe and say so. Suppose I need a job after school Friday and on Saturday. I study the want ads, dress appropriately, and with a smile of confidence, apply, believing I will get it. Be prepared with references from parents, teachers, or former employers. Show interest in the type of work and mention you would like to learn more and be an asset to the project. With such confidence, you may end up with the job. Or for a sick friend say, "Jesus will heal you. He can do it!" God will honor our faith. Help encourage the child. Assist with therapy. Tell him about Jesus' love; His friendship; that He is preparing a home for each of us and we look forward to being with Him there; and also here on earth.

ACTIVITY: List definite prayers, such as raising money for starving children overseas. Decide ways to earn the money, or a project others can donate to it. If your family is musical, put on a little concert. Put a notice in the paper or distribute leaflets to advertise it. Have a donation box and explain how much the children need help. Work out ways to "say yes" to the prayer, and God will help you bring about the answers.

†††††

DAY 27. Mark 13
         False Prophets

Prayer: Keep us alert to false cults.

Mark 13:22 For false Messiahs and false prophets will appear. They will perform miracles and wonders in order to deceive even God's chosen people, if possible. (GNB)

COMMENTS: We are to avoid false cults, Satan worshippers and such. They are workers for Satan to draw us away from God. False prophets will appear as the return of the Lord approaches.

ACTIVITY:

A.   FOR CHILDREN. There are two street signs which tell us to go the way that is God's way, not the wrong way: one is "K_____R_____." The other is "O_____ W__ _____." Print these signs for your room.

B.   FOR PRE-SCHOOLERS. Teach the street signs - Green, Yellow, and Red with Christian meanings also. (Go the right way. Think if it is the good thing to do. Stop if it is the wrong thing.)

C.   TEENS.   Make a bumper sticker with a Christian message.

†††††

DAY 28. Mark 14
         Agony

Prayer: Your will be done in our lives, too.

Mark 14:38. And He said to them, "Keep watch, and pray that you will not fall into temptation. The spirit is willing, but the flesh is weak." (GNB)

COMMENTS: It had been a long day. They walked to the Garden of Gethsemane late at night. Jesus asked His loved ones to pray with Him, but they fell asleep. He agonized in prayer for His trial and crucifixion. His battle against Satan was to happen within a few hours. Would we have stayed awake to pray with Him? Do we pray now when He urges us to intercede for someone? Oh, may we not fail to pray when God lays someone on our heart!

ACTIVITY:

A. PICTURE. Color the picture of Jesus praying and the little tab of the soldiers coming to arrest Him. This was a night scene so the sky will be dark. Attach wire to the soldiers. Reinforce the slit in the hill with tape on the back. Cut opening not as long as the back of the pull-out. Light from the moon will add a bit of yellow to Jesus' head.

B. SCENE. You may want to limit this scene to Jesus alone. Make a hillside of paper mache and a boulder for Jesus to kneel beside, head in His hands, His hands grasped tightly. The sky will be dark and scenery brown.

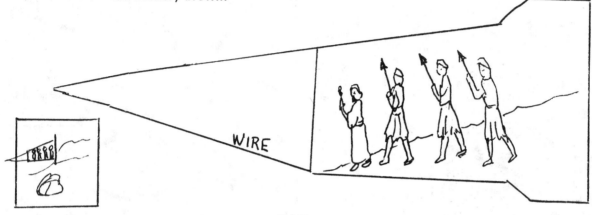

WIRE

DAY 29. Mark 15, 16
Commission

Prayer: Help us to go to all we can to tell them.

Mark 16:15,16 And He said to them, "Go into all the world and preach the gospel to every creature. He who believes and is baptized will be saved; but he who does not believe will be condemned."

COMMENTS: This command is for each of us regardless of age, ability or circumstances, but we must depend upon the Spirit to lead us in what to say, and pray for Him to work in the heart of the one we are witnessing to, then let the Spirit do His work without our pushing or being too demanding. If we can't go to others, we can write, give gifts that show God's love and our love in some way. God's Word will not return void, so let's use it, too.

ACTIVITY: Memorize John 3:16. It is the Gospel in brief, in a "nutshell." For an object lesson, use a walnut. Put a slip of paper with the verse printed on it in the shell. Attached the top of the walnut with Fun Tak (an adhesive that can be loosened and used over again).

DAY 30. Luke 1
Birth

Prayer: Thank You, Jesus, for coming to us.

Luke 1:35 The angel answered, "The Holy Spirit will come on you, and God's power will rest upon you. For this reason the holy child will be called the Son of God." (GNB)

COMMENTS: Luke, the physician, tells us details of the birth of Jesus that the other gospels omit. He also relates the miraculous birth of John the Baptist, Jesus' cousin. In his gospel, he researches matters that a doctor would note; the ancestry through Mary's line; the humble birth in a stable; the shepherds amazed at the angels; the boy's wisdom in the temple; his growth; and the parable of the Good Samaritan who treated the wounded man and took him to an inn for aid.

ACTIVITY: A. PICTURE. Color the stable picture and Mary. Attach her to the picture at the black dot with a brad, reinforcing the back with scotch tape, so she will rock the Baby.

B. SCENE. Make a cave-like paper mache stable. For a donkey, make a wire frame. Cover with twisted newspaper strips. Tape down smoothly. Paint. Add a manger and clean straw (grass). Place Joseph and Mary close together worshipping and adoring the Baby Jesus.

✝✝✝✝✝

DAY 31. Luke 2
Shepherds

Prayer: Thanks for coming to lowly shepherds as well as to wise men.

Luke 2:10, 11 But the angel said to them, "Don't be afraid! I am here with good news for you, which will bring great joy to all. This very day in David's town your Savior was born - Christ the Lord!" (GNB)

COMMENTS: Angels played a great part in the life of Jesus from birth to ascension. Recall as many incidents as you can.

ACTIVITY:

A. PICTURE. Color the picture and angel. Use wire to pull the angel from the tree. Paint night sky with stars.

B. SCENE. Make the angel tall, robed in white, with glitter on shoulders and hair. The shepherds are humbly dressed, shawls or turbans used to keep warm and wrapped around them. Make one or two staffs. Make sheep in resting positions. Make them with a wire frame, covered with twisted newspaper strips taped down and painted white. Cast the heads in flour-salt-water clay over the paper mache heads for better shaping of ears.

✝✝✝✝✝

DAY 32. Luke 3, 4
Mission

Prayer: Show us what our mission is in life that we may fulfill Your plan for us.

Luke 4:18 The Spirit of the Lord is upon Me, because He has chosen Me to bring good news to the poor. He has sent Me to proclaim liberty to the captives and recovery of sight to the blind, to set free the oppressed and, announce that the time has come when the Lord will save His people. (GNB)

COMMENTS: Jesus read the above from the scroll of Isaiah, 61.1, 2 while teaching in the synagogue. It was His calling, His mission! How well He fulfilled it! His awesome compassion for the suffering brought quick healing and changed lives. His mission is still in effect - He still cares and heals; relieves suffering and pain; binds the wounded; wipes our tears away; and sets our hearts singing. Thousands have followed in His footsteps in helping others.

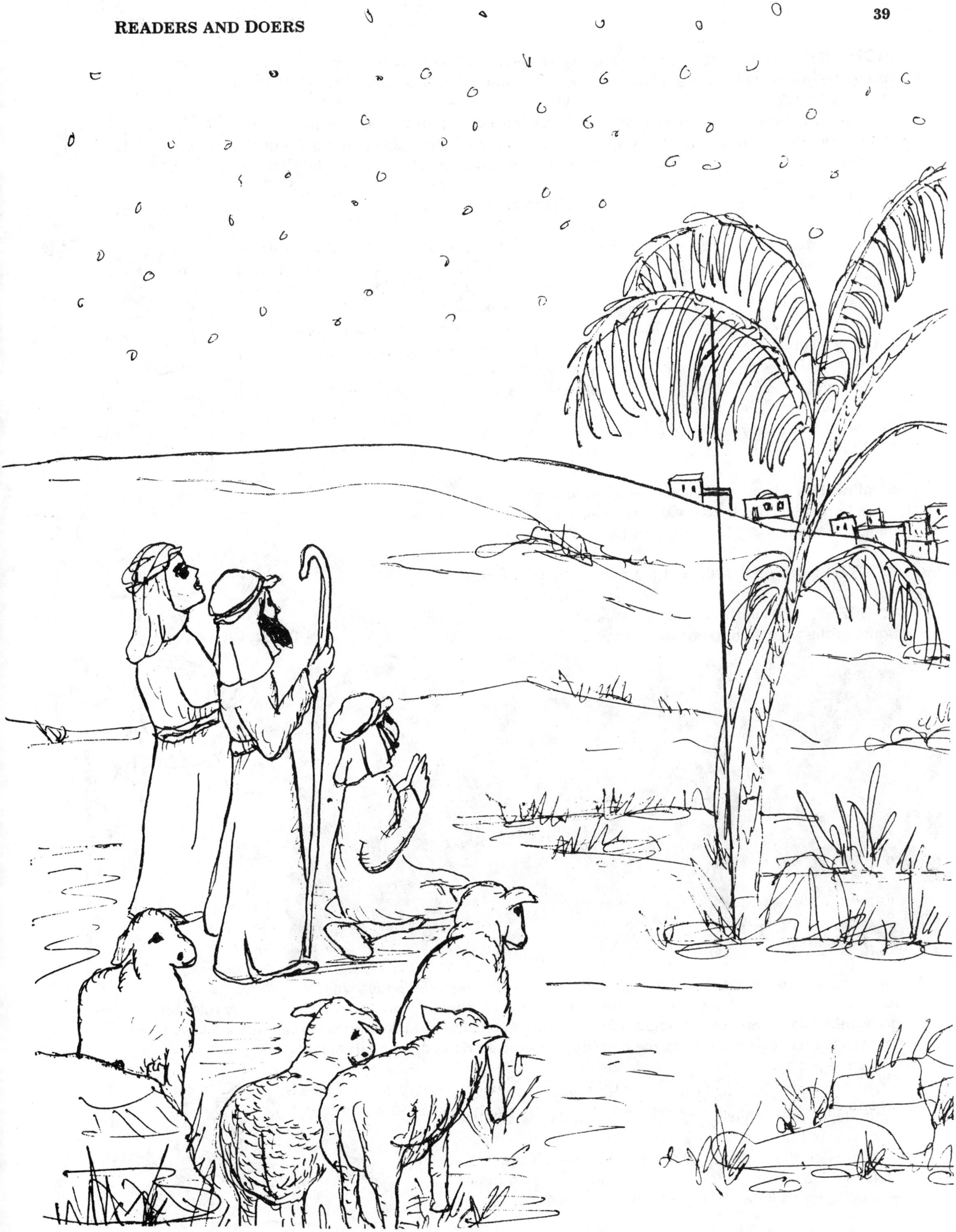

ACTIVITY: A. PICTURE. For the temple picture, Jesus talks to the priests while His parents enter (by pulling wire) to find Him. Put a patch on back of picture to hold parents in place. Keep bar behind parents longer than the slit in picture so they won't pull out too far.

B. SCENE. Jesus at 12 years will not be as tall as the priests. Look in a Bible dictionary or Sunday School papers to see priestly garb. Use a handi-wrap roll for a pillar in the temple. Make scrolls by rolling paper around a toothpick. Add clay ends and tie with cord.

✝✝✝✝✝

DAY 33. Luke 5, 6
Fishers

Luke 5:10b Do not be afraid. From now on you will catch men.

Prayer: Make us your fishers, too.

COMMENTS: Jesus used catchy expressions His people never forgot. "Follow Me, and I will make your fishers of men." (Matthew 4:19) It's fun to be God's fisherman.

ACTIVITY: A. PICTURE. Pull the fish up by the wire.

B. SCENE. Note in the photographs how the girl is bringing the background colors into the paper mache.

There are two other lessons today. 1. Luke 6:31 "Do for others just what you want them to do for you." (GNB) 2. "How are you growing?" both "spiritually" and "physically." Use a ruler for both lesson, the first verse is known as the GOLDEN RULE. "Rule" in that verse means a law. "Rule" also means measure, hence our object lesson or flannelgraph lesson.

For flannelgraph, draw a long ruler. On it, print "Golden Rule." Make several word-size cards. On two cards, print "spiritually" and "physically." On blank cards, let children print words that describe the two categories. Glue strips of flannel on the backs of all the cards and have the children place their cards on the flannelgraph board under appropriate headings, telling why they chose them.

DAY 34. Luke 7
       Faith

Luke 7:50 But Jesus said to the woman, "Your faith has saved you; go in peace." (GNB)

Prayer: We believe You!

COMMENTS: This poured out treasure is a picture of supreme love, the deep joy and gratitude for sins forgiven. The more forgiven, the greater the love.

ACTIVITY: Do you remember your great-grandmother's aroma ball hanging in her bedroom? You can make one by sticking cloves into an orange. It won't resemble an orange when finished. Carefully tie ribbon around several times to tie and hang it, or give it to an elderly person who is lonely. It's the fragrance of love.

✝✝✝✝✝

DAY 35. Luke 8
       Storm

Prayer: It is good, Lord, that you calm our storms.

Luke 8:24 The disciples went to Jesus and woke Him up, saying, "Master, Master! We are about to die!" Jesus got up and gave an order to the wind and to the stormy water; they quieted down, and there was a great calm. (GNB)

COMMENTS: Nothing equals the experience in the Lord as when He gives us that quiet peace in the midst of catastrophe - the peace that passes understanding. We never forget it. That is the peace He brought, His peace in our hearts. When He returns as King to rule on earth, there will be peace for 1000 years - that's national peace.

ACTIVITY: A. PICTURE. Color. Cut out the boat. Reinforce the brad holes with scotch tape. The boat will rock in the storm.
     B. SCENE. Paint the rolling waves with dark blue enamel paint, waves tipped with white. Make the boat of cardboard, taping the ends together. Use dowel sticks for mast and beam. Tie rolled-up sail on beam. Have the fishermen clinging to center of boat, their clothes blown back, figures bent against the wind. Jesus stands at bow, arm forward commanding the sea to be still.

ship rocks up and down in storm.

✝✝✝✝✝

Day 36. Luke 9
      Dedication

Luke 9:62 But Jesus said to him, "No one, having put his hand to the plow, and looking back, is fit for the kingdom of God."

Prayer: We want to follow You!

COMMENTS: God likes us to trust Him completely, not waver trying to make up our minds whether to follow His direction. He admires wholehearted zeal; unswerving dedication; loyalty beyond

question; and allegiance with no regrets - ready if necessary to die for Him!

ACTIVITY: Pre-schoolers tell or show how they can be like Jesus (share, help, give, love, be kind, etc.) From the following scrambled words, list the Directions for Disciples as given in verses 2, 23 and 62:

1. hrepca eht dokingm of dgo.
2. lahe het kisc.
3. nyde lefs.

4. ekta pu soscr lydia.
5. wolfol sejus.
6. nodt kolo kbca.

✝✝✝✝✝

DAY 37. Luke 10
Neighbor

Prayer: Help us to have compassion.

Luke 10:27b "You shall love the Lord your God with all your heart, with all your soul, with all your strength, and with all your mind, and your neighbor as yourself."

COMMENTS: What is our attitude if we see someone lying on the street, not knowing whether he is drunk, sick, or has been beaten - (1) indifference, don't get involved; (2) look, but don't help - let someone else do it who knows more; (3) compassion - be quick to assist in any way possible; to call for help; cover; talk to the person to find out if he is conscious; or stop flow of blood if he is bleeding? Jesus wants us to be the good neighbor, to have compassion.

ACTIVITY: A. PICTURE. Color. Cut out tab with passersby. Pull one figure at a time while telling the story.
B. SCENE. Make huge paper mache boulders. Show backs of priest and Levite having passed by the injured man. Have the Good Samaritan leaning over helping the injured man. Donkey is in the background.

tab to pull

Pull one person by at a time while telling the story

DAY 38. Luke 11
      Happy

Luke 11:38 But Jesus answered, "Rather, how happy are those who hear the word of God and obey it!" (GNB)

Prayer: Help us to put your Word in action.

COMMENTS: Our motto is, "Be doers of the Word and not hearers only." (James 1:22) How fortunate we are that we are not persecuted for reading the Bible or attending church. In countries where Christianity is banned, those who had been taught the gospel yearn for Bibles to secretly pass on His Word. Bibles are smuggled in at great risk, and they are greatly treasured, read, and passed among the people. Many are copied. Preachers are often jailed for telling others. We must encourage workers and help support missions whose aim is to get Bibles to them; financially help their families; and pray valiantly for their release. They are the persecuted church.

ACTIVITY: Draw a map on cardboard copying the one in (Appendix, Day 1). The mountains run parallel to the Mediterranean Sea coast. Between the Sea of Galilee and the Dead Sea is a valley. In fact, the Dead Sea is the lowest place on earth. The country is about 160 miles by 50 miles.

Use salt-flour-water paste to make clay. Make a relief map by piling up the clay for the mountains. When dry, paint three sections of the country: the upper Galilee, middle Samaria, and southern Judea. Mark the towns.

✝✝✝✝✝

DAY 39. Luke 12
      Riches

Luke 12:33 Sell what you have and give aims provide yourselves money bags which do not grow old, a treasure in the heavens that does not fail, where no thief approaches nor moth destroys.

Prayer: God, stretch our budgets so we can give more.

COMMENTS: The best insurance policy is to put your money into works that will have eternal value. We need to save, of course, in order to avoid paying interest, but by keeping a budget with God leading, we can find ways to give extra amounts to His work: missions, sending Christian literature to prisons, sponsoring orphans in famine areas, and helping street people. God stretches our money in unusual ways - it's exciting.

You may find this unbelievable, but it's true. Years ago I attended a mission meeting, was so impressed with the speaker that I put all my money in, including an emergency $10 hidden in my purse. I was glad to do it, and God showed His appreciation. While working among pansies in my front yard, the telephone rang. I went inside (door open) to answer and when I returned, two new $1.00 bills were lying where I had been working. No one was in view - there was no wind. I was only a few feet from the area. The next morning when I went to get in my car in the closed garage, there were another two $1.00 bills at the car door! Only an angel could have left them! That was in the depression years.

ACTIVITY: Pre-schoolers - Make banks with old cans with plastic lids. Cut a slot in each lid. Cover cans with wallpaper or contact paper, or use some pictures from their notebooks. Print "God's Money" on a paper to glue on top of the lid. The children can learn to name the coins, count them, and sort them into different piles.

Older ones can place a thin paper over a penny and with the side of a lead pencil, mark over it. The motto, In God We Trust, appears darker. This is a good motto to place on the bulletin board or in the car at the dashboard to show that we trust Him at all times.

Teens and daring pre-teens - Work the monument puzzle.

Because of Jesus' challenge to help others, many organizations have come into being, like a monument to His glory. See if you can unscramble the words in the monument to match those listed below.

There are others. Scramble any more you can think of and have the rest of the family unscramble them.

1. veterans hospitals
2. hospitals
3. orphanages
4. city missions
5. prison reforms
6. army chaplains
7. hospital chaplains
8. prison chaplains
9. homes for elderly
10. sanitariums
11. convalescent homes
12. Coffee houses
13. Deaf institutions
14. eye donors
15. blind institutions
16. travelers aid
17. blood donors
18. rehabilitation centers
19. halfway houses
20. alcoholics anonymous
21. Bible translators

isaphosit
hogorpnsea
yee nodsor
stranumsiia
lobod ndrsoo
tyic snimsois
feefoc souhes
vertsaelr dia
sprnoi merfost
mray nsplichaa
whalfay shuose
nprsoi lichapnsa
fead tinstinsotui
shemo rfo leelryd
belbi stratlorsna
nildb snuittinsito
talpisoh slapchian
sconaletenv ohmse
restevan laspihso
slocalotics ynasamuon
blitterahainio restnec

"WHOSE FOUNDATION IS CHRIST"

DAY 40. Luke 13, 14
        Humility

Luke 14:11 For whoever exalts himself will be abased, and he who humbles himself will be exalted.

Prayer: Help us not to boast.

COMMENTS: This verse does not mean we should not aspire to lead noble, worthy lives, but in doing so, to keep humble, to remember we are servants.

ACTIVITY: Pre-schoolers - Draw a picture to send to a sick child.

Older ones can try this geographical quiz: (Answers are in the Appendix)

1. Where was Jesus born?
2. What was the capital city of the land?
3. Where did the family flee to avoid Herod's anger?
4. In what town did Jesus grow up?
5. What is the main river of Palestine?
6. From what sea does it flow in the north?
7. Into what sea does it empty?
8. What was the southern territory of Palestine called?
9. The middle area? The northern country?
10. Jesus was baptized in the Jordan River near what town?
11. Where did Jesus turn water into wine, His first miracle?
12. What city did He often visit on the north shore of the Sea of Galilee?
13. What Roman city is on the west shore of the Sea of Galilee?
14. Where did He cast demons into swine on the east side of the Sea?
15. Where did Lazarus, Mary, and Martha live?
16. Where did Jesus talk with the woman at the well?
17. Where did Jesus often pray?
18. In the parable of the Good Samaritan to what city were they traveling?
19. Jesus restored life to the son of the widow of _____.
20. He prophesied doom on two seaports, _____ and _____.
21. Near what town did Jesus feed the five thousand?
22. After His resurrection, where did He walk with two disciples?
23. In what city did Jesus quietly stay before the last Passover?
24. From what mount did Jesus ascend?

✝✝✝✝✝

DAY 41. Luke 15, 16
        Rejoice

Luke 15:10 Likewise, I say to you, there is joy in the presence of the angels of God over one sinner who repents.

Prayer: We rejoice, too!

COMMENTS: Chapter 15 records three parables: the Lost Sheep, the Lost Coin, and the Lost Son. All are famous, but the first in the thoughts of most Christians is the story of the Prodigal Son, the lost one who returns to his father. When we return to God, the angels rejoice! His arms are open wide to receive us no matter how greatly we have sinned, and all heaven rejoices!

ACTIVITY: Pre-schoolers - As able, memorize name, address, and phone number. Explain how serious getting lost is, but that if they wait where they are (but not in a street or dangerous place), Mom or Dad will find them. They should call loudly if they are in a wooded area, or stick their bright cap, shawl, or some other article high in the air as a flag.

As a game, hide things to find (doll, toy) so they rejoice when they find it.

Activity: Using the locations in the previous quiz, fill in the blocks below.

DAY 42. Luke 17, 18
            Thanks

Prayer: We thank You!

Luke 17:17, 18 So Jesus answered and said, "Were there not ten cleansed? But where are the nine? Were there not any found who returned to give glory to God except this foreigner?"

COMMENTS: Ten lepers were healed, but only one thought to run back to thank Jesus. That's probably our score, too, sad to say.

ACTIVITY: Each one list all the things for which he or she is thankful. Be sure to write down the pre-schooler's list. The one with the longest list gets an extra dessert today.

Now, make a thank-you bouquet for Jesus. Purchase some pretty plastic flowers (each contributes from allowance). As prayers are answered, tag a flower, giving the prayer, date asked, and date answered. See how the bouquet grows. It will afford a conversation piece to witness to God's care.

                                    ✝✝✝✝✝

DAY 43. Luke 19
            To Save

Prayer: Thanks for saving us!

Luke 19:10 For the Son of Man has come to seek and to save that which was lost.

COMMENTS: It's so good that Jesus <u>seeks</u>. Let's answer Him quickly.

ACTIVITY: A. PICTURE. Attach a wire to the back of Zaccheus so he can be lowered from the tree. The wire goes between the two slits at bottom of tree. Attach the wire the whole length of Zaccheus to strengthen it. Remember to make a hook at the top so the wire won't pull out.

          B. SCENE. Paint background. Use small boxes like salt or cereal boxes for houses. Paint them white. Add a few lines for stones. Paint the doors and windows. Glue or attach to background with wire. Blend foreground bank of paper mache with same colors as scenery. Push a firm small branch for the tree into the bank and reinforce with clay. Put Zaccheus in the tree; Jesus and people at base.

pull Zaccheus down

                                    ✝✝✝✝✝

DAY 44. Luke 20, 21
Taxes

Prayer: Help us obey the laws of the land.

Luke 20:25 And He said to them, "Render therefore to Caesar the things that are Caesar's, and to God the things that are God's."

COMMENTS: This is an amusing incident. Jesus always gave an answer that stumped His critics. About taxes - we should be glad we can help support our good government.

ACTIVITY: Today and tomorrow we will make banners to hang in our rooms or in a Sunday School room. Think of short, inspiring verses or proverbs that have an object to portray it. For example, "The Kingdom of God is Within You" printed within a heart.

Felt, heavy cloth, and old drapery material make good backgrounds. For top bar, use old broom handle, dowel, or if banner is small, use a coathanger. Fold cloth over bar. Glue it or tack in place. Cut out red heart and glue to banner. Cut out letters of verse and glue on the heart. Add fringe or trim at the bottom.

Pre-schoolers may enjoy working on cardboard with letters and pictures to glue on. Hang with colored yarn. "Keep Smiling" with round face is easy.

✝✝✝✝✝

DAY 45. Luke 22
Satan

Prayer: Help us resist Satan.

Luke 22:22 And truly the Son of Man goes as it has been determined, but woe to that man by whom He is betrayed!

COMMENTS: Judas did a terrible thing. Jesus judged it as being the worst act mankind could commit. In John 13:2, the devil is named as the instigator, "the devil having already put it into the heart of Judas Iscariot, Simon's son, to betray Him," and in John 13:27, "Now after the piece of bread, Satan entered him." Let us beware of opening any thought to Satan's wiles, for if we do, he takes over before we know it. Have nothing to do with fortunetellers, seances, even TV shows that border on Satanic subjects. Small sins like lies and cheating can grow into shoplifting or dealing unfairly in business. Let's develop sterling character, untarnished honesty, and trustworthy values.

ACTIVITY: Continue the work on the banners. Be creative. Make some for holidays. Make cheery ones to give to the sick or elderly. Use padded applique ones for a baby gift.

✝✝✝✝✝

DAY 46. Luke 23
         Saved

Luke 23:43 And Jesus said to him, "Assuredly, I say to you, today you will be with Me in Paradise."

Prayer: Thanks, Jesus, for dying in our place!

COMMENTS: Our dear Savior was alert to win a soul, even while suffering. The understanding thief chose truth and was saved. The indifferent, uncaring one remained lost forever. A simple one-minute decision decided their fate.

ACTIVITY: A. PICTURE. This is the most important story to tell to others, so we should pray and do our best work on it. The soldiers are nailing Jesus to the cross. Put the brad at the hole near the bottom of the cross and at the circle in the open space on the picture. When the cross is raised, it shows the soldiers casting dice for Jesus' robe.

    As you tell the story, point out that He was the perfect Lamb who died once and for all people, just as the repentant people formerly brought a lamb or dove in place of their own dying for sins. The sacrifice had to be a blood sacrifice (death for sin); so Jesus had to "die" - His blood shed as the One only perfect man in place of all of us. We just have to <u>accept</u> His gift of dying for us, and <u>repent</u> of our sins - have them washed in his blood, and we become white as snow, just as though we never sinned. What a sacrifice! What love, what grace! (Isaiah 1:18) Thank You, Lord Jesus, for being our Savior. We love You for it. We give ourselves to You in return. Use us for Your glory.

    B. SCENE. Use a wider box for this scene. The sky will be dark with people railing against Jesus. Mary and John are near the cross, heartbroken. Two thieves are on crosses on each side of Jesus. Make paper mache hillside. The scene is angular and depressing. Soldiers are playing dice for Jesus' robe on the ground. One soldier with a spear is looking at Jesus.

When cross is raised, soldiers are playing dice for Jesus' robe.

✝✝✝✝✝

DAY 47. Luke 24
         Glory

Luke 24:32 And they said to one another, "Did not our heart burn within us while He talked with us on the road, and while He opened the Scriptures to us?"

Prayer: Lord, give us the feeling of Your presence.

COMMENTS: The Lord wants us all to sense His presence, for He is truly with us, always, in every circumstance. I testify truthfully, that from the time I was born again I have known He is with me - 60 years of His faithfulness. He never fails us. He ever strives to lead us on to higher ground, to an increasing knowledge of His love. Never shun the gentle working of the Spirit in your heart - welcome every touch of His presence.

ACTIVITY: Continue working on the Crucifixion scene. It will take many hours of thoughtful work to accomplish the feeling of deep sorrow - yet a sense of victory over Satan, for in His sacrificial act, Jesus won us all back to Himself - all of us who believe in what He did.

In quiet moments of meditation, as you think about the cross and the resurrection, try writing a poem or prose to express your love for Jesus.

✝✝✝✝✝

DAY 48. John 1
            The Word

John 1:1 In the beginning was the Word, and the Word was with God, and the Word was God.

Prayer: Thanks for being the Word - we believe the Word!

COMMENTS: The apostle John was closer to Jesus than the other disciples. He seemed to understand the deeper side of what He was saying. He was with Him on special occasions and was sitting (leaning) by Jesus at the last supper. He writes so beautifully of Jesus as the Son of God, the Word, the Light, the Vine, and the Good Shepherd. He includes the divine prayer of Jesus before going to Gethsemane when He prayed that we should be "one in Him as He is one in the Father." He includes detailed discourses of the deeper Christian life.

ACTIVITY: This is a brief way to tell the story of Jesus and the children can work it out through their own creativity. The ideas is to use a box for the stage, a thin white curtain, cutouts of cardboard for silhouettes, and a flashlight to make a shadow of the silhouette against the curtain.

1. Place the box on a table with an opening at back to work through.

2. Use stick for curtain hanger. Tack or pin curtain over it. Make holes in side of box near top to hold curtain bar.

3. Decide on the main events in Jesus' life. Birth, Shepherd, Healing, Crucifixion, Resurrection, Ascension, Coming Again. Find Bible verses to go with each picture. Also find hymns you or your group want to sing as part of the show.

4. Cut silhouettes of the pictures from heavy card-board, smaller than the stage opening. Put props on the back of triangle folds stapled to picture to make it stand. See if the flashlight makes a shadow of the picture on the curtain. Adjust to make it clear. Practice your show with a narrator telling the story of Jesus, and the others reading the verses and singing. Then SHOW it!!

DAY 49. John 2, 3
            Born Again

Prayer: Make us new creatures in Christ.

John 3:3 Jesus answered and said to him, "Most assuredly, I say to you, unless one is born again, he cannot see the kingdom of God."

COMMENTS: This is very important. If we are not born again, we won't see the kingdom of God, and since Jesus said the kingdom is within us, we won't know Him intimately; or if we think of the kingdom as being eternal life hereafter, we will miss that, too. I was 12 when I went forward to accept Jesus as my Savior, and that was followed by baptism and joining the church. I took new interest in the Christian life, attended preaching services (didn't like them before), and started reading the New Testament. But, my Sunday School teacher had stressed that we need to be born again - to be new creatures in Christ. This I didn't recognize. I knew I wasn't a new person. So I began praying earnestly that I might be. Days went by, and soon two months. So, I began agonizing in prayer, and even prayed in my big closet as Jesus had said in His sermon on the mount. With no avail, I finally said, "I give up; I don't know how. I don't want to go through life and miss knowing You! You do it!" And then it happened! A joy and peace came over me so that I moved from by bedside to the window which overlooked a valley, some trees and the sunset. I recognized that Jesus was looking with me, kneeling beside me. From that moment on, we talked as Friend to friend, moment by moment in a wonderful companionship! I wouldn't trade it for anything. I think it's the pearl of great price, precious, indispensable and eternal. It's even greater than falling in love. In fact, it is being in love with Jesus! So, if you haven't truly become a new person, a spiritual person, seek Him with all your heart, and He will transform you. Some leaders say you don't need to "feel anything" to be converted. Well, take my word for it, you can remain in that "more interested" way or seek to be born again and "feel it!"

ACTIVITY:

A. PICTURE. Cut out Jesus and Nicodemus. Mount on silicone or several layers of scotch tape to make them stand out from rooftop.

B. SCENE. You may decide to make this an indoor scene with an oil lamp made of clay, block furniture, some clay jars and fruit in the room. However, if you make the outdoor scene, it will be on a rooftop. There will be a stone wall around the rooftop. Paint a night sky in the background.

✝✝✝✝✝

DAY 50. John 4
            Water of Life

Prayer: Lord, give us this water of Life!

John 4:13, 14 Jesus answered and said to her, "Whoever drinks of this water will thirst again, but whoever drinks of the water that I shall give him will never thirst. But the water that I shall give him will become in him a fountain of water springing up into everlasting life."

COMMENTS: Jesus knows our lives as well as He knew this woman's. We can't hide anything from Him. He arranged to meet her, knew her needs, and gave her the victory! His Spirit, the living water, fills us and flows to others.

ACTIVITY:

A. PICTURE. Pull the jar up from the well by pulling or pushing the tab. Fold back sides of tab.

B. SCENE. Use a round oatmeal box or yogurt box for the well. Put clay around it. Add pebbles. Sketch a village in the background.

fold over to strengthen tab

DAY 51. John 5
         Authority

John 5:30 I can of Myself do nothing. As I hear, I judge; and My judgment is righteous, because I do not seek My own will but the will of the Father Who sent Me.

Prayer: We want to do Your will, Lord.

COMMENTS: Jesus is our example. If He followed minutely God's will, how much more should we! The Word shows us His way, His will.

ACTIVITY: Show pre-schoolers pictures of children obeying parents. Discuss how much fun it is to quickly obey, enjoying what task the parents have given them. Tell them how interesting it is to think of ways to do things for others.

Older ones copy the miracles of Jesus listed below in your notebook. These are the main ones - He was continually doing miracles. More are listed tomorrow. As you study miracles, you will find others performed miracles, too.

1. Water made into wine. John 2:1-11
2. Healed the nobleman's son. John 4:46-54
3. First catch of fish. Luke 5:1-11
4. Demoniac in synagogue healed. Mark 1:23-26
5. Healed Simon's wife's mother. Matthew 8:14
6. Cleansed the leper. Matthew 8:1-4
7. Healed the paralytic. Matthew 9:1-8
8. Healed the impotent man. John 5:1-9
9. Restored withered hand. Matthew 12:9-13
10. Healed centurion's servant. Matthew 8:5-13
11. Healed demoniac. Matthew 8:28-34
12. Raised widow's son. Luke 7:11-16
13. Healed a demoniac. Matthew 12:22-37
14. Stilled the tempest. Matthew 8:23-27
15. Healed diseased in Gennesaret. Matthew 14:34-36
16. Raised Jairus' daughter. Matthew 9:18, 19, 23-26
17. Healed woman with issue of blood. Matthew 9:20-22
18. Opened eyes of two blind men. Matthew 9:27-31

✝✝✝✝✝

DAY 52. John 6
         Bread

John 6:33. For the bread of God is He who comes down from heaven and gives life to the world.

Prayer: Thanks for your Bread.

COMMENTS: Bread is one of our main foods, so Jesus used it often in His messages so that we would remember each time we eat. He is the Bread of Life. When we pray, "Give us this day our daily bread," we think of both the physical and spiritual bread we need. He said on occasions, "I have bread to eat that you know not of." He referred to the inner strength He received from His Father. After an energetic day He could pray all night and the apostles marveled at His endurance. When Jesus fasted 40 days, the devil tempted Him to turn the stone into bread but Jesus refused to obey Satan, as God is the One to obey.

ACTIVITY: The younger ones can make biscuits! With supervision, let them measure, mix, roll the dough, cut, bake, time, and eat! Explain that the ingredients came from God's good earth and that our spiritual food also comes form God.

(Continue listing the miracles of Jesus in your notebook.) ·

19. Cast out devil and dumb cured. Matthew 9:32-33
20. 5000 fed. Matthew 14:15-21
21. Syrophenician's daughter healed. Matthew 15:21-28
22. Walked on sea. Matthew 14:22-33
23. 4000 fed. Matthew 15:32-39
24. Deaf and dumb cured. Mark 7:31-37
25. One blind man cured. Mark 8:22-26
26. Lunatic child healed. Matthew 17:14-21
27. Money in fish's mouth. Matthew 17:24-27
28. Ten lepers cured. Luke 17:11-19
29. Opened eyes of man born blind. John 9
30. Raised Lazarus from tomb. John 11:1-54
31. Spirit of infirmity cured. Luke 13:10-17
32. Dropsy cured. Luke 14:1-6
33. Two blind men healed. Matthew 20:29-34
34. Fig tree blighted. Matthew 21:18-22
35. Healed Malchus' ear. Luke 22:49-51
36. Second catch of fish. John 21:6

†††††

DAY 53. John 7
Rivers of Water

John 7:38 He who believes in Me, as the Scripture has said, out of his heart will flow rivers of living water.

Prayer: May the rivers flow through us.

COMMENTS: Jesus referred to the Spirit who fills us, guides, teaches, and empowers us. And, at times, we feel His overflowing joy and influence.

ACTIVITY: Let the children act out JOY - by clapping, dancing, waving arms and LOVE - by hugging, helping, being kind, holding hands, sharing, etc.

The older ones fill in the quiz on the Names and Titles of Jesus, using the New King James version (titles in some instances are different in other versions), except 1, 8, 12, and 34 which are from the King James. Think how the names declare His mission, glory, power, care, eternal state, etc. You will find that the quiz and word block in all the similar activities are excellent ways to interest a Teen Club or Neighborhood Bible Club to study doctrines:

1. We find His divine name in Romans 6:23 _____ _____ _____ _____.
2. At His baptism God called Him, "Beloved Son." (Mark 1:11) The very first prophecy regarding Him was Genesis 3:15 in which He is called the _____. (Zechariah 3:8 and Isaiah 4:2, 11:1 refer to the descendant of Jesse as a Branch.)
3. Isaiah pours forth His adoration of our coming Lord in one glorious verse: "Wonderful, Counselor, The Mighty God, the Everlasting Father, the Prince of Peace" (Isaiah 9:6), regarding His second coming. Isaiah also has a superb chapter, the 53rd, about His first coming as _____ ____ ____ _____ (Isaiah 53:3). (In 28:16 he foretells Jesus' role as a sure Foundation, a Cornerstone. In 33:21, 22 as glorious Lord, our Judge, Lawgiver, and King.)
4. In Isaiah 59:20 He is called _____.
5. Malachi proclaims, "the _____ of Righteousness shall arise with healing in His wings." (Malachi 4:2) Daniel (2:44-45) in his vision of the earthly kingdoms saw Jesus as a Stone breaking them up at the end of the age.
6. Deuteronomy 18:15, 18 says Jesus will be a _____.

7. At Jesus' first coming, the angel told Mary she would have a Son, _____.

8. Meaning, _____ _____ _____. (Matthew 1:23)

9. In Luke 1:31-35, the angel told Mary to call Him Jesus, that He would be called the Son of the Highest, the Holy One, the Son of God. As the angels sang to the shepherds, they announced Him as the _____.

10. Who is _____ ___ _____. (Luke 2:11)

11. Matthew, writing to the Jews, presented Jesus as the promised _____ _____ _____ - _____, even to the inscription written by Pilate on the cross. (Matthew 27:37)

12. Mark presented Jesus as a man of action, a divine Servant, who like the Romans accomplished things accurately and quickly. Mark 12:14 records Jesus as the _____. Isaiah 42:1 speaks of the coming Servant.

13. Luke, a Greek, interprets Jesus as the Son of _____ (Luke 5:24); and, being a doctor, his Gospel gives the viewpoint of Jesus as the One interested in each person's welfare, as One who understands human frailties. . .

14. As the _____. (Luke 5:31)

15. The most read and loved Gospel perhaps gets its first place because John loved Jesus so dearly, understanding deeper things Jesus said, and was given the inspiration to see Jesus as the _____(I John 1:1) incarnate. In I John 1:1, he adds, "the Word of Life."

16. Going through John's portrait of Jesus is a revelation in itself. Most of the names are the ones Jesus gave Himself: John 1:7 _____;

17. 1:29 Lamb of God; 1:34 Son of God; 1:41 _____;

18. 1:49 King of Israel and _____;

19. 3:2 _____;

20. 3:29 Bridegroom; 4:14 Water of Life; 6:35 _____ of Life;

21. 8:12 Light of the World; 8:58 _____ _____;

22. 10:9 _____;

23. 10:11; _____;

24. 11:25 _____; 12:15 King; 12:23 Son of Man;

25. 13:13 Teacher and Lord; 14:6 _____;

26. 14:6 _____;

27. 14:6 _____;

28. 15:5 _____;

29. 15:13 _____;

30. 21:7 _____.

31. In conclusion, John states his purpose in writing the Gospel, that readers might believe that Jesus is the _____ _____ _____. (John 20:31)

✝✝✝✝✝

DAY 54. John 8
                Light

Prayer: Thanks for lighting us.

John 8:12 Then Jesus spoke to them again, saying, "I am the light of the world. He who follows Me shall not walk in darkness, but have the light of life."

COMMENT: Receiving the light of Jesus is like receiving sight after blindness. There is a complete new dimension to living. It is exciting to see what God has for our lives, adventure, satisfaction, assurance, security, and mystery.

ACTIVITY: While the older ones continue the quiz on titles of Jesus, the younger ones play "blindfold" games to help them to sympathize with the blind:

1. Put obstacles like a small table, chair, or grocery boxes in the path for children to go around.
2. Twenty items are spread on the ground. Pick up as many as you can feel.
3. Two blindfolded children, holding hands, try to walk to a specified destination.
4. All children are blindfolded. They walk around without speaking and try to identify each other.

(Quiz on Names and Titles of Jesus continued.)

32. Acts 5:31 states God exalted Him to be a _____ and a Savior.
33. The letters written to the churches also give our Lord meaningful names: Romans 11:26 Deliverer; 1 Corinthians 10:4 _____;
34. 2 Corinthians 9:15 _____ _____;
35. Colossians 2:10 _____; 1 Timothy 1:17 King Eternal; 2:3 God our Savior;
36. Hebrews 1:2 _____;
37. Revelation 1:11 I am the Alpha and the Omega, the _____ and the Last;
38. Hebrews 4:14, 15 _____; Hebrews 12:24 Mediator;
39. 1 Peter 2:4 _____ _____; 1 Peter 2:6 Chief Cornerstone, elect, precious.
40. Song of Solomon calls our Bridegroom two dear names: 2:1 _____ _____ _____ and;
41. _____ _____ _____.
42. Revelation dramatically presents our Lord's glorious, triumphant future as Revelation 5:5 _____ of the tribe of Judah, the Root of David;
43. Revelation 13:8 _____;
44. Revelation 19:11 _____ _____ _____;
45. Revelation 19:13 Word of God; Revelation 21:6 Beginning and End; Revelation 22:13 First and Last; Revelation 22:16 _____ _____ _____ _____.

From this study of the names and titles of Jesus, we learn much about His character, ministry, purpose in coming to earth, His glorious triumphant future, our Bridegroom, Prince of Peace, and Lord of Lords! How we praise our wonderful Savior, our blessed Redeemer! Praise His Name! "At the name of Jesus every knee shall bow!" (Philippians 2:10) (Check the blanks with answers in the Appendix.)

✝✝✝✝✝

DAY 55. John 9
            Blind

John 9:3 Jesus answered, "His blindness has nothing to do with his sins or his parents' sins. He is blind so that God's power might be seen at work in him." (GNB)

Prayer: Help us to "see."

COMMENTS: Sometimes "seeing" means "insight" so that we can understand the way God works with us to increase our faith and knowledge. Often trials, illnesses, and sufferings are tests required to bring about God's glory through us.

ACTIVITY: The younger children can work the flannelgraph lesson on names of Jesus. Each one can draw one or more pictures as follows:

Then look up the references and write the word that describes the pictured name of Jesus.

Pre-schoolers can find some real objects that are like the pictures. Put the words on blank cards and place them on the flannelgraph board by the pictures:

Light - John 8:12	Lamb - Psalm 119:105	Lamp - John 1:29
Bread - John 6:48	Shepherd - John 10:11	Door - John 10:7
Star - Revelation 22:16	King - John 12:13	Way - John 14:6
Lily - Song of Solomon 2:1	Rock - 1 Cor. 10:4	Vine - John 15:1

The older ones complete the Word Block on Names and Titles of Jesus, using answers from the quiz.

NAMES AND TITLES OF JESUS

	1	2	3	4	5	6	7	8	9	10	11	12	13	14	15	16	17	18	19	20	21
1	B	R	I	G	H	T	A	N	D	M	O	R	N	I	N	G	S	T	A	R	U
2	X	F	A	I	T	H	F	U	L	A	N	D	T	R	U	E	X	X	B	S	N
3	J	E	S	U	S	C	H	R	I	S	T	T	H	E	L	O	R	D	R	O	S
4	K	N	E		A	D	R	O	L	I	V	I	N	G	S	T	O	N	E	N	P
5	I	A	E		V		Y	D	L	A	M	B	R	X	S	X	A	O	E		
6	N	M	D		I		X	X	O		A	X	E	H	E	A	D	F	A		
7	G		X		O		O	F		S	U	N		T		O	X	X	G	K	
8	O			R		R	X	T		O		S		F		A					
9	F	I	R	S	T		H	X	X	F	A	S	X	D	B						
10	T	E	A	C	H	E	R	M	E	S	M	H	L								
11	H	A	I	S	S	E	M	A	V	G	H	D	O	A	X	X	E				
12	E	P	H	Y	S	I	C	I	A	N	E	P	R	P	L	X	R	G			
13	J	E	M	M	A	N	U	E	L	X	I	V	R	I	I	R	O	C	K	X	I
14	E	T	E	H	P	O	R	P	L	X	R	I	O	I	F	D	N	E	I	R	F
15	W	X	R	E	M	E	E	D	E	R	N	N	W	Y	E	X	L	I	G	H	T
16	S	H	E	P	H	E	R	D	Y	C	X	E	S	X	A	S	I	B	B	A	R
17	C	H	R	I	S	T	T	H	E	L	O	R	D	R	O	W	T	R	U	T	H
18	R	E	S	U	R	R	E	C	T	I	O	N	G	O	D	W	I	T	H	U	S

The wonderful names and titles of Jesus, as given in the quiz on His names, are hidden in the above puzzle. See how many you can find. As you find each one, praise Him again for being our precious Lord and Savior. The 45 names are spelled forward, backwards, up, down, and diagonally.

DAY 56. John 10
             Shepherd

Prayer: Lord, You are My Shepherd!

John 10:14, 15 I am the good Shepherd;
and I know My sheep, and am known by My
own. As the Father knows Me, even so
I know the Father; and I lay down My
life for the sheep.

COMMENTS: This metaphor is one of the most blessed symbols of our Lord. We can truly know His voice. We can tell when He speaks to us. We feel His love and care. We recognize others as His sheep and rejoice being in His fold.

ACTIVITY: Feeling this unity in the family of god, let's have a "We love our family" party. This can be held at the church or for a neighborhood gathering. The children may make the invitations and deliver them. If it is near Valentine's Day, pin hearts around the room or a big sign, "We love our family!"

1. "We Love You" Get-Acquainted Game - Each one is given name tag, pencil and card. The card is lined into 20 squares. As the guests meet others, they enter the names on their card. Like bingo, later, the leader calls out the names while each checks his list. The first to get five called names in a row yells, "I love you!" and is awarded a prize (maybe a bag of heart candies all can enjoy).

2. Families Form Couples - The children also, pairing if possible with other children or friends for odd numbers. Place hearts on the floor in a circle, one less than the number of couples. As a love song is played on a tape or stereo, the couples move from heart to heart. When the music abruptly stops, the couple "without a heart" is out of the game. Continue to the last one.

3. Serenade - The husbands (fathers) go into a side room. Each decides a song to serenade his wife in a falsetto voice. The leader keeps score by number or name. Outside the wives have to guess which one was her husband who sang (one singing at a time). After all have had a turn singing, they come out and the leader announces which wives guessed right. Reverse with the wives going into the side room, singing in turn, and with the husbands guessing. Also, let the children take turns, guessing brothers or sisters. Any couples guessing each other right receive candy bars to divide, and they have to tell their favorite love song.

4. Family Roles Exchanged - (a) Children tell favorite menu he or she would prepare for dinner. (Prize for the best menu is voted on by the group - funniest). (b) Mothers write the alphabet backwards (the first one finishing wins); (c) Fathers each have to hem a square cloth (the one completing it first wins; and the one with the neatest work also receives a prize).

5. Family Workshop - Prepare ahead, a scrap wallboard square for each family (roll of embroidery thread, a hammer and bag of 20 little headless nails for each). When the time starts, the father hammers the nails around a pre-drawn heart on the square. He hands it quickly to his wife who makes and attractive string hanging by crossing the embroidery thread around the nails. The children cheer them on. The first to use up the thread wins. Also, a prize goes to the prettiest design.

6. Devotional - Use an object lesson of "Families Sticking Together" by demonstrating (1) one or two toothpicks can be broken, but (2) several can't. One member of the family may forget to take out the trash or break some rules, but if the family sticks together and helps each other, the family wins.

REFRESHMENTS: Make a large heart cake with "We Love Our Families" printed on it. Make large cookies with the names of members of individual families on them which they can take home. Red fruit punch and red jello are suggested.

✝✝✝✝✝

DAY 57. John 11
          Lazarus Raised

Prayer: Thanks for Your Power to Raise us.

John 11:25-26. Jesus said to her, "I am the resurrection and the life. He who believes in Me, though he may die, he shall live. And whoever lives and believes in Me shall never die. Do you believe this?"

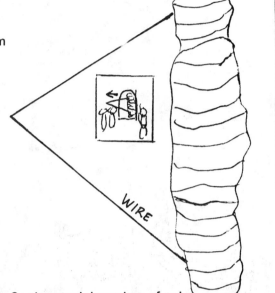

COMMENTS: How can anyone turn down the offer of eternal life which is given (not worked for) for just believing in Jesus! Oh, help us to appreciate what Jesus did for us.

ACTIVITY: A. PICTURE. For extra strength, paste the figure of wrapped Lazarus on light cardboard, then attach a wire to pull him from the cave-like tomb. Cut the slit in the picture high enough for Lazarus but shorter than the bar to prevent it from pulling out all the way.
          B. SCENE. This hillside scene will be similar to the resurrection of Jesus except it is daytime, not sunrise. There are more people assembled. Characters should show surprise, awe, hands raised, with some kneeling. Jesus stands pointing to the tomb opening. Preschoolers: Act out this story. Lazarus can be wrapped in some towels.

✝✝✝✝✝

DAY 58. John 12
          Praises

Prayer: We raise our hands in praise, too!

John 12:13 So they took branches of palm trees and went out to meet Him, shouting, "Praise God! God bless Him who comes in the name of the Lord! God bless the King of Israel!" (GNB)

COMMENTS: This is a joyful time of praising the Lord openly, just as He should have been praised all along. Yet, how horrifying that in a few days the mob cries, "Crucify Him!"

ACTIVITY: A. PICTURE. Use brads to wave the palm branches.

B. SCENE. Make a donkey as in the manger scene and wire Jesus on it. Use cardboard to cut out the wall and gate. Wire the donkey to the back of the wall.

✝✝✝✝✝

DAY 59. John 13, 14
          Greater Works

Prayer: We want to do Your greater works,

John 14:12 Most assuredly, I say to you, he who believes in Me, the works that I do he will do also; and greater works than these he will do, because I go to My Father.

COMMENTS: The 14th chapter of John is a favorite, especially for the sick and dying. Comfort and hope are in Jesus' loving words. He is preparing a home for us in heaven. He is coming back to take us to be with Him forever!

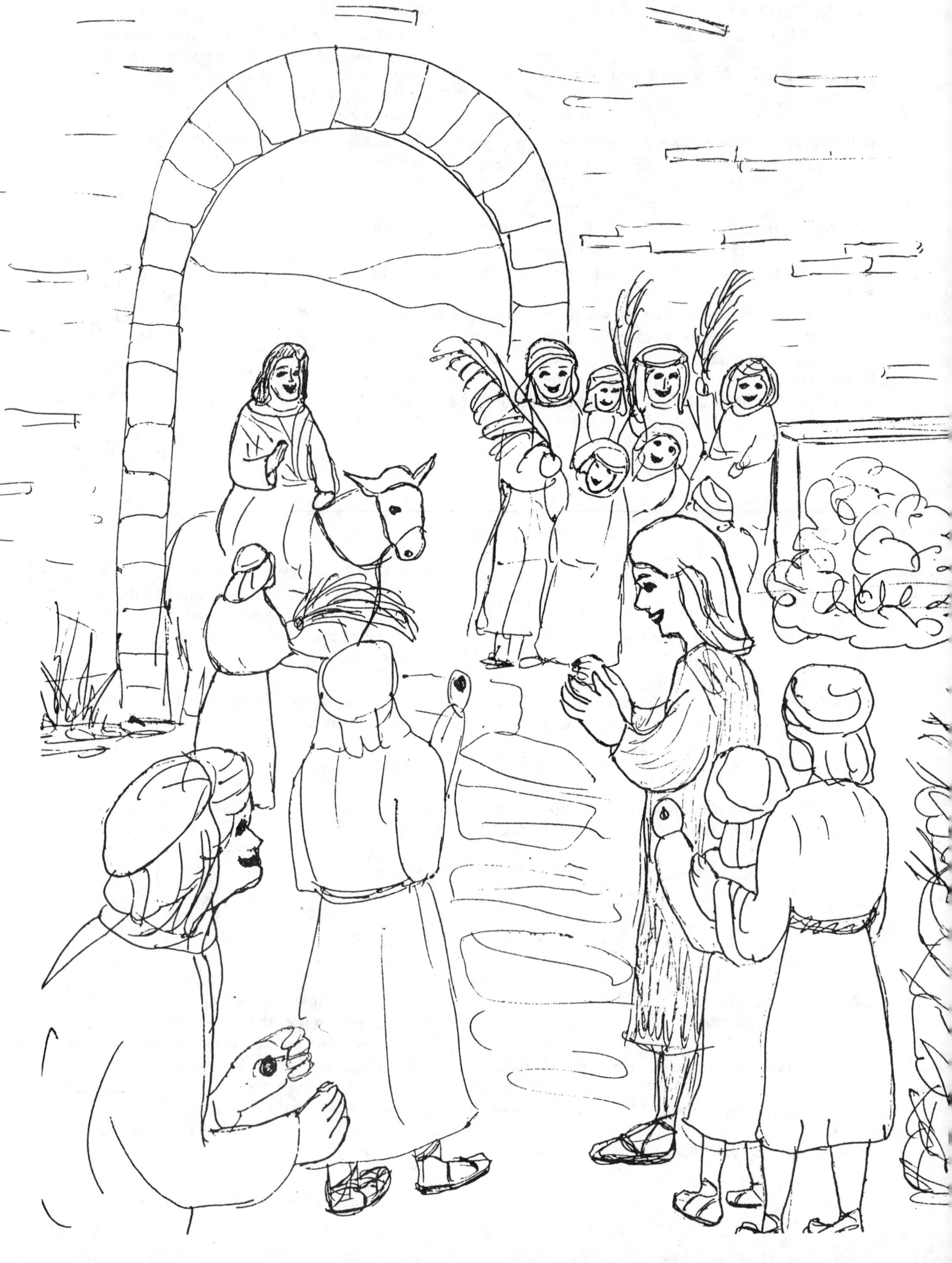

ACTIVITY: A. PICTURE. Use a brad for the arm of Jesus in the drawing of The Last Supper.

B. SCENE. All the disciples and Jesus are sitting around a long table. Us a block of wood for the table with a white cloth over it, and clay bread and cup. This is a night scene, so it will be dark through the window. Wire the men together around their waists to hold them up. Put a basin of water and towel in one corner and have an oil lamp on table or hanging on wall.

DAY 60. John 15, 16
Chosen

Prayer: Thanks for choosing us; may we be fruitful.

John 15:16 You did not choose Me, but I chose you and appointed you that you should go and bear fruit, and that your fruit should remain, that whatever you ask the Father in My name He may give you.

ACTIVITY: Pre-Schoolers - Tell each other all the things Jesus talked about. Cut out pictures to go in the file folders to use later as gifts. The older ones work the word puzzle of the sayings of Jesus. There are 2 sayings with 3 words; 6 sayings with 2 words; and 27 sayings with one word each. (Check in the Appendix to see how many you found as planned. Maybe you found more!)

Sayings of Jesus

A	B	I	D	E	I	N	M	E	W	O	R	S	H	I	P
B	E	L	I	E	V	E	M	E	P	A	T	I	E	N	T
F	T	T	E	X	P	W	I	N	S	E	R	V	I	C	E
I	H	S	T	B	O	R	N	A	G	A	I	N	T	Y	O
S	A	E	Y	L	P	E	A	C	E	G	X	S	A	T	B
H	N	N	L	H	A	P	P	Y	R	P	U	R	E	I	E
F	K	O	I	T	T	E	X	O	A	R	P	K	I	N	D
O	F	H	G	I	S	N	F	X	T	L	A	S	X	U	I
R	U	O	H	A	E	T	G	O	O	D	W	L	O	V	E
M	L	P	T	F	R	E	S	I	S	T	S	A	T	A	N
E	N	E	V	A	E	H	U	M	I	L	I	T	Y	X	C
N	F	A	U	L	T	L	E	S	S	P	R	A	I	S	E

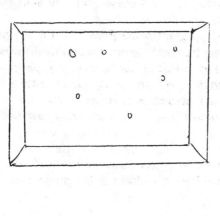

DAY 61. John 17, 18
One

Prayer: We want to be One with You, too.

John 17:21 That they all may be one, as You Father, are in Me, and I in You; that they also may be one in Us, that the world may believe that You sent Me.

COMMENTS: To me this chapter 17 is the greatest in the Bible, for it is the prayer of Jesus that we may be "one with Him as He is one with the Father." What a magnificent obsession - that we may all be one! He wants union of understanding, purpose, faith, love, joy, peace, teamwork, empathy with others, and compassion in helping others. He did the will of the Father - we are to do His will. He prayed at every opportunity - we are also to pray unceasingly. Oh, what a privilege - what a delight! No matter how humble our circumstances, no matter what race, how well educated or illiterate, Jesus wants us to be one.

ACTIVITY: Encourages the little ones to pray to Jesus as to a Friend. If you have decided to have a neighborhood or teen Bible study, you will find this study of the prayers of Jesus an interesting one.

1. The Lord's Prayer which He taught His disciples. Matthew 6:9-15, Luke 11:1-4:
    a. model prayer
    b. reverence, worship for the Father
    c. Kingdom and God's will
    d. daily needs, physical and spiritual
    e. deliverance from evil and temptation; forgive
    f. praise and allegiance

2. Thanks. Matthew 11:25, 26; Matthew 14:19; Luke 24:30:
    a. for things hidden
    b. things reveled and those to whom revealed

3. At the raising of Lazarus. John 11:41, 42:
    a. at the grave
    b. that His Father heard Him as He always does
    c. that people might believe Him

4. Intercessory prayer. John 17:
    a. on way to Gethsemane
    b. Father-Son relationship
    c. disciples - taught - pray for - keep safe
    d. truth
    e. future believers
    f. ones

5. Agonizing prayer. Gethsemane. Matthew 26:36-46; Mark 14:32-42; Luke 22:41-44; John 18:1:
    a. alone
    b. agony
    c. cup be removed - God's will
    d. angels strengthened Him

6. Calvary. Luke 23:34:
    a. forgive them
    b. forsaken. Matthew 27:46; Mark 15:34; Psalm 22:1
    c. commit Spirit into God's hands. Luke 23:46; John 19:30

7. Times and places:
    a. early in morning Mark 1:35
    b. in secret Luke 5:16, 9:18
    c. with others, Luke 11:1
    d. on mountain, Matthew 14:23

DAY 62. John 19, 20
Fulfilled

Prayer: Help us to believe!

COMMENTS: Today's drawing is Jesus appearing to His disciples the second time in the upper room with Thomas present this time. They were still in hiding, fearing they would be killed. Jesus appeared to Thomas in particular, to show His pierced side, and nail-torn hands and feet. Jesus shows each of us direct attention so that we may completely believe Him. But, He admires those who believe in Him who have not seen Him. Jesus wants us to know and love Him.

ACTIVITY: A. PICTURE. Jesus will appear through the locked door by pulling Him with the wire. Paste Him on cardboard before cutting out.
       B. SCENE. Have Jesus standing in the center with Thomas at His feet. Have scars visible.

✝✝✝✝✝

John 20:31 But these are written that you may believe that Jesus is the Christ, the Son of God, and that believing you may have life in His name.

DAY 63. John 21
About Jesus

Prayer: Thanks, Lord, for being so great and good.

John 21:25 And there are also many other things that Jesus did, which if they were written one by one, I suppose that even the world itself could not contain the books that would be written. Amen.

COMMENTS: Oh, there are so many more things to hear about Jesus when we get to heaven. For ages it will be a growing, increased knowledge of Him!

ACTIVITY: We will make a tribute to Jesus. We'll each make a cube with the four sides telling how Matthew, Mark, Luke and John wrote about Jesus. Then on top, we'll write our tribute to Him, how we see and understand Him. Matthew pictured Him as King, the promised Messiah. Mark showed Him busy working serving mankind. Luke wrote as a physician. John portrayed Him as the Son of God, the Shepherd, Vine, Bread, Life, and all the deeper aspects of God's love.

The younger children can use a block of wood or cardboard box and paste pictures on the sides to represent the 4 Gospel view of Jesus. Then have them draw a picture to show how they think of Him.

The older ones use plastic cubes like in a photo shop. It can be made into a light. Before putting the two sides together, cut a hole in one lower corner for the electric wire to enter. Set a night-light inside, holding it in place with silicone. Decide on the pictures you will use and outline them on the plastic sides with a permanent black felt pen. Fill in the colors with stained-glass paint. For the top, put something there to tell the world what Jesus means to you! Perhaps a poem or a bit of prose will best say it. Seal the cube with plastic cement.

 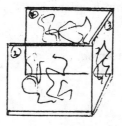 

DAY 64. Acts 1
          Power to Witness

Prayer: Empower us, Holy Spirit, to witness.

Acts 1:8 But you shall receive power when the Holy Spirit has come upon you; and you shall be witnesses to Me in Jerusalem, and in all Judea and Samaria, and to the end of the earth.

COMMENTS: Luke wrote the Gospel to his friend Theophilus, then followed it with the account of the Church and the exciting events as the Spirit transformed the followers of Jesus into a dynamic witness in Jerusalem, Samaria, and to all the then known world.

ACTIVITY: A. PICTURE. For the last picture in the booklet, show the ascension of Jesus into heaven, by pulling the wire upward. The wire will be inserted through the two small slits at the top of the page.

Now it's time to assemble the pictures. Use the list of chronological events in Jesus' life and put the pictures in order. Tape the pages back to back (page 1, birth, and page 2, shepherds) checking to see that the moving parts work easily. Punch holes to put in a binder. Now you have a book to tell others about Jesus.

B. SCENE. For the ascension, have Jesus standing on a small piece of cardboard which is covered with raw cotton representing a cloud. Attach it with wire to the back of the box. A paper mache hilltop is at the bottom with the apostles assembled around looking up at Jesus. Two angels in white apparel point up telling them that Jesus will return as He was leaving.

Arrange the diorama scenes in the order of their happening (listed in Appendix, Day 1). Bind all the edges of the boxes with masking tape. Then paint all the outsides of the boxes with a latex tan paint to obliterate any printing. Now you are ready to display them. Pray about it and contact various places that might show them: a mall, fair, hospital ward where each one will tell the story he or she made, child haven, rest home, etc. This will give people the chance to see the story of Jesus all at one time. And, if you have the opportunity, give an invitation to accept Jesus as Savior and Lord.

backing sheets

My Friend Jesus

✝✝✝✝✝

DAY 65. Acts 2
          Outpouring

Prayer: Oh, pour out Your Spirit upon us!

Acts 2:17 And it shall come to pass in the last days, says God, that I will pour out of My Spirit on all flesh; your sons and your daughters shall prophesy, your young men shall see visions, your old men shall dream dreams.

COMMENTS: This extraordinary manifestation of the Holy Spirit poured out upon the 120 believers caused many outsiders to come to see what happened. Peter, now filled with the power of the Spirit, preached so effectively that 3000 were saved. Peter was changed! At the trial, he denied knowing Jesus. Now he boldly proclaims Him as the Savior of the world. And, so it has been through the history of the Church. Transformed, we carry on the Gospel!

ACTIVITY: For the book of Acts, the children may enjoy making a scroll, drawing pictures of the events. Use a wide adding machine roll of paper or cut shelf paper in half. Staple on dowel sticks at the ends. Pictures may be glued to the roll if preferred.

✝✝✝✝✝

DAY 66. Acts 3, 4
          Miracle

Prayer: Use us, Lord

Acts 3:7 And he took him by the right hand and lifted him up, and immediately his feet and ankle bones received strength.

COMMENTS: The Spirit empowered the disciples not only to speak in tongues and preach, but to heal! They also boldly proclaimed the Word in spite of the trial and threatenings of the council. So the message was spread.

ACTIVITY: Another way to tell the stories is with flannelgraph. Sets of stories may be purchased in Christian book stores, or you may make your own.

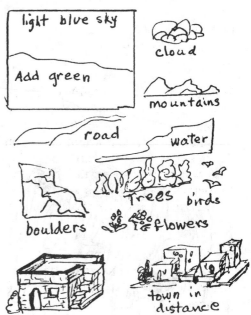

To make your own, use Sunday School pictures and characters (of about the same height). Cut out and glue scraps of flannel to their backs. Do the same with scenery: houses, trees, flowers, furnishings, animals, etc.

Buy flannel in plain colors if possible: pale blue, green, water blue, distant mountain shades of grey-blue, and tan. Or you can dye pieces of flannel. If you are artistic, draw your scenery and paint it with water or oil colors. Crayoning is possible, also, using the sides of crayons to color large areas.

Make basic backgrounds such as inside a home of just 3 lines (add separate furnishings, doors, windows); outdoor scene of countryside (add trees, town in distance, house close by, mountains in distance, river, and road). Have one dark blue flannel for night, another for dawn; half pieces of green to add on a pale blue sky background, or of tossing waves for a storm at sea.

The novelty of the flannelgraph story is moving the figures as you tell the story, adding figures or scenery, changing backgrounds, or putting another cardboard background on top with scenery already arranged.

Children love to work the flannelgraph stories. Let them take turns. Pre-schoolers spend hours at this and are learning the Bible stories.

File the pictures, characters, furnishings, backgrounds, animals, etc. in separate large envelopes or folders. Before storytime, have the figures and scenery in order on a side table to pick up quickly.

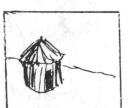

Use a fold-up easel to carry the equipment to other places such as giving a program at a hospital, rest home, school, church, Bible club, or on a picnic.

DAY 67. Acts 5, 6
         Obey God

Acts 5:29 Peter and the other apostles answered, "We must obey God, not men." (GNB)

Prayer: Keep us firm to obey.

COMMENTS: Ananias and Sapphira sinned against God as well as the church when they withheld part of the promised money. How careful we must be to keep our pledges to God and others. Also, we must not "agree" to do wrong regardless whether it is husband, wife, partner or friend. We will be held accountable on judgment day.

ACTIVITY: Think of rules that may cost you your life if you don't obey. See who can list the most (someone write the list for the pre-schoolers). Now list benefits form obeying rules and laws, particularly God's laws. All the members of the family win this time with a family treat of a picnic or tour of a fire house, museum, or other place of interest.

✝✝✝✝✝

DAY 68. Acts 7
         Standing

Acts 7:55 But he, being full of the Holy Spirit, gazed into heaven and saw the glory of God, and Jesus standing at the right hand of God.

Prayer: Thanks for standing up for Stephen.

COMMENTS: This event thrills me. Here was Stephen, the first martyr of the Church, being stoned to death for standing up for Jesus, and when he looks up toward God, he sees the glory of God and Jesus <u>standing up</u> for him! Scripture states that Jesus sits at the side of God, but for Stephen, suffering so nobly, He stands like an ovation, applauding and cheering him! Oh, thank You, Jesus, for watching our actions so intensely and helping us conquer. Stephen then does what Jesus did on the cross: submits his spirit to Jesus and asks forgiveness for those abusing him! That's the Spirit triumphing in us!

ACTIVITY: Think of modern-day martyrs, those who have given their lives for God: preachers in Russia jailed, some killed; martyred missionaries in some African countries; some by jungle tribes in South America. Read aloud *The Hiding Place* by Corrie ten Boom or Brother Andrew's *God's Smuggler*.

✝✝✝✝✝

DAY 69. Acts 8
         Travel by Spirit

Acts 8:39 When they came up out of the water, the Spirit of the Lord took Philip away. The official did not see him again, but continued on his way, full of joy. (GNB)

Prayer: Help us to be ready to witness to others.

COMMENTS: Here are remarkable miracles to list in your notebook. First, the angel directed Philip to go to someone far away who couldn't understand the Bible. Then after the man was converted and baptized, the angel caught Philip up and whisked him to another destination 50 miles away! What a way to travel. That's probably the way we'll travel when we are resurrected.

ACTIVITY: How can we take the message of God to other children in our neighborhood? One way is to have a Bible Club to meet an hour a week at a convenient time in your home. You can make the Life of Christ booklets or scenes, have flannelgraph stories, object lessons, etc. that you have already learned.

For running errands for the Lord, inviting children to come to Bible Club, we will make moccasins to carry the good news. Use old leather jackets or handbags. Draw outline of child's foot on newspaper for a pattern. Place pattern on leather. Line a half-inch wider pattern around it. Cut out. Turn pattern over and cut out another sole. Now make patterns for the upper front and heel, as in drawings.

Get an older one to punch out holes half an inch apart around the sole, front and heel. The children will use fishing line or thin leather strips for thread to sew the sole to the front and heel, carefully lining them up by starting in the middle of the back. If decorations are desired, paint them or stitch them with embroidery thread before the pieces are attached.

The teens may want to have a Teen Club to go on outings once or twice a month (hiking, biking, horseback riding, skating) with a devotional time at the end around a campfire with eats. Develop strong Christian fellowship by carrying New Testaments to read, sharing testimonies of what prayers have been answered, or using object lessons or crafts in Bible studies.

†††††

DAY 70. Acts 9
            Jesus Calling

Prayer: May we be quick to follow You when You call us, Lord.

Acts 9:4, 5 He fell to the ground and heard a voice saying to him, "Saul, Saul! Why do you persecute Me?" "Who are you, Lord?" he asked. "I am Jesus, whom you persecute," the voice said. (GNB)

COMMENTS: What a dramatic conversion Paul had. He often spoke about it in his ministry, particularly to people in authority. We must tell others, too.

ACTIVITY: Make plans for your Bible Club and Teen Club. List the ones to invite. Make invitations stating date, time, place, and activity.

For the Bible Club, arrange a meeting place in den, basement or garage with tables for crafts, materials to work with, and chairs.

For the Teen Club have an active teen-loving adult to drive or accompany them on trips. If they are older teens, they can go on their own.

You may want to start the Bible Club with a party and have some such special project at least once a month. Here are suggested games. You add others:

1. A paper straw and peanut is given to each. At starting point, each blows his peanut to the destination. First one to arrive wins.
2. Two teams for a relay race to pass clumsy objects overhead.
3. Walk on a string across the floor balancing a book on his head.
4. Line up. Give each a balloon. At signal, each blows up the balloon, ties it, then has to kick it to a destination. Turn around and bounce it back.
5. Give an object lesson or flannelgraph story. Explain that the Bible Club will meet to enjoy Bible lessons, songs, stories, and a monthly party.

†††††

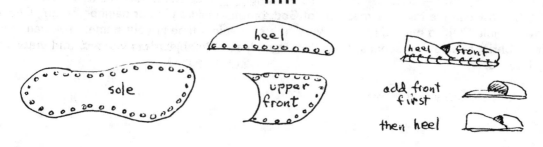

DAY 71. Acts 10
          Clean

Acts 10:15 And a voice spoke to him again the second time, "What God has cleansed you must not call common."

Prayer: Help us understand Your directions.

COMMENTS: Yesterday's unusual conversion of Paul and today's vision given to Peter to preach to the Gentiles are examples of the astonishing methods God uses to reach the lost. No wonder it is adventurous to know Him.

ACTIVITY: Younger ones work on the scrolls. Older ones work on the quiz on the Holy Spirit two days, then the answers will be in the word block on the third day.

1. The Holy Spirit has many names and duties. He is the third person of the Trinity. In Matthew 10:20 He is called the _____ ___ the _____.
(Use the New King James version as some translations have different names.)
   In Galatians 4:6 He is called the Spirit of His _____.
   As God and Christ are holy, so the third member is also holy and is called ___ ___ ___.
(Romans 1:4)

2. All the recorded great moving of God has been manifest by the Spirit:
   a. In the creation of the universe He is called the _____ ___ _____. (Genesis 1:2)
   b. He is responsible for the writing of the _____ _____. (2 Timothy 3:16)
   c. and as the _____ ___ _____ foretold the coming of Christ. (Revelations 19:10)
   d. _____ was conceived by the Spirit. (Luke 1:35)
   e. At Jesus' baptism the Spirit appeared as a _____. (John 1:32-34)
The Spirit was in Jesus' ministry, anointing Him (Luke 4:17-19) and helping with miracles. (Matthew 12:28).
   f. It was the Spirit who _____ _____ from the dead. (Romans 8:11)

3. In the last precious hours Jesus spent with His apostles He promised them that
   a. a Helper would come to _____ in them forever (John 14:16)
   b. even the Spirit of _____ (John 14:17)
   c. who would _____ them all things (John 14:26)
   d. and _____ of Him. (John 15:26)
   e. Jesus explained that the work of the Spirit is to _____ the world of sin, righteousness, and of judgement (John 16:8),
   f. to _____ them into all truth (John 16:13) and tell of things to come.
   g. The Spirit _____ _____ _____ what Jesus said (John 14:26)
   h. and when in need is there to _____ us. (Acts 9:31)
   i. We are to _____ in the Spirit (Galatians 5:16)
   j. and to exemplify the ___ of the Spirit (Galatians 5:22, 23)
   k. In our warfare against Satan and evil powers we are to use God's Word, the _____ of the Spirit. (Ephesians 6:17, 18)
   l. In so doing He will _____ us to do miracles. (Acts 1:8)
   m. As He _____ _____ individually to manifest God's works through us (1 Corinthians 12:7-11),
   n. so we find that we truly become rivers of living _____, as Jesus foretold (John 7:38)
†††††

DAY 72. Acts 11, 12
          Growing

Acts 12:24 But the word of God grew and multiplied.

Prayer: May we grow in the Word.

COMMENTS: This is a revealing story of the church's earnestness yet lack of belief. God must smile at our unbelief at times. But He uses us anyway, knowing we are slow to grow in His lessons of faith and action.

ACTIVITY: Younger ones draw this story in the scroll. Others finish quiz.

4. Dramatically, on the day of Pentecost the Spirit descended upon the 120 waiting disciples with a great _____ and tongues of _____ and they began to _____ with other tongues. (Acts 2:2-4) Peter, filled with the Spirit, preached a great sermon explaining that if they would repent and be _____ the Spirit would _____ them, too. (Acts 2:38, Ephesians 5:18)
   That was the birth of the Church (universal - all Christians)

5. As the promise of the Spirit comes _____ _____ (Galatians 3:14)
   a. we find that He works changes in us by a _____ (John 3:5) so that we can enter the Kingdom of God.
   b. The Spirit comes to _____ us. (Romans 8:11) He
   c. _____ or separates us unto the Lord. (I Corinthians 6:11)
   d. He enables us to worship God in _____ and in truth. (John 4:24)
   e. The Spirit is a _____ to us in our weakness; and
   f. when we don't know what to _____ for as we ought, the Spirit makes intercession for us with groanings. (Romans 8:26)

6. We are elevated and restored to the original position which Adam and Eve enjoyed before their fall, when we are forgiven at the cross and filled with the Spirit.
   a. God gives us the Spirit as a _____, a guarantee of our inheritance in Christ. (Ephesians 1:13, 14)
   b. We are now free from the law of sin and death by the law of the Spirit of _____ in Christ Jesus. (Romans 8:2)
   c. The Spirit bears _____ with our spirit that we are children of God. (Romans 8:16)
   d. God reveals deep truths to us by the Spirit who _____ all things. (1 Corinthians 2:9, 10)
   e. But we must be careful not to grieve the Spirit (Ephesians 4:30) for God's Spirit will not always _____ with man, (Genesis 6:3)
   f. nor speak against the Holy Spirit in blasphemy for that is the unpardonable sin (Matthew 12:31, 32). But our hearts should magnify and praise the Lord for allowing us to become sons of God by the _____ ___ _____ whereby we adoringly cry, "Abba, Father." (Romans 8:14, 15)
                                          ✝✝✝✝✝

DAY 73. Acts 13, 14   Acts 14:22 They strengthened the believers
          Encouraged   and encouraged them to remain true to the
                                                 faith. "We must pass through many troubles
Prayer: Even in troubles You are   to enter the Kingdom of God," they taught.
              with us, Lord. Thanks.   (GNB)

COMMENTS: Luke accompanied Paul on many of his journeys (note when Luke uses the word "we" he is with Paul). He carefully recorded the names of the countries and towns so that we can follow them on a map. They started churches where they stopped, stayed as long as possible, and later Paul wrote to them, letters which we call "epistles."

ACTIVITY: Find the answers to the previous quiz on the Holy Spirit in the word block.

	1	2	3	4	5	6	7	8	9	10	11	12	13	14	15	16	17	18	19	20	21
1	S	P	I	R	I	T	O	F	G	O	D	G	I	V	E	S	G	I	F	T	S
2	P				S	P	I	R	I	T	O	F	T	H	E	F	A	T	H	E	R
3	I		X	X	S	E			N	T	E	S	T	I	F	Y	B	E	F	S	A
4	R			X	A		X		D		E	M	P	O	W	E	R	A	I	E	I
5	I			X	A	R			D	W		P			B	X	I	C	L	A	S
6	T				C		X	I	E		R		X		Y		N	H	L	L	E
7	O	A	X	W	H		N	V	L		A			F		G					D
8	F	B	F	A	E	D	O	E	L		Y		X		A		S	S		X	J
9	H	I	I	T	S	D	Z	S	O	N	G		X		I		T	P		X	F
10	O	D	R	E	B	I	R	T	H	U	H	T	U	R	T		O	E		E	S
11	L	E	E	R	T	T	X	W	I	T	N	E	S	S	H	X	M	A		V	S
12	I	N	S	P	I	R	E	D	S	C	R	I	P	T	U	R	E	K	X	I	S
13	N	X	A	U	H	F	E	X	T	C	I	V	N	O	C	O	M	F	O	R	T
14	E	B	R	E	I	S	A	N	C	T	I	F	I	E	S	W	O	R	D	T	X
15	S	F	L	L	Y	C	E	H	P	O	R	P	F	O	T	I	R	I	P	S	X
16	S	P	I	R	I	T	O	F	A	D	O	P	T	I	O	N	Y	W	A	L	K

Younger Children: Plan a program for the Bible Club. Do what you think the rest of the children will enjoy: select a Bible story, songs to sing, a verse to memorize. Prepare some handwork such as coloring one of the Bible story pictures, have crayons ready, and if it is animated, have wire and scissors, scotch tape, a punch, and notebooks so they can make notebooks of the Life of Jesus, too.

Make an attendance and memory chart. List names down the paper. Draw cross and upright lines, showing dates of meetings and space to check if verse was memorized. Awards will be given to all who memorize 10 verses.

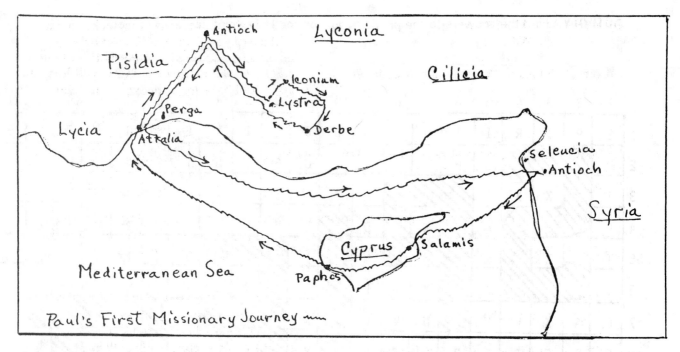

Paul's First Missionary Journey ⌇⌇⌇

DAY 74. Acts 15, 16
Guidance

Prayer: Help us to be alert to Your
call to us.

Acts 16:9 And a vision appeared to Paul
in the night. A man of Macedonia stood
and pleaded with him, saying, "Come over
to Macedonia and help us."

COMMENTS: Paul keenly followed the call of the Spirit. God leads us today by the Spirit, and as
with the Ethiopian whom the Spirit led Philip to minister to in the desert, He had prepared that
person ahead - the man needed to know and God used Philip to tell the man. God works in both
hearts, the one with the need and the one to give the needed Word. The Seed is planted and
grows.

ACTIVITY: Study the first and second missionary journeys on the two maps. Use a colored pencil
to trace the journeys. Note both the countries and cities. Teen Club plan a trip to a museum,
planetarium or place of interest.

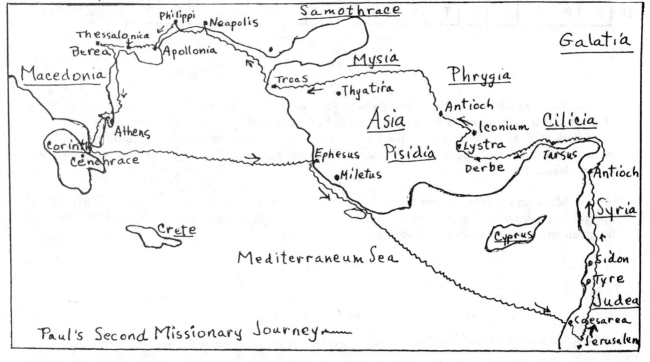

Paul's Second Missionary Journey ⌇⌇⌇

DAY 75. Acts 17, 18
        I am With You

Prayer: Thanks for Your presence with us.

Acts 18:9-10 Now the Lord spoke to Paul in the night by a vision, "Do not be afraid, but speak, and do not keep silent; for I am with you, and no one will attack you to hurt you; for I have many people in this city."

COMMENTS: The Lord is always with us to boost us on, cheer, encourage, lift, love, take care of us! Oh, what a Companion!

ACTIVITY: Look up the Parthenon in an encyclopedia. Sketch it in the scroll. Start dreaming of a trip to the Holy Land, Greece and Rome some day to see the places Jesus and the early Christians lived and ministered. Start saving. It may take years but planning is part of the fun.

✝✝✝✝✝

DAY 76. Acts 19, 20
        Keep Watch

Prayer: May we be faithful in keeping watch over ours.

Acts 20:28 Therefore take heed to yourselves and to all the flock, among which the Holy Spirit has made you overseers, to shepherd the church of God which he purchased with His own blood.

COMMENTS: This verse is one all parents, teachers, pastors and missionaries should carry in their hearts, daily reminding themselves to watch over their charge and to keep their own minds in perfect accord with our Lord. What a charge we have to dedicate our children to the Lord and to train them in loving and serving Him.

ACTIVITY: With red pen trace the third missionary journey from Antioch, to Ephesus, Macedonia, Greece, visiting churches founded on his second tour (Troas, Neapolis, Philippi, Berea, Athens), returning to Miletus where he said farewell to his friends and elders who came down from Ephesus. He then took ship to Jerusalem by way of Tyre, Ptolemais and Caesarea. With purple pen trace his final trip, as prisoner, to Cyprus stopping at Myra, Cnidus, Lasea, shipwrecked on the island of Melita, then to Rome.

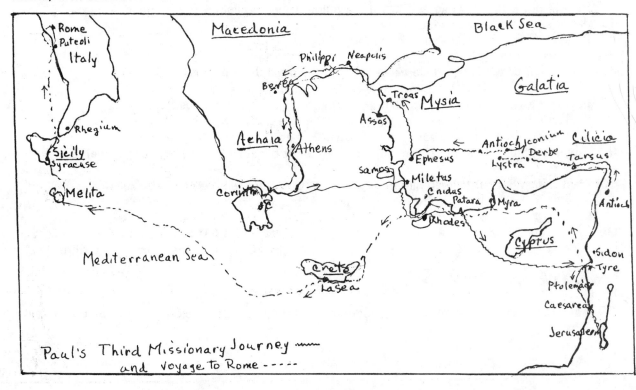

Paul's Third Missionary Journey ~~~~~~
and voyage to Rome - - - - -

DAY 77. Acts 21, 22
          Ready to Die

Acts 21:13 Then Paul answered, "What do you mean by weeping and breaking my heart? For I am ready not only to be bound, but also to die at Jerusalem for the name of the Lord Jesus."

Prayer: May we be ready to die for You, too.

COMMENTS: Are we ready to die for Jesus? He died for us! God gives His extreme grace and presence to those who suffer to Him. When we share His sufferings, we also share His glory.

ACTIVITY; Paul was bound in chains. Tie a rope or chain around ankles and hands and see how much you can do. For the brighter side, make chains for a necklace or bracelet: from paper clips, macaroni threaded with yarn, paper strips of various colors glued at the ends as they loop through another, or roll triangle cutouts of wrapping paper, glue in place and thread with yarn; loop rubber bands into a chain; and if good weather, make daisy chains or clover blossom chains.
      Dad and boys try wood carving, whittling soft wood into a chain. It's tricky. Mom and girls make clay chains, bake and paint bright colors.

†††††

DAY 78. Acts 23, 24
          Standing By

Acts 23:11. But the following night the Lord stood by him and said, "Be of good cheer, Paul; for as you have testified for Me in Jerusalem, so you must also bear witness at Rome."

Prayer: Thanks for never failing us.

COMMENTS: The Lord never failed Paul, nor will He fail us. He also gave warnings to Paul of what lay ahead, what to expect, and used this faithful servant to preach to kings and rulers. Hardships aren't as tough with Jesus!

ACTIVITY: Preschoolers: Put some cardboard boxes or styrofoam blocks in a path; blindfold a child, turn him around a couple of times, then watch him get to the destination trying to get around the boxes--it's hard!

      The older ones try this quiz about the maps we've studied:
1.   Jesus ascended into heaven on the _____.
2.   Peter and John healed a crippled man at _____.
3.   Saul was on the road to _____ when he was converted.
4.   Peter went to the home of Cornelius in _____ to tell them about Jesus.
5.   It was at _____ that the followers were first called Christians.
6.   Paul had a vision, a man calling him to "come to _____ and help us."
7.   Paul and Silas sang in prison in _____ and God freed them by an earthquake.
8.   Paul preached a sermon about the Unknown God at _____.
9.   It was at _____ that the silversmiths caused a riot because Paul's preaching hindered their sale of idols.
10. Paul's friends tried to keep him from going to _____ for fear he would be killed.

†††††

DAY 79. Acts 25, 26
          Almost Persuaded

Acts 26:28 Then Agrippa said to Paul, "You almost persuade me to become a Christian."

Prayer: We believe in You!

COMMENTS: "Almost" is not enough; God demands complete submission for us to be born again and enter His Kingdom! We cannot play it safe on the fence to drop whichever way is most convenient. God means business.

ACTIVITY: Preschoolers: An object lesson for the little ones to teach what "almost" means is to hold out a candy bar to them, but let it be almost taken. Ask them if they liked the candy, and they will reply, "I didn't get it to eat." Then explain it is the same with being a follower of Jesus; we have to listen to His Words and do them to be His child; if we don't do them, it is "almost" but not enough to "eat" His bread.

Answer true or false: (Questions may be tricky.)
1. Luke accompanied Peter on his missionary tours.
2. The disciples cast lots and chose Matthias to take the place of Judas.
3. The Holy Spirit quietly descended upon the disciples in the upper room.
4. The followers of Jesus had spent 10 days in prayer in accord before the Holy Spirit descended on the Day of Pentecost.
5. Paul preached a great sermon that day, converting 3,000 people.
6. Ananias and Sapphira were tentmakers and helped Paul on his journeys.
7. Peter and Paul had miraculous deliverances from prisons.
8. Paul had four missionary journeys, all starting from Antioch in Syria.
9. A boy fell asleep during Paul's preaching, fell out of the window to his death, but Paul brought him back to life.
10. Paul was called to preach to the Jews.

✝✝✝✝✝

DAY 80. Acts 27
Fearless

Acts 27:25 Therefore take heart, men, for I believe God that it will be just as it was told me.

Prayer: We feel safe with You.

COMMENTS: Paul's remarkable tenacity of purpose carried him and others through to victory. He is a hero may of us should emulate.

ACTIVITY: Try making a ship. The younger ones use the pattern to cut out and fold cardboard. Tape the ends together. Place on aluminum foil; bend the boil up over the boat, tucking it inside to make it waterproof. Use a plastic drinking straw for a mast. Glue a paper sail to it.
The older ones try carving a boat from soft wood. Add dowel mast and cloth sail. Or use a large cake of Ivory soap and carve a boat--it will float.

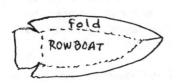   

DAY 81. Acts 28
Boldness

Acts 28:30, 31. Then Paul dwelt two whole years in his own rented house and received all who came to him, preaching the Kingdom of God and teaching the things which concern the Lord Jesus Christ with all confidence, no one forbidding him.

Prayer: In whatever circumstance, Lord, we want to serve You and others.

COMMENTS: Perhaps if Paul had not been imprisoned, he would not have had time to write those enlightening letters to the churches which help us so much.

ACTIVITY: Select some of the stories in the Bible to dramatize in the Bible Club and Teen Club. Use all the members in the groups. Have a joint session and put on the plays. Serve treats afterward.

†††††

DAY 82. Romans 1, 2   Romans 2:13. For not the hearers of the law
          Readers-Doers   are just in the sight of God, but the doers of
                                                            the law will be justified.

Prayer: Help us to be doers.

COMMENTS: Paul wrote 13 letters to the churches he started. Romans is given first, as it deals mainly with salvation; the rest follow according to spiritual growth.

ACTIVITY: Memorizing verses helps to "do" them for they are planted in our subconscious mind and come into use when we need them in trials, witnessing, in our active growth in Christ. Here are tips to help memorize.

1. Repeating often helps. Writing or typing them on small cards with the reference on the back is easy to carry with you when jogging, driving, hiking. Look at the reference and say the verse; look at the verse and say the location.

2. Each member of the family is given a card. In turn, call out reference while the rest respond with the verse; call out verse, others give reference.

3. Each member says part of the verse; others give the conclusion.

4. Print verse and use blockout cards; fill in the missing part.

5. Cut cards in half; mix; distribute. Each reads his part and the remainder is read by the one holding it.

†††††

DAY 83. Romans 3, 4   Romans 3:23. For all have sinned and fall
          All are Sinners.   short of the glory of God.

Prayer: We repent of our sins. Forgive us, Lord.

COMMENTS: Due to the disobedience in the Garden of Eden, all people have sinned--born in sin because parents sinned. We are under Satan's domain, but Jesus paid the price (died in our place) to redeem us. He bought us, and when we believe in His substitution for our sins, we are cleansed and made as white as snow through His shed blood. Thank You, precious Jesus, for saving us. Thank You for taking us into Your kingdom. Thank You for freeing us from Satan's domain.

ACTIVITY: We can use our own fingers and thumb to memorize verses on salvation. Add crayon color on the fingernails of small children.

1. Black thumb: WE NEED JESUS. All of us do wrong and wish we were perfect. Romans 3:23: "All have sinned and fall short of the glory of God." We wonder if God could love us and wish He would.

2. Red forefinger: GOD LOVES US AND WANTS US.. John 3:16: "For God so loved the world that He gave His only begotten Son, that whoever believes in Him should not perish but have

everlasting life." That's great! I want eternal life. I want Jesus as my Savior. How do I become a Christian?

3. White middle finger: OPEN OUR HEART'S DOOR. Revelation 3:20: "Behold, I stand at the door and knock. If anyone hears My voice and opens the door, I will come in to him and dine with him, and he with Me." When Jesus died on the cross for us, He was like a Lamb on an altar--a sacrifice for our sins. When we accept His sacrifice, His blood washes our sins away, and we become white as snow, just like new hearts. Now He can live in us.

4. Green ring finger: HE LIVES IN US. Galatians 2:20: "I have been crucified with Christ; it is no longer I who live, but Christ lives in me, and the life which I now live in the flesh I live by faith in the Son of God, who loved me and gave Himself for me." An easier verse for the younger children is John 1:12: "But as many as received Him, to them He gave the right to become children of God, even to those who believe in His name."

5. Yellow little finger: ETERNAL LIFE IS OURS. John 10:28: "And I give them eternal life, and they shall never perish, neither shall anyone snatch them out of My hand." We are saved! We are safe with Jesus forever! We are His children and promise to be as much like Him as possible. Thank You, Father, for making us Your helpers. Holy Spirit, teach us, fill us, so we may know, love, and serve.

✝✝✝✝✝

DAY 84. Romans 5, 6
        Gift of God

Romans 6:23. For the wages of sin is death, but the gift of God is eternal life in Christ Jesus our Lord.

Prayer: You are our Gift!

COMMENTS: This is the most precious Gift in all the world: eternal life in Christ. The Spirit indwells us. We have eternal life now and forever!

ACTIVITY: There are more verses on salvation we should learn or be familiar with. In reaching others, there are two vital means to present the Lord: (1) our personal knowledge of Him, and (2) His living Word. The Word does not return void. That's a promise from God, and though it may seem fruitless at the time, we must remember that it is the Spirit who brings the Seed to life.

Bible drills are fun and help to familiarize us with the Bible. This game may be played individually or as teams. Keep score of the person or team finding and reading the verse first. If not the called verse, the next who reads it correctly gets the point. The leader calls the verse twice while the players hold their Bibles closed (no fingers inserted), then says, "GO" or "Charge!" (we used to call it a Sword Drill from the Bible verse saying the Bible is a Sword). Try these:

1. Acts 16:30-31. And he brought them out and said, "Sirs, what must I do to be saved." So they said, "Believe on the Lord Jesus Christ, and you will be saved, you and your household."

2. John 14:6. Jesus said to him, "I am the way, the truth and the life. No one comes to the Father except through Me."

3.   John 3:3. Jesus answered and said to him, "Most assuredly, I say to you, unless one is born again, he cannot see the kingdom of God."

4.   Romans 5:8. But God demonstrates His own love toward us, in that while we were still sinners, Christ died for us.

5.   Isaiah 53:6. All we like sheep have gone astray. We have turned, every one to his own way, and the Lord has laid on Him the iniquity of us all.

6.   Revelation 22:17. The Spirit and the Bride say, "Come!" And let him who hears say, "Come!" And let him who thirsts come. And whoever desires, let him take the water of life freely.

7.   Romans 10:9, 10. If you confess with your mouth the Lord Jesus and believe in your heart that God has raised Him from the dead, you will be saved. For with the heart one believes to righteousness, and with the mouth confession is made to salvation.

8.   John 6:37. All that the Father gives Me will come to Me, and the one who comes to Me I will by no means cast out.

9.   2 Corinthians 6:2b. Behold, now is the accepted time; behold, now is the day of salvation.

10. Luke 15:10. Likewise, I say to you, there is joy in the presence of the angels of God over one sinner who repents.

11. John 14:23. Jesus answered and said to him, "If anyone loves Me, he will keep My word; and My Father will love him, and We will come to him and make Our home with him."

12. Acts 2:21. And it shall come to pass that whoever calls on the name of the Lord shall be saved.

✝✝✝✝✝

DAY 85. Romans 7, 8   Romans 8:28. And we know that all things
           For our Good   work together for good to those who love
                                               God, to those who are the called according to
                                             His purpose.

Prayer: Thanks for making all things
             turn out for good.

COMMENTS: This is a favorite verse, for it gives us faith to see the Light during darkness. After the trial, we look back and see that it was for our good.

ACTIVITY: Here is a tricky object lesson for the youngsters on trusting God. Take a strip of paper 4 feet long and about 2 inches wide. Glue the two ends together, but twist one end just before gluing. Glue them flat.

twist once   glue ends flat   cut the long way around

Explain that sometimes God gives us a test, asking us to do something or puts us in a circumstance that we think isn't right, but He says to trust Him so we do. He says to cut the paper strip loop in two the long way around. We think that to do that will make things worse. But we follow His instructions. And, lo! It didn't divide and make trouble, but made it one longer union!

one perfect large circle

DAY 86. Romans 9, 10
            Go and Tell

Prayer: Help us to truly be concerned
           for the lost.

Romans 10:14. How then shall they call on Him in whom they have not believed? And how shall they believe in Him of whom they have not heard? And how shall they hear without a preacher?

COMMENTS: These verses challenge us to tell the Good News of salvation to those who haven't heard. Are there terminal cases you know of needing to hear the way to be saved--people dying who haven't accepted Christ as Savior? Do you know of any in prison who need to know the right way to live? Any immigrants who haven't been taken to Sunday School? Ask your pastor if he knows someone who needs to know the Way, or if there is an institution where your family can witness for Christ--perhaps Juvenile Hall, rehabilitation institution, or halfway house.

ACTIVITY: If permission is given, take the Life of Christ scenes. Prepare ahead to present the story of Jesus in an attractive way. Dad will be in charge, but each member will tell some of the stories as he or she holds the scene. All sing together. Give an invitation to accept Christ as Savior, explaining that we are all sinners and need to repent and ask Jesus to come in to our hearts, that we may be born again. Then pray a simple prayer with those who want to be saved. Leave tracts or New Testaments, your name and address or phone number, if they need to contact you. Get their names to send more helpful literature and to pray for them.

✝✝✝✝✝

DAY 87. Romans 11, 12.
            Transformed

Prayer: Oh, Father, we do present
           ourselves to You that You
           will do Your mighty work
           of transformation in us!

Romans 12:1,2. I beseech you, therefore, brethren, by the mercies of God, that you present your bodies a living sacrifice, holy, acceptable to God, which is your reasonable service. And do not be conformed to this world, but be transformed by the renewing of your mind, that you may prove what is that good and acceptable and perfect will of God.

COMMENTS: Don't be conformed to the world like everyone else. Try to be like Jesus! Teens, don't let the crowd influence you to smoke, drink, try drugs. If you never take the first drink, drug or smoke, you'll never be hooked--it's impossible! It's as easy as that. Just say, "NO!" You'll be surprised that many will admire you and stick to you as a friend, and your influence will help others to say, "NO!" also.

    The best way to be transformed by the renewing of your mind is to concentrate many times each day on how Jesus would think and act, then think and act His way. Studying the Word--the valuable, fascinating philosophy of Jesus is transforming in itself.

ACTIVITY: One of the finest, most beautiful illustrations of the transformed life is the caterpillar's metamorphosis to a butterfly. From an ugly, crawling, worm-like creature, he dies to self (like we die to self and take on the new Spirit's life in us) and becomes a free, lovely creature that flies from flower to flower.

    If possible, catch a butterfly. Use some dried flowers, tiny cones, pebbles, shells. With clay arrange these in the bottom of a jar or cube for a lovely conversation piece about our New Life in Christ. We are new creatures.

DAY 88. Romans 13, 14.
            Judging

Prayer: Help us not to be a stumbling
            block to anyone.

Romans 14:12, 13. So then each of us shall give account of himself to God. Therefore, let us not judge one another anymore, but rather resolve this, not to put a stumbling block or a cause to fall in our brother's way.

COMMENTS: All of us are guilty of being critical when we did not know the true background of a person or situation. We will have to give an account of our words and actions to God; so we should be very careful how we think and speak. However, if we repent of our sins, God is faithful to forgive us and wipe them away as far as the east is from the west. With this same love and grace, we should forgive others and not judge one another.

ACTIVITY: Sometimes we misjudge by optical illusions. Are you fascinated by simple optical illusions? I am. It's astounding how we can be misled by circumstances, or in social relationships by what someone may say about another person. Let's close our ears to unkind criticism, and never criticize another unjustly.

   Look at these lines. are a and b the same length? Are the bottles c and d the same size? Are any of the lines in the third drawing the same length? Can you read a word in the line message? Measure. Were you tricked?

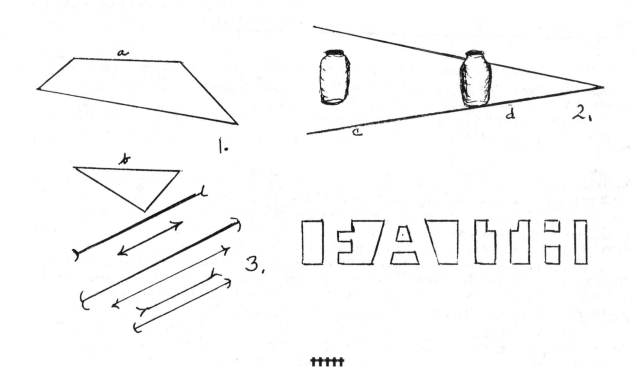

DAY 89. Romans 15, 16.
            Helpers

Prayer: We want to be helpers, Lord;
            to be good neighbors.

Romans 15:1, 2. We then who are strong ought to bear with the scruples of the weak, and not to please ourselves. Let each of us please his neighbor for his good, leading to edification.

COMMENTS: Yesterday we learned how easily we might misjudge others. Today we consider how we may help others. As we plan the programs and activities of the weekly Bible Club or Teen Club, let's pray, asking God the best way to help and guide the youngsters; to help us see their needs as He sees them; to pray for each child by name and for their families.

ACTIVITY: Some of the children may not have heard the song, "Jesus Loves Me" or "Jesus Loves the Little Children of the World." You may write some simple choruses of your own. Use a tape recorder or if you or a member of the family plays an instrument, lead in singing, for Christians are a singing people.

Make songbooks, one for each song, by cutting large grocery bags into pages, then sealing them together with masking tape. Get your picture files out and illustrate the words with related pictures. Use large print and have only a few words or a phrase on a page; as the song is sung, one of the children may turn the pages. Butcher paper or freezer paper can be folded into books.

Songbooks may be purchased in a Christian book store, but it is fun to make them. I've used some I made for decades, believe it or not!

✝✝✝✝✝

DAY 90. 1 Corinthians 1, 2
God's Power

1 Corinthians 1:18. For the message of the cross is foolishness to those who are perishing, but to us who are being saved, it is the power of God.

Prayer: Thanks for the power in the Word.

COMMENTS: This letter was written by Paul from Ephesus A.D. 57 when he was endeavoring to guide the new church in matters that the Greek culture presented: immorality, spiritual gifts, resurrection. The favorite Love Chapter, 13, is in this letter.

As we learn God's Word, we find it powerful. We also find that the basic beliefs are similar in most denominations, which strengthens our bond of Christian friendships. We are all one in Christ.

ACTIVITY: List verses you have already memorized. Consider others: Psalm 23. 1 Corinthians 13. Small children are able to memorize, "God is love," "Obey your parents," "Be kind."

Begin to learn the books of the Bible. There are 66 books in all, written over a period of 1500 years by 40 authors, all inspired by God, so that it all fits together. It is God's book to us, to show us how to live, that He is love, and how to be saved eternally.

There are 39 books in the Old Testament (the years from creation of the world until Jesus came) and 27 in the New Testament (from Jesus' incarnation until about 90 A.D.) An easy way to remember how many are in the two divisions is: 3X9 = 27. (39 and 27) There are divisions or groups of books, also. In the New Testament, there are:

4 Gospels (stories of Jesus) Matthew, Mark, Luke, John
1 History (the beginning of the Church) Acts
13 Letters by Paul (Epistles)

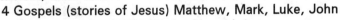

Romans	
1 and 2 Corinthians	1 and 2 Thessalonians
Galatians	1 and 2 Timothy
Ephesians	Titus
Philippians	Philemon
Colossians	

8 General Letters Hebrews   1, 2, 3 John
James   Jude
1 and 2 Peter
1 Prophecy Revelation

DAY 91. 1 Corinthians 3, 4
Teamwork

Prayer: Keep us from causing divisions
in Your ministry.

1 Corinthians 3:6, 7. I planted, Apollos watered, but God gave the increase. So then neither he who plants is anything, nor he who waters, but God who gives the increase.

COMMENTS: Keep in mind the unity of the Church (the Church which is made up of all believers) and work together as much and as often as possible. Paul knew the value of teamwork. All of us are workers in God's kingdom. Some water, some plant, some harvest, but God gives the increase!

ACTIVITY: If you have garden space, let the children plant flower seeds. Or use window boxes. each week after the Bible Club spend time in the garden, watering, weeding. When the flowers bloom, have the children make bouquets to take to the sick or elderly. Help them appreciate, "We did it together."

ттттт

DAY 92. 1 Corinthians 5, 6
Temple of God

Prayer: It's a privilege, Lord, to be Your
Temple; keep us pure for Your
indwelling.

1 Corinthians 6:19-20. Do you not know that your body is the temple of the Holy Spirit who is in you, whom you have from God, and you are not your own? For you were bought at a price; therefore, glorify God in your body and in your spirit, which are God's.

COMMENTS: How glorious it is that we are the Temple of the Holy Spirit! Knowing how beautiful the temple in Jerusalem was, we realize we must keep ourselves (hearts, minds, bodies) lovely and pure for God's sanctuary. We must let the beauty of Jesus be seen in us, His light shine through us in guiding others, His words be spoken through us to uplift others, our hands and feet His for service to others, our thoughts finding delight in our Lord.

ACTIVITY: For a flannelgraph lesson, cut an outline of red heart from cardboard or felt and put it on the flannel board. Cut out hearts about 5" wide from the leftover cardboard and glue flannel scraps on the back. Distribute them to the children. Have them print a word on their hearts, such as joy, peace, love, patience, kindness, helping, sharing, truth, goodness, forgiving. Then each puts his heart in the big heart, explaining its meaning.

Next give each child grey hearts for words that are not good: unhappiness, fear, hatred, impatience, unkindness, self-centered, selfish, lying, evil, unforgiving. As he or she puts the bad word in the heart, he takes out the good word for they can't both be there at the same time. Now we can see how horrible we appear to God and others. We don't want to be like that, so in order to get the good words back into us, we must ask forgiveness of God and the persons we have hurt, and in so doing, God plants the good word in us and the bad word is destroyed. How happy we feel then; how good and loving. We are the temple of God and must keep our hearts pure. The Spirit can't live in us if we are sinful.

ттттт

DAY 93. 1 Corinthians 7, 8
Don't Offend

Prayer: Help us not to offend.

1 Corinthians 8:13. Therefore, if food makes my brother stumble, I will never again eat meat, lest I make my brother stumble.

COMMENTS: We are constantly influencing others whether good or bad, so we must keep alert not to become a stumbling block, particularly to children.

ACTIVITY: As an object lesson, place styrofoam box cartons, odd pieces of pipe or debris along a pathway, then try walking through without stumbling. How can disaster be prevented? Remove the stumbling blocks! Place stepping stones instead; something that will help a person. The lesson is: Don't make life difficult for a child or grownup. Give him a compliment for what he has achieved. Listen, encourage, make suggestions.

✝✝✝✝✝

DAY 94. 1 Corinthians 9, 10
Temptation

Prayer: Thank You, Father, for helping us overcome temptation.

1 Corinthians 10:13. No temptation has overtaken you, except such as is common to man; but God is faithful, who will not allow you to be tempted beyond what you are able, but with the temptation will also make the way of escape, that you may be able to bear it.

COMMENTS: God is the answer to our problems--if we obey Him. To keep in the way of temptation, to go with the wrong crowd, to keep the smokes, drinks, drugs handy is only making the temptation stronger. Change course. Keep your mind on nobler things. Get busy doing something fascinating that is for good. "We are more than conquerors through Him who loved us" (Romans 8:37), if we keep in God's way of escape. Then we find that we are stronger persons because of the tests and trials.

ACTIVITY: Life is like a race (1 Corinthians 9:24-27), not against people but against Satan--all of us should help each other to win. God is there to help us, too. We are to run strong, work hard, keep pure, run straight to the goal of God's imperishable crown.

Here are party games that are races, arranged in order of age:
1. Run backwards. Run on all fours. Skip around obstacles. Jump on one foot.
2. Run with peanut in a spoon. Run with paper cup on head. (If you lose an object, pick it up and go on, for that is important in life's race--not to give up.)
3. Run with a balloon held between your knees. If outside, run with a paper cup filled with water. The one reaching the goal with the most water left wins. Run with lighted candle. Run an obstacle course, picking up the objects along the way.

Give everyone a prize in the end, for running the race (Christian bookmark).

✝✝✝✝✝

DAY 95. 1 Corinthians 11, 12
Gifts of the Spirit.

Prayer: Thanks for the gifts.

1 Corinthians 12:7. But the manifestation of the Spirit is given to each one for the profit of all.

COMMENT: In order for the Spirit to help every one of us in the Church (the Body of Christ) , He gives us "gifts" or special spiritual blessings to help each other. No one gift is superior to the others, nor is any gift for the person's "glory."

ACTIVITY: Dad and the boys make a wooden plaque "God is Love," using a jigsaw to cut out individual letters, glue on scrap wood, paint or shellac.

Mom and the girls embroider a verse to frame "Love One Another," adding flowers, birds, home. Use stitches according to age: running, chain, cross stitch.

For little ones, print L O V E on a cardboard. Punch small holes half-inch apart on the letters. With a shoelace, teach them to sew in and out of the holes. Or use yarn, making a stiff "needle" end by dipping it in glue.

DAY 96. 1 Corinthians 13, 14.
        Love

Prayer: May we truly love with Your love.

1 Corinthians 13:4-6. Love suffers long and is kind; love does not envy; love does not parade itself, is not puffed up; does not behave rudely, does not seek its own, is not provoked, thinks no evil; does not rejoice in iniquity, but rejoices in the truth.

COMMENTS: This is the Christian's measuring rod of the quality of our love. Only our Lord, loving through us, can mold us into His image, for He is Love. As we continue working on our Love plaques, think of how our "gift of the Spirit" should be used in love, for no matter how great the gift and how generously given (faith to remove mountains, give all we have to the poor), if it is not done in love, it is nothing.

ACTIVITY: Memorize 1 Corinthians 13, the Love Chapter.
        List people who are using their "gift of the Spirit" with love. Write or tell them that you appreciate their ministry, for it helps others. Thank them for their stand for Christian principles, for their faithfulness and love.

✝✝✝✝✝

DAY 97. 1 Corinthians 15, 16.
        Incorruptible

Prayer: Oh, thank You, Lord, for all the glorious mysteries You have for us!

1 Corinthians 15:51-53. Behold, I tell you a mystery: We shall not all sleep, but we shall all be changed--in a moment, in the twinkling of an eye, at the last trumpet. For the trumpet will sound, and the dead will be raised incorruptible, and we shall be changed. For this corruptible must put on incorruption, and this mortal must put on immortality.

COMMENTS: Such splendid things are to happen to us! In the twinkling of an eye, we shall have new imperishable, heavenly bodies. We travel through space faster than a space rocket. We are in the presence of Jesus and reign with Him during His Millennial reign; we dwell in the new heaven and the new earth forever!

ACTIVITY: Speaking of "fast," Dad or one of the teens should give us a report on the speed of sound, the time it takes for shuttles to orbit the earth, how long it took to get to the moon, how many light years away are some of the planets and stars.
        For the children, find out the fastest one to do his or her chores, the quickest to smile, to forgive. Often it's the youngest who forgives the quickest.

        For the Bible Club or other parties here are some "fast games."
1.   Give each a lightweight feather. Blow it to goal.
2.   Blow up a balloon and tie it.
3.   Use a stick to knock balloon to goal.
4.   Kick a jar top to goal, going around obstacles.
5.   Hammer 5 nails in a board.
6.   Eat 5 saltine crackers, then whistle, "Twinkle, twinkle, little star."
7.   Repeat the books of the New Testament.
8.   For younger ones, repeat the alphabet.
9.   Who can count to 100 the fastest?
10.   Who can jump rope the longest?
11.   Who can stand on one foot the longest?
12.   Who can do pushups the longest?

DAY 98. 2 Corinthians 1, 2
            Triumph

Prayer: Thanks for the victory!

2 Corinthians 2:14. Now thanks be to God who always leads us in triumph in Christ, and through us diffuses the fragrance of His knowledge in every place.

COMMENTS: God expects us to be winners and helps us to win. Things, circumstances, tests may seem insurmountable at times, but He shows us how to triumph over them. When we look back, we can trace how He helped us through other people, the Word, our own determination. Winning together.

ACTIVITY: This object lesson is for the younger children. One of the older children put a rubber ball in a bucket of water. Push it to the bottom--it pops up every time. Let the little ones try it. Explain that God helps us to pop up and do our job quickly and happily.
     "CHILDREN, OBEY YOUR PARENTS IN ALL THINGS, FOR THIS IS WELL PLEASING TO THE LORD." God has rewards for us in heaven for what we do right.

                                        ✝✝✝✝✝

DAY 99. 2 Corinthians 3, 4
            His Likeness

Prayer: We want to grow into Your beauty, Lord.

2 Corinthians 3:18. But we all, with unveiled face, beholding as in a mirror the glory of the Lord, are being transformed into the same image from glory to glory, just as by the Spirit of the Lord.

COMMENTS: Step by step we grow in His grace, His knowledge, and His image. It is a glorious journey as we keep our eyes on Him.

ACTIVITY: For a reminder to the little ones, paste a picture of Jesus on their mirror for them to be like Jesus, kind and sharing. For the rest, here is a study:
FIVE TYPES OF FOLLOWERS OF JESUS FOUND IN THE GOSPELS: (How far are we in Christ?)

1.   120 disciples tarried for prayer. Acts 1:14, 15.
        a. Had a desire to know the will of God but satisfied to tarry.
        b. God-empowered life.
        c. Preparation - willing to obey Him.

2.   70 disciples sent forth to serve. Luke 10:1-24.
        a. Had a desire to work but satisfied to serve.
        b. God-prospered life.
        c. Commission - willing to go for Him.

3.   12 disciples chosen to be with Jesus. Luke 9:1-10.
        a. Desire to be chosen, but satisfied to be with Him.
        b. God-planned life.
        c. Separation - willing to be called by Him.

4.   3 disciples were privileged. Matthew 17:1,2; Mark 14:33, 34.
        a. Desire to share walk with God but satisfied with special
           manifestations.
        b. God-privileged life.
        c. Revelation - willing to go with Him.

5.   1 disciple, John, followed Him all the way. John 13:23; 18:15.
        a. Desire to fulfill the will of God; satisfied only to be
           closest to Jesus.
        b. God-possessed life.
        c. Dedication - willing to stay with Him.

DAY 100. 2 Corinthians 5, 6
New Creature

2 Corinthians 5:17. Therefore, if anyone is in Christ, he is a new creation; old things have passed away; behold, all things have become new.

Prayer: We want to be new creatures in You!

COMMENTS: The new birth, when our lives take on a new spiritual dimension, is the greatest miracle we can experience; and it means not only a divine walk with Jesus on earth, but eternity with Him! For Jesus said, "Most assuredly, I say to you, unless one is born of water and the Spirit, he cannot enter the kingdom of God."

ACTIVITY: We mentioned before that the butterfly aptly represents the new birth. We will do more crafts along this line. If possible, buy real butterflies in hobby shops that come from Taiwan or Brazil. My grandchildren in New York State gathered cocoons, attached them to the ceiling of my trailer there, and my daughter took video pictures of them emerging as butterflies. They later mounted them as specimens and sent them to me to use in dried flower crafts. The flat ones go in frames with dried flowers and Bible verses. The ones in other positions are used in jars and bottles with dried flowers.

God created Us

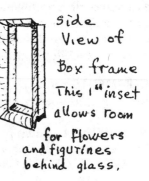
Side View of Box frame
This 1" inset allows room for flowers and figurines behind glass.

Gather all types of wild flowers, weeds, leaves; press some, let others dry in natural positions. Do the same with garden flowers. Small ones like violas, forget-me-nots, small rose buds, straw flowers work best. Keep them out of bright light in order to retain their colors.

Today we will make pictures using butterflies and dried flowers. Paint a watercolor background sky. Place flowers and butterfly in pleasant arrangement, gluing in place with small amounts of silicone or Elmer's glue. Glue a quarter-inch wooden edge around the cardboard so the arrangement won't mash. After putting it in the frame, seal the back.

straw flowers in foreground

Another idea is to use a calendar picture of pleasant scenery, add small dried flowers at the bottom and frame.

In all the pictures add a short Bible verse so as to use it as a reminder of God and as a witness when given away.

✝✝✝✝✝

DAY 101. 2 Corinthians 7, 8.
Sadness made Glad

2 Corinthians 8:9. For you know the grace of our Lord Jesus Christ, that though He was rich, yet for your sakes He became poor, that you through His poverty might become rich.

Prayer: Thanks, Jesus, for becoming poor to make us rich in You.

COMMENTS: Oh, the wonderful grace of Jesus who loves us so much. It is difficult for our finite minds to imagine the great God who created us and all the world became like us to bring us into relationship with Him! It is awesome, super-extraordinary, magnificent! How can we share such grace with others? Earlier in the chapter, the Christians though poor gave to other needy Christians. We can do that. We can share with missionaries, the Salvation Army, other ministries starving at home and overseas.

ACTIVITY: Make a missionary offering box for the Bible Club or Teen Club. Paste pictures of missionaries and natives around a coffee can with a slit cut in the plastic top. Send small gifts to the missionaries which they request (get their requests, as they know about customs duties), such as jello, powdered milk, cake mixes, balloons, crayons, embroidery materials, games, crafts.

✝✝✝✝✝

DAY 102. 2 Corinthians 9, 10
Priceless Gift!

2 Corinthians 9:15. Thanks be to God for His indescribable Gift!

Prayer: We're so glad you came, Jesus!

COMMENTS: God's Gift of Jesus to save us is beyond expression. There are so many extraordinary ways in which our Lord is made known to us. Think of these. Read again the poem, "God loved the world so very much" in the front of this book.

ACTIVITY: Draw a large diamond with many facets. Assign the following verses to be read. Write the words in the diamond describing Jesus.

Or for a program at a rest home during Christmas, have someone sing the carol as you draw or place pictures (with Fun Tak) on a large sheet of paper. Tell how the Lord meant these descriptions for you, and how He can be meaningful to them.

1. Light of the world (John 8:12)
2. Bread of Life (John 6:35)
3. Star (Revelation 22:16)
4. Door (John 10:9)
5. Friend (John 15:15)
6. Lamb of God (John 1:29)
7. Intercessor (Hebrews 7:25)
8. Vine (John 15:5)
9. Way, Truth, Life (John 14:6)
10. Savior (1 John 4:14)
11. Abundant Life (John 10:10)
12. Rock (1 Corinthians 10:4)
13. Shepherd (John 10:11)
14. Resurrection (John 11:25)
15. High Priest (Hebrews 2:17)
16. Yoke-bearer (Matthew 11:29)

✝✝✝✝✝

DAY 103. 2 Corinthians 11, 12
Sufficient

Prayer: I'm glad I am weak, for then
Your strength becomes my strength.

2 Corinthians 12:9. And He said to me, "My grace is sufficient for you, for My strength is made perfect in weakness." Therefore most gladly I will rather boast in my infirmities, that the power of Christ may rest upon me.

COMMENTS: Paul relates his sufferings in this letter more than in any other writing. His purpose is to show the power of God in his life when he was weak. This is a fresh way of looking at our failures. They aren't failures if we find God's grace is meeting our needs! Thus we are triumphant in Him!

ACTIVITY: An excellent object lesson for showing God's strength in us is to show a glove. Put your hand in the glove and it can be moved, pick up objects, etc. That is like God working through us--of our own we can do nothing of eternal value, but the Spirit empowers us to do God's work.

✝✝✝✝✝

DAY 104. 2 Corinthians 13
           Benediction

Prayer: We appreciate the blessing
           of the Trinity in our lives.

2 Corinthians 13:14. The grace of the Lord Jesus Christ, and the love of God and the communion of the Holy Spirit be with you all. Amen.

COMMENTS: This is a good benediction to use in hospitals or rest homes. In some translations, the wording is "and the fellowship of the Holy Spirit," which may better define the love between us and God and other Christians.

ACTIVITY: Memorize the benediction. Also memorize the 13 books of the Bible written by Paul as he was inspired by the Spirit to instruct the churches.

> Romans
> 1 and 2 Corinthians
> Galatians, Ephesians, Philippians, Colossians
> 1 and 2 Thessalonians, 1 and 2 Timothy, Titus (3 T's; long, medium, short)
> Philemon

✝✝✝✝✝

DAY 105. Galatians 1, 2
           Christ in Me

Prayer: Help us to put this truth
           into effect in our lives.

Galatians 2:20. I have been crucified with Christ; it is no longer I who live, but Christ lives in me; and the life which I now live in the flesh I live by faith in the Son of God, who loved me and gave Himself for me.

COMMENT: This is a dynamic statement. Memorize it and repeat it daily as a reminder that it is no longer I but Christ living in me. The old life is dead; my potential is no longer what I can do but what Christ can do through me. What possibilities there are for victorious living as we practice this truth.

ACTIVITY: Make a collection to put in a binder of true stories of God helping people in distress situations. *Guideposts* is an excellent source, as well as Drama in Everyday Life in *Reader's Digest* and stories in your church magazines or papers. Some are incredible, and we know they were miracles of God. If I feel the need of a lift, I get my collection out and read several, and I'm inspired to get busy again. Take the collection along on Teen trips; they love the stories.

✝✝✝✝✝

DAY 106. Galatians 3, 4
           One in Christ

Prayer: Thanks for the union we
           have with other Christians.

Galatians 3:26-28. For you are all sons of God through faith in Christ Jesus. For as many of you as were baptized into Christ have put on Christ. There is neither Jew nor Greek, there is neither male nor female; for you are all one in Christ Jesus.

COMMENTS: We are all one, equal in Jesus. There is no rank, color, sex, or nationality. The ground is level at the cross. Praise God!

ACTIVITY: Time for another party. It will be a clay modeling party. For any age group. Use any type clay, flour-salt-water clay, or cornstarch clay (see Appendix, Day 1). Decide on subjects to use. A good one is the verse for tomorrow, Galatians 5:22, 23, the fruit of the Spirit. Or make animals for Noah's ark, flowers, cup for "a cup of cold water." Dry in an oven or let dry overnight, then paint.

†††††

DAY 107. Galatians 5, 6
Fruit

Galatians 5:22, 23. But the fruit of the Spirit is love, joy, peace, longsuffering, kindness, goodness, faithfulness, gentleness, self-control. Against such there is no law.

Prayer: We're glad the Spirit helps us grow this way.

COMMENTS: Define these characteristics of a Spirit-led person. Let's check ourselves, using the verses as a measuring rod. Some of these we need to work on.

ACTIVITY: Memorize the verses. Paint the clay items and add verses with India ink. Use the items as gifts or for each one at the party to take home.

†††††

DAY 108. Ephesians 1, 2.
God made us.

Ephesians 2:10. For we are His workmanship, created in Christ Jesus for good works, which God prepared beforehand that we should walk in them.

Prayer: Thanks for doing such a good job in making us.

COMMENTS: Ephesians was written while Paul was in prison in Rome. It contains some of the finest "deeper life" teachings. God made us in the beginning, but He is also creating us spiritually. He has good works planned for us and is preparing us to fulfill them. Exciting, isn't it?

ACTIVITY: For an object lesson to illustrate predestination (verses in Chapter 1:4-5), make a small cardboard gate to prop on the table. On the outside print, "Come Unto Me." On the outside we are lost; when we come to Christ for salvation, we go through the gate. Then we see printed on the gate inside all that we inherit in Christ as God's children: redemption, forgiveness, adoption, love, riches of His grace, holiness, power to do His will, fruit of the Spirit, joy, peace, confidence, boldness, rest, fearlessness, on and on. God has predestined that we have all these riches in Christ. But we have to choose to go through the gate--He doesn't push us through.

†††††

DAY 109. Ephesians 3, 4
One Spirit

Ephesians 4:4-6. There is one body and one Spirit, just as you were called in one hope of your calling; one Lord, one faith, one baptism; one God and Father of all, who is above all, and through all, and in you all.

Prayer: We're glad that You have no divisions; we are all one Church.

COMMENTS: Underline the 7 "ones" in the verses above and 3 "alls." Use this as a devotional talk in the future. In your notebook under numbers, list 7 as the perfect number (4 for man and 3 for Trinity or Godhead.)

ACTIVITY: The younger children continue working with clay. Make molds of their hands. Roll clay into strips and print their names with the strips, later to be glued on a piece of board.

The older ones start a study on "Christ in Me" verses. As you study and meditate on the verses, consider the extraordinary privilege God grants us as Christ lives in us and we abide in Him. This is a good study for Teen Club or Neighborhood Bible study. The verses will be studied two days, and a word block filled in the third day using the underlined words. Verses are from New King James.

1. Colossians 1:27. To them God willed to make known what are the riches of the glory of this mystery among the Gentiles: which is, *Christ in you, the hope of glory*.

2. Galatians 2:20. I have been crucified with Christ; it is no longer I who live, but *Christ lives in me;* and the life which I now live in the flesh I live by faith in the Son of God, who loved me and gave Himself for me.

3. Ephesians 1:4. Just as *He chose us in Him* before the foundation of the world, that we should be holy and without blame before Him in love.

4. Ephesians 1:6. To the praise of the glory of His grace, by which He has made us *accepted* in the Beloved.

5. Ephesians 1:7. *In Him we have redemption* through His blood, the forgiveness of sins, according to the riches of His grace.

6. Ephesians 1:11. In whom also we have obtained an *inheritance*, being predestined according to the purpose of Him who works all things according to the counsel of His will.

7. Ephesians 2:6. And raised us up together, and made us *sit together in the heavenly* places in Christ Jesus.

8. Ephesians 2:10. For we are His workmanship, *created in Christ* Jesus for good works, which God prepared beforehand that we should walk in them.

9. Ephesians 2:15. Having abolished in His flesh the enmity, that is, the law of commandments contained in ordinances, so as to *create in Himself one new man* from the two, thus making peace.

10. Ephesians 2:18. For *through Him* we both have access by one Spirit to the Father.

11. Ephesians 2:21. In whom the whole building, being joined together, grows into a *holy temple in the Lord*.

12. Ephesians 2:22. In whom you also are being built together for a *habitation of God in the Spirit*.

13. Ephesians 3:12. *In whom we have boldness* and access with confidence through faith in Him.

14. Ephesians 3:12. In whom we have boldness and access with confidence through *faith in Him.*

15. Ephesians 3:16. That He would grant you, according to the riches of His glory, to be strengthened with might *through His Spirit in the inner man*.

16. Ephesians 3:20. Now to Him who is able to do exceedingly abundantly above all that we ask or think, according *to the power that works in us*.

17. Ephesians 4:6. One God and Father of all, who is above all, and through all, and *in you all*.

18. Ephesians 4:15. But speaking the truth in love, may *grow up in all things* into Him who is the head--Christ.

19. Ephesians 4:23. And *be renewed in the spirit* of your mind.

20. Ephesians 5:8. For you were once darkness, but now you are *light in the Lord*. Walk as children of light.

21. Ephesians 5:21. Submitting to one another *in the fear of God*.

22. Ephesians 6:1. Children, *obey your parents* in the Lord, for this is right.

23. Ephesians 6:10. Finally, my brethren, *be strong in the Lord* and in the power of His might.

24. Ephesians 6:10. Finally, my brethren, be strong in the Lord and *in the power* of His might.

✝✝✝✝✝

DAY 110. Ephesians 5, 6
              Wrestle

Prayer: Fight through us to defeat
             the enemy Satan.

COMMENTS: Paul warns us that we fight evil forces surrounding us, Satan's control of Earth includes sickness, depression, fear, drug addiction, alcoholism, insanity, crimes, perversion, lying, etc. We must put on God's armor to fight these evils. In Him we win.

ACTIVITY: Draw a large soldier on cardboard. Draw a second one on a larger cardboard or on a flannelgraph background. Cut the first one in pieces so the armor fits together like a jigsaw puzzle. Glue scraps of flannel on the back. Print the names of the armor on each piece. As you tell the story of our fight against Satan, have the children put the armor in place on the larger cardboard or flannel background. Follow carefully the Scripture definition of each piece and what it means to use it as a Christian.

This lesson is an excellent one to use in your witnessing at hospitals, rest homes, institutions, or wherever you have the opportunity.

Ephesians 6:12. For we do not wrestle against flesh and blood, but against principalities, against powers, against the rulers of the darkness of this age, against spiritual hosts of wickedness in the heavenly places.

DAY 111. Philippians 1, 2
Exalted

Prayer: We worship You, Lord,
Lord, and honor You.

Philippians 2:9-11. Therefore, God also has highly exalted Him and given Him the name which is above every name, that at the name of Jesus every knee should bow, of those in and of those on earth, and of those under the earth.

COMMENTS: Jesus deserves and will be given the greatest adulation and worship of all beings. Daily let us worship Him in spirit and in truth. People who now ridicule or reject Jesus will nevertheless one day bow to Him.

ACTIVITY: Younger ones: Act out some of the stories in your Acts scroll.
Older ones: Continue the study of "Christ in Me."

25. Ephesians 6:21. But that you also may know my affairs and how I am doing, Tychicus, a beloved brother and faithful *minister* in the Lord, will make all things known to you.

26. Ephesians 6:18. Praying always with all prayer and *supplication* in the Spirit, being watchful to this end with all perseverance and supplication for all the saints.

27. Romans 8:9. But you are not in the flesh but *in the Spirit*, if indeed the Spirit of God dwells in you. Now if anyone does not have the Spirit of Christ, he is not His.

28. Romans 8:10. And *if Christ is in you*, the body is dead because of sin, but the Spirit is life because of righteousness.

29. Romans 8:37. Yet in all these things we are more than *conquerors* through Him who loved us.

30. John 15:11. These things I have spoken to you, *that My joy* may remain in you, and that your joy may be full.

31. John 15:4. *Abide in Me*, and I in you. As the branch cannot bear fruit of itself, unless it abides in the vine, neither can you, unless you abide in Me.

32. John 15:7. If you abide in Me, and *My words abide in you*, you will ask what you desire, and it shall be done for you.

33. John 17:23. *I in them*, and You in Me; that they may be made perfect in one, and that the world may know that You have sent Me, and have loved them as You have loved Me.

34. Philippians 2:5. Let this *mind* be in you which was also in Christ Jesus.

35. Colossians 2:6. As you have therefore received Christ Jesus the Lord, so *walk* in Him.

36. Colossians 2:7. *Rooted* and built up in Him and established in the faith, as you have been taught, abounding in it with thanksgiving.

37. Colossians 2:10. And you are *complete* in Him, who is the head of all principality and power.

38. Colossians 3:16. Let the *word* of Christ dwell in you richly in all wisdom, teaching and admonishing one another in psalms and hymns and spiritual songs, singing with grace in your hearts to the Lord.

39. 1 Corinthians 15:22. For as in Adam all die, even so in Christ all shall be made *alive*.

40. 1 John 4:9. In this the love of God was manifested toward us, that God has sent His only begotten Son into the world, that we might *live* through Him.

41. 1 John 5:20. And we know that the Son of God has come and has given us an understanding, that we may know Him who is true; and we are in Him who is true, in His *Son* Jesus Christ. This is the true God and eternal life.

42. Revelation 3:20. Behold, I stand at the *door* and knock. If anyone hears My voice and opens the door, I will come in to him and *dine* with him and he with Me.

43. Genesis 1:26. Then God said, let us make man in our *image*, according to our likeness.

44. Galatians 4:7. Therefore, you are no longer a slave but a son, and if a son, then an *heir* of God through Christ.

45. 2 Corinthians 5:17. Therefore, if anyone is *in Christ, he is a new creatio*n; old things are passed away; behold, all things have become new.

46. Philippians 3:14. I press toward the goal for the prize of the *upward call of God in Christ Jesus*.

47. Matthew 18:20. For where two or three are gathered together in My *name*, there am I in the midst of them.

48. Romans 6:11. Likewise you also, reckon yourselves to be *dead* indeed to sin, but alive to God in Christ Jesus our Lord.

†††††

DAY 112. Philippians 3, 4
Run the Race.

Prayer: We yearn for Your upward call in Jesus, so we keep running.

Philippians 3:13, 14. Brethren, I do not count myself to have apprehended; but one thing I do, forgetting those things which are behind and reaching forward to those things which are ahead, I press toward the goal for the prize of the upward call of God in Christ Jesus.

COMMENTS: This illustration challenges us. We must forget our failures, and keeping our eyes on Jesus, run straight for the goal of His call to eternal life and victory in Him.

ACTIVITY: For the younger ones, play a game of running life's race, with obstacles in the way, such as: stopping, laziness, turning off, looking down, playing, etc. Give bookmarks to all who finish at the goal line, "Eternal Life."

The older ones, fill in the underlined words in the previous quiz on "Christ in Me" in the word puzzle. Words or phrases are found across, back, up, down, diagonally (slanting up).

CHRIST IN ME

	1	2	3	4	5	6	7	8	9	10	11	12	13	14	15	16	17	18	19	20	21	22	23	24	25	26
1	C	H	R	I	S	T	I	N	Y	O	U	T	H	E	H	O	P	E	O	F	G	L	O	R	Y	I
2	H	H	C	N	U	A	N	F	A	I	T	H	I	N	H	I	M	I	I	N	T	H	E	M	E	N
3	R	E	O	T	P	C	H	I	F	C	H	R	I	S	T	I	S	I	N	Y	O	U	X	X	G	H
4	I	C	N	H	P	C	I	X	C	R	E	A	T	E	D	I	N	C	H	R	I	S	T	X	A	E
5	S	H	Q	E	L	E	M	I	N	I	S	T	E	R	X	T	H	R	O	U	G	H	H	I	M	R
6	T	O	U	P	I	P	W	M	Y	W	O	R	D	S	A	B	I	D	E	I	N	Y	O	U	I	I
7	L	S	E	O	C	T	E	C	O	M	P	L	E	T	E	I	N	T	H	E	S	P	I	R	I	T
8	I	E	R	W	A	E	H	A	B	I	D	E	I	N	M	E	A	N	D	I	I	N	Y	O	U	A
9	V	U	O	E	T	D	A	L	I	V	E	D	R	O	L	E	H	T	N	I	T	H	G	I	L	N
10	E	S	R	R	I	R	V	X	X	I	N	T	H	E	F	E	A	R	O	F	G	O	D	N	X	C
11	S	I	T	T	O	G	E	T	H	E	R	I	N	T	H	E	H	E	A	V	E	N	L	Y	X	E
12	I	N	S	O	N	D	R	O	W	S	G	N	I	H	T	L	L	A	N	I	P	U	W	O	R	G
13	N	H	D	B	E	R	E	N	E	W	E	D	I	N	T	H	E	S	P	I	R	I	T	U	O	Y
14	M	I	N	D	E	A	D	R	O	L	E	H	T	N	I	G	N	O	R	T	S	E	B	A	O	O
15	E	M	A	N	O	B	E	Y	Y	O	U	R	P	A	R	E	N	T	S	L	I	V	E	L	T	J
16	H	O	L	Y	T	E	M	P	L	E	I	N	T	H	E	L	O	R	D	W	A	L	K	L	E	Y
17	X	T	O	T	H	E	P	O	W	E	R	T	H	A	T	W	O	R	K	S	I	N	U	S	D	M
18	H	A	B	I	T	A	T	I	O	N	O	F	G	O	D	I	N	T	H	E	S	P	I	R	I	T
19	C	R	E	A	T	E	I	N	H	I	M	S	E	L	F	O	N	E	N	E	W	M	A	N	N	A
20	X	X	I	N	W	H	O	M	W	E	H	A	V	E	B	O	L	D	N	E	S	S	R	I	E	H
21	N	A	M	R	E	N	N	I	E	H	T	N	I	T	I	R	I	P	S	S	I	H	U	R	H	T
22	X	I	N	C	H	R	I	S	T	H	E	I	S	A	N	E	W	C	R	E	A	T	I	O	N	X
23	T	H	E	U	P	W	A	R	D	C	A	L	L	O	F	G	O	D	I	N	C	H	R	I	S	T

✝✝✝✝✝

DAY 113. Colossians 1, 2.
All in Him.

Prayer: Help us to call on You
as Head of the church.

Colossians 1:17, 18. And He is before all things, and in Him all things consist. And He is the head of the body, the church, who is the beginning, the firstborn from the dead, that in all things He may have the preeminence.

COMMENTS: Paul's teaching in Colossians are similar to those in Ephesians. Ephesians expresses the oneness of Christ; Colossians the completeness in Christ. In Ephesians the body of the Church is emphasized; in Colossians the head, Christ.

ACTIVITY: For a flannelgraph or object lesson, make a cardboard church building explaining that Jesus often referred to His followers, His Church, as a building. The Church building is made up of all believers world-wide, all ages, all nationalities. Use the verses as you point to the parts of the church. Jesus emphatically proclaimed: "On this rock I will build My church, and the gates of Hades shall not prevail against it!" (Matthew 16:18).

1. *God's building*. 1 Corinthians 3:16. "temple" and the "Spirit of God dwells in you."

2. *Laborers together*. 1 Corinthians 3:9. "for we are laborers together with God." (KJ)

3. *Foundation is Christ*. 1 Corinthians 3:11 (KJ) "For other foundation can no man lay than that is laid, which is Jesus Christ."

4. *Joined and knit together*. Ephesians 4:16 "by which every part does its share."

5. *Door*. Matthew 11:28. "Come to Me all you who labor and are heavy laden."

6. *Windows*. Malachi 3:10. "I will open the windows of heaven and pour out a blessing that you will not be able to receive it."

7. *Tower*. Psalm 100:2. "Serve the Lord with gladness; come before His presence with singing."

8. *Cross*. Isaiah 45:22. "Look to Me, and be saved, all you ends of the earth! For I am God, and there is no other."

✝✝✝✝✝

DAY 114. Colossians 3, 4
Sing to God.

Prayer: Thank You for all the
the uplifting songs we
can sing to help each other.

Colossians 3:16, 17. Let the word of Christ dwell in you richly in all wisdom, teaching and admonishing one another in psalms and hymns and spiritual songs, singing with grace in your hearts to the Lord. And whatever you do in word or deed, do all in the name of the Lord Jesus, giving thanks to God the Father through Him.

COMMENTS: The more God's Word is studied, repeated, even played in our games, the more richly it dwells in us and we find the truths coming to our aid when decisions have to be made. The same is experienced with singing hymns and the Psalms. The Spirit puts a tune in our minds just when we need an uplift, or when we need to encourage another. Paul and Silas sang in prison; how it cheered and lifted them; and God sent an angel to set them free.

ACTIVITY: For a Teen Club party at Sunday School play some recitation games. Each one is assigned a number. When the leader calls out a number at random, that person has to do one of three things: (1) recite a Bible verse, (2) sing a chorus or hymn, or (3) say "Thanksgiving and praise to the Lord!" before the leader can count to 10. If the person doesn't start reciting before 10 is called, he is leader.

Another game to practice memory verses is to have the leader call a number, and that person has to recite verses as long as he can without a break. The one who recites the longest wins a prize. Be sure to use a timer!

Number slips of paper from 1 to 10. The pianist plays a bar of a familiar hymn, and each writes the title or first line. Those getting 10 correct receive prizes.

Gather around the piano and sing favorites; try harmonizing, quartets, duets.

DAY 115. 1 Thessalonians 1, 2.
With Power

Prayer: May the work we do for
You be done in Your power.

1 Thessalonians 1:5. For our gospel did not come to you in word only, but also in power, and in the Holy Spirit and in much assurance, as you know what kind of men we were among you for your sake.

COMMENTS: 1 Thessalonians was written at Corinth in A.D. 52. He was not able to stay in Thessalonica very long, but the church was successful so he wrote two letters to them, completing his teachings on the second coming of Christ. Paul did excellent follow-up ministry.

God's work through us may not seem successful at first, but don't despair for God promises His power to bring it to success later.

ACTIVITY: A fun way for children to spread the Word is to put typed verses in balloons. If you purchase balloons already inflated and "gassed," tie the verses on the string and also add a slip with the name and address of the sender, asking for a return letter from the finder. If you have balloons for the group to blow up, insert the verse in the balloon and all throw their balloons around in a game of keep in the air, and when a balloon breaks the person closest to it reads the verse for all to hear.

✝✝✝✝✝

DAY 116. 1 Thessalonians 3, 4
The Rapture

Prayer: Help us to win all we can
before Your return, Lord.

1 Thessalonians 4:16-18 For the Lord Himself will descent from heaven with a shout, with the voice of an archangel, and with the trumpet of God. And the dead in Christ will rise first. Then we who are alive and remain shall be caught up together with them in the clouds to meet the Lord in the air. And thus we shall always be with the Lord. Therefore, comfort one another with these words.

COMMENTS: This is the glory, the hope of the Church, the assurance we have that we will dwell with Him forever. This is to be a comfort to us when we hear of the end days, the anti-Christ, false prophets, signs of the times of tragedies, the increase of evil. During these times, the Holy Spirit increases His activities, too, and many are saved.

Foretold signs are being fulfilled in our days. The Spirit has led in the immense push of radio, TV and film ministries sending the Word to all the earth. Bible translators are busy in the remotest areas. Miracles of healing and manifestations of the Spirit are everywhere telling the world of the power of our Heavenly Father--that He's alive! It's a time to rejoice--not let Satan overshadow God's works.

ACTIVITY: Think of what will happen when the Believers, the Church, rise from the dead at the shout and the trumpet sound, and then those who are alive caught up with them in the clouds to meet the Lord in the air. We will always be with the Lord. So that means we will be with Him during the 1,000 years when He reigns as King on the earth, when there will be peace because Satan will be bound.

DAY 117. 1 Thessalonians 5
Keep Active.

1 Thessalonians 5:16-22. Rejoice always, pray without ceasing; in everything give thanks; for this is the will of God in Christ Jesus for you. Do not quench the Spirit. Do not despise prophecies. Test all things; hold fast what is good. Abstain from every form of evil.

Prayer: Help us to be kind, to rejoice, to pray always, to give thanks in everything.

COMMENTS: We need to be more diligent in our own practice of the Christian life. The above verses are excellent reminders of how to keep true to God.

ACTIVITY: Make wall plaque reminders of the above phrases. The men and boys might use wood-burning tools; the women and girls might try trimming frames with yarn wrapped around, or materials such as braid, lace. These make fine gifts.

✝✝✝✝✝

DAY 118. 2 Thessalonians 1-3.
Safe

2 Thessalonians 3:3. But the Lord is faithful, who will establish you and guard you from the evil one.

Prayer: Thanks for guarding us.

COMMENTS: We can skip worrying, for God promised to guard us from the evil one. However, we should not be lax about keeping our homes and cars locked; have fire prevention helps such as smoke alarms, sprinkler systems, a well planned escape route. We should have fire drills, take first aid courses, have emergency phone numbers in plain view, know how to use fire extinguishers, keep poisons, etc., out of reach of small children.

ACTIVITY: Read from your collection of stories of what brave persons did in emergencies, so that you will be able to profit by their experience.

✝✝✝✝✝

DAY 119. 1 Timothy 1, 2
Mediator.

1 Timothy 2:5. For there is one God and one Mediator between God and men, the Man Christ Jesus.

Prayer: Thanks for being our Mediator.

COMMENTS: Paul wrote two letters to his young pastor student, Timothy, who was already preaching in a church in Ephesus. Timothy's mother was Jewish, his father Greek. He grew up in Tarsus near Paul's home place. The information in both letters instructed Timothy in the church administration and preaching.

ACTIVITY: This short Bible drill gives answers to questions the lost may ask:

1. I don't think I am a sinner. (Romans 3:23)

2. Can I go to heaven by doing good? (Ephesians 2:8, 9)

3. I'll put it off until later. (2 Corinthians 6:2)

4. But I'm an atheist; will God accept me? (Hebrews 7:25)

5. How can I be saved? (Romans 10:9)

6. Will I be different? (2 Corinthians 5:17)

7. Do I now belong to God? (John 1:12)

8. Is this salvation forever? (John 3:16)

DAY 120. 1 Timothy 3, 4
          Youth

Prayer: Thanks for making
               youth important.

1 Timothy 4:12. Let no one despise your youth, but be an example to the believers in word, in conduct, in love, in spirit, in faith, in purity.

COMMENTS: This is excellent instruction for youth. It might be a good motto for the Teen Club. Encourage them to do noble things for the Lord. Support them in home instruction, good hobbies, educational trips, family unity and fun.

ACTIVITY: Pre-schoolers: Use 3X5" cards. Get some coloring books of animals, birds, etc., that are small enough to be traced on the cards. The children can spend some time doing the cards, and later use them as a memory game of God's creatures. Cut the cards exactly in half.

To play the game, all cards are turned over. Take turns picking up a card, see if it is a match for the 4 cards each one holds; if so, the matched card is set aside. Keep playing in turn, putting back any cards that do not match. When all cards are matched, count the sets each child has; the one with the most wins.

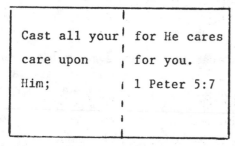

Bible and Teen Clubs: First session, the cards are printed or typed. Each 3X5" card has a memory verse, but the first half of the verse is on the left half of the card, and the remainder of the verse is on the right. Cut the cards in half. To play the game, all cards are turned upside down on the table. Each player takes 4 cards. Try to pick up a matching verse to make a set. Keep the sets; when all cards are picked up, see who has the most sets.

When a set is found, read the entire verse holding the two parts together. If it is an incorrect matching, the card has to be put back on the table and the next person takes a turn. If the match is correct, the player gets a turn until he or she doesn't find a matching verse, and the next one in turn tries.

The game is a fun way to learn verses. If the players are quite young, add a felt pen color-line across the top of the card before cutting it. Use various colors. Matching the colors helps, because small children cannot read a card at a glance, but can remember the colors to match. Reading the verse when matched is the memory trick. Use the following verses or others you want to memorize:

1. 1 Peter 5:7. Cast all your care upon Him;   for He cares for you.

2. Matthew 11:28. Come unto Me, all you who labor and are heavy laden,   and I will give you rest.

3. John 3:16. For God so loved the world that He gave His only begotten Son,   that whoever believes in Him should not perish, but have everlasting life.

4. John 14:6. I am the way, the truth, and the life,   No one comes to the Father, except through Me.

5. Philippians 4:13. I can do all things through Christ   who strengthens me.

6. Philippians 4:19. My God shall supply all your need   according to His riches in glory by Christ Jesus.

7. Colossians 3:2. Set your mind
on things above,

8. Colossians 3:17. Whatever you
do in word or deed,

9. 1 Thessalonians 5:18. In everything
give thanks;

10. Hebrews 11:6. Without faith it is impossible
to please Him, for he who comes to God

11. James 1:5. If any man lacks wisdom,
let him ask of God,

12. James 1:22. Be doers of the Word,

13. James 4:3. You ask and do not
receive, because you

14. James 4:7. Submit to God. Resist the devil,

15. James 5:15. The prayer of faith
will save the sick,

16. 2 Peter 3:8. With the Lord one day
is as a thousand years,

17. 1 John 5:7. There are three who bear
witness in heaven;

18. Matthew 5:14. You are the light of
the world.

19. Matthew 6:33. Seek first the kingdom
of God and His righteousness,

20. Matthew 7:7. Ask, and it will be
given to you; seek and you will find;

21. John 10:28. I give them eternal life,
and they shall never perish;

22. Romans 8:14. For as many as are led
by the Spirit of God,

23. Matthew 18:19. If two of you agree on
earth concerning anything they ask,

24. Mark 1:17. Come after Me,

25. Mark 8:36. For what will it profit
a man if he gains

26. Mark 10:14. Let the little children
come to Me and do not forbid them;

27. Mark 11:24. Whatever things you
ask when you pray,

28. Mark 16:15. Go into all the world and

29. Luke 12:2. There is nothing covered
that will not be revealed,

not on things on the earth.

do all in the name of the Lord
Jesus.

for this is the will of God in
Christ Jesus for you.

must believe that He is, and that He
rewards those who diligently seek Him.

who gives to all liberally,

and without reproach.

and not hearers only.

ask amiss, that you may spend
it on your pleasure.

and he will flee from you.

and the Lord will raise him up.

and a thousand years as one day.

the Father, the Word, and the Holy
Spirit; and these three are one.

A city that is set on a hill cannot
be hidden.

and all these things shall be
added to you.

knock and it will be opened to you.

neither shall anyone snatch them
out of my hand.

these are the sons of God.

it will be done for them by My
Father who is in heaven.

and I will make you fishers of men.

the whole world, and loses his
own soul?

for of such is the kingdom of
God.

believe that you receive them,
and you will have them.

preach the gospel to every creature.

nor hidden that will not be known.

30. Luke 18:27. The things which are impossible with men — are possible with God.

31. John 1:1. In the beginning was the Word, and the Word — was with God, and the Word was God.

32. John 3:3. Most assuredly, I say to you, unless one is born again, — he cannot see the kingdom of God.

33. John 4:24. God is Spirit, and those who worship Him — must worship Him in spirit and truth.

34. John 6:35. I am the bread of life, He who comes to Me — shall never hunger and he who believes in Me shall never thirst.

35. Romans 8:16. The Spirit Himself bears witness with our spirit — that we are children of God.

36. Romans 8:28. All things work together for good to those who love God, — to those who are the called according to His purpose.

37. Romans 8:37. In all these things we are more than conquerors — through Him who loved us.

38. Romans 12:21. Do not be overcome by evil, — but overcome evil with good.

39. 1 Corinthians 3:16. Do you not know that you are the temple of God — and that the Spirit of God dwells in you.

40. 2 Corinthians 12:9. My grace is sufficient for you, — for my strength is made perfect in weakness.

41. John 8:32. You shall know the truth, — and the truth shall make you free.

42. Jeremiah 33:3. Call to Me, and I will answer you, and show you — great and mighty things which you do not know.

43. Proverbs 8:17. I love those who love Me, and those — who seek Me diligently will find Me.

44. Psalm 91:1. He who dwells in the secret place of the Most High — shall abide under the shadow of the Almighty.

45. Isaiah 65:24. Before they call, I will answer; — and while they are still speaking, I will hear.

46. 2 Thessalonians 3:3. But the Lord is faithful, who will establish you — and guard you from the evil one.

47. Romans 5:8. But God demonstrates His his own love toward us, in that — while we were still sinners, Christ died for us.

48. John 15:7. If you abide in Me, and My words abide in you, you will ask — what you desire, and it shall be done for you.

49. 1 Corinthians 15:57. But thanks be to God, who gives us the victory — through our Lord Jesus Christ.

50. 2 Timothy 1:7. God has not given us a spirit of fear, — but of power and love and of a sound mind.

51. Psalm 103:12. As far as the east is from the west, — so far has He removed our transgressions from us.

52. Psalm 107:9. He satisfies the longing soul, — and fills the hungry soul with goodness.

53. Psalm 37:4. Delight yourself also
    in the Lord,
54. Hebrews 13:6. I will not fear.
55. Psalm 121:2. My help comes from the Lord,
56. James 5:8. Establish your hearts,
57. Matthew 5:9. Blessed are the peacemakers.
58. Acts 2:21. Whoever calls on the name
    of the Lord
59. Psalm 119:11. Your word I have hidden
    in my heart,
60. Psalm 119:105. Your word is a lamp to my
    feet

and He shall give you the desires
of your heart.
What can man do to me?
who made heaven and earth.
for the coming of the Lord is at hand.
for they shall be called sons of God.
shall be saved.

that I might not sin against You.

and a light to my path.

✝✝✝✝✝

DAY 121. 1 Timothy 5, 6
Fight.

Prayer: Help us win the fight
of faith, Lord.

1 Timothy 6:12. Fight the good fight of faith, lay hold on eternal life, to which you were also called and have confessed the good confession in the presence of many witnesses.

COMMENTS: What is the fight of faith? Maybe the biggest battle is overcoming our doubts and stepping out into the spiritual unknown, depending upon God instead of ourselves. In sports muscle and training pay off; in the fight of faith, complete submission to God who knows what is best for us, is the secret.

ACTIVITY: This is a baseball Bible drill. Two teams, two sets of red and blue buttons; one color at bat at a time. Bible verse is called out twice, then "Hit!" If the man at bat can repeat the verse from memory, it's a home run for his team. If he looks it up and reads it correctly, he goes to first base. Five verses are called for each team at bat. Play as for regular baseball. Team with most home runs at the end of the ninth inning wins. Use verses in Day 120. Draw a baseball diamond on paper, or use jar lids on the table for bases.

✝✝✝✝✝

DAY 122. 2 Timothy 1, 2
Sound Mind.

Prayer: Give us power, Lord.

2 Timothy 1:7. For God has not given us a spirit of fear, but of power and of love and of a sound mind.

COMMENTS: Fear, depression, unsound thinking are of Satan. Zeal, positive thinking, abounding love, fearlessness, intelligence, wisdom are of God!

ACTIVITY: Another game with the Memory Cards: Each person has 6 sets. Line them 3 top and 3 bottom. Put the second halves upside down on the table and mix all cards. In turn, each player picks up a card from center; if it matches one of his, he places it over the first half; takes another; if not a match, he replaces it in center and next one takes a turn. Try to remember where cards are to match your own. First one to get 3 sets in a row wins; also, the one to get all sets matched first wins. (Prizes: double-decker cone; triple-decker and 1 dip cones for the rest of the contestants.)

DAY 123. 2 Timothy 3, 4
Inspired

Prayer: Thanks for Your
authorship of the Word.

2 Timothy 3:16. All Scripture is given by
inspiration of God, and is profitable for
doctrine, for reproof, for correction, for
instruction in righteousness.

COMMENTS: There are many proofs that the Bible is inspired by God; one is the fulfillment of prophecies; another the continuity throughout the 1500 years of writing; lack of contradictions; personal testimonies of its vibrant influence in people's lives, verses brought to mind that helped, promises standing true, answered prayer, foundation laws of nations.

ACTIVITY: Note 2 Timothy 2:15: "Be diligent to present yourself approved to God, a worker who does not need to be ashamed, rightly dividing the word of truth." There are a number of divisions readily recognized:

1. *The Old and New Testaments*, or Old and New Covenants. Find these. Which is the largest? The Old Testament deals with the Law; the New with Grace. In the Old Testament, the people offered slain animals/birds as a sacrifice for their sins, looking forward to the promised Messiah as their Savior. In the New Testament, Jesus became the perfect Lamb, sacrificed on the Cross once for all people and all time as a substitute for our sins. He fulfilled the Old Testament law by being perfect (the only perfect sacrifice); and fulfilling the commandments to love God and neighbor.

2. *The Two Advents*. The first advent was Jesus coming to earth as our Savior; the second is when He returns as the Messiah, the reigning King for a thousand years. It is important to distinguish the two advents when reading prophecies. The people expected the Messiah at His first coming, rather than as Savior. We want to be alert to prophecies of His second coming.

3. *The Old and New Nature*. Our old nature rules us until we are born again and the Holy Spirit indwells us as our new nature. We are to be "dead" to the old and alive to the "new." (Galatians 2:20; 2 Corinthians 5:17)

4. *Jews and Gentiles*. As we study the Bible, we should discern whether the text is for Jews or for Christians. The altar sacrifices were for Jews up until Jesus' death and resurrection. The patriarchs were the important Jewish leaders of the Old Testament; the twelve apostles the chosen leaders of the Church in the New Testament. The tabernacle, temple and synagogue had to do with Jews; the Church with Christians (our body is the temple of the Spirit).

5. *Five Judgments.*

   1. Acceptance of Jesus as Savior (Lost and Saved).
   2. Daily sins as the Spirit convicts us.
   3. Believer's works when the Books are opened for rewards.
   4. Judgment of the nations.
   5. Great White Throne Judgment of the wicked dead.

List these in your Notebook for future reference and study.

✝✝✝✝✝

DAY 124. Titus 1, 2
Rescued

Prayer: We look for Your
glorious appearing.

Titus 2:13, 14. Looking for the blessed hope
and glorious appearing of our great God and
Savior Jesus Christ, who gave Himself for us,
that He might redeem us from every lawless
deed and purify for Himself His own special
people, zealous for good works.

COMMENTS: Titus was assigned to church work at Crete, following up Paul's foundation work. In a sense we are all assigned duties to follow up the work of Jesus in redeeming us. In our families, particularly, and as Bible teachers and even as young Christians we are to uplift, encourage, edify others. When God teaches us a lesson, we are to share it.

ACTIVITY: It's time for the family to witness again. What about the first party we had with the handicapped? It is appropriate to build on that foundation. Set up the scenes of the Life of Christ, perhaps in your backyard or in a large room. Roll the wheelchairs along like an exhibit at a fair with someone to explain each scene (Bible Club members). Give them time to ask questions and to give answers.

Give testimonies of what Jesus means to you. Perhaps the handicapped will testify, also. One might demonstrate the "fingers" verses on salvation and an older one give an invitation to accept Christ, just in case there is one present who hasn't had the opportunity before. If anyone responds, do follow up work: A New Testament to read, other helpful literature in child's level, visit, write, pray. See that they attend a Sunday School near them if possible.

††††

DAY 125. Titus 3.
His Mercy.

Prayer: Thanks that it is Your grace, not our works, that saves us.

Titus 3:4, 5. But when the kindness and the love of God our Savior toward man appeared, not by works of righteousness which we have done, but according to His mercy He saved us, through the washing of regeneration and renewing of the Holy Spirit.

COMMENTS: It is plainly told here that we are not saved by our goodness or works, but by the precious grace of Jesus who died in our place.

ACTIVITY: Do you note some "r's" in the Scripture above? Try an acrostic on the title "redemption." Use a "t" and list words to "testimony" or "thanksgiving."

For the pre-schoolers, use ABC blocks to introduce them to J for Jesus, G for God, C for children, and other Bible words.

For toddlers, play with all sizes of boxes, building them into towers or arranging them in a circle to walk around.

††††

DAY 126. Philemon
More

Prayer: Thanks for calling us brothers.

Philemon 1:16. No longer as a slave, but more than a slave, as a beloved brother, especially to me, but how much more to you, both in the flesh and in the Lord.

COMMENT: Paul is writing to Philemon, a prominent Christian, to take back his runaway slave, who became a Christian under Paul's ministry. He implores him to take the slave as a brother in Christ. That's what we become in our salvation: no longer slaves but friends, brothers of Jesus; not bound in sin, but free in Christ. Now we can be volunteer "bondslaves."

ACTIVITY: The older ones do the Victory block. The youngsters march like Christian soldiers around the room, carrying a banner or flag they make of a cross.

VICTORY IN JESUS

Activity:

22.
21.
20.
19.
18.
17.
16.
15.
14.
13.
12.
11.
10.
 9.
 8.
 7.
 6.
 5.
 4.
 3.
 2.
 1.

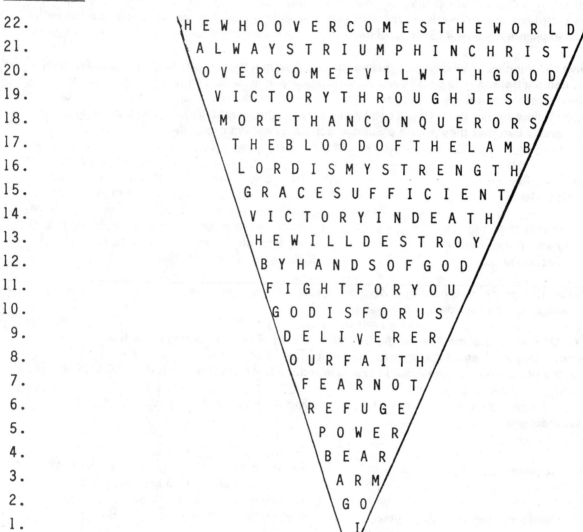

```
H E W H O O V E R C O M E S T H E W O R L D
A L W A Y S T R I U M P H I N C H R I S T
O V E R C O M E E V I L W I T H G O O D
V I C T O R Y T H R O U G H J E S U S
M O R E T H A N C O N Q U E R O R S
T H E B L O O D O F T H E L A M B
L O R D I S M Y S T R E N G T H
G R A C E S U F F I C I E N T
V I C T O R Y I N D E A T H
H E W I L L D E S T R O Y
B Y H A N D S O F G O D
F I G H T F O R Y O U
G O D I S F O R U S
D E L I V E R E R
O U R F A I T H
F E A R N O T
R E F U G E
P O W E R
B E A R
A R M
G O
I
```

MATCH THE QUOTATION WITH ITS VERSE BELOW.   READ THE ENTIRE VERSE.

I Corinthians 15:54   Isaiah 51:5   2 Corinthians 2:14
Romans 8:31   1 John 5:4   Deuteronomy 1:30
Deuteronomy 33:27   Romans 8:37   1 John 5:5
2 Corinthians 12:9   Exodus 3:20   Matthew 4:6
1 Corinthians 15:57   Exodus 15:2   Revelation 12:11
Matthew 28:19   2 Samuel 22:2   Genesis 49:24
Romans 12:21   Matthew 9:6   Isaiah 41:13
                            Deuteronomy 9:3

DAY 127. Hebrews 1, 2
No Escape

Prayer: Help us tell the lost
there's no escape if
they reject Jesus.

Hebrews 2:3. How shall we escape if we
neglect so great a salvation, which as the first
began to be spoken by the Lord, and was
confirmed to us by those who heard Him.

COMMENTS: Hebrews was written to the Hebrew Christians, about A.D. 65. The author is not known, but many think it was Paul or Apollos.

ACTIVITY: Read those two chapters with adoration to give Him honor and glory. He gives us so much--how can we treat Him lightly; how can anyone escape, if we deny Jesus?

First, God saves us, then he teaches us to live in love, service, faith, joy. It's like a pattern in our lives. Some lessons we learn step by step. Our life in Christ is like colors woven in and out in a weaving. To remind us of God's weaving of our lives, let's make a handbag for the girls and a canteen pouch for the boys. Use heavy yarn, nylon or cloth strips for the handbag and strips from an old jacket for the pouch.

1. For a base, use an upright cereal box. Wrap a cord around the top. Tie tightly.

2. Use 2' length cords of one color for the warp strands (the firm ones, hanging down). Fold in the center, slip under the tied cord, pull both ends through the loop, then down, knotting it. Repeat these knotted loops all around the cereal box. Tie strands together at the bottom.

3. The firm, downward strands are the warp. The strands woven in and out are the woof. Select colors and pattern bands. To change a color, tie the ends of the old and new, tuck them under the weaving. Weave evenly.

4. When you reach the bottom, turn inside out. Tie ends across from each other in double knots. Cut off the excess cords. Fold back the corners of the handbag like a paper bag and stitch flat. Follow the directions in the drawings, turning to right side.

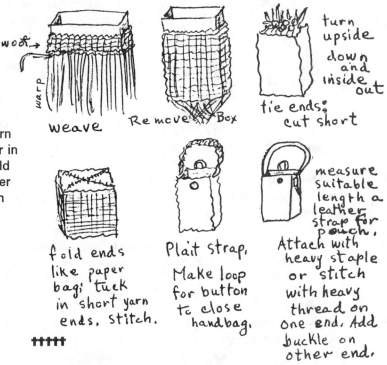

weave   Remove Box   tie ends; cut short   turn upside down and inside out

fold ends like paper bag; tuck in short yarn ends. stitch.

Plait strap. Make loop for button to close handbag.

measure suitable length a leather strap for pouch. Attach with heavy staple or stitch with heavy thread on one end. Add buckle on other end.

✝✝✝✝✝

DAY 128. Hebrews 3, 4.
Partners

Hebrews 3:14. For we are all partners with
Christ if we hold firmly to the end the
confidence we had at the beginning. (GNB)

Prayer: Thanks for being our Partner; we trust You.

COMMENTS: Dad, this verse should challenge you--Let Christ be your Partner in business. Each member of the family, let Christ be your Partner in whatever you do in life, in your sport, your hobby, your vocation.

ACTIVITY: For the handle to the handbag, cut 3' long yarn cords to plait (like braiding hair). Loop and tie the cords through one top end of the bag as you did the loops to start weaving. Plait using two cords at a time. When you reach the desired length of the handle, slip the ends through the opposite side of the bag and tie in double knots with the ends hanging like a tassel.

For the canteen pouch, make a narrow or inch-wide leather strap, stitching to one side and attaching a buckle at the other side. Punch holes to adjust strap length. Fishing line makes a strong thread to sew leather.

DAY 129. Hebrews 5, 6
Obedience

Hebrews 5:8, 9. Though He was a Son, yet He learned obedience by the things which He suffered. And having been perfected, He became the author of eternal salvation to all who obey Him.

Prayer: Help us learn
through our suffering.

COMMENTS: Although Jesus was the Son of God as well as a man, His deity didn't prevent Him from being tempted. He had to overcome and resist Satan the same as we have to. He never gave in to Satan so He became our High Priest. He constantly intercedes for us, helping us to overcome.

ACTIVITY: Obedience is a stiff lesson to learn, no matter what our age. But if we view it as a means to freedom (free from the bondage of sin), it's easier to quickly obey, cheerfully follow God's way. The results are so rewarding.

Train your pet, following directions of trainers, perhaps using a book from the library, or the advice of friends. You can condition almost any pet to eat at a certain place. Train a baby chick, duck, kitten to follow you. That is the way the Lord wants to train us, *to follow Him*--for our good and our joy.

✝✝✝✝✝

DAY 130. Hebrews 7, 8
To the Uttermost

Hebrews 7:25. Therefore, He is also able to save to the uttermost those who come to God through Him, since He ever lives to make intercession for them.

Prayer: Thanks for saving us.

COMMENTS: No matter how greatly we have sinned, Jesus saves us. He looks on our heart's desire to know Him, not on the sins we have repented of.

ACTIVITY: God saves to the uttermost! In a way, those who use scraps to make things beautiful are saving to the uttermost in a material way. If you have old clothes not good enough to distribute to the poor, cut them into inch-wide strips to use in braiding a rag rug. Old draperies are ideal.

1. Sort colors and decide on a pattern. Sew ends together to make strips long enough to work with. Take turns braiding. An older one can sew the braids together, using heavy thread and a curved needle.

2. Start at the center, make a round row, stitching closely. For an oval rug, start with an oval. For a square rug, start with a square.

3. You can make small prayer rugs for the bedside, or a large rug for the den.

Braid as flat as possible

DAY 131. Hebrews 9
         Judgment

Prayer: Help us live
           good lives.

Hebrews 9:27, 28. And as it is appointed for men to die once, but after this the judgment, so Christ was offered once to bear the sins of many. To those who eagerly wait for HIM, he will appear a second time, apart from sin, for salvation.

COMMENTS; God is love, but He is also just. He doesn't allow sin; he wants to get rid of it, even though He forgives us when we repent, and forgets. We will be judged for the sins we haven't repented of. He is constantly leading us in the right path, though we often stubbornly keep in our own way. Parents try to keep toddlers from putting fingers on a hot stove, or dashing into the street. So God is keeping us from the penalty of evil.

ACTIVITY: Explain to children in what ways they should punish their pets to keep them from harm, such as puppies chasing a car. Show them that God, too, has to train us by punishing us if we start harmful ways. So it's best to obey, start good habits, and be mindful of what might cause harm.

Here is a chart on Judgments recorded in Scripture:

WHO	WHERE	WHEN	PUNISHMENT
1. **Believer**	At the cross	Accepting Christ as Savior	Eternal Life or death
2. **Believer's daily sins** 1 Corinthians 11:31-32; Hebrews 12:7	Anywhere	Anytime during life	Forgiveness when confessed, or chastisement.
3. **Believer's works** 2 Corinthians 5:10 1 Corinthians 3:11-15	Resurrection	Book is opened.	Rewards for overcoming.
4. **Nations** Joel 3:2, 12-14; Matthew 25:31-34, 45-46.	Valley of Jehoshaphat	Christ's Coming	Some saved; some lost.
5. **Wicked Dead** 2 Thessalonians 1:6-9; Revelation 20:11-15.	Great White Throne	After Millennium Book of Life	Lake of fire, forever.

✝✝✝✝✝

DAY 132. Hebrews 10
         Patience

Prayer: We'll wait, Lord;
           help us endure.

Hebrews 10:35, 36. Therefore do not cast away your confidence, which has great reward. For you have need of endurance, so that after you have done the will of God, you may receive the promise.

COMMENTS: Thanks, Lord, for the rewards you have already poured out on us. Sometimes it is difficult to wait for God's timing, but it is always right.

ACTIVITY: We will have a World-Wide party, particularly for the Bible Club. Send invitations that have simple drawings of children of the world. Have helpers prepare games ahead for various countries; also refreshments that reflect the country. Fortune cookies (Bible verses in cream puffs); cookies in shape of elephant; cupcakes with chocolate "ants" on top; "snakes" made by dropping doughnut dough from a cookie tube into hot fat which makes curls.

Each missionary will prepare things his or her group can make, such as a hut, tepee, spears, hats. Also a dance, song, or skit. These will be shown to the other nations. Then games will be played by all the nations.

1. MEXICO. A pinata (pronounced pin-ya-ta) is lots of fun. Decorate a large plastic bottle to look like a pig. Through a slit in the top fill with candies, gum, little gifts or trinkets. Suspend it in the air from the ceiling or a branch. In turn, each child is blindfolded, given a bat and told to hit the pig in four tries. All try. When it is broken the goodies fall out and all grab them.

2. INDIA. A Hindu game is to divide into 2 teams, one called "Cheetal" (deer) and the other "Cheetah (leopard). Stand 6 feet apart, back to back. Each team faces a goal line. One in the center calls "Cheeeeee," then adds either "tal" or "tah," at which time the team with that name runs for the goal, the other team chasing. The ones caught are out. Keep playing until 1 is left.

3. BRAZIL. This grab bag game in Brazil is called Morral. Fill a paper bag with slips of paper. Each slip has something for the person to do: sing, make a speech, run around the room, hop like a frog, etc. You might also add, tell a Bible story, act out a pantomime for others to guess, recite a Bible verse.

4. JAPAN. Relay race. Each one must turn and run backwards on all fours.

5. CHINA. Amoy (catching the dragon's tail) is fun with 6-8 players in each dragon. Each holds onto the one in front. The head tries to catch the last one, the tail, but the body tries to protect the tail by twisting away.

6. GHANA. Each is given a paper cup of water, almost full. Walk to goal; if any spills, he is out. Winners are given Kool-Aid powder in their water.

End with a short devotional that Jesus loves all the children of the world. Tell a missionary story, sing a few songs, and invite new ones to attend your club.

††††

DAY 133. Hebrews 11. Faith.	Hebrews 11:1. Now faith is the substance of things hoped for, the evidence of things not seen.

Prayer: Increase our faith.

COMMENTS: This is the well loved faith chapter. Good News Bible quotes 11:1 as, "To have faith is to be sure of the things we hope for, to be certain of the things we cannot see." The Living Bible: "What is faith? It is the certainty that what we hope for is waiting for us, even though we cannot see it up ahead." The chapter states that people of great faith obeyed without seeing the results of their works. That should encourage us to keep on even though we see no present results.

ACTIVITY: Pre-schoolers: Play with clip clothespins, pinning them into funny objects, trying to make animals or buildings or chains.

Older ones: Write the answers to the quiz, finding 56 people known for faith. The questions will be in two lessons, the answers in the word block for the 3rd lesson.

1. She believed the angel who told her she would be the mother of Jesus. (Luke. 1:38)
2. This queen urged her countrymen to fast and pray for deliverance. (Esther 4:15-16)
3. The queen's cousin challenged the queen to trust God. (Esther 4:13-14)
4. An elderly man blessed Jesus when a baby, having been told by the Spirit that he would see Jesus before he died. (Luke 2:25-35)

5. God led this man to meet his brother Moses, which he did. (Exodus 4:27-28)
6. She declared allegiance to her mother-in-law's God and people. (Ruth 1:16)
7. When God called this prophet, he answered, "Here am I; send me." (Isaiah 6:8)
8. This prophet relied on God's word that he would be freed from prison.
(Jeremiah 39:15-18)
9. Another prophet traveled to the plain and saw God's glory. (Ezekiel 3:22-23)
10. In spite of illness, loss of property and family, he still worshipped God. (Job 1:20-22)
11. This man trusted God to show him the girl to select for his master's wife.
(Genesis 24:12-27)
12. A synagogue leader sought Jesus to heal his daughter. (Mark 5:22-23, 35-43)
13. A man offered a more excellent sacrifice than his brother. (Hebrews 11:4)
14. All the world recognizes the faith of the man who built the ark. (Genesis 6:13-22)
15. This man obeyed God, even offering his son as a sacrifice. (Genesis 22:1-18)
16. An altar was erected to praise God by this son of Abraham. (Genesis 26:24-25, 35:3)
17. After wrestling with an angel, his name was changed to Israel. (Genesis 32:24-28)
18. Her husband was 100 years old when they had their promised child. (Genesis 21:1-5)
19. Neither being sold, put in prison, nor holding high office turned this man from God.
(Genesis 50:19-20)
20. A mighty leader chose affliction rather than pleasures. (Hebrews 11:24-25)
21. The leader chosen to take the Israelites into Canaan knew God would give the victory.
(Joshua 3:9, 10)
22. Though a woman of disrepute, she trusted God and saved His spies. (Joshua 2:8,9)
23. God told this warrior to use only 300 men in battle and they won. (Judges 7:7)
24. This faithful spy urged the Israelites to take the land. (Numbers 13:30)
25. When she touched Jesus' robe, she was healed. (Mark 5:25-34)
26. This captain in Deborah's army sang praises for God's victory. (Judges 5:1-2)

DAY 134. Hebrews 12
Joyful Sacrifice

Prayer: We keep our eyes
You, lovely Savior
and Lord.

Hebrews 12:2. Let us keep our eyes fixed on Jesus, on whom our faith depends from beginning to end. He did not give up because of the cross! On the contrary, because of the joy that was waiting for Him, He thought nothing of the disgrace of dying on the cross, and He is now seated at the right side of God's throne. (GNB)

COMMENTS: Jesus went joyfully to the cross because of His great love for us, His future Bride (the Church). Let's face our trials joyfully because we are with Him, our Bridegroom, our Savior and Lord.

ACTIVITY: For younger children: Use a chalk-talk of two children walking toward a fence in the snow. One's footprints wandered around; the other's were like a straight line. Why? Because one kept his eyes on the goal, just as we must keep our eyes on Jesus, if we want to be like Him.

The older ones continue the quiz, writing the names of the faithful.

27. This strong man, when blind, killed more of the enemy in his death than in his life.
(Judges 16:29-30)
28. A youth of great faith defied the Philistines and killed the giant. (1 Samuel 17:45)
29. Though only a child, he answered the Lord's call in the night. (1 Samuel 3:10)
30. On Mt. Carmel God's prophet called for fire, and God answered. (1 Kings 18:32-38)
31. This prophet asked for a double portion of Elijah's spirit. (2 Kings 2:9)
32. Knowing God's faithfulness, he kept praying and was put in a lion's den. (Daniel 6:16)
33. God strengthened this man to take Israelites to Jerusalem. (Ezra 7:27-28)

34. Another, also led to restore Jerusalem, fulfilled the task. (Nehemiah 1:1)
35. She had faith to have a son and dedicated him to God's service. (1 Samuel 1:11)
36. Because of a king's faithfulness, his life was extended 15 years. (2 Kings 20:5)
37. God wrought miracles through this man and Paul. (Acts 15:12)
38. This writer argued that faith without works is dead. (James 2:18)
39. Jesus reproved this sister for worrying over serving dinner. (Luke 10:40-42)
40. The nephew of Barnabas worked with Paul and wrote a Gospel. (Acts 12:25)
41. He was the one who gave his lunch to Jesus to feed a crowd. (John 6:9)
42. God revealed the future to this apostle, which he wrote about. (Revelation 1:9)
43. This man walked on the water to Jesus. (Matthew 14:29)
44. This missionary was ready to die for Jesus. (Acts 21:13)
45. Together with Paul he sang in prison and God freed them. (Acts 16:25-26)
46. The first martyr was known as a man full of faith and the Spirit. (Acts 6:8)
47. Frightened when his prisoners were set loose, he asked how to be saved. (Acts 16:27-34)
48. When an angel told him to go to the desert, he did and led a man to Christ. (Acts 8:26-37)
49. A king's son, friend of David, believed God could save many. (1 Samuel 14:6)
50. An angel said she would have a special son and she believed. (Judges 13:2-3)
51. She gave her last meal to Elijah and God miraculously fed them. (1 Kings 17:9)
52. Because they honored God, they did not burn in the fiery furnace. They were _____,
53. _____,
54. and _____. (Daniel 3:16-17)
55. This Gentile and family were saved because he honored God, gave alms. (Acts 10:22)
56. Recognizing Jesus' authority, he told Jesus to merely say the word and his servant would be healed. (Matthew 8:5-13)

✝✝✝✝✝

DAY 135. Hebrews 13.
         Remember

Hebrews 13:3. Remember prisoners as if chained with them, and those who are mistreated, since you yourselves are in the body also.

Prayer: We remember, Lord.

COMMENTS: Yes, we must remember those in prison. Many in Communist countries are imprisoned for preaching, and their families suffer economically. Our prayers and support through caring organizations such as Underground Evangelism and Open Doors help. Also, prisoners who do not know Christ as Savior are ministered to through prison ministries in our own Christian lands. We need to support them and witness if possible.

There are great verses in this chapter, such as the 5th: "I will never leave you nor forsake you." What a comfort when going through trials day in and out as we bear a cross, as missionaries enter strange lands, as translators work among new tribes in remote areas.

ACTIVITY: Teach children about faith. Tell a child to sit in a chair. Did that take faith? No, we just knew the chair would hold him, and it didn't take any decision to test it. But some things require a step of faith when we are not sure of the outcome: to witness to a new neighbor, to make friends with a lonely person, to enter a new business, try for a scholarship, teach a class.

Read stories of faithful dogs who helped an injured person, rescued someone, traveled long distances to come home.

The older ones fill in the word block on faith with the names of the persons of great faith in the previous quiz.

ACTIVITY: 56 PEOPLE OF GREAT FAITH IN THE BIBLE

	1	2	3	4	5	6	7	8	9	10	11	12	13	14	15	16	17	18	19	20	21
1	S	S	A	M	U	E	L	X	X	C	X	N	E	H	E	M	I	A	H	J	X
2	H	X	X	J	O	S	H	U	A	M	O	R	D	E	C	A	I	S	P	O	X
3	A	R				S	X	L	C	I	S	A	I	A	H	X	J	I	E	H	J
4	D	E		X	D	X	E	A	R	X	P	H	I	L	I	P	A	M	S	N	A
5	R	H			A	B	A	S	U	M	B	J	T	X	X	A	C	E	O	B	M
6	A	T		A	V	S			T	M	A	A	A	N	X	U	O	O	J	A	E
7	C	S		A	I				H	A	O	N	R	I	A	L	B	N	H	R	S
8	H	E	B	R	D				R	M	H	O	N	L	V	R	A	H	A	B
9	M	X	O	O					Y		A	X	A	A	O	R	X	X	K	C
10	E	X	Y	N	E	L	I	S	H	A		I	R	X	H	B	R	E	X	W	E
11	S	A	R	A	H	A	N	N	A	H		M	X	K	A	S	A	M	S	O	N
12	H	E	Z	E	K	I	A	H	J	X		E				E	W	S	X	M	T
13	A	B	E	D	N	E	G	O	A	X		R	A		X	Z	X	I	X	A	U
14	C	W	I	T	H	O	U	T	I	P	X	E	B		J	E	X	L	F	N	R
15	H	X	F	A	I	T	H	X	R	X	E	J	E		O	K		A		E	I
16	D	A	N	I	E	L	I	T	U	I	S	T	L		N	I		S		L	O
17	J	O	B	I	M	P	O	S	S	I	B	L	E	O	A	E				I	N
18	T	O	X	P	L	E	A	S	E	Z	R	A	E	R	T	L		X		J	X
19	C	O	R	N	E	L	I	U	S	G	O	D	X	X	H	X		X		A	X
20	Z	A	R	E	P	H	A	T	H	W	I	D	O	W	A	M	A	R	T	H	A
21	X	X	H	E	B	R	E	W	S	G	1	1	:	6	N	E	H	P	E	T	S

See how many of the 56 people of great faith you can find in the Word Block, the names having been given in the foregoing quiz.

DAY 136. James 1, 2
Wisdom

Prayer: Thanks for giving
us wisdom liberally.

James 1:5, 6. If any of you lack wisdom, let him ask of God, who gives to all liberally and without reproach, and it will be given to him. But let him ask in faith, with no doubting, for he who doubts is like a wave of the sea driven and tossed by the wind.

COMMENTS: The James who wrote this letter is thought to be the brother of Jesus (Mark 6:3). His message stresses faith based on works. There is no conflict between Paul's statement that we are justified by faith without works and James' statement that works without faith is dead, for Paul is stating the principle of salvation, while James is explaining that the life work of a Christian is faith in action.

ACTIVITY: Give a chalk-talk on faith being like a circle, discussing the 5 subjects given in the 5 chapters. Note faith binds a Christian into the wholeness of God. It is the power in a Christian's life, like the energy that turns the wheel.

1. Trial of Faith
2. Work of Faith
3. Wisdom of Faith
4. Character of Faith
5. Triumph of Faith

✝✝✝✝✝

DAY 137. James 3, 4
Resist Satan

Prayer: Help us to fight
and resist Satan.

James 4:7-8. Therefore, submit to God. Resist the devil and he will flee from you. Draw near to God and He will draw near to you. Cleanse your hands, you sinners; and purify your hearts, you double-minded.

COMMENTS: It takes faith to resist Satan, faith knowing God is behind you.

ACTIVITY: Pray definitely for God to overcome the evil influences in our world. List such evils: drugs, alcoholism, perversion, abortion, pornography, crimes, violence on TV, child abuse, etc. Support projects for good activities.

✝✝✝✝✝

DAY 138. James 5
Healing

Prayer: Father, we pray
for the sick that
they be healed.

James 5:14-16. Is anyone among you sick? Let him call for the elders of the church and let them pray over him, anointing him with oil in the name of the Lord. And the prayer of faith will save the sick, and the Lord will raise him up. And if he has committed sins, he will be forgiven. Confess your trespasses to one another and pray for one another that you may be healed. The effective, fervent prayer of a righteous man avails much.

COMMENTS: Many Christians hesitate to pray for healing, feeling God may be allowing them to "suffer" to strengthen them. So I made a study of the Gospels, and marked every mention of healing. I am firmly convinced that God wants us to be well! It is His will! We pray, "Thy will be done on earth as it is in heaven"! There is no sickness in heaven. It is Satan who brings sickness, death, all manner of evil. But sometimes God "allows Satan to tempt us," but only to strengthen us in Him. God is *for* us, and if we team up with Him, we win.

God uses events to His glory, such as sight given to the man born blind (John 9:1-3), and He is able to give us blessings from any circumstance, and He wants to. When Jesus was asked to heal the person "if You want to," Jesus answered, "I want to heal you!" It is His desire to heal. However, Jesus could not do any great miracles in His home town because of their unbelief. Let's believe and not waiver.

Of course, we all die, so death often comes by way of illness and deterioration. Then there are a few exceptions where God uses paralysis to allow greater witnessing, such as with Joni Eareckson Tada, who has prayed for miraculous healing, but God has given her greater grace to do far beyond what is normally possible--for a greater witness to His glory. Healed, her influence may not have been as dynamic. So we do pray, "Thy will be done," but knowing that it will glorify God. Let it not be an excuse for not believing.

ACTIVITY: For a neighborhood Bible study on Prayer, or the "Prayer of Faith," consider these Scriptures. (For the children, give them the main truths.)

1. SPECIAL PROMISES AND HELPS
      If two agree (Matthew 18:19)
      Spirit intercedes for us (Romans 8:26)
      Jesus intercedes for us (John 17:9; Hebrews 7:25)
      God answers; before we call (Isaiah 65:24; Psalm 10:17; Matthew 7:9-11; Luke 11:13)

2. VARIOUS KINDS OF PRAYER
      Fellowship (Revelation 3:20; John 15:4)
      Worship (John 4:24; Ephesians 6:18; Romans 8:26-28; 1 Corinthians 14:14, 15)
      Thanksgiving (Ephesians 5:20; Philippians 4:6; Psalm 100; Ephesians 5:19, 20)
      Petition (Matthew 6:33; Matthew 7:7; ask, seek, knock; Matthew 7:9-11)
            for wisdom (James 1:5)
            for guidance (Psalm 32:8)
            for help (1 Peter 5:7)
            for needs (Luke 12:27-31)
      Intercession (James 5:16; 1 Timothy 2:1)
            for those in authority (1 Timothy 2:2)
            for the lost (1 Timothy 2:4)
            for laborers (Matthew 9:38; Colossians 4:2, 3)
            for enemies (Matthew 5:44)
            for others (James 5:16; Ephesians 6:18)
            for peace of Jerusalem (Psalm 122:6)
            for the sick (James 5:14-15)
            for nation (2 Chronicles 7:14)
            for missionaries (Ephesians 6:19-20; 2 Corinthians 1:8-11; Colossians 4:2;
                2 Thessalonians 3:2)

3. HOW TO PRAY
      with boldness (Hebrews 4:16; 1 John 5:14, 15)
      with humility (2 Chronicles 7:14)
      with faith (Mark 11:22-25; John 14:13)
      with love (1 John 3:22, 23; Matthew 5:44; Mark 11:24-25)
      with perseverance (Luke 18:1; Ephesians 6:18)
      with fervency (James 5:16; Romans 15:30; Luke 22:44)
      with righteous heart (James 5:16; Proverbs 15:29; James 4:8)
      without ceasing (1 Thessalonians 5:17; Acts 12:5)
      in the Name of Jesus (John 14:14; 16:23-26; Romans 10:13; Philippians 2:9-11)
      believing (Mark 11:24; Matthew 21:22; 1 Timothy 2:8; Hebrews 11:6; James 1:6)
      with authority (Luke 10:19; Acts 4:29-30)
      with accord (Acts 2:42, 46; 3:1; 4:24; 12:5; John 17:11; Matthew 18:20)
      with much prayer and fasting (Matthew 17:21; 1 Corinthians 7:5; Esther 4:16)
      fight Satan, principalities, power (Ephesians 6:12, 18; Daniel 10:12-13; Matthew 18:19)

4. IF NO ANSWER
     ask amiss (James 4:3; Psalm 66:18; 103:3)
     wait upon God (Psalm 46:10; Habakkuk 2:3)
     without faith (Hebrews 11:6)

It is not faith in *prayer* but in *God*.
If it is a *fact*, act on it; if a *promise*, claim the answer.

5. LORD, TEACH US TO PRAY (Matthew 6:5-15)
     in secret - privacy (Matthew 6:6)
     not vain repetitions - definite prayers (Matthew 6:7; Luke 18:41-42)
     to Father - with reverence (John 16:23-24)
     His will and plan (Matthew 26:39; Luke 5:12-13)
     for food, care, spiritual food (Matthew 6:25-27; Psalm 37:4-5)
     forgive (Mark 11:25-26)
     protect, deliver from evil (Matthew 26:41; Luke 21:36)
     worship Him (John 4:24; 9:31)

                                      ✝✝✝✝✝

DAY 139. 1 Peter 1, 2.   1 Peter 2:2. As newborn babes, desire the
             Food   pure milk of the word, that you may grow
                                         thereby.

Prayer: Thanks for our daily food.

COMMENTS: Peter wrote about A.D. 65, probably from Babylon. In 2:9 he says, "You are a
chosen generation, a royal priesthood, a holy nation, His own special people, that you may proclaim
the praises of Him who called you out of darkness into His marvelous light." He was writing to
Christians, both Jews and Gentiles. We are now God's people chosen to proclaim salvation.

ACTIVITY: For witnessing put Bible scenes in a cube or jar. Make flour-salt-water clay with green
coloring. Cut out characters from Sunday School papers, back with cardboard. Stick the figures in
the clay. Add pebbles, small straw flowers, larger
bush-like weeds, for an attractive display.
     Add the Scripture verse suitable to the
story by typing or printing it on a small strip of
paper and taping it inside the jar or cube.
     If you make several, use as gifts or prizes.

                                      ✝✝✝✝✝

DAY 140. 1 Peter 3   1 Peter 3:8, 9. Finally, all of you be of one
             Love   mind, having compassion for one another;
                                         love as brothers, be tenderhearted, be
                                         courteous; not returning evil for evil or
Prayer: Help us to fulfill   reviling for reviling, but on the contrary,
             these commands,   blessing, knowing that you were called to
             and truly love.   this, that you may inherit a blessing.

COMMENTS: This is so true in families. If we consider each other as equal spiritually before God,
each responsible to God for our own deeds for which we will be judged some day, we will be more
willing to help our partner to make a good report. Building up others in the faith is one of the facets
of a Christian's responsibility. Husbands are to respect their wives, so that their prayers will be
answered. Wives are to submit to their husbands as unto the Lord to win them through good
conduct. God loves inner beauty, the ageless beauty of a quiet and gentle spirit. Neither husbands
nor wives are to "rule" over each other. We are "one" in Christ.

ACTIVITY: Each member of the family, plan ways to make the others happy. Each check off his own list of "good deeds" at the end of the week, then fold them over as a gift "unto the Lord" with no thought of rewards, "just glad to do it for love."

†††††

DAY 141. 1 Peter 4, 5
Gifts

1 Peter 4:10. As each one as received a gift, minister it to one another, as good stewards of the manifold grace of God.

Prayer: Show us how to use our gifts.

COMMENTS: Consider your talents or gifts. They are very special--from God, entrusted to you with your own personality to best use them.

ACTIVITY: How can each of us grow as a steward of God's grace? If it's singing or playing a musical instrument, do your part at the programs the family presents when witnessing. If it's a good memory, repeat memory verses or a poem for others to enjoy in hospitals and rest homes. If it's making beautiful crafts, sewing, woodwork, pass these works on as gifts to the needy. Is it a winning smile? Smiles are contagious. Counselor? Leader? Good photographer? Artist? Neat law-mower? Good cook? Well, you know how to help others, so get busy!

†††††

DAY 142. 2 Peter 1
Prophecy

Prayer: Thanks for the Bible,
Your Word.

2 Peter 1:20-21. Knowing this first, that no prophecy of Scripture is of any private interpretation, for prophecy never came by the will of man, but holy men of God spoke as they were moved by the Holy Spirit.

COMMENTS: As we consider various prophecies of the Old Testament that were fulfilled in the ministry of Jesus, we know that the author of those books didn't make up those prophecies--they were from God. We have the same assurance for prophecies of the future, that they are from God. Only God knows the time of Jesus' second coming. But we are to watch and pray, to be ready, alert.

ACTIVITY: Make a "Signs of the Times" jigsaw puzzle for Bible or Teen Clubs, or neighborhood group. Use two poster boards, one for base, the other for pieces. Draw identical jigsaw lines on both, 16 for the 16 signs. Cut out the pieces on one board. Write a "sign" on each piece as given below. Use Fun Tak or similar removable adhesive (or make this a flannelgraph lesson). As the verses are read and discussed, place on the puzzle if it has been fulfilled. Read 1 Thessalonians 5:1-11 and 2 Thessalonians 2:1-12.

1. False Christs (Matthew 24:5)
2. Wars and rumors of wars (Matthew 24:6)
3. Famines (Matthew 24:7)
4. Pestilences, plagues, diseases (Mt. 24:7)
5. Earthquakes (Matthew 24:7)
6. Persecutions (Matthew 24:9)
7. Betrayal (Matthew 24:10)
8. False Prophets (Matthew 24:11)
9. Sin abound, love cold (Matthew 24:12)
10. Gospel to world (Matthew 24:14)
11. Wickedness as in Noah's day (Matthew 24:37)
12. Jews return to Israel (Ezekiel 11:16-17)
13. Armies at Jerusalem (Luke 21:20)
14. Unholy, selfish (2 Timothy 3:1-5)
15. Signs in sun, moon, stars (Luke 21:25-26)
16. Anti-Christ (Daniel 7; 2 Thessalonians 2:2-4; Revelation 13:4-8)

DAY 143. 2 Peter 2, 3
Not Slow

Prayer: Thanks that You
want us all.

2 Peter 3:8, 9. But beloved, do not forget this one thing, that with the Lord one day is as a thousand years, and a thousand years as one day. The Lord is not slack concerning His promise, as some count slackness, but is longsuffering toward us, not willing that any should perish but that all should come to repentance.

COMMENTS: A day with the Lord may be an extended period of time, such as a "thousand years." As I pondered the time relationship in this verse, I thought of the six days of Creation, and the seventh Day of Rest. It has been almost 6,000 years since the creation of Adam--4,000 before Jesus came and almost 2,000 years since. If we consider the next 1,000 years as the Millennium (when Jesus rules in peace), it would compare to the days of Creation and Rest. This could be another "sign of the times." If so, the time is soon.

ACTIVITY: We should be witnessing as often as possible. There are many places where people welcome something to read, such as laundry marts, bus stations. Get permission to leave Christian literature, such as church papers, Sunday School story leaflets, magazines, Bible story books your children have outgrown, tracts.

✝✝✝✝✝

DAY 144. 1 John 1, 2.
Confess

Prayer: We're sorry for our sins, Lord.

1 John 1:9. If we confess our sins, He is faithful and just to forgive us our sins and to cleanse us from all unrighteousness.

COMMENTS: Confession that we have sinned is a requisite for accepting Jesus as our Savior, for it is by His shed blood that our sins are washed away. In the Old Testament (before Christ came), the people offered a perfect animal or bird as a sacrifice in their place (the shed blood being the token of death). They offered the sacrifices often; now we pray for daily forgiveness, for Jesus died once, for all. Belonging to a church or doing good works does not save us. But our good works will bring rewards eternally.

ACTIVITY: John wrote the Gospel of John, three letters and Revelation. He lived the longest of the apostles, the others having been martyred years before. He loved Jesus the most, and his writings reflect divine love. The outline of 1 John is 3 L's as an acrostic, and all three are Jesus. Use as a chalk-talk.

Light, 1-2   John 1:9; I John 4:8; John 14:6
Love, 3-4   We reflect Him: Matthew 5:14-16.
Life, 5   John 15:12; Galatians 2:20.

✝✝✝✝✝

DAY 145. 1 John 3, 4.
Abiding in Him.

Prayer: This is so precious--
to abide in You!

1 John 4:12, 13. No one has seen God at any time. If we love one another, God abides in us, and His love has been perfected in us. By this we know that we abide in Him, and He in us, because He has given us of His Spirit.

COMMENTS: God's Spirit tells us we are His children. How we thank Him for that assurance. God doesn't see us--He sees Jesus in us. So also we see Jesus in others, not their faults. And we learn to love with His love.

ACTIVITY: So many people need love--they need Jesus! Let's spread His love around for He is in us and we represent Him today. List some who need cheering, someone in the hospital or rest home.

A surprise tree or plant is a way to love for many days. Use a firm branch of a pruned bush or tree that has many places to hang small gifts.

Plant the "tree" in a pot with pebbles or clay so that it won't fall over. Stick pencil, pen, small scissors, etc., in the "soil." Tie on the branches Scripture verses rolled up, cards, pictures, candies gum, cookies, etc. For a child add crayons, paper, small toys, balloons. Wrap the pot with aluminum foil or gift wrap. With glue and glitter, print "We love you!" and your names.

✝✝✝✝✝

DAY 146. 1 John 5
Life

1 John 5:11, 12. And this is the testimony: that God has given us eternal life, and this life is in His Son. He who has the Son has life; he who does not have the Son of God does not have life.

Prayer: Thanks for Abundant
Life we have in You.

COMMENTS: If we have not felt God's presence, His leading, His love, we should earnestly seek it. Don't go through life missing what God has for you!

ACTIVITY: At times you can make the gift with the person, which adds delight. Such is this macrame hanging plant.

Use flour-salt-water clay to form beads around a pencil. Dry in a 200 degree oven about an hour. Make the beads various sizes; paint them with bright colors with felt pens or model paints.

For the pot, select a large plastic pot and a smaller one to fit into it for drainage. Punch a few holes in the smaller pot at the bottom. Paint over any printing on the pot. Use the large pot for the macrame hanger and the small one for a plant. Punch 4 holes around the top of the large pot.

For the hanger, plait 4 double cords. At intervals slide on a bead, then divide the cords, braid, adding smaller beads on each cord. Continue braiding until you reach A in drawing, and add a large bead.

Continue braiding about a foot and thread each cord into one of the holes in the large pot at B. Tie.

Divide the 4 cords to make 8 cords, twisting them down several inches to meet opposite cords at C, and put a bead, joining at 4 places. Divide again to D; add bead at each joint. Then bring them all to one big bead beneath the pot at E. Tie ends firmly and make a tassel with the hanging ends. Trim.

Slip your plant in the smaller pot and carefully lower it into the larger pot. If you want, draw little smiling faces or print Bible verses in the open spaces on the large pot. Spray with clear acrylic paint for protection.

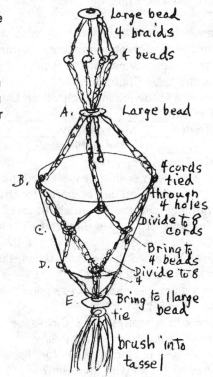

DAY 147. 2 John
        Live in Love

2 John 1:6. This is love, that we walk according to His commandments. This is the commandment, that as you have heard from the beginning, you should walk in it.

Prayer: Thanks that You are Love.

COMMENTS: Living in love and praying in love is an exciting way to live. If you are on a bus, train, plane, whatever, start praying for the people you see. They may feel it and turn their heads. Pray for the teens who seem to be getting into trouble, for the alcoholic neighbor, abused or neglected children, those with burdens, the happy child skipping along.

ACTIVITY: Make large prop-up cards to distribute. Use calendar pictures, Bible story pictures, or church bulletin pictures. Paste on cardboard like a round, oval or square frame. Print your favorite Bible verse on the bottom. Each member of the family sign, with "We love you!" and give to the sick, lonely, etc.

✝✝✝✝✝

DAY 148. 3 John
        Faithful in Love

3 John 5, 6. Beloved, you do faithfully whatever you do for the brethren and for strangers, who have borne witness of your love before the church. If you send them forward on their journey in a manner worthy of God, you will do well.

Prayer: Make us a blessing
              to others.

COMMENTS: John constantly wrote about love. It would be wonderful to be remembered as one who is spilling over with love--to God, to family, to others, to the lost.

ACTIVITY: Pre-school children: Make little plastic flower bouquets for the sick; or use fresh flowers to put in a small jar. Tie with ribbon.

For the others, here is a quiz on Love:

1. What family opened their home to Jesus near Bethany?
2. What are the two great commandments on love?
3. Repeat the favorite verse of the Bible.
4. Where is the Love Chapter found?
5. Complete the following instructions on love:
   a. Perfect _____ casts out _____. (1 John 4:18)
   b. If you _____ Me, keep My _____. (John 14:15)
   c. _____ is the fulfillment of the _____. (Romans 13:10)
   d. God loves a cheerful _____. (2 Corinthians 9:7)
   e. Eye has not seen, nor ear heard, nor have entered into the heart of man the things which God has prepared for those _____. (1 Corinthians 2:9)
6. What warnings did Jesus give about love?
   a. The love of _____ is a root of all kinds of evil. (1 Timothy 6:10)
   b. Do not love the _____ or the things of the _____. (1 John 2:15)
7. What disciple denied Jesus three times, then later Jesus asked him three times, "Do you love Me? (John 21:15-17)
8. Jesus told a parable about love, saying the one who loved the most had been _____ the most. (Luke 7:41-43)
9. Name some love stories in the Old Testament.
10. Name some great friends in the Bible.
11. In John 17, the prayer of Jesus for His followers, what divine request did Jesus ask of the Father for all who love Him?
12. What is the greatest way love can be given?
13. Which writer of the Bible wrote the most about love?
14. What warning did Jesus give the church of Ephesus in Revelation 2:4?

DAY 149. Jude
Benediction

Prayer: Thanks for Your blessings, Lord.

Jude 1:24, 25. Now to Him who is able to keep you from stumbling, and to present you faultless before the presence of His glory with exceeding joy, to God our Savior, who alone is wise, be glory and majesty, dominion and power, both now and forever. Amen.

COMMENTS: This is a beautiful benediction. The most glorious part is for the Church. Here is Christ presenting His Bride (the Church) to the Father in Heaven, without spot or wrinkle--perfect in Him! He's proud of us! He bought us with His own blood. He has cherished us, worked over us until we are perfect enough to reign with Him forever--as His Bride! Maybe I am overly romantic, but the love Jesus pours out in John 14-17 as the Bridegroom wooing His loved ones to abide in Him overwhelms me with awe. He's coming back to get us to dwell in the mansions He's building for us; to let the Holy Spirit comfort us while He is gone, and to tell us about Him, praying over us that we be "one in Him as He is One in the Father!" How we adore Him, our Prince of Glory!

ACTIVITY: This is a flannelgraph lesson on LOVE. Make a large red heart and print on it GOD IS LOVE (1 John 4:16). Make 10 smaller hearts and write verses on them. The children place them on the board, reading them.

> Jeremiah 31:3 - I have loved you with an everlasting love.
> 2 Corinthians 13:11 - The God of love and peace will be with you.
> John 15:13 - Greater love has no one than this, to lay down one's life for his friends.
> Proverbs 17:17 - A friend loves at all times.
> Proverbs 10:12 - Love covers all sins.
> Matthew 22:37 - Love the Lord your God with all your heart, with all your soul, and with all your mind.
> John 13:34 - Love one another, as I have loved you.
> Song of Solomon 2:4 - His banner over me is love.
> Matthew 5:44 - Love your enemies.
> Ephesians 3:19 - The love of Christ passes knowledge.

✝✝✝✝✝

DAY 150. Revelation 1
Blessing

Prayer: We're glad to read it, Lord.

Revelation 1:3. Blessed is he who reads and those who hear the words of this prophecy, and keep those things which are written in it; for the time is near.

COMMENTS: Revelation is the last book in the Bible and the most difficult to understand, yet it is the only one that pronounces a blessing on all who read or hear it. We know that the Holy Spirit will help us understand it.

The vision of Jesus which John saw is so glorious. Read 13-17 again.

ACTIVITY: If you have an artist in the family, try drawing this glorious picture of Jesus in the middle of the seven lampstands. Use fluorescent chalk and black light (ultra-violet) for the picture to glow in the dark. For more information regarding chalk-talk art, write Ren Dueck, 16428 Harvest Ave., Norwalk, CA 90650.

When giving this chalk-talk, explain that the book of Revelation is a series of visions given to John on Mt. Patmos when he was about 90 years old.

The first vision is of Jesus as He appears in heaven. In His right hand He holds 7 stars (angels of the churches), stands among the 7 churches, and out of His mouth comes a sharp two-edged sword (Word of God). (Hebrews 4:12)

DAY 151. Revelation 2
Testing

Prayer: Help us to be
faithful unto death.

Revelation 2:10. Do not fear any of these things which you are about to suffer. Indeed, the devil is about to throw some of you into prison, that you may be tested, and you will have tribulation ten days. Be faithful until death, and I will give you the crown of life.

COMMENTS: To each church Jesus pays a compliment for good points, warns about their shortcomings, and challenges them to overcome so as to receive outstanding awards. We all, as a group of Christians in a local church, and as individuals can learn a great deal from these messages.

ACTIVITY: We will play a game of toss. Three boxes are to be marked, first the Good Points, second the Bad Points, third Rewards. Use jar lids. There are 7 churches; make 3 taped slips for each church and put them on the jar lids, stating their good points, the bad and the rewards if they overcome. There will be 21 lids in all; each person tries to throw the lids in the right boxes. High score wins. This game will help us remember what God expects of us, what to avoid, and His rewards.

✝✝✝✝✝

DAY 152. Revelation 3
Fellowship

Prayer: Come into my heart, Jesus.

Revelation 3:20. Behold, I stand at the door and knock. If anyone hears My voice and opens the door, I will come in to him and dine with him, and he with Me.

COMMENTS: This is my favorite verse, for it tells how precious Jesus is, inviting us to have fellowship with Him, how He listens as well as discusses issues. What an invitation! That we can dine with the Prince of Peace, the King of kings and Lord of lords, the Savior of the World!

ACTIVITY: The New King James translation gives headings for the churches:

1. The Loveless Church
2. The Persecuted Church
3. The Compromising Church
4. The Corrupt Church
5. The Dead Church
6. The Faithful Church
7. The Lukewarm Church

In what category would you place the church group you attend? Are there warnings that your group should heed and put in correct course in order to carry out our mission to win the lost? Is the church in a rut, no vision, no outside ministry, looking to its own needs instead of the world's needs?

✝✝✝✝✝

DAY 153. Revelation 4, 5
Throne

Prayer: It will be glorious
to see Your beautiful
throne!

Revelation 4:2, 3. Immediately, I was in the Spirit; and behold, a throne set in heaven, and One sat on the throne. And He who sat there was like a jasper and a sardius stone in appearance; and there was a rainbow around the throne, in appearance like an emerald.

COMMENTS: We will see this beautiful throne with the rainbow halo. The glory, majesty, mightiness of it all is beyond our comprehension! And the One on the throne is our Lord! And we will see His glory--that glory that He prayed in the upper room that we would see. Thank You, Lord, that You want to share that with us. Your love--the height, depth, width--is beyond our understanding. We praise You!

ACTIVITY: Make a chalk-talk of this magnificent throne scene, the sea of glass, the lightnings, lamps of fire, 24 elders, and 4 living creatures.

DAY 154. Revelation 6, 7
Living Water

Prayer: Thank You for the
living fountains.

Revelation 7:16, 17. They shall neither hunger anymore nor thirst anymore. The sun shall not strike them, nor any heat, for the Lamb who is in the midst of the throne will shepherd them and lead them to living fountains of waters. And God will wipe away every tear from their eyes.

COMMENTS: The Lamb was the only One who could open the Book. As He breaks open the 7 seals, marvelous and fearful things happen. Read Billy Graham's book, *The Approaching Hoofbeats*, and contemporary books on prophecy when you have spare time.

1. White Horse - the Anti-Christ
2. Red Horse - war
3. Black horse - famine
4. Green horse - sword/famine
5. Souls slain for the Word
6. Earthquake, sun black, moon red, stars fall
(parenthesis re: 144,000: ones saved)
7. Silence for half hour in heaven

These are some of the "signs of the times" predicted by Jesus in Matthew 24.

ACTIVITY: Continue the chalk-talk drawings. In your notebook page for numbers, list these groupings of 7's.

✝✝✝✝✝

DAY 155. Revelation 8, 9
Prayer Incense

Prayer: May our prayers ascend
with fragrance to You.

Revelation 8:4. And the smoke of the incense, with the prayers of the saints, ascended before God from the angel's hand.

COMMENTS: After the seals were opened, then the 7 angels with the 7 trumpets were heard and other dramatic events took place:

1. Hail, fire with blood
2. Great mountain on fire
3. Great star from heaven
4. 1/3 sun, moon, stars are black
5. Star from heaven, key to bottomless pit - locusts
6. River Euphrates; army of 200,000,000 slays 1/3 men.

ACTIVITY: This drawing will be a mural with so many catastrophic events.

✝✝✝✝✝

DAY 156. Revelation 10
Rule forever.

Prayer: Help us to witness.

Revelation 10:9. And I went to the angel and said to him, "Give me the little book." And he said to me, "Take and eat it; and it will make your stomach bitter, but it will be as sweet as honey in your mouth."

COMMENTS: This is another parenthesis. John is told not to write of the 7 thunders; but to eat the bitter book; to measure the temple and altar.

ACTIVITY: We are to witness as often as possible. Have the children show their Life of Christ animated books, telling the stories.

DAY 157. Revelation 11
Rule forever.

Prayer: Thanks for Your
Reign forever.

Revelation 11:15. Then the seventh angel sounded; and there were loud voices in heaven, saying, "The kingdoms of this world have become the kingdoms of our Lord and of His Christ, and He shall reign forever and ever!"

COMMENTS: Some Bible scholars think Moses and Elijah may be the two witnesses who have power against the Beast for 3-1/2 years. The Beast kills them; the Spirit takes them to heaven. People are glad and exchange gifts. There is a great earthquake; 7,000 men are slain by it.

ACTIVITY: The people at that predicted time will be exchanging gifts for an evil happening. Let's give good gifts to celebrate how good God is.

We'll make bookmarks using dried flowers and Bible verses. Print the verse at the bottom of the card. Arrange some flat flowers at the top. Put wax paper over the flowers and press with a warm iron. Trim. Add braid around the edge, stitching with embroidery thread by hand, or with a zig-zag stitch on a sewing machine.

Here are some suggested verses:

Philippians 4:19 - My God shall supply all your need according to His riches in glory by Christ Jesus.

Philippians 4:13 - I can do all things through Christ who strengthens me.

Psalm 37:4 - Delight yourself also in the Lord, and He shall give you the desires of your heart.

1 Peter 5:7 - Cast all your care upon Him, for He cares for you.

1 Thessalonians 5:17 - Pray without ceasing.

Hebrews 13:5 - I will never leave you nor forsake you.

Psalm 23:1 - The Lord is my shepherd; I shall not want.

✝✝✝✝✝

DAY 158. Revelation 12.
Victory

Prayer: Thanks for giving us victory.

Revelation 12:11. And they overcame him by the blood of the Lamb and by the word of their testimony, and they did not love their lives to the death.

COMMENTS: This portion gives the account of the war in heaven between Michael and his angels against the dragon and his angels. The dragon is defeated, and he and his angels are not allowed to stay in heaven but are cast out.

ACTIVITY: Help the youngsters do some weaving. If you have a potholder weaving frame, use that; if not, make one by hammering short nails at the top and bottom of a wooden frame about 8" X 8". Use heavy yarn or cord. Tie a knot at one corner, then weave the cord up over the nail, down under the nail, and continue until all the nails have been circled. Tie a knot.

Thread a large-eye needle with yarn. Weave the thread in and out of the upright cords going back and forth until you reach the end. Tie a knot; make a loop for hanging the potholder; tie again.

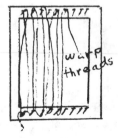

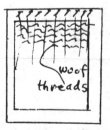

DAY 159. Revelation 13
Mark of the Beast

Prayer: May the beast
be defeated.

Revelation 13:16-18. And he causes all, both small and great, rich and poor, free and slave, to receive a mark on their right hand or on their foreheads, and that no one may buy or sell except one who has the mark or the name of the beast, or the number of his name. Here is wisdom. Let him who has understanding calculate the number of the beast, for it is the number of a man: His number is 666.

COMMENTS: Note that in Chapters 6 and 7, there were 7 seals; in Chapters 8-11 there were 7 angels with 7 trumpets. Now in Chapters 12 and 13 there are 7 personages:

1. Woman (Israel?)
2. Great red dragon (devil, Satan)
3. Man child (Jesus) rules with rod of iron
4. Archangel Michael
5. Jewish remnant
6. Beast, Anti-Christ - out of the sea, political 3-1/2 years.
7. Another beast - out of earth - religious; mark of 666 needed to buy, sell.

This mark is a warning. Followers of God are not to take the mark of the beast or they will be killed, eternally lost. The ones who do not take the mark 666 come to life and rule as kings with Christ for 1,000 years (Revelation 20:4).

ACTIVITY: The children may enjoy making a box of 5 woven potholders. The sides may be of different colors, or some other design the children choose.
Stitch the sides of the potholders together with large overcast stitches of heavy thread.
The box makes a holder of pens, pencils, crayons; or a plant may be placed in it.
To make a lid, stitch another potholder across one end. Chain-stitch a loop to attach to the middle of the opposite end. Sew on a round head to hold the loop.

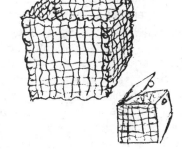

✝✝✝✝✝

DAY 160. Revelation 14
Angels news

Prayer: Give us understanding of these
prophecies.

Revelation 14:6, 7. Then I saw another angel flying in the midst of heaven, having the everlasting gospel to preach to those who dwell on the earth--to every nation, tribe, tongue, and people--saying with a loud voice, "Fear God and give glory to Him, for the hour of His judgment has come; and worship Him who made heaven and earth, the sea and springs of water."

COMMENTS: This is another parenthesis telling of the vision of the Lamb and 144,000 virgins with the Name in their foreheads (Name of the Lamb). Six angels appear:

1. Angel - preaching the Gospel
2. Angel "Babylon is fallen"
3. Angel "those worship the beast and his mark--to be punished"
4. Angel "Son, thrust in sickle and reap."
5. Angel - with sharp sickle
6. Angel with power over fire; blood to the horse's bridle - the wrath of God.

ACTIVITY: Youngsters: Make an angel with a clothespin (or popsicle stick) and a paper doilie.

Cut the doilie in half. Put one-half around the neck of the clothespin for the robe. Tie at the waist with a gold-colored cloth, ribbon or yarn.

Draw a pleasant face on the head, using felt pens for color.

Cut the other half doilie in two. Roll one piece to make the arms. Staple on the back of the angel in the middle of the roll for arms to extend on each side.

Accordian pleat the other piece of doilie, pinch at the center, and flatten the wings on each side. Staple it over the arm roll.

Scriptures do not state that angels have wings, except Cherubims, but for children it explains the angels' ability to travel through space. These angels make nice Christmas tree decorations. Add yarn hair or a wreath halo.

The quiz on angels includes information from all parts of the Bible, about their mission, who they are, and fascinating contacts with people. The answers are given in the Appendix Day 160 according to the first number. Tomorrow you will fill in the answers in the crossword puzzle using the numbers in parentheses.

1. God sends many angels on errands; they might be called m_____. (1 across)
2. An angel told Mary her baby would be called _____. (Luke 1:31 (6a)
3. An angel appeared to distraught _____ in the desert. Genesis 16:7-12 (10a)
4. H_____ angels celebrated Jesus' birth. Luke 2:13 (11a)
5. There are many groups of angels of which the archangel Michael is_____. Jude 9 (15a)
6. Angels _____ battles, and at one battle killed 185,000 men. 2 Kings 19:35 (16a)
7. An angel delivered _____ from jail. Acts 12:6-11 (17a)
8. God's angels are _____. Matthew 25:31 (19a)
9. An angel appeared as a _____ in a bush to Moses. Exodus 3:2 (20a)
10. Elijah's servant's _____ were opened to see an army of angels protecting them.
       2 Kings 6:14-17 (22a)
11. Two angels led _____ and family out of a wicked city. Genesis 19:1-17 (23a)
12. An angel called to _____ at a mountain altar of sacrifice. Genesis 22:11-18 (24a)
13. _____ dreamed of angels going up and down a ladder. Genesis 28:10-12 (25a)
14. _____ saw an angel with sword drawn, a battle being fought. 1 Chronicles 21:15-16 (26a)
15. An Angel protected ____ from lions. Daniel 6:21-22 (27a)
16. All angels were not good and fell from heaven whose leader was the beautiful angel S_____.
       Revelation 12:9 (28a)
17. An angel told _____ God would make him strong. Judges 6:11-23 (29a)
18. An angel directed _____ to meet an Ethiopian. Acts 8:26-27 (30a)
19. _____ was struck dead by an angel for not honoring God. Acts 12:21-23 (31a)
20. An angel blocked the way of ____'s donkey. Numbers 22:22-35 (32a)
21. At Jesus' _____ two angels said He would return as He went. Acts 1:10-11 (33a)
22. Angels are immortal; they _____ _____. Luke 20:36 (34a)
23. Jesus said angels are not like us as they ____ _____. Mark 12:25 (35a)
24. They always worship and _____God. Psalm 148:2 (36a)
25. They _____ over every sinner who repents. Luke 15:10 (GNB) (37a)

26. At the end of the world angels will cast the _____ into fire. Matthew 13:49, 50 (38a)
27. An angel told ___ she would be the mother of Jesus. Luke 1:26-38 (1d)
28. He said Jesus was sent to be the ___ of the world. John 4:42 (2d)
29. The angels are also called ___ ___ ___. Job 1:6 (KJ) (3d)
30. The angel who spoke to Mary was named ___. Luke 1:26 (4d)
31. This same angel told ___ he would have a son. Luke 1:11-20 (5d)
32. This son was to be called ___. Luke 1:13 (6d)
33. An angel fed ___ who ran from a wicked queen. 1 Kings 19:5-7 (7d)
34. Angels appeared to ___ in a field. Luke 2:8-15 (8d)
35. God orders His angels to ___ and protect us. Psalm 91:11-12 (9d)
36. Two angels heralded Jesus' resurrection at the ___. Matthew 28:1-7 (12d)
37. An angel told ____ not to be afraid. Acts 27:23 (13d)
38. An angel told ____ and his wife they would be parents of Samson. Judges 13:6-24 (14d)
39. _____ was told by an angel that God would answer his prayer. Acts 10:3-7 (18d)
40. When questioning what to do, an angel told ____ to marry Mary. Matthew 1:20 (21d)

✝✝✝✝✝

DAY 161. Revelation 15, 16
        Song of the Lamb

Prayer: How beautiful that song will be, Lord!

Revelation 15:3 And they sing the song of Moses, the servant of God, and the song of the Lamb, saying: "Great and marvelous are Your works, Lord God Almighty! Just and true are Your ways, O King of the Saints."

COMMENTS: The angels with the last plagues are presented with 7 gold bowls filled with the anger of God.

ACTIVITY: Youngsters work on picture files. Older ones, do puzzle from quiz. Use for answers the numbers in parentheses; answers may not fill all the blanks.

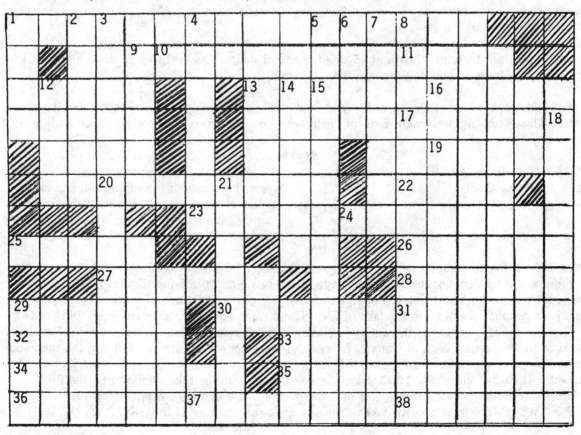

DAY 162. Revelation 17, 18
               Victory of the Lamb

Prayer: Glory to the Lamb, the Overcomer!

Revelation 17:14 These will make war with the Lamb who will overcome them, for He is Lord of lords and King of kings; and those who are with Him are called, chosen, and faithful.

COMMENTS: The great Babylon falls and the merchants bewail the loss.

ACTIVITY: As we think of God's triumph over evil as we come to the end of Revelation, and as we realize we have read through all of the New Testament, it's time to celebrate with a party. It will be a Sunday School party, divided into two groups, one for the younger children, and the other for the teens and older members of the family. Games are given in the following days for the two groups. At the conclusion of the games all will join for refreshments and devotional time.

GAMES FOR YOUNGER GROUP:

1.   Jesus grew in wisdom and stature and in favor with God and man.
      a.   Wisdom. Prize to the one reciting the most memory verses.
      b.   Stature. Stretch hand the highest, standing on toes. Tallest gets prize. Shortest gets prize. Rest get apple or other fruit to grow on.
      c.   Favor with God and man. Have copies made of Luke 10:27 printed in large letters on sheet of paper, with jigsaw lines, to cut up into puzzles. Put each cut-up puzzle into envelope. Prize to one assembling it first.

2.   If party is outdoors, use a volley ball; if inside, use a balloon. Game "to keep unspotted before the world" is for one in center of ring to keep from being hit with the ball or balloon. If hit, he changes places or is out of the game (depending upon the number of children playing -- if only a few, take turns). To play with teams, the team is in center of circle.

3.   Disciples sent forth. Large circle, marching around. Several articles (book, note pad, plastic dish, etc.) are handed to various ones and they start passing them on. When music stops, those with articles are out of the game.

4.   Each given plastic cup, straw and 15 dried beans of peas. The first to pick up all the beans by sucking on the straw and putting them in the cup wins.

5.   Put Bible story pictures on the wall, numbered. Give paper and pencil to each. List the title of the story (Jesus healing blind man, Birth of Jesus, etc.) by number on the paper. Ones with perfect score win bookmarks.

✝✝✝✝✝

DAY 163. Revelation 19,20
               Praise God!

Prayer: Praise Your Name, Alleluia

Revelation 19:6 And I heard, as it were, the voice of a great multitude, as the sound of many waters and as the sound of mighty thunderings, saying, "Alleluia! For the Lord God Omnipotent reigns!"

COMMENT: The 19th chapter tells of the Second Coming of Christ with alleluias in heaven; great multitude, and 24 elders announce the marriage of the Lamb and the Bride (Church). The battle of Armageddon follows - White horse, the Word of God, King of kings, Lord of lords, - fight. The Beast, false prophet are put into the lake of fire. The devil is bound 1000 years in the bottomless pit. There is peace, people live the entire 1000 years in happiness. Nations do not war. Revelation 20 tells of the Millennial Reign of Christ. Those who were beheaded for Christ during the tribulation (who did not take the mark of the Beast) will reign with Christ 1000 years. This is the first resurrection. At the end of the 1000 years, Satan is loosed, brings the nations to battle; fire devours them; Satan is cast into the lake of fire with the Beast and false prophet forever. The Great White Throne judgement takes place with the resurrection of the dead (the second resurrection). The books are opened and the Book of Life. Judgement is rendered according to works. All who are not in the Book of Life are cast into the lake of fire.

ACTIVITY: GAMES FOR OLDER GROUP:

1. According to number of guests, set up dart games against wall. Be careful darts aren't thrown toward people. Mark circles: center 25 points, next 20, 15, 10, 5. Paper to keep scores. The thrower has to answer according to circle he hits: 25 - quotation or saying of Jesus: 20 - a miracle of Jesus; 15 - a parable; 10 - a city He visited; 5 - name a disciple.

2. Two teams. Start spelling the books of the Bible starting with Genesis -- anyone on team can answer; but if spelled wrong, he or she has to sit down. Ask teams alternately. If you need more words to spell, use geographical names in Holy Land, characters, etc. Team with last member standing wins. Bag of candy as prize.

3. Give each member a paper with alphabet listed on it. At signal each one writes in a Bible name, place or object, such as A - ark; B - Bethlehem. One completing alphabet first wins (if correct).

4. Prize to any person able to say the books of the Bible backward correctly.

5. Two teams, balloon for each person. Each has to blow up the balloon, tie it and kick it to goal. Bag of cookies to team finishing first.

6. Two tables and two teams. A plastic cup given to each one. At signal first one in each team puts his cup on table upright; next one puts his cup balanced rim to rim on the first cup. Build a tower of Babel. The tallest without it falling wins. If large group of people, keep teams to 15 people.

7. For fun select one "fun-type" person. Blindfold him after placing a number of objects in the pathway. As he is turned around, members remove the objects quietly. Then they direct him, "Go right to miss the chair," ""Now left," "Ooh, you just missed it," etc. When he reaches a goal, applaud, and remove the blindfold.

8. Jigsaw verse prepared as illustrated. Each in envelope. At signal the puzzles are assembled; the first to finish and tell what the five objects are wins. All read the verse together. (Door, Shepherd, Cross, Light, Bread)

9. Two teams. Cracker to each one. At signal first one eats cracker and whistles a hymn tune the next in line has to guess; if he guesses right, then he eats cracker, whistles, etc. First line finishing wins box of Oreos.

†††††

DAY 164. Revelation 21, 22
Come!

Revelation 22:17 And the Spirit and the bride say, "Come!" And let him who hears, say, "Come!". And let him who thirsts come. And whoever desires, let him take the water of life freely.

Prayer: Oh, we want You to come, Lord Jesus.

COMMENTS: This is the final, dramatic invitation in the Bible to come to Christ. Chapter 21 tells of the new heaven and the new earth; the new Jerusalem descends as the Bride. No more tears, death, sorrow, crying or pain for us. Jerusalem is described in all its splendor: wall of jasper; 12 gates of pearl for the 12 tribes of Israel; foursquare, 1500 miles each way; foundation of precious stones; street of gold; God and the Lamb are the Temple and the light.

Chapter 22 describes the river of crystal--water of life; tree of life with 12 fruits; no more curse; His servants see His face, His name in their foreheads; no night there; reign forever.

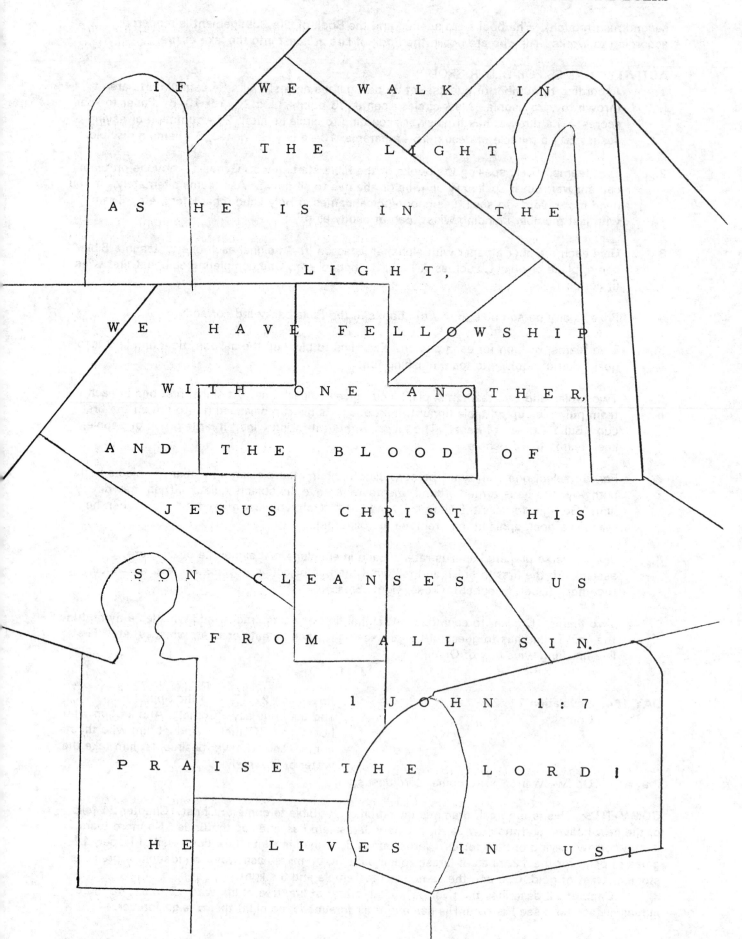

IF   WE   WALK   IN

THE   LIGHT

AS   HE   IS   IN   THE

LIGHT,

WE   HAVE   FELLOWSHIP

WITH   ONE   ANOTHER,

AND   THE   BLOOD   OF

JESUS   CHRIST   HIS

SON   CLEANSES   US

FROM   ALL   SIN.

1   JOHN   1:7

PRAISE   THE   LORD!

HE   LIVES   IN   US!

John ends the report of his Revelation with the warning not to add or take away from the Book. He declares, "He who gives His testimony to all this says, 'Yes, indeed! I am coming soon!' So be it. Come, Lord Jesus!"

ACTIVITY: For a devotional at the close of the Sunday School party when both groups are together, members of your family present "Christ in Me - the Open Door," based on Revelation 3:20, "Behold, I stand at the door and knock. If anyone hears My voice and opens the door, I will come in to him and dine with him, and he with Me."

Using the drawings as a guide, cut out a house with the separate room from cardboard. If that seems too difficult, use a child's doll house and point to the door, etc. Dad might do the talking, or divide the parts among the family.

1.   The Door. Jesus knocks on our heart's door through the urgings of the Holy Spirit. It's up to us to open to Him. He doesn't force Himself upon us. When we open our minds and hearts to Him He's like sunshine as He enters, a golden love filling the room, flooding the windows of our soul, and friends recognize a difference in us. The Son of God has entered--we'll never be the same again; we're new, born again! (Use Fun-Tak to hold the sections together.)

2.   Living Room. As we sit by the fireside talking, we find He is a precious, understanding Friend, gentle, kind, dependable, knowing the innermost yearnings of our hearts, recognizing our mistakes but showing us the Way to overcome, trading our former fears for His peace, erasing our sins and making us white as snow, presenting us with a clear slate to start life anew, an abundant life in Him. The warmth of His presence is heavenly, and we sit and learn of Him.

3.   Dining Room. Remembering to be hospitable, we enter the dining room to eat, and we find that the food is His Word, that He is the bread of life and He is the water of life. We see the pattern He has for each of us that we are to be "one" in Him as He is one in the Father, seeing things from His viewpoint, carrying on His work in helping others. He speaks lovingly: "Abide in Me; let My words abide in you; continue in My love. Love Me with all your heart, soul, mind, body, strength, and spirit. Love others as much as you love yourself." We grow like Him.

4.   Library. He beckons us to the library so that we can dig deeper into His Word--His library of 66 books. As we get a bird's-eye view of the Bible, we see His life in every book, like a golden thread. So many things come to light which we found difficult before. Our Conqueror, Jesus, explains that life on earth is a constant battle against the evil forces around us, but the Spirit gives us power to overcome, and our joint faith in him and He in us becomes a joyous victory.

5.   Kitchen. Here Jesus shows us how to prepare the Word to feed the hungry, those who will be lost forever if we do not feed them. We roll up our sleeves and work with Him, shoulder to shoulder, giving, sending, going to all the world.

6.   Bedroom. But He warns us that we must rest in Him, wait upon Him for direction, not to run ahead. He leads us beside still waters to refresh us with His peace that is past understanding. He knows that this rest will help us in the heat of the battle. We bask in His Light, are saturated with His fullness, His Spirit.

7.   Fireplace. Our morning talks here fire us, challenge us for the day's work.

8.   Windows. Through the windows of His sight we see those who need our help and take the Word with us, giving cups of cold water and the meat of the Word. Through us He lifts the fallen, renews the discouraged, heals the sick.

9.   Roof. As we leave the house and look up at the roof, we see that His banner over us is love. He shelters us under His wings. From the rooftop we glimpse the mansions He is building us in heaven; the glories we will share with Him forever. So we travel our pilgrim journey through life hand in hand with our Lord.

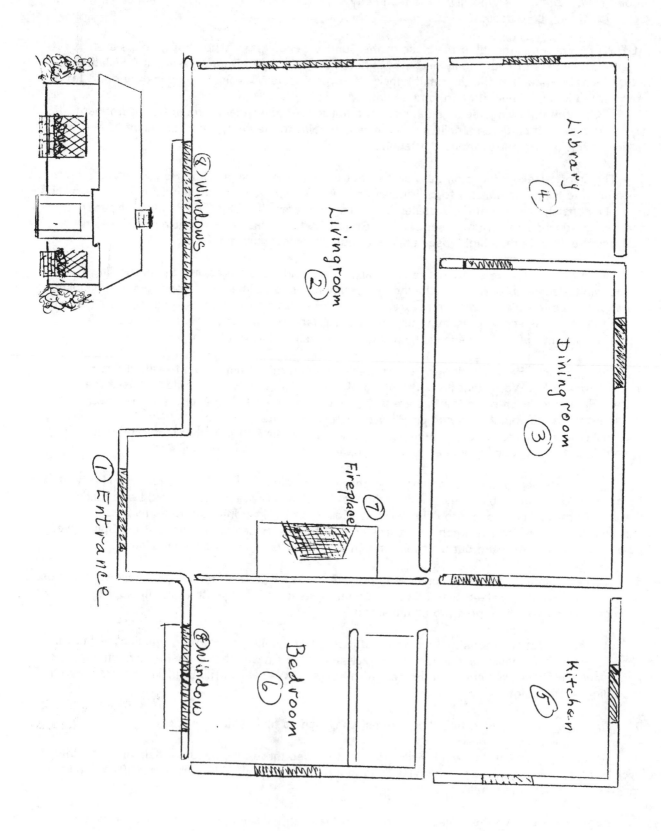

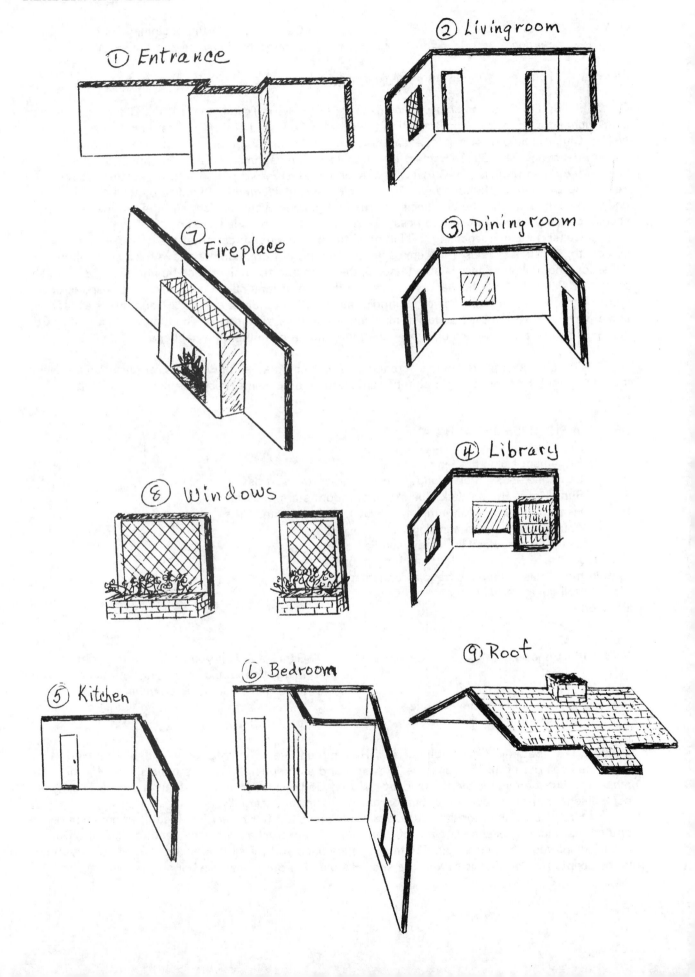

① Entrance

② Livingroom

⑦ Fireplace

③ Diningroom

④ Library

⑧ Windows

⑨ Roof

⑥ Bedroom

⑤ Kitchen

DAY 165. Genesis 1,2
          Creation

Genesis 1:1 In the beginning God created the heavens and the earth.

Prayer: Thank You for making us in Your image.

COMMENTS: For Christians our vital guidance is in the New Testament, but the Old Testament has many riches for us, also. It is interesting to see who God used in the Old Testament days to be a type of Christ (Joseph, for instance) and how the tabernacle and temple symbolized the ever-present Jehovah. The Old Testament Law (the Ten Commandments), the foundation of all justice, was perfected and fulfilled by Christ, the only one who never sinned. The Old Testament Law (the Ten Commandments), the foundation of all justice, was perfected and fulfilled by Christ, the only one who never sinned. The prophecies of His first coming were fulfilled, and the prophecies of His second coming are yet to come to pass. So the New Testament is based on the Old.

Genesis means beginning. Think of all the beginnings: creation of the universe, life, family, sin, death, sacrifice for sins. The time span for the days of creation may have been six 24-hour days, for God's almightiness is able to speak the word and the universe come into being; or it might be as in 2 Peter 3:18 "a thousand years as one day," or it may have been trillions of years as one day. "Time" has only the space of a pinpoint as related to endless eternity. God always existed and always will, so the brief period of mankind's history is as nothing. The glorious fact is that <u>God created</u>! It didn't just happen or evolve any more than a computer just happened.

ACTIVITY: Our craft for today is a "creation candle" using a fish bowl or similar glass bowl. Divide into six upright sections, using a strip of cardboard as a guideline. Use permanent color felt markers.

DRAW A PICTURE FOR EACH DAY:
1.   Light (golden) rays
2.   Firmament - blue heaven
3.   Earth and seas - brown land, blue sea, green trees, grass
4.   Sun, Moon, Stars - dark blue sky with moon, stars, and dawn
5.   Fish, fowl, birds - fish jumping at water's edge, swan, birds
6.   Animals, man - man and dog
       Use a tin spray can lid for the candle holder.
Drop melted wax in bottom of lid and bottom of bowl to hold the candle. Now you have a conversation piece to tell guests at dinner that God Created the world.

✝✝✝✝✝

DAY 166. Genesis 3, 4
          Sin

Genesis 4:7 If you had done the right thing, you would be smiling; but because you have done evil, sin is crouching at your door. It wants to rule you, but you must overcome it. (GNB)

Prayer: Keep us from the evil one.

COMMENTS: Satan is responsible for sin. He tempted Eve, who believed him instead of God. That has been our problem ever since. Physical and eternal death was the punishment, for all mankind. But the remarkable thing about it is that God still loves and wants us to be His companions, not only now during our journey on earth, but eternally.

First, He planned for those who were repentant to offer a sacrifice (death) of an animal or bird so that blood was shed in place of their own. That foreshadowed the death of the only One, Jesus, who would be perfect, and be the Sacrifice once and for all time and all people. Everyone who accepts His sacrifice is saved. He shed His blood in our place. He bought us; we are His.

ACTIVITY: Let's make a terrarium--a miniature Garden of Eden. Find a glass container with small opening at the top (if opening is large, put plastic over it). Plants will manufacture their atmosphere in this way. It is like the earth was before the flood, watered by the dew, no rain.

Put gravel, soil, small stones and the plants in the bottom of the bowl. Select bright, short plants such as violets, pansies, some greenery. Arrange artistically. A few small shells will be attractive.

If you have tiny animals, birds, etc. place them around the plants. You need not water for several months.

✝✝✝✝✝

DAY 167. Genesis 5, 6
          Ark

Prayer: Thanks, Lord, for being our Ark.

Genesis 6:18 But I will establish My covenant with you; and you shall go into the ark--you, your sons, your wife, and your sons' wives with you.

COMMENTS: The Living Bible translates that verse: "But I promise to keep you safe in the ship, with your wife and your sons and their wives."How comforting! Safe in the ship, safe amid turmoil, storms, stress. Many people find God in times of trauma; others blame God for their trials and turn away. But He is there to watch over and help at all times. "I will never leave you nor forsake you," He promised. (Hebrews 13:5). We must look to Him; trust Him; build an ark of faith in Him.

Imagine the faith it took for Noah to build that huge boat (450' long, 75' wide, 45' high) taking 120 years, with the taunts of the people. It had never rained; there had never been a flood; the earth had been watered by dew. It is estimated 7000 species of animals could stay in such a boat for a year.

ACTIVITY: We'll make a Noah's Ark scene for several days. Use a box with diagonal sides. Paint a clear sky. Make only the front of the ark using flexible cardboard, taping the pieces together. Paint it dark brown. Cut a ramp opening in the side for the animals to enter. God shut the door.

The ark is three stories high with overhanging roof sheltering the windows.

Using the flour-salt-water clay make animals in sets of two; paint them when dry. Keep them small in comparison to the 45' height of the ark. If the children are young, use small cutout animals, backed with cardboard.

tape sides a & b.
together with c
in between

← window

box for housing.

✝✝✝✝✝

DAY 168. Genesis 7,8
          Flood

Prayer: Thanks that You warn us and save us.

Genesis 7:17 Now the flood was on the earth forty days. The waters increased and lifted up the ark, and it rose high above the earth.

COMMENTS: In your notebook page on numbers note that 40 is a testing number (Jesus fasted 40 days, the children of Israel wandered 40 years).

Noah was 600 years old when he entered the ark; the water was 22 feet above the highest peak and covered the earth 150 days; the ark landed on the mountains of Ararat. A few explorers have seen its shape from the air, in the snow top peaks, and have climbed the mountain claiming to have seen some of the wood. Noah sent out his birds in periods of seven days. A year after the flood he opened the ark window and saw dry ground.

ACTIVITY: Cut out figures from Sunday School papers for Noah and family. Add backing and stand. Staple to bottom of box. Add paper mache areas with twigs, flowers. A work bench and sticks for the men to use will add to the scene.

DAY 169. Genesis 9,10
Rainbow

Prayer: Your rainbow has always been a beautiful covenant. Thanks for the rainbows in our lives.

Genesis 9:13-15 I set My rainbow in the cloud, and it shall be for the sign of the covenant between Me and the earth. It shall be, when I bring a cloud over the earth that the rainbow shall be seen in the cloud; and I will remember My covenant which is between Me and you and every living creature of all flesh; the waters shall never again become a flood to destroy all flesh.

COMMENTS: God keeps His covenants with us. He has kept a covenant with me for over 50 years of driving. When I was 18 and taking my Junior boys Sunday School class on a trip from Washington, D.C. to Philadelphia to visit the Franklin Institute, etc., we left very early. Coming to a super highway with no traffic in sight I exceeded the speed limit--and was stopped by a local sheriff. I learned my lesson well, for as I thought how terrible it would have been if I had an accident, I would never have gotten over it. So I prayed earnestly, like a covenant with God, that I would never be in an accident or the cause of an accident. It was like God sent an angel down to watch over me. There have been many miraculous deliveries from any harmful accident. Even when traveling in foreign countries on various conveyances. When on a tour to Machu Pichu in Peru, traveling slowly on a locomotive on a one-way track through the jungles with steep mountain side on the right and a deep ravine with raging river below on the left, the train jerked to a stop. The engine had hit a boulder and derailed, breaking the track--but no one was hurt. The train didn't fall against the mountainside nor down the ravine! Another time returning by plane from a world tour, the plane's wheels wouldn't unlock, but finally they did and we had a safe landing. Another time returning from shopping on a two-lane road in New York with two little grandchildren on the front seat with me, a trailer-truck swerved to evade hitting a car and flopped over on its side in my lane right in front of me. If I had been two seconds ahead (I timed it later) we would have been demolished! I praise Him for His care! I figured all my miles of driving (crossed the United States and Canada alone over 20 times) and world travels by various means, I must have traveled almost a million miles, and my angel has guarded me every mile of the way! Thank You, Heavenly Father, and thank you, guardian angel!

ACTIVITY: Complete the scenes of the ark. Practice telling the story so that when you have an opportunity to give a program as a family, you will each take part.

Explain that we, too, have an ark, our Savior and Lord, Jesus. If we trust God's Word as Noah trusted Him, we will give our lives to Jesus, go into His Way, Truth, and Life, and we will be safe from the storms of life. He will feed, shelter and protect us. He wants every one to be safe in His arms. He will keep His covenant promises with us, and His banner of love will be the rainbow.

✝✝✝✝✝

DAY 170. Genesis 11,12
Babel

Prayer: Help us not to run ahead of You in going our own way.

Genesis 11:9 Therefore its name is called Babel because there the Lord confused the language of all the earth; and from there the Lord scattered them abroad over the face of all the earth.

COMMENTS: This event was how God started all the different languages and scattered the people over the earth. Ham's descendants settled in Africa; Japheth's in the north toward Europe; Shem's remained in the east and were the ancestors of the Hebrew people. The genealogies listed in the Bible have a purpose--for one thing, it traces the background of Mary, the mother of Jesus, and for another it proves in one way that the Bible is true and historical.

One day I wondered if Methuselah died in the flood. With the genealogies I worked out a chart, discovering a number of facts. Using the ages given in Genesis 5; 9:28,29; 10; 11:10-32; 25:7; 35:28, I designate the time as "BA", _beginning with Adam_. To my knowledge no one else has made such a study, so you can skip it if you want, but I found it helped me get facts straight.

Adam was created 1 BA (the years starting with Adam) and died 930 BA. Seth was born to Adam when Adam was 130 years old so Seth's birthday was 130 BA. Seth lived 912 years making his death in 1042 BA (130 BA plus 912 years = 1042 BA).

The chart gives the descendants of Adam, showing when each was born in BA, how many years he lived, and the date he died in BA. The notation in parenthesis gives the reference to how old his parent was, from which the date of his birth is calculated. So when reading the chart, read the person's name and only refer to the parenthetical information if you want to know how his birth date is determined.

For approximately 2000 years from Creation to the Chosen People, God dealt with all mankind (Genesis 1-11). Then for approximately another 2000 years He dealt with Abraham's descendants (Genesis 12 to Malachi). When Jesus was on earth, He dealt with the Chosen People (Gospels). Since Pentecost, the Holy Spirit has dealt with all people, particularly the Church.

ACTIVITY: While the older ones study the chart and answer the quiz, the young ones make a family "tree" of family and relatives.

Draw a tree with large trunk and branches, one for each child in the family. On the trunk write the names of Mom and Dad; on the branches the names of the children. If any children are married, add the spouse's name and any children's name.

If small photos are available, add them where the names appear.

Frame the family tree and hang for all to see.

If your family has only a few members, start with the grandparents and add uncles and aunts, cousins on the branches, with your family as one branch.

CHART OF THE ANCESTORS OF JESUS
From Adam to Isaac

(not official--worked
out by Fern Ritchey)   BA means Beginning with Adam

	Adam was Created 1 BA,	lived 930 years,	died 930 BA
(when Adam was 130 years)	Seth was born, 130 BA,	lived 912 years,	died 1042 BA
(when Seth was 105)	Enosh was born, 235 BA,	lived 905 years,	died 1140 BA
(when Enosh was 90)	Kenan was born, 325 BA,	lived 910 years,	died 1235 BA
(when Kenan was 70)	Mahalalel was born, 395 BA,	lived 895 years,	died 1290 BA
(when Mahalalel was 65)	Jared was born, 460 BA,	lived 962 years,	died 1422 BA
(when Jared was 162)	Enoch was born, 622 BA,	was taken when 365 years,	987 BA
(when Enoch was 65)	Methuselah was born, 687 BA	lived 969 years,	died 1656 BA
(when Methuselah was 187)	Lamech was born, 874 BA,	lived 777 years,	died 1651 BA
(when Lamech was 182)	Noah was born, 1056 BA,	lived 950 years,	died 2006 BA
(when Noah was 502)	Shem was born, 1558 BA,	lived 600 years,	died 2158 BA

(Noah was 600 at the time of the Flood, 1656 BA)

(when Shem was 100)	Arphaxad was born, 1658 BA,	lived 438 years,	died 2096 BA
(when Arphaxad was 35)	Shelah was born, 1693 BA,	lived 433 years,	died 2126 BA
(when Shelah was 30)	Eber was born, 1723 BA,	lived 364 years,	died 2087 BA
(when Eber was 34)	Peleg was born, 1757 BA,	lived 239 years,	died 1996 BA
(when Peleg was 30)	Reu was born, 1787 BA,	lived 239 years,	died 2026 BA
(when Reu was 32)	Serug was born, 1819 BA,	lived 230 years,	died 2049 BA
(when Serug was 30)	Nabor was born, 1849 BA,	lived 148 years,	died 1997 BA
(when Nabor was 29)	Terah was born, 1878 BA,	lived 205 years,	died 2083 BA
(when Terah was 70)	Abraham was born, 1948 BA,	lived 175 years,	died 2123 BA

(Abraham was 75 when he went to Canaan, 2023 BA)

(when Abraham was 100)	Isaac was born, 2048 BA,	lived 180 years,	died 2228 BA

Bible genealogy quiz (using the foregoing chart)

1.   Who was the oldest man who ever lived?
2.   When did he die?
3.   What happened that year?
4.   How old was Noah at the time of the flood?
5.   How old was Adam when he died?
6.   How many of his descendants in the line on the chart could Adam have talked to directly (if they lived close by) telling the history of the world?
7.   Who were they?
8.   How old was Methuselah when Adam died?
9.   How old was Lamech when Adam Died?
10.   How long did Noah live?
11.   How many of the descendants in Jesus' line could Noah have talked to directly (if they lived close by), telling of the history, the flood, up to his death?
12.   Who were they?
13.   How many years was it from Adam to the Flood?
14.   How many years from Adam to Abraham settling in Canaan?
15.   Although this may not have happened, as they may not have lived in the same area, Adam could have told Lamech, father of Noah; Noah could have told Abraham--just three people for retelling the history of man from creation to settling in Canaan, over 2000 years. When did man's life span begin to shorten?

††††††

DAY 171. Genesis 13, 14
           Covenant

Prayer: Thanks for keeping Your covenants.

Genesis 13:15-16 For all the land which you see I give to you and your descendants forever. And I will make your descendants as the dust of the earth; so that if a man could number the dust of the earth, then your descendants also could be numbered.

COMMENTS: This is referred to as the Abrahamic Covenant. God kept His covenant--the Chosen People are still a distinctive nationality, and though scattered throughout the world since the time of Jesus, they are still a race.

Abraham is known for his great faith. Sarah, too, is listed in Hebrews 11 chapter of faith ("By faith Sarah herself also received strength to conceive seed, and she bore a child when she was past the age, because she judged Him faithful who had promised." Hebrews 11:11) There were times that Abraham and Sarah lacked faith to wait for God's timing, but as they learned to depend upon God, their faith became strong. It is true with all Christians--we grow in all dimensions: love, faith, peace, joy, zeal, service, submission, patience.

ACTIVITY: Trace this map for your notebook and mark Abraham's journey to Canaan.

DAY 172. Genesis 15, 16
          Ishmael

Genesis 16:11 And the Angel of the Lord said to her "Behold, you are with child, and you shall bear a son. You shall call his name Ishmael, because the Lord has heard your affliction."

Prayer: Help us not to scheme, but follow You.

COMMENTS: Abraham and Sarah had waited long for their promised child, and growing impatient had planned for the maidservant to have the child--taking the matter into their own hands instead of waiting for God's miracle, or His timing. Even so, God watched out for Hagar and her son, Ishmael. Ishmael's descendants are now known as the Arabic race (2 Chronicles 17:11).

ACTIVITY: Here is an object lesson on "timing". We may want a seed or plant to grow overnight, but God's timing isn't according to our desires but His laws. Nature is a good example. Let the children watch some of nature's seeds take on new life.

1. Onions sprout quickly without water or soil. Put one in a small container.
2. Plant a peach kernel in the yard, make a circle of stones so no one will molest the area with mowing.
3. Plant bird seed in a small container on the window sill.

Make use of commercial time on TV by:
1. Read a Psalm.
2. Recite the Books of the Bible.
3. Sing a hymn.

Use time at a stop light:
1.   Look at several people around and pray for something definite about them--are they worried, happy, need money or love? Pray for God's care for them.
2.   Memorize a verse a day and report it at every stop light.

✝✝✝✝✝

DAY 173. Genesis 17, 18
          The Land

Genesis 17:8 Also I give to you and your descendants after you the land in which you are a stranger, all the land of Canaan, as an everlasting possession; and I will be their God.

Prayer: Thanks that Your plans work out.

COMMENTS: The Covenant also included the land of Canaan, which would be the prophesied place of Jesus' birth and the land from which Jesus will reign as King for 1000 years. Even though the Jewish people were dispersed for almost 2000 years, the land promised to Abraham and his descendants is still known as Israel. It is one of the fulfilled signs of the times that they returned to their land in 1948.

ACTIVITY: Answer true or false to this quiz on angels:
1.   Angels never take on human form.
2.   Angels can open locked doors.
3.   They are messengers of God.
4.   They are not created beings of God.
5.   We become angels in heaven.
6.   Some angels have names.
7.   All angels are good.
8.   Good angels worship God.
9.   They assist, protect, deliver people.
10.   Angels ministered to Jesus.

DAY 174. Genesis 19
               Judgment

Prayer: Keep us from evil.

Genesis 19:29 And it came to pass, when God destroyed the cities of the plain, that God remembered Abraham, and sent Lot out of the midst of the overthrow, when He overthrew the cities in which Lot had dwelt.

COMMENTS: It is so important not to associate with persons bent on evil nor hang around places that are questionable. Avoid drug users, bars, adult book shops, R-Rated movies, violence, crime, shoplifters, gangs that get into trouble, gossipers, vandals, those who tell dirty jokes. Before you know it, their evil doesn't seem so bad and you begin to drift in the same way. God punished the sins of Sodom and Gomorrah with fire and brimstone--using Satan's tools against Satan.

ACTIVITY: Make a list of all the good activities to get involved in, then get involved. Have the Teen Club earn money toward a trip to a Christian camp or other place of interest. Do some volunteer work at a Fire House, Salvation Army, Nurses Aid, or playground work. Read David Wilkerson's *The Cross and the Switchblade*.

ᵗᵗᵗᵗᵗ

DAY 175. Genesis 20, 21
               Watchcare

Prayer: We're grateful for Your care.

Genesis 21:17, 18 And God heard the voice of the lad. Then the angel of God called to Hagar out of heaven, and said to her, "What ails you, Hagar? Fear not, for God has heard the voice of the lad where he is. Arise, lift up the lad and hold him with your hand, for I will make him a great nation.

COMMENTS: God cares for us no matter how unhappy and insecure our circumstances may be. In this case He raised Hagar and Ishmael to a much higher level than slavery and starvation as outcasts. Sometimes He uses us to rescue a child from death be sponsoring him through one of the many Child Care programs. He may use us to help a spiritually hungry person nearby.

ACTIVITY: A candy village is a unique and attractive way to raise money for overseas relief. My Junior High Sunday School class, Good News Club, grandchildren, and daughter's missionette group have made such villages, for donations to World Vision and World-Wide Missions. The one my grandchildren and I made several years ago brought in $1475 to our amazement. The contributions were mostly in change. It was displayed in a large mall at Christmas time. They were only three to eight years old. To make a village see the directions in the Appendix.

Author and grandchildren with village they made in 1982 (ages at that time 3 to 8), displayed in the mall near Elmira, N.Y. $1475 was received in donations for World Vision and World Wide Missions. (Most of the money was in change-- incredibly heavy for us to carry out!)

Below: Village made by my Good News Club in Rocky Mountain House, Alberta, in December 1986, and displayed in Red Deer and Rocky Mountain House. Donations: $1068. Ages of children: 7 to 12. This project is not only delightful to create, but delicious to eat after the display.

Adding the finishing touches at Rocky. Photograph by "The Mountaineer" photographer, Ronald Pigeon, Rocky Mountain House. (In December 1987 the Good News Club children, ages 5 to 11, made a Christmas scene of Bethlehem, nativity stable, and shepherd's field with host of angels, displayed in Rocky supermarket.)

DAY 176. Genesis 22,23
         Sacrifice

Genesis 22:12 And He said, "Do not lay your hand on the lad, or do anything to him; for now I know that you fear God, since you have not withheld your son, your only son, from Me."

Prayer: Oh, help us to have such trust in You.

COMMENTS: No wonder Abraham is called the man of faith. When God asked him to sacrifice his son, he willingly followed orders, knowing God would provide another sacrifice. God truly admires those who trust Him. God's tests are not easy. Isaac had great faith, too, to climb up on that altar. It is a picture of God giving His only Son, and Jesus willing to die for us.

ACTIVITY: This is a good story to make a scene. Make the altar of pebbles. With paper mache make a small mound to one side; stick bushes in the clay; make a clay ram and put it in the bushes.
         Make the figures of Abraham and Isaac of wire, so they will be able to bend over to make the altar.
         If you desire, you can act out the story with the figures: have them discuss where the sacrifice is; then they build the altar (use Fun-Tak or other removable stickum); then place Isaac on the altar, Abraham ready to strike when the angel stops him, and shows Abraham the ram in the bushes.
         Explain that this is a type of God, offering Jesus as our sacrifice.

✝✝✝✝✝

DAY 177. Genesis 24
         Answered Prayer

Genesis 24:27 He said, "Praise the Lord, the God of my master Abraham, who has faithfully kept His promise to my master. The Lord has led me straight to my master's relatives." (GNB)

Prayer: Thanks for always answering prayer.

COMMENTS: This is one of the most remarkable and beautiful stories of faith and obedience in the Bible. Added is the romantic angle which reminds us that God created romance in the beginning.

ACTIVITY: Unscramble the following names of those who showed faith in this story:
ascai cherbace telubeh tansrev balna mabhraa
         Continue work on the Faith scene. Sew clothes of plain or striped material. To have the figures stand, put small squares of magnet on the soles of their feet, and before making the paper mache bottom of the box, put a tin or metal cookie sheet as the base. Then the man and boy can stand and be moved around.

✝✝✝✝✝

DAY 178. Genesis 25, 26
         Family Heritage

Genesis 25:34 And Jacob gave Esau bread and stew of lentils; then he ate and drank, arose, and went his way. Thus Esau despised his birthright.

Prayer: Thanks for our family.

COMMENTS: Discuss as a family what each member should consider his or her birthright. Dad and

Mom might each discuss their family's heritage, accomplishments, homes they built with love, what the other members of their families are doing, how loyalty to the family name is an honorable trait.

ACTIVITY: If your family has a coat-of-arms, discuss its meaning, the symbols, and what they represent. Or if the ancestors had a certain costume or other distinguishing trademark, discuss that. If you have nothing of that type in your background, why not make a design, pattern or coat-of-arms that will picture what your family stands for. All members discuss the design, help draw and paint it. The men make a suitable frame.

†††††

DAY 179. Genesis 27, 28
　　　　　　Promises

Genesis 28:15 Behold, I am with you and will keep you wherever you go, and will bring you back to this land; for I will not leave you until I have done what I have spoken to you.

Prayer: Thanks for staying with us always.

COMMENTS: We can depend upon our God of promises. Though Jacob was deceitful at times, God still had a plan for his life. His name meant supplanter or deceiver. Later God changed his name to Israel, meaning Prince with God.

ACTIVITY: Make a "Jacob's Ladder" flannelgraph lesson. Cut out two flannel poles and 10 horizontal rungs of cardboard backed with flannel scraps. Print the following Old and New Testament promises on the ten rungs. Compare them, the New fulfilling the Old; the promises in Genesis 28:15 fulfilled in Christ.

1. I will be with you
2. Protect you wherever you go
3. Bring you back to the land
4. Will not leave you
5. Will finish what I promised

1. lo, I am with you always - Matthew 28:20
2. To Him who is able to keep you from falling - Jude 24
3. I will come again and receive you unto Myself-John 14:3
4. I will never leave you - Hebrews 13:5
5. He who promised is faithful - Hebrews 10:23

†††††

DAY 180. Genesis 29, 30
　　　　　　Love Journey

Genesis 29:20 So Jacob served seven years for Rachel, and they seemed but a few days to him because of the love he had for her.

Prayer: Thanks for love that's forever.

COMMENTS: All the world is interested in true love. Mom and Dad might tell of their romance, how they met, when they knew they wanted to share their lives together, the fun, the hard times, the growth in love, understanding, and companionship during the years. Tell of the things done together, building the home, painting, papering, whatever--it will be of value to the children.

ACTIVITY: Play the game Jacob's Journey for Marriage. Use buttons for the players and a spinner. Travel the number spun, following the arrows. If the player lands on a circle (blessing) advance two spaces; if on a block wall (obstacle), go back two spaces. They are the obstacles and blessings Jacob encountered on his journey.

　　　If you don't have a spinner, make one. Draw a circle on a cardboard. Divide into numbered portions. Bend a 2" wire into a hook. Put another wire through it and through hole in center of circle, bend the ends underneath like a brad.

JACOB'S JOURNEY FOR MARRIAGE

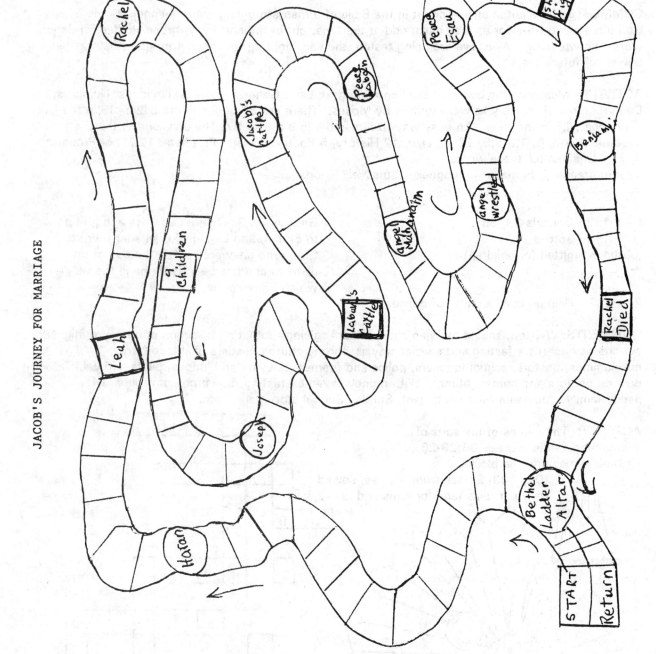

DAY 181. Genesis 31, 32
Wrestling

> Genesis 32:28 And He said, "Your name shall no longer be called Jacob, but Israel; for you have struggled with God and with men, and have prevailed."

Prayer: Lord, we want to prevail, too.

COMMENTS: This is the only account in the Bible of a man struggling with an angel. Some of God's tests and trials for us may seem odd at the time, but in the end the purpose He has for us is worth the wrestling. When we are being tested, the very fighting for the victory gives us mightier power for future tests.

ACTIVITY: Memorize the books of the Pentateuch, or Law: Genesis, Exodus, Leviticus, Numbers, Deuteronomy. These books were written by Moses. There are 66 books in the Bible; 39 in the Old Testament, 27 in the New. An easy way to remember is 3 x 9 = 27. The divisions of the Old Testament are: 5, 12, 5,5, 12: 5 Law, 12 History, 5 Poetry, 5 Major Prophets, 12 Minor Prophets.
     Unscramble these words:
  ynomdtreeou   bumersn   esgneis   tuscveili   odxeus

✝✝✝✝✝

DAY 182. Genesis 33, 35
               36:6-8
(portions omitted for children)

> Genesis 35:3 Then let us arise and go up to Bethel; and I will make an altar there to God, who answered me in the day of my distress and has been with me in the way which I have gone.

Prayer: Help us build an altar of praise.

COMMENTS: We, too, should build an altar of thanksgiving--but let's put action into it. We might set one day apart for fasting and special prayer: for the church, leaders of the country, missionaries, pastors, school teachers, police and firemen, lawyers and judges, pilots and vehicle drivers, doctors and nurses, others. With money saved by fasting, buy a box of groceries for a needy family. Include a New Testament, Sunday School story paper, etc.

ACTIVITY: The names of the sons of Jacob are given in Genesis 35:23-26. Fit their names into the blocks.

(Day 183) Smock from old ties, sewed together, bias tape for arms and neck.

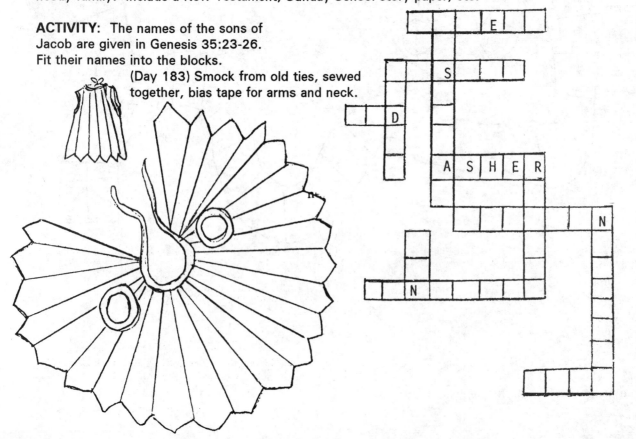

DAY 183. Genesis 37, 38:1-5
Coat of Colors

Genesis 37:7 There we were, binding sheaves in the field. Then behold, my sheaf arose and also stood upright; and indeed your sheaves stood all around and bowed down to my sheaf.

Prayer: Thanks for the plans You have for our lives.

COMMENTS: Joseph was favored because he was Rachel's firstborn, so his brothers disliked him, and his dreams of superiority did not help matters any.

ACTIVITY: Make a smock, a coat of many colors, for each of the younger children. Sew odd scraps of material together in strips without rhyme or reason or color. Measure the length needed, then cut 3 front and 3 back panels wider at the bottom than the top; and two shorter panels for the sleeves. Sew panels together. Add pockets. If the neck is too big, gather to right size and bind with bias tape long enough to tie in the back. Hem sleeves and skirt. The children may help with pinning and basting.

This is a smock of Love. Think of doing good deeds and acts of love when wearing it.

✝✝✝✝✝

DAY 184. Genesis 39, 40
Helping

Genesis 39:23 The keeper of the prison did not look into anything that was under Joseph's hand, because the Lord was with him; and whatever he did, the Lord made it prosper.

Prayer: Be with us, Lord, to be good workers.

COMMENTS: God helps us to be successful if we give Him the freedom to mold and guide us. Joseph spent many years in prison, and though he had a right to be bitter for he had done no crime, he wasn't. He worked hard, was obedient, and God rewarded him. He never forgot that God was in charge of his life.

ACTIVITY: Make large flowers for an elderly person. Use thin paper, preferably colored. Print a short verse on each outside petal. Twist the petals at the bottom, like a rose, and wrap with green strips of cloth or yarn. Glue or tie in place.

Make two leaves and short stem; put the flower on a tray with pen, note pad, and a few such things. If a child has helped with this, it will be precious treasure to the recipient.

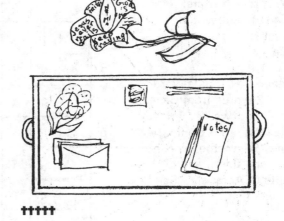

✝✝✝✝✝

DAY 185. Genesis 41-43
Spirit-filled

Genesis 41:38 And Pharaoh said to his Servants can we find such a one as this, a man in whom is the Spirit of God?"

Prayer: May the Spirit be seen in us.

COMMENT: Do you suppose a non-Christian can see God's Spirit in us? Let's pray that the beauty of Jesus may be seen in us.

ACTIVITY: Pre-schoolers: Make a gift tag to accompany your flower tray by cutting out a small flower and pasting it on a little card.

The older ones have Bible searching to do. Look up the verses and write in the similarities between Joseph and Jesus. Joseph was a type of Christ.

	Joseph		Jesus
1.	Genesis 37:3	_____	Matthew 3:17
2.	37:4, 37:20	_____	John 15:25, 5:16
3.	37:23	_____	Matthew 27:28
4.	37:28	_____	Matthew 26:15
5.	40:21-22	_____	Luke 23:33
6.	40:15	_____	Luke 23:47
7.	41:38	_____	John 18:36-37
8.	41:40	_____	Revelation 3:21
9.	41:45	_____	Acts 15:14
10.	41:46	_____	Luke 3:23

✝✝✝✝✝

DAY 186. Genesis 44-46:1-7, 26-34
           Prophecy Fulfilled

Prayer: Thanks for Your plans.

COMMENTS: What insight Joseph had to see God's planning in his life to save his family from starving. He was a man of sterling character, avoiding self-pity, condemnation of others, involvement with sin of any sort.

ACTIVITY: Pre-schoolers: dress up in old clothes and act out some of the stories in the Bible.

Others: Here is a word block with 42 words from Genesis: 19 across, 7 backwards; 9 down; 2 up; 2 slanting up; 3 slanting down. They follow the account of creation, sin, flood, and the descendants of Abraham. See how many you can find.

Genesis 45:5 But now, do not therefore by grieved or angry with yourselves because you sold me here; for God sent me before you to preserve life.

	1	2	3	4	5	6	7	8	9	10	11	12
1	G	E	N	E	S	I	S	J	U	D	A	H
2	A	V	G	O	D	C	A	I	N	X	D	O
3	R	E	U	B	E	N	T	A	E	S	A	U
4	D	A	Y	X	S	T	A	R	S	X	M	S
5	E	X	W	O	M	A	N	X	T	R	E	E
6	N	I	G	H	T	E	L	I	F	E	A	I
7	O	N	I	S	V	N	X	B	I	R	D	S
8	O	O	X	A	U	D	E	A	T	H	A	A
9	M	A	E	S	N	M	A	H	A	R	B	A
10	A	H	T	H	G	I	L	X	A	X	E	C
11	R	A	C	H	E	L	M	H	A	E	L	E
12	K	H	P	E	S	O	J	A	C	O	B	R
13	R	E	B	E	C	C	A	H	L	O	T	I
14	R	A	I	N	B	O	W	X	H	S	I	F

DAY 187. Genesis 47; 48; 49:1-3,
5, 10, 13-16, 19-33;
50:1-10, 15-26
Blessings

Prayer: Bless us, too, Lord, that we
may be a blessing to others.

Genesis 50:24 And Joseph said to his
brothers, "I am dying; but God will surely
visit you and bring you out of this land to
the land of which He swore to Abraham, to
Isaac, and to Jacob."

COMMENTS: Genesis starts with "in the beginning" and ends "in a coffin." The book covers a period of over 2000 years. From Exodus to the end of the Old Testament is another 2000 years. All the recorded facts are true, and the Holy Spirit inspired the authors to write these books. They are in accord.

ACTIVITY: See how good you are at Bible arithmetic!

1. To the number of people in the ark,
    Add the total number of books in the Bible,
    Divide by the main divisions of the Bible,
    Multiply by number of books of Law. What is your answer?

2. Divide the number of Jacob's sons
    By the number of the Trinity;
    Multiply by the number of each kind of clean animals in the ark,
    and subtract the days God rested after creation.

3. Multiply the number of years Jacob worked for Leah
    By the number of years he worked for Rachel;
    Add the days it rained during the flood
    And subtract the number of chapters in Genesis.

4. To the number of Isaac's sons Add the
    number of sons of Noah; Multiply by the age
    of Jonah at the time of the flood. And divide
    by the sons of Joseph. Did you make A?

✝✝✝✝✝

DAY 188. Exodus 1,2
Moses' Youth

Prayer: Help us to put You first in our lives.

Exodus 1:20, 21 Therefore God dealt
well with the midwives, and the people
multiplied and grew very mighty. And so it
was, because the midwives feared God, that
He provided households for them.

COMMENTS: Exodus means departure and recreates the detailed adventures of the children of Israel escaping Egypt and wandering in the desert 40 years. We see how God prepared the great patriarch Moses for this tremendous undertaking (leading about 3,000,000 people and their belongings and animals on a 40 year journey). He saved Moses at birth, schooled him in Pharaoh's house 40 years, set him apart 40 years, used him to lead the people to Canaan 40 years. Note these three 40-year periods in your notebook page on numbers.

ACTIVITY: Children love to act the story of baby Moses. Now they can make the baby's basket. Cut an oval cardboard about a foot long. Punch holes 1/2 inch apart around the edge. Insert plastic drinking straws and bend in the bottoms under the cardboard and tape.
    Use long strips of old pantyhose for waving in and out of the straws. When near the top, bend the straws inward and tack. To put it in water, cover outside with aluminum foil.

DAY 189. Exodus 3,4
           Moses' Call

Prayer: Help us to hear You when You call us.

Exodus 3:14 God said to Moses, "I AM WHO I AM." And He said, "Thus you shall say to the children of Israel, "I AM has sent me to you."

COMMENTS: The I AM name of God declares His holiness, almightiness, omnipotence, omnipresence, omniscience, Supreme Being over all, eternal! What a glorious God we have!

ACTIVITY: The Burning Bush scene is novel. Make paper mache rocks, and vegetation on the sides. For the burning bush tape red cellophane over the front of a small flash light. Insert the flashlight through a hole in the back of the box to protrude to the middle of the "burning bush." The bush is a firm tree branch set in clay, with copper colored cleaning pad like Kurly Kate for the foliage. Turn on the flashlight when telling the story.

flashlight side view

DAY 190. Exodus 5, 6
           Chosen

Exodus 6:7 I will take you as My people, and I will be your God. Then you shall know that I am the Lord your God who brings you out from under the burdens of the Egyptians.

Prayer: Thanks for choosing us as Your children.

COMMENTS: Pharaoh was a very stubborn, hard-hearted ruler, but God used that characteristic to demonstrate God's power. His power would have meant nothing against a weak, retreating person, Teaming up with God means victory. You may be called a "square" for your sterling stand for the right, but consider it a compliment.

ACTIVITY: How many "squares" are in this circle?
Are you a square in God's circle?

DAY 191. Exodus 7, 8
           Miracles

Exodus 7:5 And the Egyptians shall know that I am the Lord, when I stretch out My hand on Egypt and bring out the children of Israel from among them.

Prayer: Do miracles among our sick, Lord.

COMMENTS: Imagine how Moses felt as he undertook the immense task of moving millions of people. Yet God was in charge and Moses had been prepared and he was bold to proclaim the miracles.

ACTIVITY: Talk about any miracles you have personally encountered. Relate some you have read or heard about. God does His miracles today. List any people who need miracle healings, and start praying for them, believing!

DAY 192. Exodus 9, 10
           Plagues

Exodus 10:22-23 So Moses stretched out his hand toward heaven, and there was thick darkness in all the land of Egypt three days. They did not see one another; nor did anyone rise from his place for three days. But all the children of Israel had light in their dwellings.

Prayer: Help us to follow Your directions.

COMMENTS: God gives His people light, even the Light of the World, Jesus. John 8:12, "I am the Light of the World. He who follows Me shall not walk in darkness, but have the light of life."

ACTIVITY: Sit in a dark room and light a small candle. Have the children stand as far away as the reflection of the candle light is on their hands. Use a flashlight and check its ability to light the room. Now turn on the electric lights. We may be small but even our candle-size light helps; as we grow in Christ and witness for Him, our light is more effective. Read Matthew 5:16.

†††††

DAY 193. Exodus 11-13
        Passover

Prayer: Thanks that Jesus' blood covers us.

Exodus 12:13 Now the blood shall be a sign for you on the houses where you are. And when I see the blood, I will pass over you; and the plague shall not be on you to destroy you when I strike the land of Egypt.

COMMENTS: The passover is one of the most significant events in the Bible. It looks forward to the cross (the blood on the door top and sides form a cross just as Jesus hung on the cross with head and hands bleeding for us). If Jesus is covering us, the death angel passes over us. What a precious symbol from the Old Testament to the New.

ACTIVITY: It was Passover celebration when Jesus instituted the Lord's Supper. At the next Communion Service at church sit together as a family and remember that your family, like the families in Egypt, is safe under the shed blood of Jesus. The Israelites were saved from brick making, slavery, poverty and brought to freedom in their own land. List the things that we are brought from as we enter our new life in Christ.

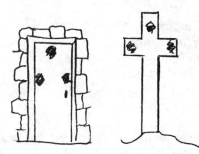

    This makes an effective chalk-talk. Draw the door with the red blood stains for the angel to pass over, then the cross with its stains.

†††††

DAY 194. Exodus 14, 15
        Red Sea Miracle

Prayer: We praise You for Your miracles.

Exodus 14:13 And Moses said to the people, "Do not be afraid. Stand still, and see the salvation of the Lord, which He will accomplish for you today. For the Egyptians whom you see today, you shall see again no more forever."

COMMENTS: Probably the most dramatic miracle was the opening to the Red Sea, the millions of Israelites crossing over on dry ground, followed by the smashing waters on the Egyptian army. Cecil B. DeMille must have had divine direction to produce such a mighty movie as "The Ten Commandments."

ACTIVITY: Unscramble these two sentences telling of miracles of Jesus on the sea:
Sjeus dwelak no het treaw. Usesj dias "ceepa eb listl" ot eht morst ta ase.

†††††

DAY 195. Exodus 16, 17
        Food and water.

Prayer: Thanks for water.

Exodus 16:35 And the children of Israel ate manna forty years, until they came to an inhabited land; they ate manna until they came to the border of the land of Canaan.

COMMENTS: It is incredible how God provided food and water for the millions in the desert for 40 years. Their shoes never wore out. God tells us not to worry about food and clothes, yet we like the Israelites often murmur and fail to thank Him for His daily care.

ACTIVITY: During the summer vacation time conduct a Playground Club in a park or playground where there are children playing to invite. Use the Life of Christ scenes, about five a day, to tell the stories of Jesus. The children love it. Sing a few songs with the music recorded, and have volunteer children turn the pages of the song books you made for Good New Club. Explain the message of salvation at the end, inviting children to accept Jesus as their Savior.

Select a game or object lesson for each day. I found that using Miniature Golf on the Christian's life was wonderful drawing card, especially for the boys. That will be explained on Day 250, but it is wise to prepare for it early and advertise the Club in the newspaper or on bulletin boards in stores. I have found it wise to have 4- or 5- Day clubs in several parks for four weeks, scheduling the time for one hour each day either from 2 to 3 p.m. or after supper, 7 to 8 p.m. In Canada the evenings remain light until late.

Keep records of names, addresses, phone numbers, ages, and if they attend a Sunday School. If numbers of children do not attend a church, do some follow-up work in the homes to take them to a church of their choice near them. I was able to have some join my Good News Club. One year the GNC made a Palestine village (Bethlehem), nativity stable scene in center, and shepherds and angels in the field on the right. It was displayed in the supermarket during December 1988. (See Day 338). The children were 5 to 11 years old.

✝✝✝✝✝

DAY 196. Exodus 18, 19
           Wanderings

Exodus 18:10-11 Praise the Lord, who saved you from the king and the people of Egypt! Praise the Lord, who saved His people from slavery! Now I know that the Lord is greater than all the gods, because He did this when the Egyptians treated the Israelites with such contempt. (GNB)

Prayer: How we praise You, Lord, for saving and keeping us.

COMMENTS: If the Israelites had not complained, they would have reached the Promised Land within a few months; but instead they wandered in the desert 40 years. The original adults died on the way. Only the youth and Joshua and Caleb made it all the way. Are we reaching the goals God has set for us?

ACTIVITY: Pre-schoolers: prepare for a trip with dolls, lunch, pretend to go by car or plane, buying tickets, etc.

The rest of the family mark on the map the journey the children of Israel made, and with another felt pen draw a line how they could have made a short journey.

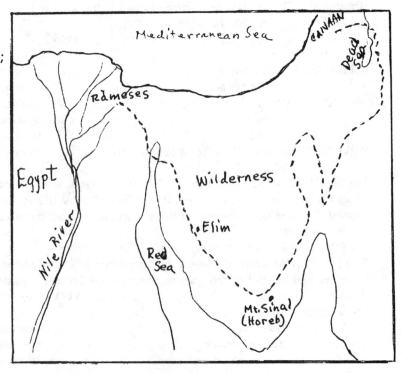

DAY 197. Exodus 20, 21
              Ten Commandments

Exodus 20:20 And Moses said to the people, "Do not fear; for God has come to test you, and that His fear may be before you, so that you may not sin."

Prayer: Help us to keep Your laws.

COMMENTS: The Ten Commandments are the basic laws on which our nation and most countries rule.

ACTIVITY: Print the commandments on a poster board. Braid three cords (representing the Trinity) for the edging, glue in place. God the Father wrote the laws, God the Son fulfilled them, and God the Holy Spirit instructs us in righteousness.

THE TEN COMMANDMENTS (abbreviated)

Worship no god but me.
Do not bow down to any idol.
Do not use my name for evil purposes.
Observe the Sabbath and keep it holy.
Respect your father and mother.
Do not commit murder.
Do not commit adultery.
Do not steal.
Do not accuse one falsely.
Do not desire another's house or anything he owns.

††††

DAY 198. Exodus 22, 23
              Angelic Leader

Exodus 23:20 Behold, I send an Angel before you to keep you in the way and to bring you into the place which I have prepared.

Prayer: Thanks for our guiding angel.

COMMENTS: Again God is using an angel to guide and protect all His people. There are several contemporary books on Angels. Bill Graham authored one. Read one to find out more about the angels God uses for our benefit.

ACTIVITY: Write a list of the directions the people were to follow as found in Exodus 23:20-33.

††††

DAY 199. Exodus 24; 25:1-26,
              29, 31-33; 26:1-14,
              31-37 God Speaks

Exodus 24:17 The sight of the glory of the Lord was like a consuming fire on the top of the mountain in the eyes of the children of Israel.

Prayer: Thanks for Your glorious appearing, and your watch care.

COMMENTS: In this glorious setting God gave Moses instructions to make a place of worship for the people. A courtyard 150 x 75' was to be within the midst of the city of tents. Curtains on poles would border it. A tent or tabernacle, 45 x 15', would be the building to hold an ark in the Holy of Holies room. The larger room would be the Holy Place, containing the altar of incense, table of bread, and candlestick. Curtains were to be hung before each entrance.

Outside in the courtyard a large bronze altar would stand with a laver or bowl of cleansing closer to the door of the tent. The tent was to face east and be covered with three large curtains: the first goat skins, the middle red ram's skins, and the top leather. All the articles, furnishings and poles were to be covered with gold. It cost millions and was made from the treasures brought from Egypt.

ACTIVITY: For several days we will construct the
Tabernacle. Use a board to hold the 20 x 30"
courtyard. The fence around the area will be made
with short dowels for posts, and a white strip of
cloth attached around it. The 4" entrance in the
fence is at the east.

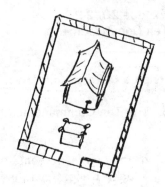

      With flour-salt-water clay or cardboard construct
the ark, altar of incense, table of show bread, candlestick,
and laver. See drawings.

𝌆𝌆𝌆

DAY 200. Exodus. Portions
           listed beneath the
           furnishings.
           Tabernacle

Exodus 27:21 In the tabernacle of meeting,
outside the veil which is before the
Testimony, Aaron and his sons shall tend it
from evening until morning before the Lord.
It shall be a statue forever to their
generations on behalf of the children of
Israel.

Prayer: You are our Tabernacle, Lord, our heart Your throne.

COMMENTS; The first item the person saw as he entered the courtyard was the <u>altar of burnt
offering</u>. The priests sacrificed the offerings brought by the people on this altar daily. The altar and
sacrifices pointed to the cross and Jesus as the Perfect Lamb slain in our place.

      The second item was the <u>laver</u>, in which the priest washed his hands before making the
sacrifice, representing cleansing and purity. Jesus, pure, is our High priest. He is our Mediator;
another priest is not needed.

      The third item was the <u>candlestick</u> with seven lamps, representing Christ and the believers
as light to the world. The oil for the lamps represents the Spirit.

      The fourth item was the <u>altar of incense</u> before the veil where the priest placed coals of fire
from the altar of burnt offering on the small altar; then added incense representing the work of
Christ and the prayers of the people. (Revelation 8:2-4)

ACTIVITY: Continue the construction as given in the Appendix, Day 200.

𝌆𝌆𝌆𝌆𝌆

DAY 201. Exodus 32, 33
           Depravity

Exodus 33:14 And He said, "My Presence
will go with you, and I will give you rest."

Prayer: Thanks for Your Presence.

COMMENTS: With such a promise from God it is difficult to understand how the Israelites forgot
God and His Presence, asking for the gods of Egypt. Aaron took their gold, formed a bull-calf
which they were worshiping and dancing around, then God told Moses they had sinned. Moses,
upon seeing their terrible sin, threw down the tablets of stone, breaking them. He remelted the idol
and made the people drink the water he poured the gold into. Returning to God, he pled for his
people, saying he was willing to die in their stead, which was symbolic of Christ's love for us.

ACTIVITY: God returned to the Tabernacle Tent in a cloud. Use raw cotton for the cloud over the
tent; and if possible, hide a tiny flashlight in it to shine at night.

      Use the tabernacle scene for Bible studies when an opportunity arises, explaining that it was
forerunner of the Temple, and later of Christ living in us. Our hearts are the temple of the Holy
Spirit, Christ is on the throne; He is our High Priest. The curtain at the entrance to the Holy of
Holies was torn open by God the Father at His son's sacrifice, so that we come boldly to him.

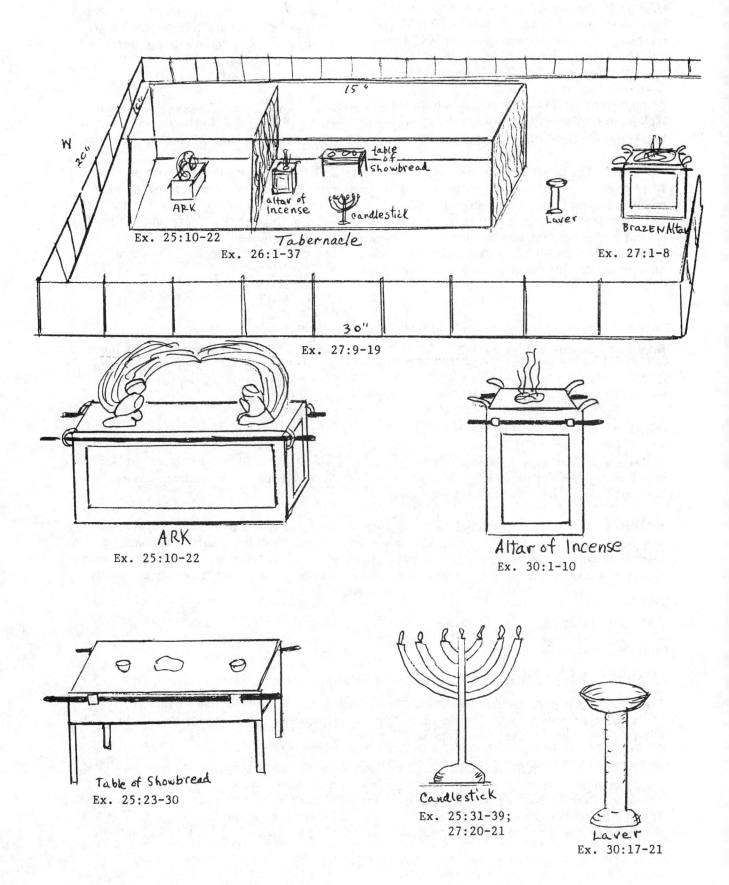

15"

W 20"

table of showbread

altar of incense

candlestick

Laver

BrazeN Altar

ARK
Ex. 25:10-22

Tabernacle
Ex. 26:1-37

Ex. 27:1-8

30"

Ex. 27:9-19

ARK
Ex. 25:10-22

Altar of Incense
Ex. 30:1-10

Table of Showbread
Ex. 25:23-30

Candlestick
Ex. 25:31-39;
27:20-21

Laver
Ex. 30:17-21

DAY 202. Exodus 34, 35
Moses Shines

Exodus 34:12 Take heed to yourself, lest you make a covenant with the inhabitants of the land where you are going, lest it be a snare in your midst.

Prayer: We pray for our family members.

COMMENTS: God knew the heart of man, that associating with the wrong people caused man to take on their sins. Living with the Egyptians led to accepting their gods. God warns them not to repeat this sin by making covenants with the people in the land where they will settle.

ACTIVITY: The priest had a breastplate with 12 gems in it, representing the 12 tribes of Israel, which was to remind him to constantly pray for them. From old jewelry select a stone for each member of your family. Place them neatly in clay. Add a hook in the center top so that it will hang like a necklace. Bake or let dry overnight. Brighten the clay with glaze or model paint. This will remind you to pray for each member of your family. Of course you want to pray for them whenever they are about: working, playing, reading, doing homework; or for those away, a photograph in a prominent place will be a reminder.

✝✝✝✝✝

DAY 203. Exodus 36:1-6; 37:1-2
38:1-16, 22-31;
39:1-3, 8-14, 21, 24-25,
42-43; 40:17, 32-38

Exodus 36:35 And he made a veil woven of blue and purple and scarlet yarn, and fine linen thread; it was woven with an artistic design of cherubim.

Prayer: We worship You, Lord.

COMMENTS: God must love beautiful things: linen, embroidered work, bright colors, articles which took skill and time to achieve. God's beauty is displayed in hummingbirds, peacocks, sunsets, flowers, butterflies, all His creation.

ACTIVITY: It would be nice to have a prayer room in the home where any member of the family may have private time for Bible study, meditation and prayer. Make it a prayerful atmosphere. One member might make a cross, another an embroidered scarf for the table, a plaque with a verse on prayer, the small children's pretty stone, sea shell, or vase of flowers. Add taped hymns to play.

✝✝✝✝✝

DAY 204. Leviticus, portions below
Offerings

Leviticus 6:13 A perpetual fire shall burn on the altar; it shall never go out.

Prayer: Here are our offerings, Lord.

COMMENT: The purpose of sacrifices was for cleansing from sin; and animal's death in place of one's deserved punishment. If no sacrifice, then no forgiveness. It is the same today: no acceptance of Jesus' salvation, no eternal salvation.

ACTIVITY: As you study the types of offerings in your Scripture readings listed under each altar, the children may pretend that they were living thousands of years ago as they present their offerings. One will be the priest going through the motions of washing his hands in the laver, etc. The others mention their sins of dishonesty, complaining, working on the Sabbath, etc. This skit should be followed by today's confession of sins; kneeling by the chair, talking to God directly.

SWEET OFFERINGS

burnt offering
Lev. 1:1-5, 14

grain offering
Lev. 2:1, 9, 13

peace offering
Lev. 3:1, 16, 17

NON-SWEET OFFERINGS

sin offering

trespass offering

priest 4:1-3, 12
congregation 4:13, 14
ruler 4:22-33
common people 4:27

trespass 5:1-7, 15-17
restitution 6:1-6, 13;
7:1, 2, 11-13

✝✝✝✝✝

DAY 205. Leviticus, portions
8:1-13, 33-36; 9:6-9,
22-24; 10:1-3, 9-11;
11:1-4, 45; 12:6;
13:45-46; 14:1-4;
15:14
Consecration of Priests

Leviticus 9:6 Then Moses said,
"This is the thing which the
Lord commanded you to do, and
the glory of the Lord will
appear to you."

Prayer: Your glory is great, Oh Lord.

COMMENTS: At times we may sense the glory of the Lord. Some Christians when receiving a
miracle healing have seen a dazzling light or heard His voice.

ACTIVITY: For the home altar find a lovely candlestick and golden candle to remind you of the
Light of the World, and that the Word is a lamp unto our feet and light unto our path. Start a
spiritual diary, recording special prayers, answers, verses of personal meaning, ones to pray for,
goals.

✝✝✝✝✝

DAY 206. Leviticus, portions.
16:1-4, 29-34; 17:10-12;
18:1-5; 19:1-4, 9-18, 31,
34, 36; 20:6-8, 23-24;
21:6-21; 22:1-2, 24,
32-33.
Behavior

Leviticus 20:7 Sanctify yourselves therefore,
and be holy, for I am the Lord your God.

Prayer: We desire holiness; make us holy.

COMMENTS: God expects His people to be holy; to keep our minds pure, our ways spotless.
There is a special reward for those who are pure in heart for they shall see God. (Matthew 5:8)
        Here is a verse that explains God's reason for blood sacrifices; Leviticus 17:11, "For the
life of the flesh is in the blood, and I have given it to you upon the altar to make atonement for
your souls; for it is the blood that makes atonement for the soul."

ACTIVITY: Family photographer, it is your turn. Compose a picture that will express worship and
praise. Pray about it that it will be good enough to use as a Christmas card or for framed gifts.

DAY 207. Leviticus, portions below.
Festivals

Leviticus 20:7 Sanctify yourselves therefore, and be holy, for I am your God.

Prayer: Thanks that You like festival days, too.

COMMENTS: God set special days for festivals so that the people would remember His laws; assign portions to read explaining the types of festivals:

23:1-3	Sabbath	23:6-8	Unleavened Bread
23:10-11	Firstfruits	23:15-18, 22	Wave-loaves or Harvest
23:23-25	Trumpets or New Year	23:27-32	Day of Atonement
23:33-36	Tabernacles or Shelters	24:2, 4	Care of Lamps
25:2-6	Sabbatic Year	25:10, 33, 54	Year of Jubilee
26:1-9, 12	Blessing	26:26-33, 40-42	Confess
23:4-5	Passover	27:30-31	Tithe

ACTIVITY: Pre-schoolers: gather small boxes for tomorrow. Others do Word Block: There are 41 words relating to the tabernacle, offerings, festivals - use NKJ.

X	U	X	A	L	T	A	R	X	F	O	R	G	I	V	E
B	P	N	X	X	P	A	S	S	O	V	E	R	X	D	A
X	U	F	L	O	U	R	B	X	L	A	M	P	S	O	T
X	R	L	K	E	E	P	X	E	T	L	A	M	B	O	O
F	E	I	L	X	A	G	O	D	R	K	L	A	W	R	N
T	I	T	H	E	X	V	X	X	U	N	P	E	A	C	E
H	G	R	A	I	N	X	E	X	M	X	A	X	V	O	M
O	X	X	S	H	E	E	P	N	P	A	N	C	E	N	E
L	E	V	I	T	E	B	X	R	E	S	T	X	L	F	N
Y	X	P	N	X	F	U	X	X	T	D	X	F	O	E	T
X	H	I	G	H	P	R	I	E	S	T	B	I	A	S	D
W	X	G	L	T	X	N	U	D	O	V	E	R	V	S	A
X	O	E	A	O	X	T	R	I	R	A	M	E	E	X	Y
B	L	O	O	D	V	O	X	X	T	T	L	A	S	A	X
X	G	N	D	X	L	E	T	R	E	S	P	A	S	S	D

1:5   2:2   5:6   25:4   3:8   20:8   4:20   1:10   2:13   24:2

2:12   23:5   2:7   24:4   4:3   1:8   2:12   5:33   5:15   1:14

19:18   3:7   21:10   23:24   1:6   3:12   11:44   1:14   23:7   1:7

1:1   27:30   5:15   26:40   1:5   1:5   3:1   1:5   23:27   6:16

18:4

DAY 208. Numbers 1-8 Census.
One read ahead and tell:
1:1-4, 16-19. 46-54; 2:2, 17, 34;
3:13-16, 44-51; 4:15;
5:6-7; 6:2, 3, 8, 12, 23-27;
7:1-5, 89; 8:1-7, 25, 26

Numbers 6:24-26 The Lord bless you and keep you; the Lord make His face shine upon you, and be gracious to you; the Lord lift up His countenance upon you, and give you peace.

Prayer: Thank You for blessing us.

COMMENTS: The tents in which the people lived were arranged by tribes, one tribe for each of the sons of Jacob. There were three groups on each side of the tabernacle while settled. While marching, six tribes went before the tabernacle and six behind, showing God was always in the midst of them. And He dwells within us today, in the Church universal, and individually.

ACTIVITY: Memorize the blessing above.
   Youngsters make "Our Town." Usually a town is set up with church in the center; stores, hospital, schools around; and the houses on the outskirts. Use various boxes for the buildings, cut the ends of facial tissue boxes for the houses. Paint with latex (washable) or tempera colors.
   Get a good-sized board. Mark off the streets with chalk (erase when you want to change the arrangement). Decide where the buildings and homes will be.
   Bring out small cars, trucks, etc., to drive around. Have fire and police stations. Add cutout trees; small people pasted on cardboard.
   Hours can be spent on this activity, so use it for occasions when the older ones are busy on long projects. Keep it for Bible time as a special incentive.

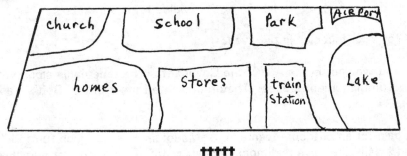

†††††

DAY 209. Numbers 9-11
Cloud of God's
Presence

Numbers 11:23 And the Lord said to Moses, "Has the Lord's arm been shortened? Now you shall see whether My word will befall you or not."

Prayer: Thanks for Your arm!

COMMENTS: This is an interesting portion to read in full. It gives a clear picture of traveling complaints, problems, Moses' difficulty in leading, and God's prevailing power to meet the needs or punish when needed.

ACTIVITY: When traveling, sketch a beautiful scene. Then when home, make a box lamp like it. Use a wooden box about 10" deep. Paint background. Attach a night light in center. Put a glass in front of it with smaller bushes, foliage to hide the light. Add dried flowers, etc. to make it more realistic. Have the cord from the night light enter from a hole in the back of box. Fit a frame on the front and you have your own unique lamp. Add a Bible verse at bottom.

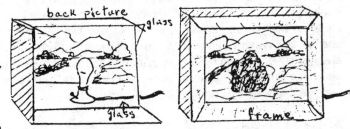

DAY 210. Numbers 12-14
Spies

Prayer: We want to be positive thinkers, Lord, trusting Your victory.

Numbers 14:7,8 And they spoke to all the congregation of the children of Israel, saying, "The land we passed through to spy out is an exceedingly good land. If the Lord delights in us, then He will bring us into this land and give it to us, a land which flows with milk and honey."

COMMENTS: The 10 spies were sent out for 40 days to see whether Israel could conquer the Promised Land. Joshua and Caleb were the only ones with a positive-thinking answer. The others said it was impossible, looking on the giants instead of God's powerful arm. The unbelievers died in the wilderness. Joshua and Caleb were appointed to lead the younger generation into the land. How much depends upon our strong belief that all things are possible with God.

ACTIVITY: Let's play a family game today to be the "good spies" in all we do; that is, we will maintain a positive attitude. "Yes, God can do it through us!" "We can win today!" "I'm not worried about the exam--I'll relax and concentrate." "I'm enthusiastic about the conference at the office." "I'll sing hymns while doing the chores." "I'll giggle while I pick up my toys." "I like this!"

†††††

DAY 211. Numbers 15-17
Aaron's Rod

Numbers 17:8 Now it came to pass on the next day that Moses went into the tabernacle of witness, and behold, the rod of Aaron, of the house of Levi, had sprouted and put forth buds, had produced blossoms and yielded ripe almonds.

Prayer: Thanks for Your miracles in our lives.

COMMENTS: This rod was put in the Ark of the Covenant in the tabernacle along with some manna and the Ten Commandment stones. They represented the types of God's leadership, care, and righteousness.

ACTIVITY: Time again for an outdoors teen event. Mountains are so much fun to hike to the top, eat and sing around a campfire, give testimonies, relate victories in Christ, or miracles you've read about. Make it a challenging time.
     Plan a Bible Club hike to watch birds, pick flowers, gather some to dry.

†††††

DAY 212. Numbers 18-21
Disobedience

Numbers 20:12 Then the Lord spoke to Moses and Aaron, "Because you did not believe me, to hallow Me in the eyes of the children of Israel, therefore you shall not bring this congregation into the land which I have given them."

Prayer: We want to be obedient, quick to do Your will.

COMMENTS: Even a super-leader like Moses didn't do everything perfectly. He should have spoken to the rock as God commanded, but he struck it, as if by his own power. Or was it his anger at the people, as when he broke the Ten Commandment rocks? His act displeased the Lord and Moses wasn't allowed to enter the land he worked so hard to lead the people to. But God always gives a blessing anyway, and when Jesus was transfigured, He let Moses and Elijah (who also was weak at one time) appear to Jesus in the Promised Land. God deals with us similarly: we fall, He picks us up, we go on.

ACTIVITY: Rock is one of Jesus' titles. Peter's statement was called the Rock, the Rock of my salvation, and there are other references about the Rock.

Have you ever collected rocks? Find out all you can about rocks and gems from an encyclopedia or gem book. Gather various colored rocks and pebbles, square, round, triangle, heart shape, special designs in the rock; maybe you can find fossil rocks or crystals. If you have a slicer and polisher, try polishing some stones for gifts. ✝✝✝✝✝

DAY 213. Numbers 22-24
          Balaam

Numbers 23:19 God is not a man, that He should lie, nor a son of man, that He should repent. Has He said, and will He not do it? Or has He spoken, and will He not make it good?

Prayer: Thanks that Your Word is good.

COMMENTS: This is an unusual story. Balaam is characterized as a false prophet, doing things for reputation or money. However, he tried to follow God's directions. God used him to save Israel from battle, and talked through a donkey! Again, I think God has a keen sense of humor! Balaam may not have.

ACTIVITY: Let's make a puppet show of this story. Use a large box for the stage; set it on a card table with cover to the floor. Work from the back, and make stage opening for the front. Add a curtain on a string with paper clip hangers.

Use old socks for puppets or sew cloth ones as shown in the drawings. For the donkey add ears of felt, button eyes, red circle mouth stitched in place. Do this by cutting a slit, then add an oval-shaped piece of red cloth. Add black yarn mane; felt nostrils.

Use white sock for the angel; add yellow yarn hair, button eyes, felt mouth, felt wings.

The prophet will have a turban and beard. King Balak a small crown of cardboard, and his princes rolled turbans.

Use the Bible for conversations. Make as many scenes as needed to tell the whole story. If it turns out well, show it at your visits to rest homes, etc.

Use a shallow box and narrow table to allow children's arms space to work puppets

✝✝✝✝✝

DAY 214. Numbers 25-27
          Joshua

Numbers 26:52-53 Then the Lord spoke to Moses, saying: "To these the land shall be divided as an inheritance, according to the number of names."

Prayer: Thanks for the things you give us.

COMMENTS: The priests, Levites, did not own land for their duties were at the tabernacle or temple. The Levites' portion and Joseph's portion were given to Joseph's two sons, Ephraim and Manasseh.

ACTIVITY: Make a relief map of the Promised Land using flour-salt-water clay. The mountain ranges run parallel to the Mediterranean Sea, the Jordan valley lowers at the Dead Sea, and mountains are on the east side of Jordan.

After the map dries, line sections as in the drawing, for the tribes. Outline the Sea of Galilee, the Jordan River flowing down to the Dead Sea, which is the lowest place in the world, 1300 feet below sea level.

Paint the sections with water colors. Print the names.

The land is about 150 miles long and 50 miles wide, a small land to have influence throughout history and world-wide.

It is a desert area for the most part, but since the modern technology, with irrigation, there are orange groves and many agricultural products. The desert has blossomed as the rose, as prophesied. When I visited Jordan and then Israel, the difference was remarkable--Jordan as in the days of the Bible, Israel modern. This is due not only to Israel's water availability, but money put into it by well-to-do Jews.

✝✝✝✝✝

DAY 215. Numbers 28-30
Offerings.

Prayer: We want to keep our word with You, Lord.

Numbers 30:2 If a man vows to the Lord, swears an oath to bind himself by some agreement, he shall not break his word; he shall do according to all that proceeds out of his mouth.

COMMENTS: God keeps His promises; We should keep ours.

ACTIVITY: Use the following Promise verses as a Bible drill. As you read the verse, stand if it is something you are to do; sit if it is something God does.

Hebrews 7:25	Psalm 84:11	Isaiah 26:3
1 Peter 2:2	John 5:24	Phillipians 4:19
Romans 8:17	Luke 21:33	James 5:15
1 John 1:9	John 6:35	Matthew 18:19
Psalm 31:24	Isaiah 40:31	Acts 16:31
Psalm 55:22	John 8:12	Romans 8:28
John 1:12	Revelation 3:20	James 4:8

✝✝✝✝✝

DAY 216. Numbers 31-33
Inherit the Land

Prayer: Help us to make use of the things You give us.

Numbers 33:51-52 Speak to the children of Israel and say to them: "When you have crossed the Jordan into the land of Canaan, then you shall drive out all the inhabitants of the land from before you, destroy all their molded images, and demolish all their high places."

COMMENTS: These where direct commands, yet hard to obey.

ACTIVITY: In the accompanying game start in the middle block above the name of the son of Jacob you choose. Use two small buttons of the same color for each player. Use felt pens to color the buttons. Play on the blocks to the right, and when returning to the place you started, travel upward to Canaan.

WANDERING IN WILDERNESS

From 2 to 8 players (Jacob's sons). Use spinner or dice. If player stops on block (complaints), go back 3 spaces; if on circle (blessing), go ahead 3 spaces. If stop on space another is on, that player goes back to start. Each player has 2 captains. First to get both to Canaan, wins.

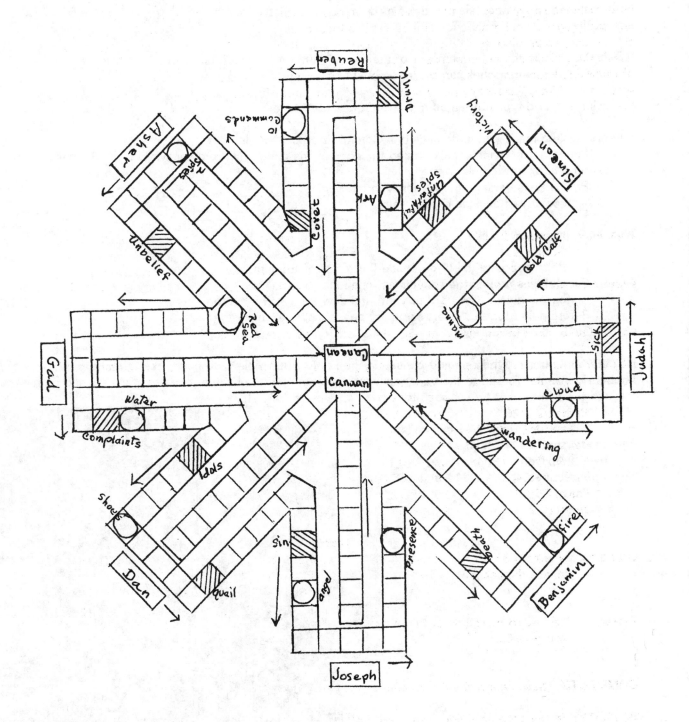

DAY 217. Numbers 34-36
             Boundaries

Prayer: Keep our families honorable, Lord.

Numbers 36:7 So the inheritance of the children of Israel shall not change hands from tribe to tribe, for every one of the children of Israel shall keep the inheritance if the tribe of his fathers.

COMMENTS: The land was divided as equally as possible. Cities of refuge were established. Moses was one of the greatest men of the Bible and carried out the most stupendous tasks the Lord assigned to anyone. He had more miracles in his ministry than any other person in the Bible except Jesus.

ACTIVITY: While the older members of the family work on the word block of 28 miracles in the life of Moses, the younger ones can make tambourines.

We will make two types of tambourines, both of paper plates.

The first will be made with little bells (the Christmas-type of jingle bells).
    Punch holes an inch apart around the edge of the plate. With flower wire attach the bells by making a hook in the hole to the bell.
    Print a Bible verse in the center with felt pen.
    Add color and designs if you desire.

The second type will be like a rattle.

    Print and decorate the two outside (bottoms) of the plates.
    Punch holes around the two plates, one inch apart.
    Match the holes. Use cord or yarn, and sew the two plates together.
    Before going too far, insert some dry beans inside to make the rattle.
    Tie the ends securely.

Use the tambourines when singing praises to the Lord. Your Bible Club might like to make a tambourine band. To add to the variety of musical instruments, put thin paper over combs and hum through the comb, beat two spoons together, tap a metal bar, etc.

Here is one of the bright Mexican children who made the Life of Christ scenes in Tijuana, Mexico in 1984.
See other pictures at Days 314 and 348.

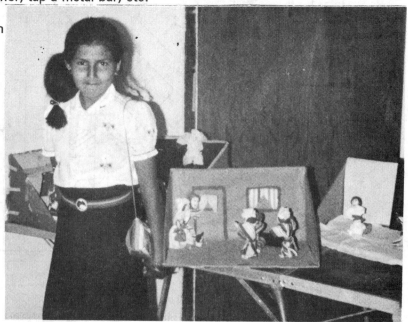

Activity: 28 Miracles in the Life of Moses

	1	2	3	4	5	6	7	8	9	10	11	12	13	14	15	16	17	18	19
1	X	M	O	S	E	S	S	H	I	N	I	N	G	F	A	C	E	Y	F
2	S	D	U	B	D	O	R	S	N	O	R	A	A	X	R	N	X	M	I
3	R	K	C	O	R	M	O	R	F	R	E	T	A	W	X	O	N	R	R
4	D	E	A	T	H	O	F	F	I	R	S	T	B	O	R	N	G	A	E
5	A	S	D	O	O	L	B	X	R	O	D	L	O	C	U	S	T	S	M
6	R	E	B	S	W	E	E	T	E	N	E	D	W	A	T	E	R	X	S
7	K	R	O	R	E	D	N	U	H	T	G	N	I	N	T	H	G	I	L
8	N	P	I	L	L	A	R	C	L	O	U	D	O	F	F	I	R	E	I
9	E	E	L	T	T	A	C	X	Y	S	O	R	P	E	L	I	A	H	A
10	S	N	S	F	L	A	M	I	N	G	B	U	S	H	I	I	X	X	U
11	S	T	K	E	L	A	M	A	F	O	T	A	E	F	E	D	C	X	Q
12	X	S	M	I	R	I	A	M	S	L	E	P	R	O	S	Y	X	E	X
13	M	O	S	E	S	E	Y	E	S	S	T	R	E	N	G	T	H	X	X

Exodus 3:2	9:3	14:21	19:16
4:2	9:9	14:24	34:29
4:6	9:18	15:25	Numbers 12:12
7:19	10:4	16:4	11:1
8:3	10:21	16:13	17:8
8:16	11:15	17:6	21:8
8:21	13:22	17:13	Deuteronomy 34:7

Of the 28 miracles, 16 are given in 1 word; 5 in 2 words; 6 in 3 words; 1 in 4 words.

DAY 218. Deuteronomy - Moses
One read ahead and tell:
1:5-38; 2:2-7, 13-18; 3:1-4,
12-19, 21-28; 4:1-2, 5-13,
23-31, 35-39

Deuteronomy 3:24 O Lord God, You have begun to show Your servant Your greatness and Your mighty hand, for what God is there in heaven or on earth who can do anything like Your works and Your mighty deeds?

Prayer: Thanks for Your care.

COMMENTS: Moses reminded the people how God had lovingly taken care of them through the 40 years and brought them to the brink of the Chosen Land. Much of this review was for the younger generation who must conquer the land in the power of God and to keep the land free from idolatry.

ACTIVITY: Try speech-making. Choose a subject you like or one of these: How God has blessed our family. How God blessed me. My most wonderful spiritual experience. What God means to me. The most important thing in my life. How might I tell others about Jesus.

DAY 219. Deuteronomy 5; 6:1-19;
7:2-9; 8:2-7, 19-20
Signs

Deuteronomy 6:5-9 You shall love the Lord your God with all your heart, with all your soul, and with all your might. And these words which I command you today shall be in your heart; you shall teach them diligently to your children, and shall talk of them when you sit in your house, when you walk by the way, when you lie down, and when you rise up. You shall bind them as a sign on your hand, and they shall be as frontlets between your eyes. You shall write them on the doorposts of your house and on your gates.

Prayer: We do love You, Lord, and will express it in all the ways we can.

COMMENTS: These are commands, and it is fun to fulfill them.

ACTIVITY: There are many slogans on T-shirts, etc., so we will do the same. Use fabric color pens that are waterproof. Print on a belt, "Keep in the Circle of God's Love"; on a scarf or T-shirt, "Praise the Lord!", "God is Love", "God Keeps His Promises". On jewelry kits, use words: Love, Faith, Joy.

DAY 220. Deuteronomy 9:4-5; 10:14-22; 11
The Lord's

Deuteronomy 10:14 Indeed heaven and the highest heavens belong to the Lord your God, also the earth with all that is in it.

Prayer: Thanks that all is Yours.

COMMENTS: Use words that are meaningful to you so that you can give a testimony when friends question your writings. Use a concordance of verses.

ACTIVITY: Wall hangings with Bible verses catch our attention. Use calendar pictures for the background, add straw or pressed flowers in appropriate foreground, frame. Make frames of your own design. Cloth frames tacked over heavy cardboard are unique. Use thick latex paint on an old frame, then with a toothpick mark designs in it. Scraps of wallboard make unusual backing. Buy old frames at auctions and decorate them. Add designs and verses to one side of a mirror.

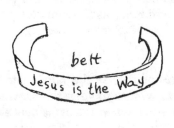

belt
Jesus is the Way

beaded headband or bracelet

Use fabric pens

framed dried flowers

Pressed dried flowers under wax paper

Love Chapter 1 Corinthians 13

ZIG-ZAG sewing fancy stitches over plastic cover - dried flowers

It is more blessed to give than to receive. /////

Placemat - overcast yarn stitching holding together 2 clear plastics with pressed flowers between

Plastic cheese container with butterfly and dried flowers sealed in.

small pine cones, pebbles

Candy jar sealing butterfly and dried Roses

feathered bird, red berries

sea shells and starfish

DAY 221. Deuteronomy 12:1-11; 13:12-18; 14:28; 15:1-4, 9-15
Follow Him

Deuteronomy 13:4 You shall walk after the Lord your God and fear Him, and keep His commandments and obey His voice, and you shall serve Him and hold fast to Him.

Prayer: We'll obey You, Lord.

COMMENTS: Have a family "council" meeting to decide standards and guidelines the family should follow. List them. The children may have suggestions about their toys, where to keep them, which to give to the poor, which to share with friends. Teens may desire a schedule when the car is available so as to plan ahead, how they can share home responsibilities, career possibilities, good manners.

ACTIVITY: Make arrangements in jars with your own dried flowers or ones you purchased. Add pebbles, small shells, butterflies you collected, or small feathered birds (from hobby shop). Small pine cones, bits of dry moss or bark are also nice additions. Use the flour-salt-water clay in the bottom of the jars, or use silicone. Print a favorite Bible verse on clear plastic. Attach it in the bottom of the jar or near the rim, by scotch tape.

✝✝✝✝✝

DAY 222. Deuteronomy 16:1-3, 9:19; 17:6-20; 18:1-5, 9-15, 20-22
Fair and Just

Deuteronomy 16:20 You shall follow what is altogether just, that you may live and inherit the land which the Lord your God is giving you.

Prayer: Help us to treat others justly.

COMMENTS: Consider ways to be loyal, fair, just to your family, nation, all.

ACTIVITY: To make placemats, draw or trace designs, flowers, or scenery. Print the Bible verse with India or indelible ink. Spray with clear plastic. Or use some of your pressed flowers and leaves, cover with heavy plastic like overhead projector transparencies. Bind with wide tape or machine stitch with a wide zig-zag stitch. Make greeting cards with pressed flowers using album stickum paper, with zig-zag stitch edges. Bookmarks with pressed flower and short verse, covered with waxed paper and sealed with warm iron are handy reminders of God.

✝✝✝✝✝

DAY 223. Deuteronomy 19:1-4, 15-21; 20:1-18; 21:18-21
Witnesses

Deuteronomy 19:15 One witness shall not rise against a man concerning any iniquity or any sin that he commits; by the mouth of two or three witnesses the matter shall be established.

Prayer: May we be true witnesses.

COMMENTS: Witnesses often do not agree; the more witnesses the better.

ACTIVITY: Here are some suitable verses, some abridged:
What God has promised He is able also to perform. Romans 4:21
Live the life that pleases God who calls you to share His kingdom. 1 Thessalonians 2:12

God said, "I will never leave you or forsake you." Hebrews 13:5
Have faith in God. Mark 11:22
Faith is the substance of things hoped for, the evidence of things not seen. Hebrews 11:1
Without faith it is impossible to please God. Hebrews 11:6
No one who believes in Him shall be disappointed. Romans 10:11 (GNB)
Do not be afraid or discouraged, for I, the Lord your God, am with you wherever you go. Joshua 1:9 (GNB)
God will supply all your needs. Phillipians 4:19 (GNB)
We are His workmanship, created in Christ Jesus for good works. Ephesians 2:10
The grass withers, the flower fades, but the word of our God stands forever. Isaiah 40:8
I can do all things through Christ Jesus who strengthens me. Phillipians 4:13
You will seek Me and find Me when you search for Me with all your heart. Jeremiah 29:13
The prayer of faith will save the sick, and the Lord will raise him up. James 5:15
I am the resurrection and the life. Whoever believes in Me will live. John 11:25 (GNB)
If we confess our sins, He is faithful and just to forgive us our sins. 1 John 1:9
I have come that they may have life and have it more abundantly. John 10:10
I am the Good Shepherd. The Good Shepherd gives His life for the sheep. John 10:11
The wages of sin is death, but the gift of God is eternal life in Christ Jesus our Lord. Romans 6:23
I am the Way, the Truth, and the Life. John 14:6
If you love Me, keep My commandments. John 14:15

✝✝✝✝✝

DAY 224. Deuteronomy 22:1-2, 9-12; 23:14, 21-25; 24:19-22; 25:1-5, 14-16
Clean Camp

Deuteronomy 23:14 Keep your camp ritually clean, because the Lord your God is with you in your camp to protect you and to give you victory over your enemies. (GNB)

Prayer: We want to keep clean.

COMMENTS: Keeping things clean around the house and yard is a testimony to neighbors; keeping minds clean is a testimony to all the world. Daily resist reading, seeing, or listening to trashy, evil, dishonest, unworthy matters.

ACTIVITY: Check books, magazines, and destroy anything spiritually unclean.

✝✝✝✝✝

DAY 225. Deuteronomy 26:1-13; 27:1-8; 28:1-20, 45-52, 64-65
Obedience

Deuteronomy 28:1 If you obey the Lord your God and faithfully keep all His commands that I am giving you today, He will make you greater than any other nation on earth. (GNB)

Prayer: Thanks for that promise.

COMMENTS: We can depend on God--He won't leave or forsake us!

ACTIVITY: Add to the genealogy chart on Day 170 in your notebook: Isaac lived to be 180. He was 40 when Jacob and Esau were born. Jacob lived to be 147 (Gen. 50:26). In Genesis 15:13-14 God prophesied Abraham's descendants would be slaves, cruelly treated 400 years, the nation punished, and they would take riches with them. The Bible does not state how old Jacob was when Joseph was born, but we can discover this by the following:

Joseph was 30 when he served the king of Egypt at the start of the 7 years of plenty (Gen. 41:46). His brothers came for food the second year of the 7 years of famine. (Gen. 45:6) (Joseph would have been 39 then.)

Jacob stayed in Egypt 17 years before dying at age 147 (Gen. 47:28), so Joseph would have been 56 at Jacob's death (39 + 17). Jacob would have been 91 at Joseph's birth (147 - 56 = 91).

Now add this to your chart:

When Abraham was 100, Isaac was born	2048 BA	lived 180 years	died 2228 BA
When Isaac was 40, Jacob was born	2088 BA	lived 147 years	died 2235 BA
When Jacob was 91, Joseph was born	2179 BA	lived 110 years	died 2289 BA

Joseph was 39 when Jacob and family moved to Egypt, (2179 + 39 = 2218 BA) God prophesied they would be in Egypt 430 years. (Exodus 12:40) So it was about 2648 BA when Moses delivered them. He was called to do this at age 80, (so he would have been born in 2568) He lived 120 years and died in 2688 BA.

✝✝✝✝✝

DAY 226. Deuteronomy 29:1-13; 30:1-20; 31:1-26 Strong

Deuteronomy 31:6 Be strong and of good courage, do not fear nor be afraid of them; for the Lord your God, He is the one who goes with you. He will not leave you nor forsake you.

Prayer: Thank You, Lord, that You will never leave us nor forsake us. We praise You for that!

COMMENTS: We write that promise in our hearts and it strengthens us.

ACTIVITY: The 70 descendants of Jacob who moved to Egypt in 2218 BA (Gen. 46:27) multiplied to 603,500 males above age 20 exclusive of Levites according to the Mt. Sinai census. If 4 in a family that would be 2,414,000 who left Egypt.

✝✝✝✝✝

DAY 227. Deuteronomy 32:1-10, 29-31, 45-52, 33:1-4, 26-29; 34:1-12 God's Arms

Deuteronomy 33:27 The eternal God is your refuge, and underneath are the everlasting arms; He will thrust out the enemy from before you, and will say, "Destroy!"

Prayer: Thanks for Your loving arms.

COMMENTS: Moses was a type of Christ as we find in the comparisons below:

Moses	Comparison	Jesus
Exodus 3: 7-10	chosen	Luke 4: 18,19
Exodus 2:11-15	rejected; turns to Gentiles	Mark 12:10-12
Exodus 4:29-31	accepted as Deliverer	Romans 11:26
Acts 3:22-23	prophet	Acts 3:22-23
Exodus 17:1-6	intercessor	Hebrews 7:25
Exodus 32:31-35	advocate	1 John 2:1-2

ACTIVITY: Fanny Crosby wrote the famous hymn, "Safe in the Arms of Jesus." She was blind but had great spiritual sight. Borrow a book from the church on how hymns were written and be uplifted by the stories. Use the stories in some of your witnessing programs. Tell how certain hymns have helped you when in need of guidance, encouragement, or when you just wanted to praise the Lord.

Day 228.   Joshua 1 - 4
             Cross the Jordan

Prayer: In You we will not be afraid
               nor dismayed for You are with us.
prosperous, and then you will have success.

Joshua 1:8-9 This Book of the Law shall not depart from your mouth, but you shall meditate in it day and night, that you may observe to do according to all that is written in it. For then you will make your way

Have I not commanded you? Be strong and of good courage; do not be afraid, nor be dismayed, for the Lord your God is with you wherever you go.

COMMENTS: It's time for a Bible Club party and we will play games of the Bible stories in the Old Testament, particularly the traveling to the promised land. Joshua led the way after Moses and he lived up to God's expectations. The Canaanites, descendants of Noah's son Ham, worshipped the sun god, Baal. Understandably, God decreed that Baal worship and the worshippers were to be wiped out of the land. To do this there were three campaigns covering a period of 7 years in which Israel conquered 7 nations.

ACTIVITY: Send invitations to the Bible Club party with a drawing of Noah's Ark. For refreshments prepare a Noah's Ark cake, cookie animals, and rainbow punch. Draw animals from a coloring book, cut and use as a cookie pattern. The family will enjoy doing this together. After baking, use a decorator to outline an animal head, etc.

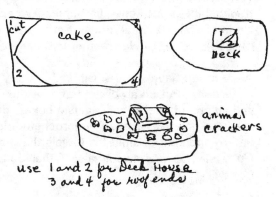

Bake the chocolate cake in a rectangular pan. After baking, cut one end like a boat and round off the other end. Put these extra pieces on top of the house. Use frosting to hold in place; decorate roof, sides, window, door, and add animal crackers. Before eating the cake, use it as the devotional, emphasizing obedience to God, His care, and the rainbow promise.

GAMES:

1. <u>Going to Canaan</u>.   As in Going to Jerusalem, use chairs, one less than children playing. To music "Onward Christian Soldiers" sit in one chair after the other so that when the music stops, one person is left without a chair. He is out. This continues with a chair being removed each time, and finally only one child is left.

2. <u>Traveling</u>.   Each one is given a plastic bag representing the Israelites with all their possessions. At the word "manna" they are to hunt for hidden mints. At the stop signal, the one with the most wins, the prize a package of Life Savers.

3. Two teams with Joshua and Caleb as leaders. This is a <u>relay race</u> to pass overhead all kinds of fruit (cutout cardboard or plastic fruit). The team getting all the fruit in the bag first wins. Prize for team, small boxes of raisins.

4. <u>Name the Animals</u>.   Sit in a circle. Leader starts with, "I built the Ark and the animals and birds went with me, including --- (then add name of one beginning with A)". The next in line repeats the saying and adds a name beginning with B; and so on through the alphabet.

5. <u>Charades</u>.   Joshua and Caleb teams go to separate corners and each team picks two plays to perform in pantomime for the other team to guess. Time each play so that the team guessing the plays in the shortest total time wins. Plays are to be in Old Testament up to the time of Joshua.

6. Give a prize to those who can repeat the Ten Commandments, or tell the days of creation, or name the 12 children of Jacob. If none can do it, give prizes to the person reciting next best.

DAY 229. Joshua 5-8
5.;6.;7:1-13,19-21,
25;8:1-24,30-35
Jericho Falls

Prayer: Help us tear down bad
walls and build up.

Joshua 6:20 So the people shouted when the priests blew the trumpets. And it happened when the people heard the sound of the trumpet, and the people shouted with a great shout, that the wall fell down flat. Then the people went up into the city, every man straight before him, and they took the city.

COMMENTS: After God's great demonstration to the Israelites of the parting of the Jordan River, they were ready to follow His directions to capture Jericho. God sent a Commander of the Army to instruct Joshua how to take the city. He no doubt was an angel. It was a dramatic victory for the whole country to hear and fear the God of the Israelites.

ACTIVITY: This is a terrific story, one the Bible Club should dramatize. Read the story, ask for volunteers for the Commander, Joshua, trumpet blowers, priests, etc. The simple props can be made of cardboard (trumpets, etc.), box for the Ark, a cover tied across the hallway for the wall. This is also good for the family. Think of walls. Now each list kinds of walls to build (friendship, an attractive partition between a room where a doorway is no longer needed); and kinds of walls to break down (Berlin wall, wall of unforgiveness, a garden wall no longer needed). Now decide whether you can do anything about your lists.

Also, if you have some small wall space you would like to use, here are some ideas: Children's play room. Put up an oilcloth and let the children waterpaint. Install wall brackets for holding collections of shells, bells, music boxes, dried flower jars containing dried vegetables and fruits ready to use. Hang exquisite crocheted doilies (pin them on colored squares or circles). Make an arrangement of linen tea towels that have pictures on them. Tools in the shop. Cookie Cutters. Nails, screws in jars. Other Collections.

††††††

DAY 230. Joshua 9-12
9; 10:5-26, 40-43;
11:1-8, 20, 23; 12:1,24
Sun Stood Still

Prayer: Thanks for Your miracles.

Joshua 10:13 So the sun stood still, and the moon stopped, till the people had revenge upon their enemies. Is this not written in the Book of Jasher? So the sun stood still in the midst of heaven, and did not hasten to go down for a whole day.

COMMENTS: In this short period of time, 7 years, God performed some unusual miracles, including the earth standing still for part of a day-- or the sun--or whatever really happened. It reminds us of the 7 years Tribulation period in Revelation when remarkable things will happen.

ACTIVITY: List all the miracles in the Bible you can remember. List any you can remember that have happened since Bible days. Longest list wins extra dessert.

††††††

DAY 231. Joshua 13-19
13:1, 7, 33; 14:6-13; 15:63;
16:10; 17:12-13, 17-18;
18:1-10; 19:49-51
Territories

Joshua 13:33 But to the tribe of Levi Moses had given no inheritance; the Lord God of Israel was their inheritance, as He had said to them.

Prayer: Thanks that we are joint heirs with Christ.

COMMENTS: Joshua unselfishly took no portion of the land for himself. Caleb, now old, instead of accepting a reward for his services, asked for the privilege of conquering the most difficult hill country near Hebron. The Tabernacle was set up in Shiloh. Later, when David was king, he arranged for the Tabernacle to be set up in Jerusalem, the capital and religious center of the nation.

ACTIVITY: We are joint heirs with Christ. Fill in the blanks in the "heirs" verses below; then make a list of all we share with Jesus.

1. For as many as are _____ by the _____ of God, these are _____ of God. For you did not receive the spirit of _____ again to _____, but you received the Spirit of _____ by whom we cry out, 'Abba, Father.' The Spirit Himself bears _____ with our spirit that we are _____ of God, and if children, then _____ heirs of God and _____ heirs with Christ, if indeed we _____ with Him, that we may also be glorified together. Romans 8:14-17

2. And if you are Christ's, then you are _____ seed, and _____ according to the _____. Galatians 3:29.

3. And because you are _____, God has sent forth the _____ of His Son into your _____, crying out, 'Abba Father!' Therefore you are no longer a _____ but a _____, and if a son, then an _____ of God _____ _____. Galatians 4:6-7

4. In whom also we have obtained an _____, being _____ according to the _____ of Him who works all things according to the counsel of His _____, that we who first _____ in _____ should be to the _____ of His _____. In _____ you also trusted, after you heard the word of _____, the gospel of your _____; in whom also, having _____, you were _____ with the Holy _____ of _____, who is the _____ of our _____ until the _____ of the _____ _____, to the praise of His glory.
Ephesians 1:11-14

5. That having been _____ by His _____ we should become _____ according to the hope of _____ life. Titus 3:7

6. Are they not all _____ _____ sent forth to minister for those who will _____ _____? Hebrews 1:14

†††††

DAY 232. Joshua 20-24
20:1-3; 21:1-3, 41-45;
22:1-6, 11-34; 23; 24.
Joshua's Farewell

Prayer: Thanks for keeping Your promises!

Joshua 23:14 Now my time has come to die. Every one of you knows in his heart and soul that the Lord your God has given you all the good things that He promised. Every promise He made has been kept; not one has failed. (GNB)

COMMENTS: The verse today is one to memorize - the last sentence. He's great!

ACTIVITY: Make a wall plaque with the part you memorized. Use a circle to represent everlasting for the background - maybe wood, cloth, cardboard, or glass.

†††††

DAY 233. Judges 1-3
Israel's Idols

Prayer: May we worship only You, Lord.

Judges 3:10 The Spirit of the Lord came upon him, and he judged Israel. He went out to war, and the Lord delivered Cushan-Rishthaim, king of Mesopotamia into his hand.

COMMENTS: Soon after Joshua's death the people began to serve Baal instead of God. They lost wars and sinned against the Lord in many ways. Yet God found a few good men who still loved and served him.

ACTIVITY: Make a poster of today's idols (cars, TV, movie stars, etc.) on one side and put opposite pictures of how we can serve God (helping, giving, etc.)

✝✝✝✝✝

DAY 234. Judges 4-5
Deborah

Judges 5:3 Hear, O kings! Give ear, O princes! I, even I, will sing unto the Lord; I will sing praise to the Lord God of Israel.

Prayer: Bless our girls and women in serving You.

COMMENTS: The yoke of the Canaanites was finally broken by Deborah and Barak, bringing about 40 years of peace. Deborah was a remarkable woman, full of patriotic courage and zeal for the Lord.

ACTIVITY: Among God's beautiful handiworks are shells. Enjoy along the beach gathering them and admiring the intricate craftsmanship. It's fun to glue shells into shapes: birds, little animals, flowers; decorate a jewelry box.

✝✝✝✝✝

DAY 235. Judges 6-8
Gideon

Judges 7:22 When the 300 blew the trumpets, the Lord set every man's sword against his companion throughout the whole camp; and the army fled to Beth Acacia.

Prayer: Thanks for this lesson on faith.

COMMENTS: We often hear the expression, "put out a fleece," meaning a test (as Gideon did) to determine if it is God's will to do a certain thing. This extra "yes" gives us courage to step out in faith to do the impossible. I have found that God is pleased to give us signs, and He is faithful to keep His word.

ACTIVITY: Fill a jar with dried beans. Each member of the family guess how many are in the jar. Then divide them in portions for each to count. When 300 are counted put them back in the jar to use for a party game later on. The people guess, and the closest to 300 wins. It is an opportunity to tell of Gideon.

Sew bean bags for games. Use heavy material. Make one a circle, another a square, and one a triangle. They represent eternal life, honest people, the Trinity. Use 3 boxes, marked circle, square, or triangle. The person throwing the bags in the correct box wins.

Try juggling the bean bags.

Throw the bags between your legs into the boxes behind you.

With chalks draw a series of blocks like a ladder, and draw circle, square, triangle in some of the blocks. Hop on one foot, drop the bag in the correct block, and on to the end, then still hopping, return, picking up the bags. If you fall, start over, but it is one point against you. Earn two points for each bag dropped or picked up. Top scores wins.

Play softball with the bags and a paddle or board, a team game.

DAY 236. Judges
9:1-24, 50-56;
10:6-18; 11; 12:7
Repentance

Prayer: Forgive us for our sins, too, Lord.

Judges 10:15-16 Then the children of Israel said to the Lord, "We have sinned! Do to us whatever seems best to You; only deliver us this day, we pray." So they put away the foreign gods from among them and served the Lord. And His soul could no longer endure the misery of Israel.

COMMENTS: What do you think of judges and lawyers today? Is it right to defend a criminal, striving to free him in spite of what he may do in the future - such as someone who has murdered many people? What do you think about laws that allow sinning in moderation? What about peddling dope, especially on school grounds? Are the penalties strict enough to wipe out such deplorable crimes? What about drunk drivers? How strict should their penalty be? How can we help to have just laws and just punishments?

ACTIVITY: Make a poster of what should be done in the case of

1. FIRE

2. BURGLARY

3. ACCIDENT OR SICKNESS

Plan strategies in each case. Check for bad wiring, places where fires could start; install fire alarms, extinguishers, smoke alarms, sprinklers. Have a plan of escape from various rooms. Emergency phone numbers handy. What should the family do to prevent burglary? Practice first aid.

†††††

DAY 237. Judges 13-16
Samson

Prayer: Keep us strong in You.

Judges 13:24-25a So the woman bore a son and called his name Samson; and the child grew, and the Lord blessed him. And the spirit of the Lord began to move upon him.

COMMENTS: The Spirit did many mighty things through Samson to deliver Israel. Study his story so you can find words about him in the accompanying word block.

ACTIVITY: Pre-schoolers: See how strong you are. Play tug-of-war; who can carry the most toys back to the toy box; and who can straighten the furniture.

†††††

DAY 238. Judges 17-21
17; 18; 19:1-4; 20:12-48;
21:15-25
Apostasy

Prayer: Give us wisdom to follow You.

Judges 21:25 In those days there was no king in Israel; everyone did what was right in his own eyes.

COMMENTS: Israel as a nation was far from what God intended it to be. Idolatry prevailed. Except for a few godly men and women, the situation was deplorable.
ACTIVITY: The total years ruled by judges was 300; 3 of them served 40 years each. The pre-schoolers line up their crayons and judge which colors match.
The rest fill in the following blanks with names from the book of Judges:

1. God gave_____ strength in his long hair; when cut, he was as weak as others.
2. The Spirit of the Lord came upon _____ and gave him victory in Mesopotamia.
3. With trumpets and torches _____ won a battle with only 300 men.
4. _____ tied the tails of foxes in pairs, added torches with fire, which burned the enemy's field.

Activity: Can you find 34 words from the story of Samson in the puzzle below?

	1	2	3	4	5	6	7	8	9	10	11	12	13	14
1	P	J	P	X	B	L	I	N	D	X	B	P	C	N
2	H	A	I	R	I	D	D	L	E	X	U	O	O	A
3	I	W	S	O	I	M	O	T	H	E	R	W	L	Z
4	L	B	N	P	E	S	A	G	O	D	N	E	U	A
5	I	O	I	E	K	Y	O	N	F	X	E	R	M	R
6	S	N	A	T	N	N	E	N	O	I	D	Y	N	I
7	T	E	H	F	O	X	E	S	D	A	E	E	L	T
8	I	X	C	S	T	R	O	N	G	N	H	L	S	E
9	N	G	M	X	S	X	C	X	O	A	I	U	D	E
10	E	A	N	G	E	L	X	H	C	M	R	R	X	V
11	S	T	A	I	L	S	W	E	E	T	X	X	G	O
12	D	E	L	I	L	A	H	X	I	S	R	A	E	L

blind	lion	rope	strong
burned	Delilah	mother	foxes
chains	Israel	God	honey
torches	power	eyes	mill
trust	column	Manoah	love
Philistines	Nazarite	field	gate
jawbone	hair	Samson	angel
prison	riddle	grind	tails
knots	sweet		

5. The army general _____ fought Sisera who had 900 iron chariots.
6. _____, the son of a godly judge, turned against God, killed his 70 brothers, and was an evil ruler.
7. A ballad of victory and praise was sung by _____ and _____.
8. An angel appeared to _____ _____, saying she would have a son.
9. _____ used wool and morning dew to test whether God was directing him.
10. _____ made a foolish vow if he won a battle, to sacrifice the first person coming from his house.

✝✝✝✝✝

Day 239. Ruth 1-4
          Beauty
          Read as a play; assign
          reader and characters.

Ruth 1:16 But Ruth said: "Entreat me not to leave you, or to turn back from following you; for wherever you go, I will go; and wherever you lodge, I will lodge; your people shall be my people, and your God, my God."

Prayer: We'll follow You, Lord.

COMMENTS: The culture of the Israel nation was that the oldest son, as heir, was to have a child to carry on the tribal line. Since Ruth's husband had died, Boaz was the proper male in line to take her as wife. He followed the custom of seeking the elders' advice. Boaz and Ruth are listed in Jesus' genealogy.

ACTIVITY: Make a box-like wall hanging for your kitchen using grains, seeds, bark, twigs, etc. Sketch a landscape, mountains, lake, hillsides, road, wheat field. Color rice blue for the sky and lake, spread glue in those areas, then press the rice into the glue. Use barley for ground, wheat heads for field, black beans for rocks, green peas for grass, and so on. The picture shows God's abundance.

✝✝✝✝✝

DAY 240. 1 Samuel 1-3
           Samuel and Eli

1 Samuel 2:2 There is none holy like the Lord, for there none beside You, nor is there any God like our God.

Prayer: Let us hear Your voice.

COMMENTS: Hannah was another beautiful woman of faith whom God honored with a child. Samuel's father was a Levite priest, so it was natural for Samuel to continue this line of duty under Eli, the high priest. God also used Samuel as a judge. The other judges were assigned definite places, but Samuel enlarged the ministry by establishing a circuit court in order to judge the whole nation.

ACTIVITY: God is constantly weaving a pattern in our lives as we interrelate with others. With this in mind, we will do some more weaving. This time we will make an oblong frame for placemats, 18" x 12". Select yarn or strips of cloth. Use colors to blend with your china.

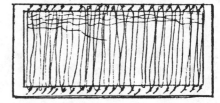

Sew ends together as you weave, to fit your color pattern. Weave in and out of the vertical threads, pushing up with a pencil to keep the lines straight.

When you have completed the weaving, tie at the end. Tack underneath any end knots that show.

Day 241.   1 Samuel 4-7
              Ark

Prayer: Help us build a
              testimony to You.

1 Samuel 7:13 So the Philistines were subdued, and they did not come any more into the territory of Israel. And the hand of the Lord was against the Philistines all the days of Samuel.

COMMENTS: Eli, a leader for 40 years, dropped dead at age 98 when he heard of the capture of the Ark of the Covenant and the death of his sons. The nation who held the Ark was punished and finally returned it with gifts to express sorrow for their sin. It stayed 20 years in Kiriath Jearim. Samuel exhorted his people to destroy their idols and worship God. After that an alter was made called, "The Lord has helped us all the way." What a testimony!

ACTIVITY: Each one make a Treasure Box or Testimony Box to hold your spiritual diary, special items the Lord has blessed you with, and covenants or resolutions. Print a favorite verse on the top and decorate. Jesus has given me tokens I've kept. Once when troubled, I looked down and there was a heart-shaped stone. Another time a butterfly landed on my shoe and stayed there - I kept it and it is in one of my tabletop displays. He has demonstrated His presence many times.
✝✝✝✝✝

DAY 242.   1 Samuel 8-10
              Saul

Prayer: Empower us, Lord.

Samuel 10:6 Then the Spirit of the Lord will come upon you, and you will prophesy with them and be turned into another man.

COMMENTS: We are changed, too, when the Spirit teaches, leads, changes us.

ACTIVITY: Today we will weave a picture, a landscape, about 8" x 12". Tack half-inch headless nails a quarter-inch apart on a frame. The warp or vertical threads will be blue.

Sketch a scene on paper: mountain, lake, road, bushes, a simple design of large areas of color. The foreground colors are bright and green; the background more blue and lighter in shade.

Use embroidery thread. Weave a long, wide-eyed needle. Weave back and forth with one color at a time. Tie knots in the back.

Since this is intricate work, the children will make potholders and tack on felt flowers or butterflies.

If the woven picture seems flimsy, spread with Elmer's glue on the back before removing from the frame. Put in a glass frame, add a verse and your name on the back.
✝✝✝✝✝

Day 243.   1 Samuel 11-13
              Prayer for others.

Prayer: Bless our loved ones and our neighbors.

1 Samuel 12:23 Moreover, as for me , far be it from me that I should sin against the Lord in ceasing to pray for you; but I will teach you the good and the right way.

COMMENTS: According to this verse, the sin is against the Lord when we fail to intercede for someone He has placed on our hearts. God uses us in prayer, maybe many of us, to fight Satan's hold on another's life. If we fail, it takes longer to win the victory and prolongs the suffering for the one under trial.

ACTIVITY: Look at your prayer-answer bouquet of flowers. Have you remembered to add flowers when prayers were answered? If not, catch up on the ones you recall. Look at the prayer list. If someone needs more prayer, maybe fasting, pray more earnestly and faithfully. Add on the vase "It is a sin not to pray."

✝✝✝✝✝

Day 244. 1 Samuel 14-15
Obedience

Prayer: We want to obey You, Lord.

1 Samuel 15:22 Then Samuel said: "Has the Lord as great delight in burnt offerings and sacrifices, as in obeying the voice of the Lord? Behold, to obey is better than sacrifice, and to heed than the fat of rams."

COMMENTS: List spiritual and material gains for being obedient. (Strong character, peace of mind, satisfaction, job well done, etc.)

ACTIVITY: See how many words you can make out of the saying:

"It is better to obey than sacrifice." (Example: beet, fire, say, batch)

✝✝✝✝✝

DAY 245. 1 Samuel 16-18
Goliath
Read as a play.

Prayer: We believe in Your name and Your power.

1 Samuel 17:45 Then David said unto the Philistine, "You come to me with a sword, with a spear, and with a javelin. But I come to you in the name of the Lord of hosts, the God of the armies of Israel, whom you have defied."

COMMENTS: David was young when he was anointed king; a mere youth when he fought the giant. God uses young people who believe in Him! Don't be afraid to stand up for the Lord and His ways among your friends, everywhere.

ACTIVITY: Start a scene of David and Goliath. Goliath was about 9' tall, so use a dowel stick for the extra height and add a popsickle stick for David. Goliath will have full warrior uniform: aluminum foil spear and shield, breastplate, helmet; leather or felt leggings, tunic. David wears a simple shepherd's tunic, turban, belt.

King Saul will have a kingly armor and the soldiers (small in the distance) breastplates over leather skirts and spears.

✝✝✝✝✝

DAY 246. 1 Samuel 19-21
Jonathan

Prayer: May our love be as strong as theirs.

1 Samuel 20:17 And Jonathan again caused David to vow, because He loved him; for he loved him as he loved his own soul.

188   READERS AND DOERS

COMMENTS: The friendship between David and Jonathan was God-given. It would have been difficult for David to survive in Saul's reign without Jonathan's care. God gives us good friends, too, and we should appreciate them.

ACTIVITY: Make the background scenery, with hillside and valley with stream in the middle; Philistines on the left, and Israelites on the right.

✝✝✝✝✝

DAY 247. 1 Samuel 22-24   1 Samuel 23:16 Then Jonathan, Saul's son
           Encouragement   arose and went to David in the woods and
                                                strengthened his hand in God.

Prayer: Bless our friends.

COMMENTS: Practice telling the story as it will be a favorite to use at playground Bible Clubs, or when visiting institutions or hospitals - for anyone who needs a strong, victorious God.. The Good News Bible translated the above verse: "Jonathan went to him there and encouraged him with assurances of God's protection." God often uses friends to encourage and strengthen us.

ACTIVITY: Write letters of encouragement to some leaders, the President or governor, or people under stressful situations.

✝✝✝✝✝

DAY 248. 1 Samuel 25-27   1 Samuel 24:17 Then he said to David:
           Loyalty   "You are more righteous than I; for you have
                                                rewarded me with good, whereas I have
                                                rewarded you with evil."

Prayer: We want to be loyal to You and others, Lord.

COMMENTS: It was good of Saul to acknowledge David's compassion. And how noble David was, honoring God's appointed king. Nobleness is an admirable virtue; strive to be noble, honorable, loyal.

ACTIVITY: Decide in several ways the family can support the community: block parent, solicit for heart, or cancer funds, invite children after school whose parents are working, keep area clean and beautiful with sharing flowers.

✝✝✝✝✝

DAY 249. 1 Samuel 28-31   1 Samuel 29:5 Is this not David, of whom
           Saul's Death   they sang to one another in dances, saying,
                                                "Saul has slain his thousands, and David his
                                                ten "thousands"?

Prayer: Thanks for taking care of us.

COMMENTS: Seeking information from a fortuneteller, witch, or medium is sinful in God's sight. He offers us His wisdom without charge. Trust in the Lord. He knows the future and guides us daily. Pray for the fortunetellers that they may come to know the Lord and be a witness for Him.

ACTIVITY: In this quiz on anger, fill in the name of the person who was angry.

1. _____ killed Abel. (Genesis 4:5-8)
2. _____ threw a spear at David. (1 Samuel 18:10-11)
3. _____ tied foxes tails to destroy field of the Philistines. (Judges 15:3-5)
4. _____ had children under 2 years slain. (Matthew 2:16)
5. _____ threatened Elijah for slaying the prophets of Baal. (1 Kings 19:1-3)

6. _____ was angry because God forgave the Ninevites (Jonah 4:1-2)
7. _____ hardened his heart against Moses and God. (Exodus 9:34)
8. _____ threw down the Ten Commandments when his people sinned. (Exodus 32:19)
9. _____ wanted to hang Mordecai because he didn't salute him. (Esther 3:5)
10. _____ will punish Satan and wicked angels. (Revelation 15:7)

✝✝✝✝✝

DAY 250.   2 Samuel 1-3
              Tragedies

2 Samuel 1:23. Saul and Jonathan were beloved and pleasant in their lives, and in their death they were not divided; they were swifter than eagles, they were stronger than lions.

Prayer: Minister through us.

COMMENTS: Considering Saul's depression and jealousy, this is a praiseworthy epitaph. What would our epitaph be? Let's live to make it a worthy one.

ACTIVITY: Good friendship can grow around a miniature golf course. I found it a splendid activity at a playground cub or church youth group. try it with the Bible Club and Teen Club working together.

Decide on a theme. I used "The Christian Life." If it is to be a one-time afternoon game, make temporary obstacles from all kinds of objects: boxes, juice cans with open ends, pipes (all large enough for a ball or jar lid to pass through), styrofoam blocks with cutouts, scrap carpet, linoleum or wallboards.

If it is to be more permanent, such as at a campground, make wooden or concrete obstacles. Scrap wallboard makes smooth runways for each hole.

Set up the course with each "hole" having a signpost with the Scripture verse on it and the "title" so that the course has spiritual meaning.

For a Sunday School class game after the lesson, I took some simple cardboard obstacles, lath sticks and jar lids. The students set up the course in a circle on the floor, taping down the obstacles, then played the game twice. Afterwards they could recite the events in the Christian's journey and enjoyed it.

For my playground clubs I prayed about getting clubs and balls, and God answered; then I set up more permanent obstacles which I could arrange on the lawn and carry in my station wagon. The children helped set up and put away.

For themes you could have "Jesus Walks through Israel," or "World Trip."   A charge of $.25 a game would earn money for missions or a sponsored child.

The Christian's Journey Through Life
1. Cross - John 3:16
   from death to life;
   drive ball through long
   narrow box, like cross.

2. Narrow Gate - Matthew 7:13-14
   Several choices gates: My way,
   Fortune, Pleasure, Fame, Narrow Gate.

3. New Life - 2 Corinthians 5:17
   Several juice cans; one with
   hole in both ends.

4. Prayer - Revelation 3:20
   Types of prayer: thanks, worship
   intercession - go through all.

5. Bible - Psalm 119:11
   Choices of books, one being the Bible.

6. Faith - Philippians 4:13
   3 choices: I Give Up;
   Hope I Can; In Christ I Can

7. Service - Galatians 5:13
   Choices: Myself, pleasure,
   indifference, others.

8. Witness - Mark 16:15
   Pray, Give, Go

9. Tests - 1 Peter 1:7a
   Several twists, sand, blocks

10. Heaven - Revelation 2:10b
    Crown of Life - ramp into circle

18 Holes for the Holy Land course, following Events in Jesus' Life:

1. Bethlehem, birth in stable

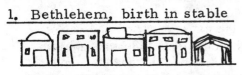

shoot ball into stable door

2. Flight to Egypt

via pyramids

3. Nazareth carpenter shop

shoot for shop entrance

4. Baptism in Jordan River

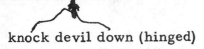

through bushes at bank

5. Mt. of Temptation

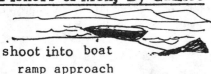

knock devil down (hinged)

6. Fishers of Men, By Galilee

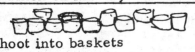

shoot into boat
ramp approach

7. Sermon on Mount, 5000 Fed

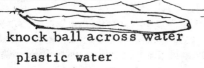

shoot into baskets
ramp approach

8. Crossing Galilee

knock ball across water

plastic water

9. Cast out Demons

swine on hinges, knock down

10. Samaria, Woman at Well

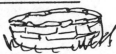

ramp approach
ball into well

11. Transfiguration, Mt. Herman

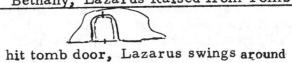

flexible pipe cut in half
making ditch trail
shoot up the mountain trail

12. Healings

go through Faith door; spring releases

blind, deaf, crippled, sick to stand.

13. Jericho, Zaccheus

tree hinged at bottom
knock Zaccheus out of tree

14. Bethany, Lazarus Raised from Tomb

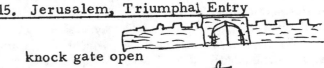

hit tomb door, Lazarus swings around

15. Jerusalem, Triumphal Entry

knock gate open

16. Crucifixion

kneel at the cross, drop into hole

17. Resurrection

empty tomb, go through it

18. Ascension, Mt. of Olives

hit hard, ball bounces in air when landing
on a spring

Each player is given score card with the map

of the course. Low score wins; 1 point for

each try to get ball through goal.

DAY 251. 2 Samuel 4-6
            Jerusalem

Prayer: Thanks for being with us.

2 Samuel 5:10 So David went on and became great, and the Lord God of hosts was with him.

COMMENTS: David captured Jerusalem, established it as the nation's capital and center of worship. David was 30 (the same age as when Jesus began His ministry) and he ruled 40 years.

ACTIVITY: Find out facts about Jerusalem from Bible dictionaries and travel brochures. Start planning for a trip to the Holy Land some day, saving money for a few years in a special fund.
        When I went, I hiked up the Mt. of Olives to see the sunrise, leaving my hotel room in Jerusalem at 4:00 A.M. I passed the Garden of Gethsemane and on my return spent some time in there in prayer. During the sunrise I read all the Scriptures about that area--Jesus ascending, and to return again on that spot. Later at Gethsemane I picked up some hollyhock seeds on the ground and planted them at home. When I reached Galilee, I also rose early to watch the sunrise and saw a fishing boat coming in, and read the Scriptures pertaining to that area.

                                    ✝✝✝✝✝

DAY 252. 2 Samuel 7-9
            How Great Thou Art

Prayer: We praise You, too,
            for being so wonderful!

2 Samuel 7:22. Therefore, You are great, O Lord God. For there is none like You, nor is there any God besides You, according to all that we have heard with our ears.

COMMENTS: Remember, David was poetic, sensitive to God's presence.

ACTIVITY: For this Bible drill, as a person reads the verse he also draws part of the face: the oval, eyes, hair, etc. Make it a smiling face.

1. 1 Kings 2:4
2. 1 Chronicles 22:10
3. 2 Chronicles 7:14
4. Zecharian 12:8
5. Amos 9:11
6. Psalm 89:34
7. Jeremiah 33:3
8. Luke 1:32

9. Psalm 119:1
10. Micah 5:4
11. Isaiah 9:6-7
12. Psalm 132:11
13. 1 Samuel 12:4
14. 1 Peter 2:9
15. Acts 2:25
16. Revelation 5:5

                                    ✝✝✝✝✝

DAY 253. 2 Samuel 10-12
            Bathsheba

Prayer: Forgive us for our
            many sins, Lord,
            both known and unknown.

2 Samuel 12:22-23. So he said, "While the child was still alive, I fasted and wept; for I said, 'Who can tell whether the Lord will be gracious to me, that the child may live?' But now he is dead; why should I fast? Can I bring him back again? I shall go to him, but he shall not return to me."

COMMENTS: This was David's greatest sin. It discolored his outstanding life. He broke three of the Ten Commandments: coveting, adultery, murder. His remorse was great; he was forgiven, but the punishment was severe, causing others to suffer also. Some of the Psalms were written at this time, such as Psalm 32 and 51. Sin slips up on us so easily. We must keep alert.

ACTIVITY: We are apt to judge serious crimes such as murder, torture, and overlook little sins such as pride, boasting, worrying, selfishness, gossiping, telling white lies, wanting too many things. Make up a story about the results of little sins. Choose one of the following, or one you originate.

1. Bobby found a dime on the table, did not ask whose it was but kept it.
2. Mary wanted to see her boy friend but knew her parents objected to his wild ways, so she arranged to meet him at the library, unbeknownst to her parents.
3. Mother answered the phone. Her neighbor told her that so-and-so was seen entering a bar.
4. Dad wanted a raise but would have to work on Sundays to get it.

☩☩☩☩☩

DAY 254. 2 Samuel 13-15
          Absalom

Prayer: Bless and keep our
               loved ones from harm.

2 Samuel 15:21. But Ittai answered, "Your Majesty, I swear to you in the Lord's name that I will always go with you wherever you go, even if it means death. (GNB)

COMMENTS: In spite of David's troubles, God forgave him and blessed his memory. He is known as "the man after God's own heart." He is spoken of in the New Testament more than any other Old Testament character.

ACTIVITY: As we think of kings, we usually think of crowns. There are a number of crowns mentioned in the Bible. Most are rewards for great achievements. When the angel in Revelation speaks of the rewards being laid down at the Lamb's feet, it is the crowns that are given. Jesus promised the crown of life to those faithful unto death (Rev. 2:10; 4:10). Then there is the saddest crown of all, the crown of thorns our Savior wore for us. God punished Adam (Genesis 3:18), saying he would work hard, bearing thorns and weeds. Jesus bore thorns on His head for us.

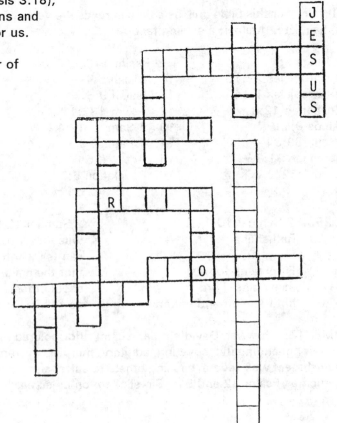

Pre-schoolers: Make crowns to wear of cardboard, coloring them brightly.

The rest, try this word puzzle, using the words in italics.

Psalm 8:5. Jesus crowned with *glory* and *honor*.
Job 31:36. *head* crown (GNB)
Proverbs 4:8-9. *wisdom* will be your crowning glory. (GNB)
Proverbs 16:31. Grey *hair* is a glorious crown.
Revelation 4:10. Elders cast their crowns before the *throne*.
1 Corinthians 9:25 crowned with *wreath* (GNB)
2 Timothy 4:8. Crown of *righteousness.*
Isaiah 28:1. Crowns of *flowers* (GNB)
Matthew 27:29. Crown of *thorns*.
1 Peter 5:4 *glorious* crown.
Revelation 19:21. *Jesus'* crown.
Revelation 2:10 crown of *life*.

DAY 255. 2 Samuel 16-18
                 Grief

Prayer: Only You know, Lord,
                 the anguish of our souls.

2 Samuel 18:33. Then the king was deeply moved, and went up to the chamber over the gate and wept. And as he went, he said thus: "O my son Absalom-if only I had died in your place! O Absalom my son, my son!"

COMMENTS: David's grief was unbearable. Sometimes grief can be overpowering and our only comfort is in the everlasting arms of God. He alone can lift us.

ACTIVITY: Unscramble the following names from 2 Samuel:

> hbeipmohhtse   bahse
>
> vaddi   lestniphiis
>
> baalmos   hhebbaats
>
> bajo   nolsoom
>
> berna   hatann

†††††

DAY 256. 2 Samuel 19-21
                 Remembered

Prayer: We want to help others.

2 Samuel 19:27. He lied about me to your majesty, but you are like God's angel, so do what seems right to you. (GNB)

COMMENTS: David's compassion was still great when it came to Mephibosheth, the crippled grandson of Saul. He kept his pledge to care for Jonathan's children.

ACTIVITY: Do something for the handicapped children you know. Take them on an outing to the beach, to a ball game, camping, whatever you can work out with the parents. Prepare foods they can eat; see that their special needs will be taken care of. Make it a restful and inspiring time, full of love and friendship. Read the Bible, sing around the campfire, give testimonies.

†††††

DAY 257. 2 Samuel 22-24
                 Song and Census

Prayer: We sing praises to You
                 for Your goodness.

2 Samuel 22:3-4. The God of my strength, in Him I will trust, my shield and the horn of my salvation, my stronghold and my refuge; my Savior, You save me from violence. I will call upon the Lord, who is worthy to be praised; so shall I be saved from my enemies.

COMMENTS: Again David sinned. This time the pride of life overtook him. How often we pass God's test on a certain thing, only later to be ensnared again. But ultimately God triumphs in our lives and we are His forever!

ACTIVITY: Try this numerical quiz:

1. To the number of books of Law,
   Add the sons of Jacob;
   Multiply by the years David reigned;
   And subtract the number of times God parted the waters.

2. From the number in Gideon's army,
   Subtract the number of books of Old Testament history;
   Add the number of years the Israelites wandered in the wilderness;
   Multiply by the number of items in the Ark of the Covenant.

3. To the number of books Moses wrote,
   Add the sons of Isaac;
   Multiply by the number of years Samson was judge;
   And divide by the number of faithful spies.

4. From the number of foxes Samson tied together,
   Subtract the number of the tribes of Israel;
   Add the number of Hannah's children;
   And multiply by the number of times the angel saw Manoah's wife.

                              ✝✝✝✝✝

DAY 258. 1 Kings 1-3
            1:1-30, 49-53; 2:1-25; 3
            Wisdom
            (Read ahead and tell)

1 Kings 3:9. Therefore, give to Your servant an understanding heart to judge Your people, that I may discern between good and evil. For who is able to judge this great people of Yours?

Prayer: Give us wisdom, also.

COMMENTS: 1 Kings continues the history of the kings. The author of 1 and 2 Kings is believed to be Jeremiah. From now on, have an adult handle the readings.

Solomon loved God and asked for wisdom which God greatly honored and bestowed upon him. He was given the task of building the Temple. His downfall was his love for women, many of his wives being foreigners who led him into idol worship. This wisest of men wasn't wise enough.

ACTIVITY: We have similar tests--idols or God. Write down for your Treasure Box what your choice is. Ask God for wisdom, understanding, a pure heart and mind, a noble and dedicated life, to be a blessing to many people.

Pre-schoolers: From their box of crayons, assemble all the same colors in piles. The ones who are able, count the crayons in each pile.

The others play tic-tac-toe, using the names of the New Testament books. They have to be recited in their right order, and each player in turn says one book. If one misses, he just misses his turn to put an "x" or an "o" on the drawing. Each one has to use the alternate "x" or "o". The one who happens to get 3 in a row is the winner, but out of the game. Continue through the books. Do as many games as needed.

                              ✝✝✝✝✝

DAY 259. 1 Kings 4-6
            Temple

1 Kings 6:21. So Solomon overlaid the inside of the temple with pure gold. He stretched gold chains across the front of the inner sanctuary; and he overlaid it with gold.

Prayer: Help us make the
           temple of our hearts
           beautiful.

COMMENTS: The cedars of Lebanon have been one of the wonders of the world. Hiram loved God and cooperated with Solomon in providing the beautiful wood for the temple.

ACTIVITY: The pattern of the temple was similar to the tabernacle, the Holy Place, 60' long, the Most Holy Place 30' square. The building was 3 stories high with rooms on each side.

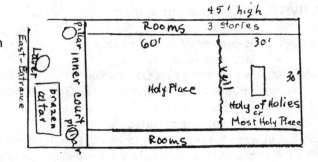

DAY 260. 1 Kings 7-9
7:1-10, 15-26, 40-51; 8; 9
Glory and Wealth

Prayer: What a glorious sight--Your Shekinah glory!

1 Kings 8:10-11. And it came to pass, when the priests came out of the holy place, that the cloud filled the house of the Lord, so that the priests could not continue ministering because of the cloud; for the glory of the Lord filled the house of the Lord.

COMMENTS: The wealth and splendor Solomon brought to the nation put it in top place. People from all over the world visited Solomon to hear his wisdom and to admire the wealth of the nation of Israel. There was peace for the 40 years of his reign.

ACTIVITY: We will do some amateur candle making. For molds use narrow jars, cans, milk cartons. For wax, use old candles or paraffin. For color add old crayons. Grease the molds with petroleum jelly.

tie wick on pencil

1. Melt the paraffin or candles in a double-boiler.

2. Since the candle is upside down in the jar, tape extra string (wick) to the bottom of the jar. At the top put a pencil across and tie the string to it.

3. Cool wax to pouring temperature, 190 degrees F.

4. Pour the wax down the center of the jar.

5. Let wax set for 8 hours.

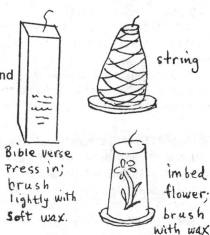

string

Bible verse press in; brush lightly with soft wax.

imbed flower; brush with wax

6. Slide candle out of the mold by turning it upside down and tapping it. If stubborn, run warm water over the outside of the mold.

7. Try different decorations: add string wrapped around; a pressed-in dried flower, brush thin wax over the flower; beads; glitter; marbles.

Add verse to jar lid rim.

candles formed in muffin tin then placed on metal jar lid for safety.

8. For variety pour wax in shallow paper cup with upside down birthday candle in the center. Put the unmolded candle in a jar lid for a holder. Or let it float in water for centerpiece. "Let your light shine." (Matthew 5:16)

†††††

DAY 261. 1 Kings 10-12
10; 11; 12:1-7, 25-30
Idolatry

Prayer: Keep us shining for You.

1 Kings 11:9. So the Lord became angry with Solomon, because his heart had turned from the Lord God of Israel, who had appeared to him twice.

COMMENTS: It is difficult to understand how the people could turn from God to idols so quickly, but that proves the constant tempting of Satan over men who do not trust God. Those trusting God have His inner strength to overcome.

ACTIVITY: Try putting typed Bible verses around the bottom of the candles, brushing with melted wax thin enough to read through. Make a lovely candle for the prayer room altar.

DAY 262. 1 Kings 13-16
Punishment
13; 14:1-18, 25-26;
15:1-4, 9-12, 14-16, 25-29;
16:23-26, 29-34

1 Kings 16:26 For he walked in all the ways of Jeroboam, the son of Nebat, and in his sin by which he had made Israel sin, provoking the Lord God of Israel to anger with their idols.

Prayer: Keep us from idolatry.

COMMENTS: God's punishment was to divide the kingdom of Israel into two portions after the death of Solomon, the southern land called Judah, the norther, Israel. They fought each other, and God allowed them to be captured by Babylon and Assyria.

ACTIVITY: If we keep busy with clean fun, helping others, witnessing for the Lord, studying God's Word, there isn't much chance we will be worshipping idols. Plan activities with the neighbors--a barbecue, picnic with baseball, fishing trip, boat trip, or ski trip to build up Christian friends.

✝✝✝✝✝

DAY 263. 1 Kings 17-19.
Elijah

Prayer: We want to be daring like
Elijah in living for You.

1 Kings 18:36. And it came to pass at the time of the offering of the evening sacrifice, that Elijah the prophet came near and said, "Lord God of Abraham, Isaac, and Israel, let it be known this day that You are God in Israel, and that I am Your servant, and that I have done all these things at Your word."

COMMENTS: What remarkable miracles God performed through Elijah. Elijah had great faith that God would send down the fire; he made it impossible from natural laws for the sacrifice to be burned knowing that God would do the impossible The people were amazed and believed! Then God sent the long-withheld rain. What power and glory He demonstrated that day.

ACTIVITY: This is a dramatic scene to use in witnessing. Mt. Carmel parallels the Mediterranean Sea above the Haifi seaport. If you visit Israel, be sure to drive to the ridge to enjoy the view Elijah had that day. It is part of the city now. To make the scene, paint the background with mountains. Make paper mache hilltop, the altar of pebbles, ditch around it; separate the altar in background for Baal's prophets. Make clay ram, and 4 jars.

DAY 264. 1 Kings 20-22
          Prophets

Prayer: Oh, we look forward to
              seeing You on Your throne!

1 Kings 22:19. Then Micaiah said,
"Therefore, hear the word of the Lord: I saw
the Lord sitting on His throne, and all the host
of heaven standing by, on His right hand and
on His left."

COMMENTS: Ahab was the most despicable of the kings, greatly influenced by his wicked wife
Jezebel.

ACTIVITY: Elijah will be dressed in a white robe and turban; Ahab in more regal clothes; Baal's
prophets in darker clothes.

Put a tin bottom in the center part of the scene so that you can add magnets to the feet of
Elijah and move him around. One of the younger children can move him so hands won't block the
drama. Tape the wailing of Baal's prophets and Elijah's comments. Have a few stones for Elijah
to put on the altar, then the bull, wood, then pour the jars of water over the altar and into the ditch.
Use a red cellophane flame wrapped around a glove to reach down from the back of the scene to
turn up the sacrifice (take it away).

Then the people shout, "The Lord is God! The Lord alone is God!"

†††††

DAY 265. 2 Kings 1-3.
          Translated

Prayer: Oh, what wonderful
              experiences You give
              Your heroes!

2 Kings 2:11. Then it happened, as they
continued on and talked, that suddenly a
chariot of fire appeared with horses of fire
and separated the two of them; and Elijah
went up by a whirlwind into heaven.

COMMENTS: The school of priests which Samuel had initiated was still training prophets, but
Elisha was God's choice to take over the "mantel" of Elijah. He was allowed to witness the great
translation of Elijah to heaven, and his request for a double portion of Elijah's spirit was granted to
him. Their lives seemed to be a double exposure of God's miracles.
It is noteworthy that 900 years later Elijah appeared with Jesus
on the Mount of Transfiguration.

ACTIVITY: This is an animated scene.
Cut out the chariot of fire. Wire it
to pull up through the 2 slits
(reinforced with scotch
tape on the back).
Color the pieces.
Cut out Elisha
and mount
him on the
right.

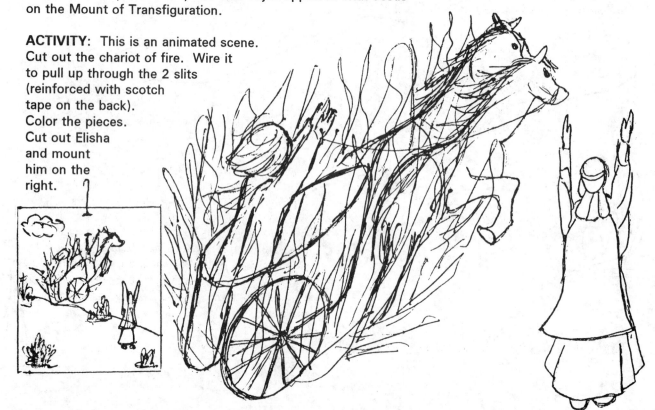

DAY 266. 2 Kings 4-7
Elisha

Prayer: Open our eyes, Lord,
that we may see Your
Mighty power.

2 Kings 6:16-17. So he answered, "Do not fear, for those who are with us are more than those who are with them." And Elisha prayed and said, "Lord, I pray, open his eyes that he may see." Then the Lord opened the eyes of the young man and he saw. And behold the mountain was full of horses and chariots of fire all around Elisha.

COMMENTS: Don't you love this eye-opener? Oh, how great and caring our God is! To think that whenever we are in danger, there are angels all about us, ready to help in our time of need.

Elisha had no malice nor fear--he knew God's power; so instead of having the enemy army killed, he had them blinded, led them to the king of Israel, suggested they be fed and allowed to return home! He returned good for evil. They made a peace pact; no one was hurt, and all praised God!

ACTIVITY: The miracles God performed through Elisha were awesome. To tell about them, we will make a 10-page accordian booklet. Use shelf-lining paper; fold pages about 8" wide, back and forth like a pleated skirt.

Each page will describe one miracle, using a title, Scripture reference, and merely a suggestion of the miracle for curiosity and suspense. Cut pictures from magazines for the suggestions.

1.	Salt in the Spring	2 Kings 2:19-22	box of salt
2.	Mean boys	2:23-24	boys making ugly faces
3.	Ditches filled	3:4-19	road with ditches
4.	Oil aplenty	4:1-7	jars, bowls
5.	Miracle son	4:8-37	boy
6.	Good stew	4:38-41	pot of stew
7.	Barley bread	4:42-44	loaves of bread
8.	Naaman healed	2 Kings 5	Sunday School picture
9.	Ax floats	6:1-7	cut picture of ax and place it on water.
10.	Angel army of chariots	6:8-23	Sunday school picture, or draw.

✝✝✝✝✝

DAY 267. 2 Kings 8-10
Jehu

Prayer: May we not depart from
Your holy ways, O Lord.

2 Kings 10:30-31. And the Lord said to Jehu, "Because you have done well in doing what is right in My sight, and have done to the house of Ahab all that was in My heart, your sons shall sit on the throne of Israel to the fourth generation." But Jehu took no heed to walk in the law of the Lord God of Israel with all his heart; for he did not depart from the sins of Jeroboam, who had made Israel sin.

COMMENTS: Elisha was a great prophet as well as miracle worker. Some of the prophecies fulfilled were:

1. famine - 2 Kings 8:1-6;
2. Jehu to be King - 2 Kings 9 to 10:17;
3. death of Jezebel and Ahab's relatives - 2 Kings 10:17;
4. King Jehoash to defeat Syrians - 2 Kings 13:14-20.

ACTIVITY: Complete the book on Elisha. Practice telling the stories.

✝✝✝✝✝

DAY 268. 2 Kings 11-13
Joash

Prayer: I'm glad You
know our hearts.

2 Kings 13:3 Then the anger of the Lord was
aroused against Israel, and He delivered them
hand of Ben-Hadad, the son of Hazael, all into
the hand of Hazael, King of Syria, and into
the their days.

COMMENTS: God sees through all our plans. He know our hearts. We should try to check
ourselves, take time to consider the motive behind our actions to be sure we keep in God's will.

ACTIVITY: Use this type of candle-making as an object lesson of the way we want to appear as
representatives of Jesus.

1. Use a clear glass or bowl in which a candle
placed later.
2. Draw with a felt pen a circle with a smiling face.
Draw other circles around the glass. Print a short
Bible verse, motto, or other drawing to represent what
you like to do for Jesus. Color with felt pens.
Spray liquid plastic on the circles.
3. Melt paraffin in double boiler; cool till there's
scum on the top. Beat up melted paraffin with egg
beater until it gets frothy.
4. With spatula apply the paraffin froth all over
the jar except the circles.
5. When dry, place candle in bowl, and your
message will shine through.

Or use a small flashlight in a can be
cardboard box with cutouts of a
smiling face drawn on clear
plastic for character to "shine"
through.

✝✝✝✝✝

DAY 269. 2 Kings 14-17
Israel Captured
14:1-14, 23-27;
15:1-5, 8-9, 12, 19-20;
29, 32-35; 16:1-18;
17:5-12, 24-33.

2 Kings 17:23 Until the Lord removed Israel
out of His sight, as He had said by all His
servants, the prophets. So Israel was carried
away from their own land to Assyria, as it
is to this day.

Prayer: Help use keep true to you.

COMMENTS: Israel, in the north, was taken captive by Assyria. Later Judah, in the south, was
taken by Babylon. God had warned; now their judgment came.

ACTIVITY: Use the picture candle as an object lesson. What do people see in us? Are we smiling,
Christlike, having our lights shining for Jesus? Do we reflect His actions, His gentle, forgiving
ways? Draw a grumpy face in the circle; then remove it for a happy face to show how much more
pleasant it is to smile.

DAY 270. 2 Kings 18 - 20
Hezekiah

Prayer: Again we thank You
for Your mightiness.

2 Kings 19:35 And it came to pass on a certain night that the angel of the Lord went out, and killed in the camp of the Assyrians one hundred and eighty-five thousand; and when people arose early in the morning, there were the corpses--all dead.

COMMENTS: Because Hezekiah was a godly king, God blessed him with an additional 15 years of like when he prayed not to die. There were 4 outstanding accomplishments in his reign: 1. the temple and the land purified; 2. worship of God restored; 3. the Passover celebrated; 4. the people reformed. God was pleased with Hezekiah.

ACTIVITY: There were fewer good kings than bad. Unscramble their names:

1. lasu

2. vidda

3. loosnom

4. saa

5. hejspathoah

6. sojha

7. zamihaa

8. zahuiz

9. hojatm

10. hezheika

11. sajhoi

✝✝✝✝✝

DAY 271. 2 Kings 21 -25
Judah Captured
21:1-6, 10-16; 22;
23:1-9, 21-27;
24:1-2, 8-17;
25:1-5, 8-11,15-16.

2 Kings 23:2 And the king went up to the Lord with all the men of Judah, and with him all the inhabitants of Jerusalem--the priests and the prophets and all the people, both great and small; and he read in their hearing all the words of the Book of the Covenant which had been found in the house of the Lord.

Prayer: It's so great to read
Your word, Lord.

COMMENTS: Josiah was a good king like Hezekiah. He cleansed the temple, reinstated the Passover, but foolishly interfered with the war between the Egyptian and Assyrian armies. The kingdom declined rapidly after his death.

ACTIVITY: What kind of a king or a queen would you be? Take turns for each family member to be a King or a Queen for a day, with the right to request special food, book to be read from, game to play, good deed to do, and to be a blessing. Note the lands which captured Israel and Judah: Assyria, Babylon, Media-Persia.

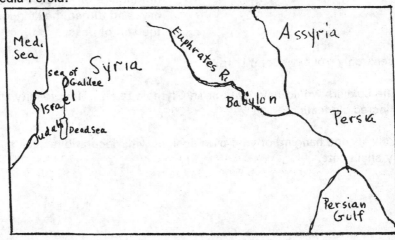

DAY 272. 1 Chronicles 1-9
Genealogies
1:28-32; 2:55;
3:1-9; 4:10, 21-23;
5:1-2, 20-22;
6:31-34, 49, 64;
7:4-11, 40; 8:40;
9:1-3, 9, 13, 21-30

1 Chronicles 4:10 And Jabez called on the God of Israel saying, "Oh, that You would bless me indeed, and enlarge my territory, that You would keep me from evil, that I may not cause pain!" So God granted him what he requested.

Prayer: Bless us as a family, Lord; keep us from evil.

COMMENTS: The genealogies served to assign the Jews to their tribes and their land on their return to Canaan.

ACTIVITY: We will make a window hanging from plexiglass or heavy plastic.

1. Glue a wide bias tape of bright color around the edge of the plastic, leaving a loop at the top for hanging.
2. Select from scrap materials brown cloth for the boat, white for the sail. Glue them on the plastic.
3. Glue on a dowel stick for the mast.
4. Add a bright flag at the top, and a white cloud.
5. For waves, make wavy lines for water with Elmer's glue. Quickly sprinkle blue glitter on the wet glue, shake off excess, and let dry.
6. On the back of the plastic, use waterpaint for a light blue sky and water.
7. Add a verse at the bottom, of "God is My Pilot."

ttttt

DAY 273. 1 Chronicles 10-13
David's Soldiers
10; 11:1-25;
12:8, 16-22, 38-40;
13.

1 Chronicles 10:13-14 So Saul died for his unfaithfulness which he had committed against the Lord, because he did not keep the word of the Lord, and also because he consulted a medium for guidance. But he did not inquire of the Lord; therefore He killed him, and turned the kingdom over to David, the son of Jesse.

Prayer: We seek only Your wisdom, Lord.

COMMENTS: The soldiers would have won in an Olympic team. Their loyalty to David and God helped them do incredible feats.

ACTIVITY: Make a second hanging of your own design, with decorations such as glitter, sequins, small beads, tiny shells, etc.

DAY 274. 1 Chronicles 14-17
    Ark
    14; 15:1-3, 11-16, 25-29;
    16:1-4, 7-43; 17

1 Chronicles 16:29 Give to the Lord the glory due His name; bring an offering, and come before Him. Oh, worship the Lord in the beauty of holiness.

Prayer: We worship You, Lord.

COMMENTS: God's great care of the Ark was to impress upon the people His mightiness, not to be taken lightly; and that He keeps His law and promises.

ACTIVITY: Today we work with scrap tiles. You may be able to get a variety at a low price from a hardware store. Separate the colors.

1. Sketch a pattern: bird, flowers, a scene. Use thin wall board for base. Use patching plaster or other prescribed mix for cementing tile.
2. Glue broken tile bits into the design.
3. Use square tiles for the border.

DAY 275. 1 Chronicles 18-23
    Victories
    18:1-4, 14-17; 19;
    20:5-8; 21; 22;
    23:1-6.

1 Chronicles 22:12 Only may the Lord give you wisdom and understanding, and give you charge concerning Israel, that you may keep the law of the Lord your God.

Prayer: Give use wisdom and insight.

COMMENTS: All the treasures David gathered for the temple he passed on to Solomon, as he was not allowed to build the temple, being a warrior. We may not be able to complete our goals, but we can help others to do so.

ACTIVITY: Beautify old flower pots with tile.

†††††

DAY 276. 1 Chronicles 24-29
    Temple Duties
    24:1-5; 25:1-7;
    26:26-29; 27; 28;
    29

1 Chronicles 29:9 Then the people rejoiced, because with a loyal heart they had offered willingly to the Lord; and King David also rejoiced greatly.

Prayer: We truly want to help You.

COMMENTS: God wants us to be happy in our work; appreciates willingness to tackle the job with zest. After all, it's our attitude that counts.

ACTIVITY: Another craft idea with tiles is to make a bird bath. Use an old trash can lid or plastic tray. Place on a sawed-off log. Glue broken tiles into a design, filling all spaces with cement. Add a dowel or branch for birds seed. The birds will soon fill your yard with music.

DAY 277. 2 Chronicles 1-4
            Wisdom

Prayer: We want wisdom, too.

2 Chronicles 1:7 On that night God appeared to Solomon, and said to him, "Ask! What shall I give you?"

COMMENTS: God opens His arms to us, to give us what we ask. What should we request? God gave Solomon more than he asked for because he didn't ask for riches, honor, long life, the life of his enemies, but for wisdom to rule well. Let's follow his example and seek the Lord's way to win souls.

ACTIVITY: We'll make a birdhouse out of a large milk carton.
Put a wire through the top for hanging.

1. Cut an opening to fold down, turning back the corners like a triangle. Glue in place.
2. Punch a hole in the back, opposite door, and insert a dowel stick for a perch.
3. Spray paint the birdhouse a pretty color.

fold cut out portion to make a perch

†††††

DAY 278. 2 Chronicles 5-9
            Pray for our Nation
            5; 6; 7; 8:1-9;
            9:1-4, 21-28

Prayer: Lord, we do humble ourselves, and seek forgiveness.

2 Chronicles 7:14 If my people who are called by My name will humble themselves, and pray and seek My face, and turn from their wicked ways, then I will hear from heaven, and will forgive their land.

COMMENTS: This command is certainly for us today. Our nation has grown so far from God and His righteous way of living. We, the careless Christians, are at fault according to this verse. We are to humble ourselves, pray and seek God's forgiveness. We have to straighten our lives, do our part in the community, vote for godly leaders, pray for our leaders, support programs for moral issues, and do our part. And God will do His, and bless our nation.

ACTIVITY: This game will help us to think of ways to help our country. Each one write 2 ways to improve out community, school, country. (Small children tell how the family could be better.) Fold the paper and put it in a bowl. Each one pick one (not their own) and discuss the suggestions. For more fun, scramble the words of the suggestion (keep it short) before putting it in the bowl.

†††††

DAY 279. 2 Chronicles 10-18
            God's Strength for Us
            10; 11:1-4; 12:1-14;
            13; 14:1-12; 15;
            16:1-10; 17:1-12; 18

Prayer: We're glad You hunt for us.

2 Chronicles 16:9 For the eyes of the Lord run to and fro throughout the whole earth, to show Himself strong on behalf of those whose heart is loyal to Him.

COMMENTS: When the Judeans saw they were surrounded (13:14-16), they used God's strategy of making a loud noise as though there were many more warriors. Then they attacked and scattered the enemy. When God tells us to resist the devil, we can rebuke Satan with a loud noise, too, and he will flee from us.

ACTIVITY: Our good deed today for the birds is to make a hanging bird treat. Buy bird seed. Use applesauce as a base; spread the seeds over a layer of applesauce on a cookie sheet. Add crumbs. Bake at low temperature until dry like leather.

    Cut into cone shapes. Roll. Stick a dowel through the bottom for perching; this also keeps its shape.

    Hang where the squirrels won't eat it, and protect it from the rain.

✝✝✝✝✝

DAY 280.   2 Chronicles 19-28
       God's Battle
       19:1-7; 20:1-29;
       21:4-7, 10-15; 22:1,4,7,10-12;
       23:1-3, 11-18; 24:1-3, 17-18;
       25:1-2,14,23-24; 26:3-5,16-20;
       27:1-2,6; 28:1-5,24-25

2 Chronicles 20:15b Thus says the Lord to you: "Do not be afraid nor dismayed because of this great multitude, for the battle is not yours, but God's.

Prayer: Thanks, Lord, that the battle is Yours, not ours.

COMMENTS: How wonderful that god fights our battles for us.

ACTIVITY: Explain to the little ones that if we are on God's side (doing His will), He will give us the right answers and the right way to live. Let them draw some pictures of living God's way. The others fill in the blanks on this Quiz on God. Use the New King James. (Note: KJ stands for King James)

1. God is above all, He is ___ ___. (Genesis 17:1)
2. He is all powerful, a term theologians call <u>omni</u>____. (Genesis 18:14)
3. Because He knows all, He is <u>omni</u>____. (Psalms 139:14-17)
4. And because He is everywhere at all times, He is <u>omni</u>____. (2 Chronicles 2:6)
5. He cannot sin but is <u>g</u>____. (Psalms 25:8)
6. Since He is ___, He wants us to be ___. (Matthew 5:48)
7. Everyone on earth and all heavenly creatures praise Him for He is <u>h</u>___. (Psalms 147:17 KJ)
8. He is ___ of ___,
9. and ___ of ___. (Revelation 17:14)
10. God had no beginning and has no end for He is ___. (Deuteronomy 33:27)
11. There is no evil in Him for He is just and ___. (Psalms 7:9)
12. God told Moses that He is the great ___ ___. (exodus 3:14)
13. In the Old Testament times He is also known as <u>J</u>____ God. (Exodus 6:3 KJ)
14. Hannah called upon God as ___ ___ ___. (1 Samuel 1:11)
15. The Psalmist hails Him as ___ ___. (Psalms 50:1 KJ)
16. In the first verse if the Bible He is acknowledged to be <u>C</u>___. (Genesis 1:1)
17. The Israelites knew Him as the ___ ___ ___ ___. (2 Kings 19:22)
18. No one has seen God, just manifestations of Him for He is <u>i</u>____. (Exodus 33:20)
19. All of us who have a personal appreciation of Him call Him our ____. (Matthew 6:9)
20. In praying the Lord's prayer, we praise Him for ___ and ___. (Matthew 6:13)
21. God is just; at the end of the world He is the strict <u>J</u>___. (Revelation 20:12)
22. That is why we rest assured in His decisions for He is <u>u</u>____. (Psalms 25:8)

23. All children know that God is _____. (1 John 4:16)
24. Those in trouble find He is a _____. (Deuteronomy 33:27)
25. We realize how far above He is yet how close when we pray ____ ____. (Matthew 6:14)
26. It is difficult for us to comprehend that He had no beginning and has no ending, but is ____. (Psalms 90:2)
27. We can trust the truth of the Bible for God is the ____. (John 1:1)
28. We can trust Him because he know what is r___. (Hosea 14:9)
29. He is a God of great m____ when he sees our frailty. (Numbers 14:18)
30. He is ____ in keeping his promises. (2 Thessalonians 3:3)
31. So we seek Him for He is our h____ in time of distress. (Psalms 115:10)
32. He is our ____ of security. (Deuteronomy 32:4)
33. God is also our ____ and ____ to brighten and protect us. (Psalms 84:11)
34. There will be no need of a church in heaven fir He is the ____. (Revelations 21:22)
35. He commanded us to baptize in the name of the ____, ____ and ____. (Matthew 28:19)
36. Yes, we can truly bow before Him as the ____ ____ ____. (Genesis 14:18 KJ)
37. God is ___ in heart and mighty in strength. (Job 9:4)
38. God is faithful and ____ to forgive our sins. (1 John 1:9)

✝✝✝✝✝

DAY 281. 2 Chronicles 29-36
One Heart
29:1-10, 18-19, 28-29;
30:5-27; 31:20-21; 32:1-17;
33:1-3, 11-17; 34:1-3, 14-33;
35:1-6, 20-24; 36

2 Chronicles 30:12 Also the hand of God was on Judah to give them singleness of heart to do the commandment of the king and the leaders, at the word of the Lord.

Prayer: Keep us steadfast on Your side.

COMMENTS: If the Lord gives us "singleness of heart" to do His will as a family, the vision is there, the team spirit is at work, and the incomparable Christ will give the victory.

ACTIVITY: The older ones complete the word block on GOD from quiz blanks. The pre-schoolers will enjoy making some fans like the ones shown, using the steps listed:

1. Use a paper plate or cut out a circle from cardboard.
2. Draw or trace a pretty pattern on it. Color it.
3. Or paste some wallpaper, giftwrap paper, or a cutout picture on it.
4. Staple a tongue depressor or stick to the bottom for a handle.
5. Add a Bible verse you like. Cut a printed one and glue it on at the bottom.
6. To make another one, use some pretty yarn. Make loops like daisy petals, and glue them on the fan.
7. This is a nice token of love to give to an elderly person. They may use it or hang it on the wall.

Activity: With the answers to the quiz on God (Appendix Day 280) fill in the

WORD BLOCK ON G O D

	1	2	3	4	5	6	7	8	9	10	11	12	13	14	15	16	17	18	19
1	F	A	T	H	E	R	S	O	N	H	O	L	Y	S	P	I	R	I	T
2	L	H	E	A	V	E	N	L	Y	F	A	T	H	E	R	O	C	K	C
3	O	O	J	U	D	G	E	V	E	R	L	A	S	T	I	N	G	X	E
4	R	L	E					M	O	S	T	H	I	G	H	G	O	D	F
5	D	Y	H		I	R	E	F	U	G	E	X	C	R	E	A	T	O	R
6	O	O	O			X	X	A	L	M	I	G	H	T	Y	G	O	D	E
7	F	N	V	A				I						G	O	O	D	O	P
8	H	E	A		M			I			L	J	M	E	R	C	Y	M	O
9	O	O	H					H			O	U	N	H	E	L	P	N	M
10	S	F	A	T	H	E	R	F			V	S						I	N
11	T	I	G	L	O	R	Y	U			E	T			H	W		S	I
12	S	S	H	I	E	L	D	L							O	I		C	P
13	R	R	E	W	O	P	L	A	N	R	E	T	E		L	S		I	O
14	I	A	L	O	R	D	O	F	L	O	R	D	S		Y	E		E	T
15	G	E	X	R	I	N	V	I	S	I	B	L	E					N	E
16	H	L	X	D	K	I	N	G	O	F	K	I	N	G	S	U	N	T	N
17	T	E	M	P	L	E	U	P	R	I	G	H	T	E	O	U	S	X	T

DAY 282. Ezra 1 - 4
        Return to Jerusalem
        1; 2:1, 63-70;
        3; 4

Ezra 1:3 Who is there among you of all his people? May his God be with Him! Now let him go up to Jerusalem which is in Judah, and build the house of the Lord God of Israel (He is God), which is in Jerusalem.

Prayer: Help us build Your house, Your Church.

COMMENTS: Within 7 months of Cyrus' command, a group of exiles had returned to Jerusalem, taking with them gifts from neighbors to pay for the work, and the golden temple utensils which Nebuchadnezzar had taken.

        Ezra and Nehemiah describe the return to Jerusalem in several deportations form Persia. The political policy of Persia was wiser than that of Babylon. Babylon made slaves of its captives, but Persia, led by God, sent the people back to their own country. They let them restore God's temple and government under the leadership of the Jews, subject to the headship of the Emperor of Persia. The first emperor to send them back was Cyrus, then Artaxerxes (Ar-ta-xerx'-es) and Darius (Da-ri'-us).

ACTIVITY: Your home and garden is your castle. With the Israelites' joy find some little jobs that need attention and work as a family to "rebuild."

        Add the following chart of dates in your notebook:
721 BC (Before Christ) Israel was taken captive by Assyria.
606 BC Judah was taken captive by Babylon.
536 BC Zerubbabel led back 442,360 Jews, 7,337 servants, 200 temple singers, carrying
        5,400 gold and silver utensils of the temple.
520 BC Haggai, Zechariah, prophets of God, worked there.
478 BC Esther became Queen and gave the Jews more liberty.
457 BC Ezra, priest, with 1,754 men returned.
444 BC Nehemiah, governor, returned and worked with Ezra, rebuilding the wall.

                                             †††††

DAY 283. Ezra 5 - 7
        Temple Restored

Prayer: Help us to beautify
               our house of worship.

Ezra 7:27-28 Blessed be the Lord God of our fathers, who has put such a thing as this in the king's heart, to beautify the house of the Lord which is in Jerusalem, and has extended mercy to me before the king and his counselors, and before all the king's mighty princes.

COMMENTS: Ezra, a priest, as a descendent from Aaron, had a special desire to rebuild the temple and its worship in Jerusalem, which he was able to do with God's help.

ACTIVITY: Imagine hundreds of joyful singers rendering beautiful music as they worked on the wall and the temple. "Make a joyful noise unto the Lord, all ye lands, serve the Lord with gladness; come before His presence with singing." (Psalms 100:1,2 KJ) Let's learn to sing as we work. Practice some special music to use when you give your next program at a rest home or hospital.

        There are choruses and hymns from Israel, also tunes put to Psalms which are nice to learn, especially as we are studying the Old Testament. Often on TV news of Israel the people are dancing and singing--beautiful songs and dances probably handed down for thousands of years.

DAY 284. Ezra 8 - 10
Repentance
8:15-36; 9;
10:1-17

Ezra 9:9 For we were slaves. Yet our God did not forsake us in our bondage; but He extended mercy to us in the sight of the kings of Persia, to receive us, to repair the house of our God, to rebuild its ruins and to give us a wall in Judah and Jerusalem.

Prayer: Thanks that You call us friends.

COMMENTS: How quickly Ezra anguished, prayed, and brought the people to repentance over their inter-marriage with foreigners.

ACTIVITY: Memorize the Old Testament books in their divisions:

(5) Law, (12) History, (5) Poetry, (5) Major Prophets, (12) Minor Prophets. Repeat the books of Law, History, and begin learning the books of Poetry.

††††††

DAY 285. Nehemiah 1 - 5
Wall Rebuilt
1; 2; 3:1-2;

Nehemiah 4:14b-15 "Do not be afraid of them. Remember the Lord, great and awesome, and fight for your brethren, your sons, your daughters, your wives, and your houses." And it happened, when our enemies heard that it was known to us, and that God had brought their counsel to nothing, that all of us returned to the wall, everyone to his work.

Prayer: Lord, we do remember our family members in prayer for Your blessing.

COMMENTS: Because of the constant threat of the enemy, the workers wore swords and worked in shifts to keep the area safe. God gave the victory. Walls were a main source of protection and considered of great importance. The walls around Jerusalem, even today, lend a sense of beauty and strength.

ACTIVITY: This "Prayer Wall" flannelgraph lesson is for the Bible and Teen Clubs and for use as a devotional at a rest home. Use construction paper for the "stones" and glue scrap flannel on the back. On each stone write one of the words below. The children put them on the board as they are discussed.

1. <u>Reverence</u>. Much depends upon our attitude when we pray. We must have respect and reverence for God. Matthew 6:9
2. <u>Communion</u>. It is not a one-way conversation. We must also listen to God's instruction for us. Revelation 3:20, John 15:4
3. <u>With Humility</u>. We remember that unless Christ died for us we would not be worthy of this divine friendship with God. Ephesians 1:7
4. <u>Joyfully</u>. He wants us to share His joy. John 15:11
5. <u>Thanksgiving</u>. We thank Him for answered prayers and for future ones He is yet to answer. Philippians 4:6
6. <u>Don't Worry</u>. This same verse, Philippians 4:6, emphasizes not to worry but to make our requests with thanksgiving.
7. <u>Faith</u>. Jesus told us to have faith in God, that we must believe that He is answering when we ask. Mark 11:22-23
8. <u>Believe in the answer</u>. Mark 11:23-24 exhorts us to actually say that we are getting the answer and believe it has been answered.
9. <u>With forgiveness</u>. We must forgive others, or prayer will not be answered. Mark 11:25-26

10. <u>With repentance</u>. We must confess any sins we know and seek forgiveness. 1 John 1:9
11. <u>Wait</u>. We wait upon His answer, expectantly, patiently, for His timing may be different than ours. Isaiah 40:31
12. <u>Search His Word</u>. As He answers, sometimes He shows us details, guidance and explanations in His Word. Jeremiah 29:13
13. <u>With whole heart</u>. This same verse in Jeremiah stresses that we must seek God with all our heart, not half-heartedly.
14. <u>Intercede for others</u>. We must not forget others in our prayers. 1 Samuel 12:23; James 5:16
15. <u>For those in authority</u>. We are to pray for those in leadership, kings, presidents, rulers (even in Communist countries). 1 Timothy 2:1-2
16. <u>Laborers</u>. Pray for workers to go to witness. Matthew 9:38
17. <u>For enemies</u>. One of the first things Jesus preached was to pray for our enemies, those who despitefully use us. Matthew 5:44
18. <u>For the sick</u>. The prayer of faith will save the sick. James 5:14-16
19. <u>In the Spirit</u>. The Spirit prays through us to conquer the evil one. Eph.6:18
20. <u>Without Ceasing</u>. We must never give up praying, and be constantly in the attitude of prayer. 1 Thessalonians 5:17

✝✝✝✝✝

DAY 286. Nehemiah 6 - 9
Festival
6; 7:1-6, 63-73;
8; 9.

Nehemiah 8:10 Then he said to them, "Go your way, eat the fat, drink the sweet, and send portions to those for whom nothing is prepared; for this day is holy to our Lord. Do not sorrow, for the joy of the Lord is your strength."

Prayer: Your joy is our strength.

COMMENTS: The last phrase of this verse has been written as a chorus. We learn verses this way, and also find their messages coming alive within us.

ACTIVITY: Let your children sing some of their action songs, then join them. Try writing some choruses to tunes you know.

✝✝✝✝✝

DAY 287. Nehemiah 10-13
Confession
10:28-39; 11:1-3;
12:27-47; 13

Nehemiah 12:27 Now at the dedication of the wall of Jerusalem they sought out the Levites in all their places, to bring them to Jerusalem to celebrate the dedication with gladness, both with thanksgivings and singing, with cymbals and stringed instruments and harps.

Prayer: We sing praises to You.

COMMENTS: We can visualize the marching singers on the top of the wall of Jerusalem, going in opposite directions and returning. When you go to Israel you will see what a gigantic task they completed.

ACTIVITY: March around your recreation room singing praises to the Lord. Use your tambourines. Divide and go in opposite directions. Clap your hands and use a skipping dance, as the Israelites did. (Tambourines made on Day 217) If any of you play musical instruments, have a band for the Lord. The little ones can use jingling bells.

DAY 288. Esther 1-4
Willing to Die
Make this a play;
assign parts.

Esther 4:16 Go, gather all the Jews who are present in Shushan, and fast for me; neither eat nor drink for three days, night or day. My maids and I will fast likewise. And so I will go to the king, which is against the law; and if I perish, I perish!

Prayer: Thanks for Esther's bravery; help us to be brave, too.

COMMENTS: This story tells of a beautiful Jewish girl who saved her people. The event occurred during the return of the Jews to Canaan to rebuild the capital city Jerusalem. The Jews were no longer slaves but in bondage.

ACTIVITY: For this play use the Good News Bible for the conversations. Use a tape recorder for background crowds, etc. Shorten the Reader's parts.

Five scenes: 1. Vashti, 1-4:10 - throne room (plush material over chair)
                2. Esther 4:10-17 - simple room, 2 chairs, window (can be picture)
                3. King 5:1-8 - throne/banquet room, table, chairs
                4. Haman 5:9-14 - Haman's home, 2 chairs, window
                5. King 6-10 - throne/banquet

Costumes: King - crown, robe
            Vashti and Esther - tiara (make with florist wire and white beads)
            Mordecai - white robe, turban tied with cord
            Haman - nice attire; servants - simple tunics

PLAY
Scene 1 - Reader: 1:1-14
          King: 1:15
          Memucan: 1:16-20   Scene 2 -
          Reader: 1:21-22; 2:1-2a   Esther: 4:11
          Adviser: 2:2b-4a   Mordecai: 4:12-14
          Reader: 2:4b-3:7   Esther: 4:16
          Haman: 3:8-9   Reader: 4:17
          Reader: 3:10   (CHILDREN: Play with your town, having the
          King: 3:11   families shop, go to church, play, go to
          Reader: 3:12-4:10   school, etc.)
                                                   (Play continues next two days)

                                    ✝✝✝✝✝

DAY 289. Esther 5 - 7
Petition

Esther 7:3 Then Queen Esther answered and said, "If I have found favor in your sight, O king, and if it pleases the king, let my life be given me at my petition, and my people at my request."

Prayer: Help us to be brave like Esther.

COMMENTS: How brave, bold, and clever the queen was. The Lord helped her to say the right thing at the right time.

ACTIVITY: Continue the play:
Scene 3 - Reader: 5:1-2   Scene 4 - Reader: 5:9-11
          King: 5:3   Haman: 5:12-13
          Esther: 5:4   Wife: 5:14
          Reader: 5:5
          King: 5:6
          Esther: 5:7-8

Scene 5 -   Reader: 6:1-2   King: 6:10   Esther: 7:6a
               King: 6:3a   Reader: 6:11a   Reader: 7:6b-8a
               Servants: 6:3b   Haman: 6:11b   King: 7:8b
               King: 6:4   Reader: 6:12-7:1   Reader: 7:8c-9a
               Servants: 6:5a   King: 7:2   Servant: 7:9b
               King: 6:5b-6a   Esther: 7:3-4   King: 7:9c
               Haman: 6:6b-9   King: 7:5   Reader: 7:10

✝✝✝✝✝

DAY 290. Esther 8 - 10   Esther 10:3 For Mordecai the Jew was
          Honored   second to King Ahasuerus, and was great
                                               among the Jews and well received by the
                                               multitude of his people and speaking peace
                                               to all his kindred.

Prayer: Thanks for joy!

COMMENTS: Think of it! God planned feast, fun and festival days! He's joyful!
 ACTIVITY: Scene 5 continued:

Reader: 8:1-4   Reader: 8:9-9:11   If you enjoyed reading the play, consider doing it
Esther: 8:5-6   King: 9:12   in your own words for church or where you witness.
King; 8:7-8   Esther: 9:13   The younger ones hold card Scenes, etc.
                   Reader: 9:14-10:3

✝✝✝✝✝

DAY 291. Job 1 - 3   Job 1:8 Then the Lord said to Satan, "Have
          Job tested   you considered My servant Job, that there
                                               is none like him on the earth, a blameless and
                                               upright man, one who fears God and shuns
                                               evil?"

Prayer: Thanks for Your tests.

COMMENTS: The next five books are called books of Poetry: Job, Psalms, Proverbs, Ecclesiastes (E-cle'-ze'-as-tez), Song of Solomon. Job is considered the oldest book of the Bible, the author probably Moses. Since Job's life span was 200, he must have lived after the flood.

The remarkable fact is that God allowed Satan to test Job, knowing Job would remain faithful, and allowed only what Job was able to endure, then rewarded Job with twice as much as he had before. We must remember Job when we are tested, knowing God is in charge, thinks we are special, and has a crown for us. We note that Job's friends patiently listened, but their advice wasn't always the best.

Assign parts as follows, and read as a play, the children playing with the town.

ACTIVITY:
Reader: 1:1-6 God: 1:8   Reader: 1:13-20   God: 2:2a
God: 1:7   Satan: 1:9-11 Job: 1:21   Satan: 2:2b
Satan: 1:7b   God: 1:12   Reader: 1:22, 2:1   Job: 3:3-5, 20-26

✝✝✝✝✝

DAY 292. Job 4 - 20   Job 19:25 For I know that my Redeemer
          Friends   lives, and He shall stand at last on the earth.

Prayer: We know that You live!

COMMENTS: With our Redeemer with us we can bear the trials.

ACTIVITY: While the older ones read the Scripture portions, the children will enjoy making pompons the colors of the rainbow, to remind us that as with Noah, God gives us a test, and when we follow Him through it all, He gives us a beautiful rainbow to remind us He is faithful to carry us through to victory.

Eliphaz 4:1-8; 5:8-12,17,18	Zophar 11:1-3, 7-10	Job 16:1-5; 17:1,16
Job 6:1-4,8,9; 7:17	Job 12:1-3,9-16; 13:13-18	Bildad 18:1,2,20-21
Bildad 8:1-3,9	14:1-2, 14	Job 19:1-6, 22-27
Job 9:1-3,20-21; 10:12	Eliphaz 15:1-9	Zophar 20:1, 27-29

CHILDREN: Rainbow pompons to tell that God watches over our trials and helps us.
1. Tie 15" yarn or embroidery thread colors together.
2. Wind it around an 8x11" card; tape ends down.
3. Thread a wide-eyed needle with short cord, and go through the loops on the card and tie tightly.
4. Cut the upper edge of loops. Use to decorate hat, gloves, shoes, etc.

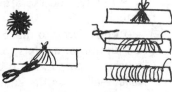

†††††

DAY 293. Job 21 - 32
Job Wonders

Job 23:10 But He knows the way that I take; when He has tested me, I shall come forth as gold.

Prayer: Thanks for making us golden!

COMMENTS: Friends may not know the best; God does! Trust His word and way.
ACTIVITY: Job 21:1,
17 Eliphaz 22:1, 21-27
Job 23:1, 3-12
Zophar 24:22-25

Bildad 25:1, 4-6
Job 26:1-14; 27:10-11; 28:12-13,20-28;
29:1-5; 30:15-16; 31:6,35-36
Reader 32:1-5   Elihu 32:6-13

CHILDREN: Make cap with pompon on top.
1. Cut 6 pieces of cloth like the pattern; sew together.
2. Measure a band to fit your head with room for seam.
Print "God Cares" on it. Attach to cap. Add pompon.

†††††

DAY 294. Job 33 - 42
God Answers

Job 42:10 And the Lord restored Job's losses when he prayed for his friends. Indeed the Lord gave Job twice as much as he had before.

Prayer: Bless our friends, Lord.

COMMENTS: Job won victory when he prayed for his friends, forgetting himself.
ACTIVITY: Elihu 33:4, 23-26; 34:15; 35:11;
36:2, 6, 21-26; 37:5, 14-18
God 38: 39:13-15, 19-20
Job 40:3-5

Reader 40:6
God 40:7-10; 41:1
Job 42:1-6
Reader 42:7-17

CHILDREN: Gather and dry flowers to use as gifts. Find fresh,
dry ones (no dew), small such as pansies, violas.
1. Get dry sand, or Silica Gel (from hobby shop), or use mixture of
2 parts Borax to 1 part sand; or 1 part Borax to 2 parts corn meal. Use
cans or boxes.
2. Slowly sift sand into box, then place flowers head down in box,
sift more, then add more flowers, etc. Seal and date. Keep 2 weeks. Then
pour out sand carefully so as to protect flowers. Store them in dark place.

†††††

DAY 295. Psalms 1 - 9 <u>Book 1</u>

Psalms 9:1 I will praise You, O Lord, with my whole heart; I will tell of all Your marvelous works.

Prayer: We praise You!

COMMENTS: There are 5 books in the 150 Psalms; some Psalms are prophetic, foretelling the suffering of Christ and His kingdom; some patriotic, or historical. They proclaim through song and music praise, thanksgiving, trust, hope, faith.

We will read more pages of Psalms each day to get the real feel of them, and they are easy reading for meal time, between TV programs, while driving as a group. Sing as many as you know. Memorize the ones you enjoy.

ACTIVITY: While reading Psalms, we will make a two or three-wing screen to display pictures with Psalm verses to match. This is especially for the photographers of the family, and the artists, with help from the rest of the members.

An easy way to make a screen so it can be moved around is to use 6 uprights (dowels, pipe, old mop handles); and 6 cross pieces (dowels, curtain rods) to be joined to the upright poles.
1. Have all poles the same height; bottoms smooth or capped so as not to scratch floor.
2. For hinges, use heavy cord, wrapped in figure 8 pattern around the upright sections. Tack at both ends of the cord. Coat with 2 coats of brushing lacquer.

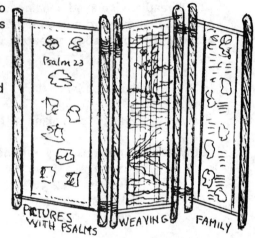

ttttt

DAY 296. Psalms 10 - 18

Prayer: Thank You for these songs Your people wrote so many years ago.

Psalms 16:8-9 I have set the Lord always before me; because He is at my right hand I shall not be moved. Therefore my heart is glad, and my glory rejoices; my flesh also will rest in hope.

COMMENTS: Our hearts sing in tune with David the composer. He has written most of these songs. Select outstanding verses to use in the screen show.

ACTIVITY: For the 3 panels inside the 3 sections of the folding screen, measure the exact length, plus sufficient overlap top and bottom to fasten.

Make panels which can be changed for variety, some of burlap, damask, cardboard sections from shipping crates on which to paste wallpaper, plastic.

Another idea is to use the center frame for macrame weaving. Many modern designs shown in hobby shops or art exhibits are made of heavy, uneven wool yarns tied in artistic uneven knots and designs.

ttttt

DAY 297. Psalms 19 - 27

Prayer: This 23rd Psalm is our prayer.

Psalms 23:1 The Lord is my shepherd; I shall not want.

COMMENTS: Psalms 22, 23, and 24 are our Lord's Cross, Crook, and Crown in poetry. They portray His suffering as Savior, His care as Shepherd, and His glorious appearing as King of kings.

ACTIVITY: Use this subject as an Easter chalk talk: the cross, crook, crown. Draw simple outlines of the three, and read the related parts from the Psalms. What a precious Savior, Lord and King we have to go through overwhelming experiences for us: His incarnation, becoming lower than the angels to take our form, His taking our sin, burying it and rising victorious over death, His coming again.

DAY 298. Psalms 28 - 35

Psalms 34:7 The angel of the Lord encamps all around those who fear Him, and delivers them.

Prayer: Thanks for Your angels who
             deliver us.

COMMENTS: If you have felt that angels have protected you or your loved ones at times, write the list of thank-yous to the Lord for them, and keep it in your Treasure Box. As you read or hear of others who have been kept or delivered by such a presence, include that in your list.

ACTIVITY: On the screen panels, make one of the cross, crook and crown pictures. On another draw or make cloth or felt angels such as might have been on the Temple curtain. (Exodus 26:31, 36:8)

††††

DAY 299. Psalms 36 - 41

Psalms 37:4 Delight yourself also in the Lord, and He shall give you the desires of your heart.

Prayer: Oh, we do love and adore You;
             we delight in You and Your love.

COMMENTS: When we delight in the Lord, our heart's desire is to know Him better, love Him more, serve Him, obey Him, rejoice in Him, claim Him as the Prince and King of our lives.

ACTIVITY: It's time to plan for another Good News Bible Club party. This time it is a baking party. Borrow extra rolling pins and cookie sheets. Make the cookie recipe a week ahead to be chilled and taken out the morning of the party. Children are to come in casual clothes that can be spattered with icing.

1 pound brown sugar
1 pound soft butter or margarine
1½ teaspoons vanilla
1½ cups unsifted flour

With mixer cream sugar, butter and vanilla until fluffy. Work in the flour at slow speed. Shape into smooth ball, cover and chill a week. Make several batches.

    Have a card table for every two children; rolling pins, flour, dough, etc. Have patterns to use as cookie cutters, the designs cut from coloring books of animals, house, bell, heart, bird, church, etc. Demonstrate to the group how to roll the dough and cut the pattern, then have enough helpers to work with the younger ones. Cut around the edge of the pattern with paring knife. Each child makes 4 cookies with initials in the corner of each. When baked, they eat one and put 3 on a cookie sheet they brought, or on a cardboard, cover with plastic wrap, to take home. To bake, put on cookie sheet, ungreased, about 15 minutes at 300°. Warn children about not touching hot oven or cookie sheets.
    Have games prepared for waiting time (see next day). After cookies have cooled let the children decorate them. Have sandwiches and fruit drink for lunch.

††††

DAY 300. Psalms 42 - 51
         Book 2

Psalms 47:1 Oh, clap your hands, all you peoples! Shout to God with the voice of triumph!

Prayer: Praise the Lord! Praise You
             for Your goodness!

COMMENTS: God appreciates our singing with joy and all our strength. Sing as a family group, sing when alone. Make up songs to sing to Him of your love, your joy in Him, your peace, your delight in having Him as your Friend. Climb to a hilltop to view His handiwork, raise your arms in praising Him.

ACTIVITY: Have some active games such as skipping or hopping to goal, jumping tope, follow the leader -- to relax from the cookie making.

Each blow up a balloon and then keep it in the air, bouncing it, the longest. Line up at goal and try to walk to destination with the balloon between your knees.

With felt pens carefully print "God Loves Me" on the balloon, and a smiling face. Have sufficient balloons for those who break them, to tie on a string to take home.

End with a short devotional time, a chalk-talk or object lesson, and prayer.

✝✝✝✝✝

DAY 301. Psalms 52 - 63

Psalms 51:10 Create in me a clean heart, O God, and renew a steadfast spirit within me.

Prayer: We pray this prayer, too.

COMMENTS: The more we grow spiritually, the greater our desire to be pure.

ACTIVITY: Let's put the cameras to work again. Find subjects to photograph which portray purity, clean hearts, goodness, nobleness, godliness. God is the author of all goodness, beauty, love. Make a series of slides or movies to go with Psalm verses that praise the Lord for His goodness and beautiful handiwork to show at rest homes, hospitals, institutions, Bible Club, Teen Club, church.

✝✝✝✝✝

DAY 302. Psalms 64 - 72

Psalms 70:5 But I am poor and needy; make haste to me, O God! You are my help and my deliverer; O Lord, do not delay.

Prayer: Thanks for Your goodness to us.

COMMENTS: Consider and list God's "daily load of benefits" (Psalms 68:19).

ACTIVITY: Make a series if photographs using your list.

✝✝✝✝✝

DAY 303. Psalms 73 - 77

Psalms 73:26 My flesh and my heart fail; but God is the strength of my heart and my portion forever.

Prayer: Help us to be cheerful.

COMMENTS: What a comfort and consolation this verse is to those growing old, or those in hospitals. Remarkably, He is all we need; He strengthens us!

ACTIVITY: Today the children will have a gift to make for an elderly or sick neighbor. Make a scrapbook of lovely pictures, not only of pretty scenes but of children at play, babies smiling, a boy and his dog, kitty, animals.

Add Bible verses or verses from the Psalms. Take it personally with your love.

✝✝✝✝✝

DAY 304. Psalms 78 - 84

Psalms 84:10 For a day in Your courts is better than a thousand. I would rather be a doorkeeper in the house of my God than dwell in the tents of wickedness.

Prayer: We love Your Church,
            Oh, heavenly Father.

COMMENTS: Some Psalms appear to be pleading for God to destroy the enemy. Actually, at that time God's dealing with His chosen people, He was urging them to wipe out idol worship that the land would be completely God's promised haven. It's sin we are fighting; we want to save the people from sin. Whatever we can do to alleviate the sin of drugs, alcohol, murder, violence, torture, and other evils of Satan is a blessing to the world and to every child growing up. We must fight such evils and pray for sin to be abolished. We must pray for the sinners that their hearts be turned to the Lord and know His saving grace and transforming power.

ACTIVITY: Ask God in prayer today what the family can do to help wipe out sin in the community. Are there drug peddlers at school? Pornographic magazines in the stores? Are there groups fighting these evils? Put your shoulder to the task, your vote on the line for clean-up in town, your dollars to enforce the effort.

✝✝✝✝✝

DAY 305. Psalms 85 - 89

Psalms 87:1 High on His holy mountain stands Jerusalem, the city of God, the city He loves more than any other! (LB)

Prayer: Bless and enrich our missionaries, Lord, that they may help others.

COMMENTS: Put a world map on the screen. Mark locations and names of missionaries you know, or children you sponsor. On another panel add pictures of them and the people they are working with. Put a list of their needs, a list of when you have written to them and what you sent in parcels.

ACTIVITY: Make a picture with scraps of materials. Sketch a flower. Cut out stem, leaves, blossom from suitable colored cloth. Glue the parts in place. Or sketch a mountain, lake scene and cut out the mountains, sky, hills, lake from scraps and glue in place. Put them on the panels of the screen.

✝✝✝✝✝

DAY 306. Psalms 90 - 101
        Book 4

Psalms 91:11-12 For He shall give His angels charge over you, to keep you in all your ways. They shall bear you up in their hands, lest you dash your foot against a stone.

Prayer: Thanks for Your care.

COMMENTS: Praise God! He is not dead, but alive, and giving His angels charge over us to keep us from stumbling. Put this verse in your car, cabin or house.

ACTIVITY: While on vacations or trips, gather seashells, moss, twigs, weeds that are durable for art displays, butterflies, driftwood, pebbles and stones.

✝✝✝✝✝

DAY 307. Psalms 102 - 106

Psalms 103:12 As far as the east is from the west, so far has He removed our transgressions from us.

Prayer: Oh, thanks for Your forgiveness.

COMMENTS: How magnificent is God's forgiveness. Our sins are wiped out, forever! We don't have to worry about the past -- that door is shut.

ACTIVITY: Make cheerful pebble scenes, using the other materials for the background: bushes, flowers, pebble mice gossiping. One scene could be mice nibbling on cheese (stone painted yellow). Another could be a band made of shells glued in shape of people. Group shell birds on a piece of driftwood.

DAY 308. Psalms 107 - 117   Psalms 116:1 I love the Lord, because
        Book 5   He has heard my voice and my supplications.

Prayer: We love You, Lord.

COMMENTS: So often it is the little everyday prayers which God answers that build our faith in Him. Then when the big tests come we don't falter -- we trust His judgment all the way. His answers often cause us such joy we keep repeating, "Thank You, Lord! Thank You!"

ACTIVITY: For a change of pictures on your folding screen, gather snapshots of your family. Give a section to each member, showing his or her favorite hobbies, sports, ribbons won, news clippings, little poems, cartoons, jokes, tributes, accomplishments. It's a nice way to pat each other on the back for "just being you" and "We not only love you, but like and admire you!"

╫╫╫

DAY 309. Psalms 118 - 119   Psalms 119:11 Your word I have hidden in
                                                   my heart, that I might not sin against You.

Prayer: We love Your Word!

COMMENTS: Psalm 119 is the longest chapter in the Bible. It contains 176 verses. Each one is about the law or God's Word -- sometimes called statutes, commandments, precepts, judgments, testimony or ordinances. It has 22 stanzas of 8 lines each. In the King James version, the Hebrew alphabet is used at the top of each stanza. The shortest chapter in the Bible is 117, and it is also the middle of the Bible.

ACTIVITY: We will make an English alphabet on God's Word for Bible study or drill. You may think of better verses to use; if so, substitute them.

A - <u>All</u> scripture is given by inspiration of God. 2 Timothy 3:16
B - <u>Book</u> of law - meditate day and night. Joshua 1:8
C - <u>Continue</u> in My Word. John 8:31 (KJ)
D - Rightly <u>dividing</u> the Word of Truth. 2 Timothy 2:15
E - God's Word is <u>eternal</u>. "The Word of our God stands forever." Isaiah 40:8
F - The Truth will set you <u>free</u>. John 8:32
G - <u>Glorify</u> the Word. Acts 13:48
H - <u>Holy</u> Scriptures. Romans 1:2
I - <u>Inspired</u> by God. 2 Timothy 3:16
J - The <u>judgments</u> of the Lord are <u>just</u>. Psalms 19:9 (GNB)
K - Blessed are they that <u>keep</u> it. Luke 11:28
L - Word of <u>life</u>. Philippians 2:16
M - Pure <u>milk</u> of the Word. 1 Peter 2:2
N - <u>Never</u> pass away. Mark 13:31
O - <u>Oracles</u> of God. Romans 3:2
P - Every word of God is <u>pure</u>. Proverbs 30:5
Q - Word of God is <u>quick</u> and powerful. Hebrew 4:12 (KJ)
R - Blessed is he that <u>reads</u> the Book. Revelations 1:3
S - Word of God as the <u>sword</u>. Ephesians 6:17
T - Word is <u>truth.</u> John 17:17
U - What was written was <u>upright</u>. Ecclesiastes 12:10
V - Shall not return to Me <u>void</u>. Isaiah 55:11
W - The <u>Word</u> was God. John 1:1
X - How preach <u>except</u> they be sent? Romans 10:15 (KJ)
Y - Word of God abides in <u>you</u>. 1 John 2:14
Z - Out of <u>Zion</u> shall go forth the law. Isaiah 2:3

DAY 310. Psalms 120 - 135   Psalms 134:2 Lift up your hands in the
                                                  sanctuary, and bless the Lord.

Prayer: We raise our hands and bless You, Oh Lord.

COMMENTS: There are many positions in prayer: kneeling, face to the ground, face upraised, hands lifted, eyes closed, eyes open. Position does not matter as much as reverence and fervor.

ACTIVITY: "Hands" is a good theme for photos. Baby's, child's, workman's, artist's, scrubwoman's, elderly couple holding hands, hands in prayer, pilot's hands on controls, ditch-digger's hands on shovel, etc.

With the multitude of photographs needed for advertising and illustrating magazines and books, there must be a great demand for artistic, sensitive photography. Look into the market available, pray about taking and submitting a group of pictures; and maybe you'll earn some money for college or a teen trip.

Rest of family: Use plaster of paris and mold hands of each family member indicating name and date. When friends come, have them guess whose they are.

✝✝✝✝✝

DAY 311. Psalms 136 - 142   Psalms 139:16 Your eyes saw my
                                                  substance, being yet unformed. And in Your
                                                  book they all were written, the days
Prayer: That You know our lives are   fashioned for me, when as yet there were
               satisfying, Lord.   none of them.

COMMENTS: That verse sounds like a mystery. The Good News Bible tells the answer to the riddle: "You saw me before I was born. The days allotted to me had all been recorded in Your book, before any of them ever began." According to that verse, God has our ages listed in His Book. The dates of our birth and death are in His records. Knowing this, we can concentrate on living well; living every day as unto the Lord; making each day a specialty in God's album.

ACTIVITY: My husband was a camera hobbyist all his life. He furnished our family with a history of photographs that are priceless. We have made our Christmas cards from the beginning--Now it is a quick record of our family. On our 45th anniversary I compiled a 6-page photo album of pictures of our life which would not have been possible without his photographs.

You can do the same for your family. Keep albums by subjects; an album for each child; of friends, relatives, etc.

Start making your Christmas cards. See the Appendix on "Christmas Cards."

✝✝✝✝✝

DAY 312. Psalms 143 - 150   Psalms 145:18 The Lord is near to all who
                                                  call upon Him, to all who call upon Him in
                                                  truth.
Prayer: Thanks for hearing us.

COMMENTS: Psalms starts with "happy" and ends with "Praise the Lord!" It is truly a blessed hymnbook--songs from the heart, from the emotions.

ACTIVITY: Help the younger children make another song book for the Bible Club. Select a song find pictures to match the words; print with large letters about one bar or phrase on a page. Use shopping bags cut for as large a page as possible. Tape the pages together, so they open flat. Children love them.

Activity: <u>PSALMS OF PRAISE</u>. Fill blanks with 36 phrases/words
from NKJ Scriptures listed below at numbered locations in word block.

	1	2	3	4	5	6	7	8	9	10	11	12	13	14	15	16	17	18	19	20	21
1	P	R	A	I	S	E											S				X
2							T	H	A	N	K	F	U	L			H				X
3									L	O	R	D					O		X		
4					X												U				
5	L						J	O	Y	F	U	L					T				
6	O								G				P								
7	R								O				R								
8	D								D				P	L							
9		R											I	E			L				
10		E	P										S	A	P		O				
11		S	R				B						E	D	R		R				
12		T	A				L							S	A		D				
13		O	I				E								I				L		E
14		R	S				S	P							S				I		V
15		E	E				S	R							E				G		E
16		S						A			T				S				H		R
17			M					I			R								T		L
18			A					S			U		X								A
19			D					E			M										S
20			E								P										T
21	X										E										I
22	X										T										N
23	S	I	N	G																	G

1. 23:1 2-1d
2. 23:1 11-5d
3. 23:2 6-15d
4. 23:3 7-2d
5. 23:4 20-14d
6. 23:5 20-15d
7. 23:5 19-20d
8. 93:1 6-12d
9. 93:4 17-12d
10. 93:5 20-16d
11. 98:1 23-1a
12. 98:4 1-17d
13. 98:8 5-5a
14. 100:3 3-5a
15. 100:3 5-4d
16. 100:3 9-6d
17. 100:4 2-5a
18. 100:4 11-7d
19. 100:5 3-21d
20. 100:5 4-6a
21. 146:1 1-1a
22. 146:2 5-3d
23. 146:5 6-8d
24. 146:6 6-10d
25. 146:6 4-20u
26. 146:8 6-14d
27. 147:1 6-13d
28. 147:6 6-18d
29. 147:7 6-9d
30. 147:7 6-16d
31. 148:2 6-20d
32. 148:3 6-19d
33. 150:1 14-8d
34. 150:3 6-11d
35. 150:4 14-10d
36. 150:5 13-9d

DAY 313. Proverbs 1 - 4

Prayer: We do seek Your guidance daily.

Proverbs 3:5-6 Trust in the Lord with all your heart, and lean not on your own understanding; in all your ways acknowledge Him, and He shall direct your paths.

COMMENTS: Proverbs was written almost entirely by Solomon. It is a book of wise and practical sayings, often quoted. Psalms is our relationship to God; Proverbs our relationship to man. The advice is as timely today as when written 3000 years ago. Like Psalms, many verses should be memorized.

ACTIVITY: This project will be our handsomest craft. The idea came to me when we were first married. My husband was making wrought iron end tables with glass tops; I was making silhouette pictures with dried flowers behind glass, in frames. My brother, serving in the Engineer Corps in the South Pacific, sent me a gorgeous huge blue butterfly. I needed a safe place to keep it, yet show it off. Why not put it under the glass in the end table, with silhouettes of children playing around the border, and dried flowers and the butterfly in the center, with shiny fluffy milkweed as a background? It was a lovely success. We'll try it now.

Get some supplies ready.   The <u>milkweed</u> may be difficult to get; if so, use a soft-color background paper. <u>Pictures</u> to make the silhouettes from. My Junior High Sunday School class in Rocky Mountain House, Alberta, made tables to sell for our first trip to Los Angeles to see the Rose Parade. There were many subjects, but (as our custom was) we added Bible verses as a witness and to fulfill the verse that whatever you do, do all to the glory of God. Pressed <u>flowers</u> or straw flowers. <u>Butterflies</u>, if possible. India <u>ink</u>, <u>brushes</u>, permanent black felt markers. <u>Silhouettes</u> to relate to <u>Bible verses</u>. See drawings in the Appendix. Scissors and scotch tape. <u>Tables</u> to work on. Work together or make individual pictures. If making the pictures, be sure your <u>glass</u> fits the <u>frame</u>, that you add a cord or narrow stick around the border under the frame to protect the flowers from crushing. If making a table, buy a heavy <u>plastic</u> top instead of glass; use a <u>wallboard</u> for the background, and narrow <u>edging</u> of ¼ inch wood to keep flowers from crushing.

†††††

DAY 314. Proverbs 5 - 8

Prayer: Give us wisdom, Lord.

Proverbs 8:11 For wisdom is better than rubies, and all the things one may desire cannot be compared with her.

COMMENTS: James 1:5 excitedly states, "If any lack wisdom, let him ask God for it." Wisdom is so much more powerful than knowledge.

ACTIVITY: The table is attractive immediately upon seeing it, not only because it is unique, but it is brightly colored. The black pictures on the silky background, with rich-colored flowers and butterflies is a lovely display.

Measure your pictures and Bible verses so that they will fit into the border on the 4 sides without overlapping.

If using children as a theme select verses: God is Love; Be kind; Help your neighbor, etc. See drawings in Appendix, Day 313.

This is one of the 60 sweet Mexican children in a new Tijuana church (constructed by missionaries Jim and Sondra Peppers) who learned to make the Life of Christ scenes one Easter weekend with my Junior High Sunday School class--neither knowing the other's language. How they loved one another! (4/84)

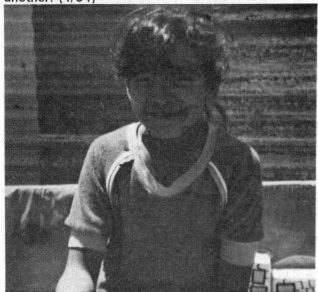

Above table made for World-Wide Missions, Pasadena, CA, who let us stay in their missionary apartment on our first trip to Los Angeles. Our class supported a WWM orphan boy in Madras, India. Our Rocky Mountain House, Alberta class took 3 trips to Los Angeles.

1.

frame

2.

heavy glass or plexiglass

ink silhouettes on underside
  above the Scripture verses

Add narrow wood strips at edge.

3.

board
Place Scripture slips around
the border under the glass.
Arrange flowers, butterflies

4. Carefully lower glass on top of board, noting that flowers, butterflies, etc. are not mussed. Tape around edges with wide adhesive tape to prevent air inside, sealing glass and board together.

5.

Place frame over the glass art picture. Seal it around the back securely.

6. Make a separate table for the art pictures to rest on, adding an edge of wood so it will not slip off. Use heavy plywood for the table. Screw legs underneath.

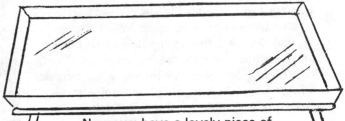

Now you have a lovely piece of furniture which also is a witness to God's lovely handiwork.

DAY 315. Proverbs 9 - 12

Proverbs 10:30 Righteous people will always have security, but the wicked will not survive in the land. (GNB)

Prayer: We feel safe and secure in You, Lord.

COMMENTS: Every day we make choices. Our life depends upon our decisions: right or wrong, God or Satan, good or evil, self or others, purity or impurity, caring or indifference. We can't escape temptation, but our outcome depends upon how we direct our lives. If we allow the Spirit to lead us, we'll keep in God's way; if we follow the crowd, most likely we'll go astray into worldly ways.

ACTIVITY: Draw your outline pictures on thin paper, exactly as they are to appear on the border. Turn upside down, and slip it under the glass. Using the permanent pen, carefully make outlines of the drawings on the glass. After all the outlines are finished, fill in the spaces with brush and India ink. Don't let the ink run outside of the lines; if it does, quickly wipe it off with facial tissue. Once the ink sets, it won't rub off.

Since it is very difficult to print backwards, use strips of firm transparent plastic; cut perfectly straight the distance needed for each border. Print the verses on it. Attach it, upside down, under the pictures, and use scotch tape to hold in place along the edge of the glass. Be sure that the printing and pictures are not covered by the picture frame. Keep it about an inch within the border.

††††††

DAY 316. Proverbs 13 - 16

Proverbs 13:24 He who spares his rod hates his son, but he who loves him disciplines him promptly.

Prayer: Help us to discipline promptly.

COMMENTS: Tests show that children raised without teachings on right and wrong have great difficulty in life. Many have no guilt feelings about hurting others. Obedience must be taught at an early age; the sooner the child learns to obey the easier it is on everyone. It is damaging to allow the child to do wrong; on the other hand punishment must not be too severe, and without malice. Be sure the child understands what is wrong with disobedience, and the advantages of doing what is right.

ACTIVITY: The pre-schoolers can teach their dolls how to obey, and the harm caused if the doll touches a hot stove, etc.

The most difficult part of the display in the table is putting the milkweed on the background. First, put the edging around the border.

Then start in upper left corner of board and open one milkweed pod at a time. There must be no draft as the fluffy part floats around the room. Hold the fluffy part down with one hand while gently removing the seeds with the other. Spread the feathery remainder as far as it will go without showing wood beneath. Do another pod, and so on till the area is covered.

Next carefully place the butterflies in the center. Add the dry flowers where they will show

Silhouette   Pressed flowers

Be kind to one another.

see silhouette patterns in Appendix

above the drawings. Tape down edge, if necessary. Then gently lower the glass over the whole scene. Snip off protrudings. Tape around the edge of the glass, sealing it to the back board.

If your table top is large, you may want to follow the directions of making a separate table for it to sit on as in the drawings. If it is an end table, screw it to the table top from underneath, in such a way that the screws go into the frame without breaking the glass.

Now you have a work of art that is your own creation as well as a witness.

✝✝✝✝✝

DAY 317. Proverbs 17 - 20   Proverbs 20:1 Wine is a mocker, intoxicating drink arouses brawling, and whoever is led astray by it is not wise.

Prayer: Help us always to say NO to drinking and drugs.

COMMENTS: The Good News Bible says: "Drinking too much makes you loud and foolish. It's stupid to get drunk." If a doctor ordered us to take drugs that would damage our minds, we would sue him; but so many people thoughtlessly take drugs "for fun!" They're flirting with death. Once hooked it is almost impossible (except with God's help) to quit. Alcoholism takes a little longer, but is soon a habit almost too difficult to conquer. Just say NO!

ACTIVITY: List the results of alcoholism and drugs: accidents, jail, dirty hangouts, stealing, unkempt appearance, frightened children, poor grades, fear, hatred, suicide attempts, brutality, crimes, ruined homes, ruined lives.

Now that is what happens if you take drugs. Think of the good side of lie, what God gives. List things to do instead of worldly pleasures. There are lots of exciting, adventurous, worthwhile things to do with God leading. Trust Him with your life, your goals, with eternity.

✝✝✝✝✝

DAY 318. Proverbs 21 - 24   Proverbs 22:1 A good name is to be chosen rather than great riches, loving favor

Prayer: We choose you, Lord;   rather than silver and gold.
not riches or the world.

COMMENTS: A person can gain great wealth but without a good reputation he won't be trusted or admired. We hear many testimonies on Christian TV, "I had everything: fame and money, but lacked something--Jesus Christ!" Prestige, pleasure, wealth never measure up to Him. He satisfies longing hearts.

ACTIVITY: Team for a Bible Club part! An Indian Party in the park. Divide into tribes with a chief for each. Each tribe will decide on a name, a dance, a tent to decorate with tribal drawings, a yell.

Paint faces with jelly beans. Make head bands of braid, pinning with safety pins and adding a feather if available or make one of cardboard.

Each tribe will perform for the others. Then the team relays begin. Scores are added for all the games, and in the end the highest score will be the Great Chief.

The invitation should indicate wearing casual clothes.

Games. 1. Boys sit back; girls back to back. As a pair, they are to stand up. First doing so, wins. Arms must be kept locked together.

2. Beading. Teams. Chiefs are given bowls of popcorn, needle and thread. Each one in line threads 4 popcorn kernels, then pass to next, until last one ties knot.

DAY 319. Proverbs 25 - 28

Proverbs 27:1 Do not boast about tomorrow, for you do not know what a day may bring forth.

Prayer: Help us not to boast.

COMMENTS: It is a good habit to say, "If God wills, I will do so and so." Our plans may not work out as well as we hoped, so it's better not to boast about the future. Working day by day toward a goal is more certain.

ACTIVITY: 3. Basket Race. Each chief is given a basket or bucket of equal number of potatoes. At destination is an empty basket for each team. At start signal each chief runs to goal, carrying one potato which he puts in his basket, returns, and next in line does the same until the line getting all in basket wins.

4. Target Practice. Have a number of dowel sticks for each tribe. Target is a cardboard bear. Each in turn has 3 tries to spear the bear. Keep score. Rerun those who tie until one is a winner.

5. Corn Meal. Each tribe is given a bowl, and each contestant 5 kernels of corn. Toss the kernels in the bowl; high score wins. Prize: cracker jacks.

Keep prizes as much like Indian fare as possible: candy corn, sunflower seeds, fruit, raisins.

Suggested names for Chiefs: Chief Brave One; Chief Know the Most; Chief Fastest Runner; Princess Smiling Face; Princess Pleasant Helper.

Suggested Yell: We are Indians bold and free, wah, wah, wah, wah,

We are happy as can be, wah, wah, wah, wah,

Bible Clubs are what we love

For they tell of God above, wah, wah, wah, wah, wah!

At the end have a campfire, pot of boiling water with corn on the cob, candied apples, popcorn balls, apple juice or fruit drink.

††††††

DAY 320. Proverbs 29 - 31

Proverbs 29:18 Where there is no revelation, the people cast off restraint; but happy is he who keeps the law.

Prayer: Give us vision, Lord.

COMMENTS: The Good News Bible puts it this way: "A nation without God's guidance is a nation without order. Happy is the man who keeps God's law." King James says: "Where there is no vision, the people perish; but he that keepeth the law, happy is he." Whichever way we want to memorize it, it is good to have a vision of what God wants us to do and we'll be happy fulfilling it.

ACTIVITY: Pre-schoolers. If outdoors, have several bowls of water and have the children toss pebbles into bowls. One bowl is marked "God's Way" and the one who tosses the most pebbles into that bowl wins.

Make a peg-board game called, "Christ, the Goal of Life." Hammer 3" nails at the various locations on the board. Print below the one on the center, "The Way," and other names such as money, fun, fame, my way, under the other nails. Use curtain rings to throw, each one having 5 throws. Start with 25 points, add 10 each time The Way is pegged, lose 2 points when a worldly way is pegged. High score wins.

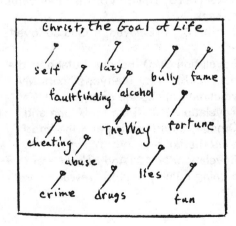

DAY 321. Ecclesiastes 1 - 4

Prayer: It's reassuring that You are in charge, Lord.

Ecclesiastes 3:14 I know that whatever God does, it shall be forever. Nothing can be added to it, and nothing taken away from it. God does it, that men should fear before Him.

COMMENTS: We go to our graves empty-handed except what we have done through God for others. With that key, let's store up treasures in heaven.

ACTIVITY: Let's also hide God's Word in our hearts, for there may be a day when we will not have the freedom to read the Word, if persecution comes in the last days. But if there are memorized verses, no one can take them from us.
        Make more cards for the Memory Game (Day 120).

61.   Ephesians 4:32 Be kind to one another, tenderhearted, forgiving — one another, just as God in Christ also has forgiven you.

62.   Ephesians 6:11 Put on the whole armor of God, that you may be able — to stand against the wiles of the devil.

63.   Romans 12:2 Be not conformed to this world, but be transformed by the renewing of your mind, — that you may prove what is that good and acceptable and perfect will of God.

64.   Romans 12:5 We, being many, are one body in Christ, — and every one members of one another.

65.   John 7:38 He who believes in Me, as the Scripture has said, — out of his heart will flow rivers of living water.

66.   John 8:12 I am the light of the world; he who follows Me — shall not walk in darkness but have the light of life.

67.   John 10:14 I am the good Shepherd; and I know My sheep, — and am known by My own.

68.   John 11:25 I am the resurrection and the life; he who believes — in Me, though he may die, yet he shall live.

69.   John 12:32 And I, if I am lifted up from the earth, — will draw all men to Myself.

70.   John 15:12 This is My commandment, that you love one another — as I have loved you.

71.   John 17:15 I do not pray that You take them out of the world, — but that You keep them from the evil one.

72.   Romans 6:23 For the wages of sin is death, — but the gift of God is eternal life.

73.   Luke 19:10 The Son of Man has come to seek — and to save that which is lost.

74.   1 John 4:11 Beloved, if God so loved us, — we also ought to love one another.

75.   Revelation 3:20 Behold, I stand at the door and knock. If anyone hears My voice and opens the door, — I will come in to him and dine with him and he with Me.

76.   Revelation 1:8 "I am the Alpha and Omega, the Beginning and the End," says the Lord, — "Who is and Who was and Who is to come, the Almighty."

77.   Revelation 22:12 And behold, I am coming quickly, and My reward is with Me, — to give to each one according to his work.

78.   Matthew 6:14 If you forgive men their trespasses,   your heavenly Father will also forgive you.

79.   Matthew 6:20 Lay up for yourselves treasures in heaven, where neither moth   nor rust destroys and where thieves do not break in and steal.

80.   1 Corinthians 13:13 Now abide faith, hope, love, these three;   but the greatest of these is love.

81.   Galatians 5:22, 23 The fruit of the Spirit is love, joy, peace, longsuffering,   kindness, goodness, faithfulness, gentleness, self-control.

82.   Galatians 6:2 Bear one another's burdens,   and so fulfill the law of Christ.

†††††

DAY 322. Ecclesiastes 5 - 8

Prayer: We promise to keep our promises.

Ecclesiastes 5:4 So when you make a promise to God, keep it as quickly as possible. He has no use for a fool. Do what you promised to do. (GNB)

COMMENTS: Ecclesiastes was written when Solomon was old. He departed from God when he worshipped idols with his foreign wives, and now as he reviews his life, he finds it all in vain. He remembers his promise to God and knows to be wise, one has to keep his promise to the Eternal One.

ACTIVITY: With a jigsaw cut out a hand from scrap wood, with the forefinger pointing outward. Tie a durable cord on the finger. On the hand print, "Keep your promise to God."

†††††

DAY 323. Ecclesiastes 9 - 12

Prayer: We desire to do Your work quickly and well.

Ecclesiastes 9:10 Whatever your hand finds to do, do it with your might; for there is no work or device or knowledge or wisdom in the grave where you are going. Do what you promised to do. (GNB)

COMMENTS: There is no nonsense in this verse. We measure up or we don't make it. Solomon summarizes his contemplations in 12:13-14. "Let use hear the conclusion of the whole matter: Fear God and keep His commandments, for this is the whole duty of man. For God will bring every work into judgment, including every secret thing, whether it is good or whether it is evil."

ACTIVITY: Consider some work you can do voluntarily for a just cause, in the community, in the church, in the home. The church or school appreciates helpers to file, write reports, keep records, mail envelopes. For the neighborhood, seek other volunteers and clean up the area, cut shrubs, plant flowers to beautify the area. Is there a need for a playground for the children? Provide equipment, using old tires for swings, barrels to walk through, bars to climb.

Do your teens need a clubhouse workshop and volunteer instructors in crafts, leather work, woodwork, science projects, fixing up cars? Work out schedules with other parents. Busy teens in good projects build character and happiness.

Neighborhood fairs are fun for everyone. Include art shows, crafts, needle work, garden produce, flowers, baked goods.

DAY 324. Song of Solomon
1:1-4, 15-17; 2:1-4, 8-17;
3:9-11; 4:7-16; 5:10-16;
6:1-3; 7:10-13; 8:5-7

Song of Solomon 2:1 I am the rose of
Sharon, and the lily of the valleys. (KJ)

Prayer: We love you for being so beautiful and good.

COMMENTS: Song of Solomon is Solomon's love song. Bible scholars attribute parts to represent the Bridegroom and Bride relationship of Christ and the Church in the New Testament, and to God and Israel in the Old Testament. Others state it is a drama of Solomon and one of his lovers.

ACTIVITY: Make a poster of Marriage and the Family with pictures of happy activities: working, playing games, vacationing, sailing, driving, attending church, patriotic observances. List qualities of a good family relationship: honesty, loyalty, fairness, consideration, love, cleanliness, encouragement. Plan future outings, goals, improvements in house and yard.

†††††

DAY 325. Isaiah 1 - 5
White as Snow
1:1-4, 15-20; 2:1-4,
10-21; 3:13-15;
4:2-6; 5:20-24

Isaiah 1:18 "Come now, and let us reason together," says the Lord, "though your sins are like scarlet, they shall be as white as snow; though they are red like crimson, they shall be as wool."

Prayer: Search our hearts, Lord, and make us white as snow.

COMMENTS: For the prayer time, consider what a tremendous blessing it is to be cleansed by Jesus' blood, and thus be white as snow.

Isaiah was the greatest of the prophets, telling more about Jesus, the Messiah, to come. He was also a great statesman who often took political leadership. He was a contemporary of Hosea, Nahum and Micah, 745-695 BC. The prophets are the remaining books of the Old Testament: 5 Major Prophets and 12 Minor Prophets. Memorize them. Fulfillment of prophecies is one of the main proofs of the truth of the Bible.

ACTIVITY: In Jerusalem at the Shrine of the Book are the Dead Sea Scrolls. Isaiah is the best preserved and is laid out under glass around the inside of the building--a marvel to see. God has seen to it that His Word was not mistranslated, though over 2000 years.

As with Acts, we will make a scroll of the prophets, drawing pictures of importance with Scripture references and titles. Print today's verse as a start. You will want to record outstanding prophecies in your notebook, also.

†††††

DAY 326. Isaiah 6 - 12
Throne
6; 7:1-17; 8:11-19;
9:2, 6-7; 10:20-22;
11:1-12; 12

Isaiah 6:8 Also, I heard the voice of the Lord, saying: "Whom shall I send, and who will go for Us?" Then I said, "Here am I! Send Me."

Prayer: Here we are, Lord. Send us!

COMMENTS: Isaiah's experience must have been fantastic. Can you picture the throne and the fiery creatures with 6 wings, 2 covering the face, 2 the body, and 2 to fly with? How quickly Isaiah answered, "Here am I."

The prophecies begin. The Branch refers to Jesus in 4:2-6. Chapter 5 predicts the capture of the Assyrians. It happened that year.

ACTIVITY: Buy some potter's clay from the hobby shop. Make a water jar like the ones used by the women to carry on their heads. Use it to hold your scroll. The Dead Sea scrolls were found in such jars.

Start with coils of clay, a circle for the bottom, and adding coils upward. Press flat as you work and keep the jug round. Make the neck narrower. Add two handles.

Bake the jug according to directions for the type of clay you bought.

Paint with a glaze or tempora paints. Coat the jug with a plastic spray coating.

✝✝✝✝✝

DAY 327. Isaiah 13 - 18
Lucifer
13:1-5, 14:12-15; 15:1,
16:5; 17:7; 18

Isaiah 14:12 King of Babylon, bright morning star, you have fallen from heaven! In the past you conquered nations, but now you have been thrown to the ground. (GNB)

Prayer: Teach us these lessons.

COMMENTS: Verses 12-17 of Chapter 14 refer to Satan, or Lucifer, the devil. He desired to become greater than God which God cannot endure. He tries to get all earthly men and women to reject God. That is why there is such a battle of God against Satan and his angels and demons-- to save us from Satan's clutch.

ACTIVITY: With the clay that is left, sculpture a lamp or other vessels used at the time. The lamps resembled a shallow pitcher, with the wick in the sprout. Try your lamp with olive oil (used then) when it is dry.

Have a copy made for your notebook of these prophecies:

A. <u>First Coming, as Savior</u>

1. Isaiah 7:14 virgin birth   fulfilled Luke 1:26-27, 30-31
2. 9:1-2 Galilean ministry   Matthew 4:13-16
3. 9:7 ministry both advents   Luke 1:32-33
4. 40:3 John's ministry   John 1:23
5. 50:6 maltreated   Matthew 26:67; John 19:1
6. 53:3 rejected   Luke 23:18; John 1:11
7. 53:5 vicarious sacrifice   Romans 5:6, 8
8. 53:7 silent to accusations   Mark 15:4-5
9. 53:9 buried with rich   Matthew 27:57-60
10. 53:12 crucified with thieves   Mark 15:27-28
11. 61:1-2 heal brokenhearted   Luke 4:18-19

B. <u>Second Coming, as King</u>

1. 2:4, 10-21	5. 24:21-23	9. 32:1-8, 15-20	14. 51:5
2. 9:2-5, 7	6. 25:4-9	10. 33:5-6, 20-22	15. 60:19-20
3. 11:6-11	7. 26:19-21	11. 34:4, 16	16. 65:17-25
4. 16:5	8. 27:6,13	12. 35:1-2	17. 66:1-2, 15-16
		13. 45:23	

C. <u>Other prophecies in Isaiah</u>:

1. 9:2 great light	8. 32:15	15. 46:4	22. 61:1-3, 10-11
2. 9:6 many names	9. 35:5-6,8,10	16. 49:6-7	23. 63:1-3, 8-9
3. 11:1-5 twofold nature	10. 40:3,8-11	17. 52:13-15	
4. 12:2	11. 42:1-8	18. 53	
5. 19:20	12. 43:25	19. 54:5	
6. 28:16	13. 44:3, 22-23	20. 59:20	
7. 29:18	14. 45:15	21. 60:16	

DAY 328. Isaiah 19 - 23
Egypt
19:1, 20-25; 20;
21:11-12; 22:1-14;
23:1-4, 11, 15-18

Isaiah 19:24 In that day Israel will be one of three with Egypt and Assyria, even a blessing in the midst of the land.

Prayer: Thanks for Your prophecies which give us guidance and assurance.

COMMENTS: The more we see prophets fulfilled, the more we know that God is in charge of the nations and the world history. Watch current events happening around Israel. It is still God's land and Jesus will return there.

ACTIVITY: God has no problems with His memory; His prophecies come to pass like clockwork. Our memories are unreliable. Try these games at a party:

1. Place a tray of all sorts of objects on a table for 1 minute. Remove the tray. See who can list the most objects.
2. Describe your church. The person with the most descriptive details wins.
3. Recall what happened on Sunday 2 weeks ago. Last July 4th.

✝✝✝✝✝

DAY 329. Isaiah 24 - 27
Victory over Death
24:1-3, 21-23;
25:1-9; 26:1-9,19-21;
27:1-6, 13

Isaiah 25:8 He will swallow up death forever, and the Lord God will wipe away tears from all faces; the rebuke of His people He will take away from all the earth; for the Lord has spoken.

Prayer: What a promise; no tears.

COMMENTS: Have you ever thought about the small crosses on graves being "plus" signs? Jesus changes death from a minus to a plus. "Victory over death" refers to Jesus triumphing over death when He was buried and took the keys to death. We do not need to fear dying.

ACTIVITY: Pre-schoolers: Play with your village.
As we read through the Bible, we see God's plan. Try this quiz: (2 days)

1. Genesis 1:31, 2:7 The Bible tells us that man was:
    a. created perfect; b. evolved from apes; c. always sinful

2. Genesis 1:27 God created man:
    a. with a mind of his own; b. on the third day; c. in God's image

3. Genesis 2:16-17 God didn't want robots so he gave man:
    a. free will; b. lots of energy; c. a super ego

4. Genesis 2:19 As one of Adam's first jobs he:
    a. built a house; b. named animals; c. planted a garden

5. Genesis 2:21-22 God knew Adam was lonely so He made:
    a. a garden of Eden; b. Eve from Adam; c. woman from dust

6. Genesis 3:23 God sent them from the Garden because:
    a. Adam and Eve sinned; b. they outgrew it; c. Satan was there

7. Romans 3:23 Because they disobeyed God:
   a. only they were judged; b. that didn't effect anyone else; c. all sinned (every descendant)

8. Romans 5:12 When sinned entered man, the judgment was:
   a. hiding; b. death; c. forgiveness

9. John 3:16 God worked out a plan of salvation because:
   a. God loved us; b. He hated Satan; c. He was sorry He made man

10. Ephesians 2:8-9 In accepting Jesus' death in our place, we are saved by:
    a. being good; b. joining the church; c. grace, not works

11. Romans 10:9-10 Tells us how to be:
    a. satisfied; b. saved; c. saints

12. From what angle does Joel 2:32 explain salvation?
    a. who?; b. what?; c. where?

13. 2 Corinthians 6:2 tells when to be saved:
    a. age of accountability; b. now; c. before you die

14. What is the first step in being saved? (Acts 3:19):
    a. read the Bible; b. repent; c. wait until you are better

15. John 3:18 Jesus told Nicodemus if he believed, he would thereafter have:
    a. nothing to do; b. no problems; c. no condemnation

16. In Revelation 3:20, Jesus says that in order for Him to enter our hearts, we must have:
    a. attitude of humility; b. excellent character; c. open the door

17. In John 6:35, Jesus said in Him we shall never hunger for He is:
    a. bread; b. rich; c. generous

18. In John 18:12 He also represents Himself as:
    a. light; b. fruit; c. strength

19. Matthew 5:16 Because He lives in us we are to:
    a. wait for Him; b. hide; c. shine

20. John 10:14 Jesus said His followers would know Him because He is the Good:
    a. Samaritan; b. Shepherd; c. Savior

21. John 21:17 When Jesus talked with Peter after his denial, He said:
    a. feed my sheep; b. be faithful; c. confess your sin

DAY 330. Isaiah 28 - 31
Confidence
28:9-17, 29:11-24
30:1-3, 15-25; 31-4-7

Isaiah 30:15 For thus says the Lord God, the Holy One of Israel: "In returning and rest you shall be saved; in quietness and confidence shall be your strength."

Prayer: We confidently believe.

COMMENTS: Being at rest in Him gives us confidence, peace, assurance. Another memorable verse is Isaiah 26:3, "You will keep him in perfect peace, whose mind is stayed on You, because he trusts in You."

ACTIVITY: Continue the quiz on Man. The answers will be used in the word block.

22. In Matthew 7:17 Jesus said we shall be known by our:
    a. faces; b. freedom; c. fruit

23. Mark 12:30-31 Jesus' two great commandments deal with:
    a. prayer; b. love; c. work

24. Romans 8:35-39 states nothing can separate us form the love of God for through Him we are more than:
    a. good soldiers b. conquerors; c. followers

25. John 14:12 Jesus said if we believe in Him we can do His:
    a. speaking; b. will; c. works

26. John 15:5 Since He is the vine and we the branches, He says:
    a. abide in Me; b. confess; c. rejoice

27. 1 Corinthians 9:24-27 Life is a winning matter when we:
    a. climb the mountain; b. run the race; c. meet the goal

28. 1 Corinthians 10:13 God helps us in many ways, one of which is:
    a. over-confidence; b. temptation; c. shyness

29. Galatians 2:20 When we die to self, it is no longer I, but:
    a. power; b. love; c. Christ in me

30. 2 Corinthians 6:16 We should keep our bodies pure for we are His:
    a. people; b. children; c. temple

31. Revelation 2:10 If faithful through tribulation, we will receive:
    a. crown; b. reward; c. salvation

32. Isaiah 61:10 shows Christ's church as His:
    a. congregation; b. bride; c. building

33. John 17:23 records Jesus' prayer that we be:
    a. one; b. thankful; c. workers

34. 1 Thessalonians 4:16-17 When Christ comes we will:
   a. meet him in the air; b. fall down; c. rejoice

35. Philippians 3:21 Our transformation seems impossible, but He is:
   a. hopeful; b. trying; c. able

36. Mark 9:23 Jesus said to those who believe we can expect:
   a. some things; b. all things c. a few things

37. Psalms 37:7 tells us not to fret but in the Lord we are to:
   a. forgive; b. repent; c. rest

✝✝✝✝✝

DAY 331. Isaiah 32 - 36
   The King
   32:1-8, 15-20; 33:1-2, 5-6, 13-22
   34:1-4, 16; 35; 36

Isaiah 35:1 The wilderness and the wasteland shall be glad for them, and the desert shall rejoice and blossom as the rose.

Prayer: We look for Your coming!

COMMENTS: Verse 33:17 proclaims, "Your eyes will see the King in His beauty; they will see the land that is very far off." One day we'll see Him!

ACTIVITY: Use the answers on the previous quiz for the word block on man.

Word Block on M A N

	1	2	3	4	5	6	7	8	9	10	11	12	13	14	15	16	17	18	19
1	C	R	E	A	T	E	D	P	E	R	F	E	C	T	H	T	A	E	D
2	I	N	G	O	D	S	I	M	A	G	E	F	R	E	E	W	I	L	L
3	E	A					A	D	A	M	E	V	E	S	I	N	N	E	D
4	V	M					A	L	L	S	I	N	N	E	D	N	O	W	G
5	E	E					X	X	X	G	O	D	L	O	V	E	D	R	
6	F	D		X	A			X	B	O	X	O	X	S	A	V	E	D	A
7	R	A		L	T						N	P				X	M	A	C
8	O	N	L	E	E	I					E						T	E	E
9	M	I	E	L	D	E			X		N			T			S	R	N
10	A	M	B	E	N	T	E	M	P	L	E	D			S	X	I	B	O
11	D	A	B	I	D	E	I	N	M	E	X	O		E	F		R	L	T
12	A	L	H	T	E	M	P	T	A	T	I	O	N	R	T	W	H	O	W
13	M	S	H	E	P	H	E	R	D	X	X	R	U	H	X	X	C	V	O
14	F	E	E	D	M	Y	S	H	E	E	P	I	G	T	N	E	P	E	R
15	N	O	C	O	N	D	E	M	N	A	T	I	O	N	W	O	R	C	K
16	S	R	O	R	E	U	Q	N	O	C	L	R	U	N	R	A	C	E	S

DAY 332. Isaiah 37 - 40
      Jerusalem
      (Read and tell)

Isaiah 37:35 For I will defend this city, to save it for My own sake and for My servant David's sake.

Prayer: Thanks for miracle healings, Lord, that You do today also.

COMMENTS: These chapters recount Hezekiah's reign as given in 2 Kings 18-20 and 2 Chronicles 32. God still heals. He never disappoints. He is faithful.

ACTIVITY: We can learn something about Jerusalem from this quiz.
1. How many hills was the city built on?
2. Who captured and started the city?
3. Why is it attributed to be the City of God?
4. Two thousand years earlier, a son was sacrificed on the hill which later became the temple area. Who was that?
5. This rock is now enshrined by the Moslems in their mosque called _____.
6. What more important Son was also killed on a hill near Jerusalem?
7. Why didn't David build the temple?
8. Who built it?
9. What did Jesus say about the temple?
10. Who will reign in Jerusalem for 1000 years?

                                    †††††

DAY 333. Isaiah 41 - 48
      Strength
      41:1-4, 8-20; 42:1-10, 15-16, 21-22;
      43:1-19, 25; 44:1-8, 21-28; 45;
      46:4, 9-10; 47:13-14; 48:9-19

Isaiah 40:31 But those who wait on the Lord shall renew their strength; they shall mount up with wings like eagles, they shall run and not be weary, they shall walk and not faint.

Prayer: Thanks for Your challenge to keep going.

COMMENTS: If this verse is a commentary on a person's life in Christ, the early enthusiasm is like taking flight, the years of growing in the Lord are like running, and the later years are steady and sure. The reference to a voice crying in the wilderness is John the Baptist.

ACTIVITY: Make a wall plaque for the verse for today.
Use a scrap of wallboard, perhaps in a triangular shape.
Arrange straw or plastic flowers across the bottom; glue
and tape in place.

Take a narrow board; with jigsaw carve the top into
scallops. Add an extra ¼" block on each end to raise the
narrow board off the stems of flowers. Fasten it to the main
board. Add Bible verse.

For another version of the verse, make an abstract
painting of the wings like eagles, running light-heartedly,
walking steadfastly. Or make a collage picture combining
the three phases of the Christian life.

Put all the works of creative art on the folding screen.

DAY 334. Isaiah 49 - 55
Final Victory
49:1-13; 50:4-7;
51:1-16; 52:7-15;
53; 54:13-17; 55

Isaiah 51:6 Lift up your eyes to the heavens, and look on the earth beneath. For the heavens will vanish away like smoke. The earth will grow old like a garment, and those who dwell in it will die in like manner; but My salvation will be forever, and My righteousness will not be abolished.

Prayer: Thanks for Your salvation which is eternal.

COMMENTS: God has promised a new heaven and a new earth. We like the present ones very much, but the new ones will be even more splendid as we read in the last chapters of Revelation.

ACTIVITY: In verse 49:16 God says He has written the names of Israel in the palm of His hands. Jesus has the nail prints in His hands for us. What marks do we bear in the service for others?
     Let's do some hard work for someone who needs a strong arm. If there is someone needing the lawn mowed, garden harvested, or assistance in moving furniture, we could be the angel of mercy today. Why not assist someone in painting or papering their rooms, doing some repair work around the place, some mending, a drive to the doctor or hospital, a nourishing bowl of soup? I'm sure we don't need to look very far to brighten someone's heart and home!

✝✝✝✝✝

DAY 335. Isaiah 56 - 66
Lamb of God
56:7-8; 57:15-19;
58:1-2, 6-14; 59:1, 21;
60:1, 19-22; 61; 62;
63:3-10; 64:4-8; 65:17-19,
24-25; 66:1-2, 22-23

Isaiah 53:4-5 Surely, He has borne our griefs and carried our sorrows; yet we esteemed Him stricken, smitten by God, and afflicted. But He was wounded for our transgressions, He was bruised for our iniquities; the chastisement for our peace was upon Him, and by His stripes we are healed.

Prayer: Oh, Lamb of God, we come!

COMMENTS: We are made whole by Jesus' suffering for us. Just as we are, we can momentarily be made clean and whole because Jesus died in our place! Praise you, Lord Jesus! Thank You, Lamb of God, for healing us!

ACTIVITY: As we grow in Christ, we find that Isaiah 64:8 is an excellent illustration. Print the verse in 3 sections and put it on the folding screen.
(1) But now, O Lord, You are our Father;
(2) We are the clay, and You our Potter;
(3) And all we are the work of Your hand.
     Transform a cardboard box into a kiln with a door on the front.
     If you have a real potter's wheel, use it. If not, use a lazy-daisy turntable on a small table. For tools, use paring knife, small spatula, etc. A few jars and paints and brush complete the setting. The clay with pebbles in it is on the floor. Before the talk, make a finished vessel and put it in the oven.

Follow the 3 parts of the verse as you work. First, God the Father finds us in our earthly hiding place, lifts us out, removes pebbles and dirt (made clean by the blood of the Lamb). Next He works on us as the Potter and we must yield to Him, become pliable in His hands. If we remain hard in heart, we won't make a durable vessel. Trials spin us around (on the wheel) and we wonder just what goes on, but then we find He has made a workable vessel out of us.

Encouraged, we submit to His leading, only to find that life is not all joy and beauty as He paints us with dark colors. Finally, He puts us in a fiery furnace test (like the 3 men in the fiery furnace); But lo! Jesus is with us, even there! It is worth the test for that closeness with our Lord. Then when we are taken out, we find our dark colors have turned to gold! Even our shape reflects talents we did not realize we had before.

The day by day life in Him becomes more blessed as He takes us in His loving hand and gives a cup of cold water to a weary traveler, or bread to the hungry, and the Word of Life to new ones in Christ.

✝✝✝✝✝

DAY 336. Jeremiah 1 - 6
Crossroads
1; 2:1-12; 3:1, 11-19;
4:1-2; 5:18-19; 6:16-17

Jeremiah 6:16 The Lord said to His people, "Stand at the crossroads and look. Ask for the ancient paths and where the best road is. Walk in it, and you will live in peace." But they said, "No, we will not!" (GNB)

Prayer: Lord, we choose Your way willingly.

COMMENTS: Jeremiah was called before birth (1:5), commanded not to marry (16:2), forbidden to enter the house of joy and feasting (16:8), and everyone was against him except good King Hezekiah. He suffered 40 years during the wicked reigns of Jehoahaz, Jehoiakim, Jehoiachin, and Zedekiah. Contemporary prophets were Ezekiel, Daniel, Habakkuk, Nahum, and Obadiah.

ACTIVITY: Use a chalkboard illustration of a crossroads with signs pointing to Fame, Fortune, Pleasure, etc. but one golden sign to God's Way. Tell about Jesus, the Way to Abundant Life, fulfillment, adventure, joy, peace, purpose.

✝✝✝✝✝

DAY 337. Jeremiah 7 - 12
Boasting
7:1-11, 21-24; 8:18-22;
9:13-16, 23-24; 10:6-10,
23-24; 11:18-23; 12:14-17

Jeremiah 9:24 "But let him who glories glory in this, that he understands and know Me, that I am the Lord, exercising loving kindness, judgment, and righteousness in the earth. For in these I delight," says the Lord.

Prayer: Let us glory in You, Lord.

COMMENTS: The Israelites were being punished by God because they left Him to worship idols. They were taken captives to Babylon and did not heed Jeremiah.

ACTIVITY: During the study of Jeremiah we will construct a Palestine village. Use a large plywood board, narrow enough to carry through a doorway. The Bible Club will enjoy working on it with the family. Make a hill on the left with mounds of crumpled paper taped down and strips of paper dipped in flour-water and smoothed over it. Leave flat areas around the hill for the Palestine houses. When dry use latex paint with some sandy coloring. In flat areas, the temple will be placed, or the nativity stable scene, or other changes when telling various stories.

✝✝✝✝✝

DAY 338. Jeremiah 13-19.
Power
13:1-11, 23-25;
14:1-15; 15:21;
16:21; 17:7-10; 18:1-12; 19:1-11

Jeremiah 16:21. Therefore behold, I will this once cause them to know, I will cause them to know My hand and My might and they shall know that My name is the Lord.

Prayer: We know the power of Your name, Lord.

COMMENTS: God previously judged Israel in the north; now He is judging Judah, the southern tribe of God's chosen nation.

ACTIVITY: Cut off each end of facial tissue boxes to make the houses. Paint with the latex paint, and with black felt pen mark outline of stones, doors and windows. For some add stairway and upper room. Arrange the houses around the hill, with pathway, pebbles, small plastic flower-bushes, etc.

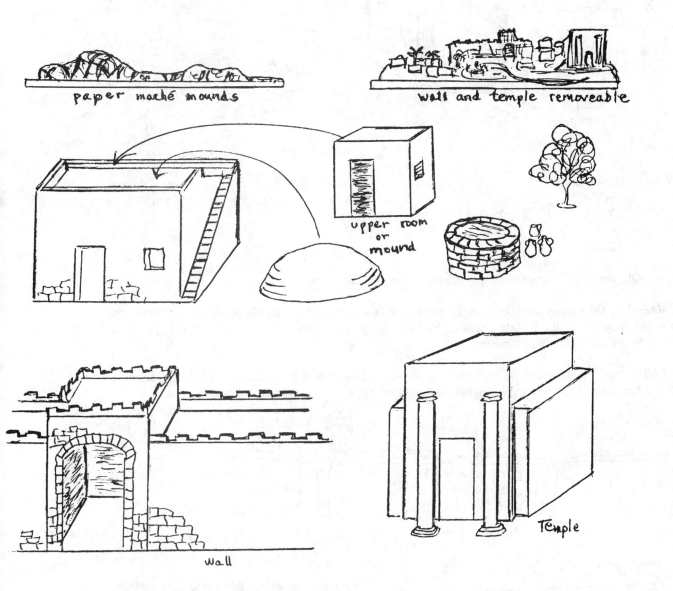

paper maché mounds

wall and temple removeable

upper room
or
mound

wall

Temple

DAY 339. Jeremiah 20-26
Choice
20:1-6; 21:1-10;
22:1-5; 23:3-8; 24:1-10;
25:1-12; 26:1-19.

Jeremiah 21:8. Now you say to this people, "Thus says the Lord: Behold, I set before you the way of life and the way of death."

Prayer: Thanks, Lord, for Your way.

COMMENTS: We have the same choice. Choose God! God uses such excellent visual aids. After the demonstration of the broken jar, they would always remember the lesson. Our visual aids work, too.

ACTIVITY: This village can be used for Jerusalem by adding a part of the wall, or Capernaum by the Sea of Galilee by adding blue plastic for the water, or Bethlehem by adding the cave stable for the nativity scene, etc. Put a well in a central area of the houses. Use a round box covered with pebbles indented in flour-salt-water clay.

ttttt

DAY 340. Jeremiah 27-32
Seek
27:1-8, 21-22; 28; 29:1-13
30:1-3, 18-22; 31:1-13, 31-34;
32:2-20, 36-42

Jeremiah 29:13. And you will seek Me, and find Me, when you search for Me with all your heart.

Prayer: Oh, we seek You with all our heart, and want to follow You.

COMMENTS: God loves a whole-hearted person; one who acts with all his strength and zeal. As you recall men He chose for hard tasks, they were vigorous men. The same with the girls and women--ones who stood up for Him.

ACTIVITY: Use facial tissue boxes taped together for the wall of Jerusalem. Use one in upright position for gate, cutting out the opening. Add strips cut out for parapets along the top.

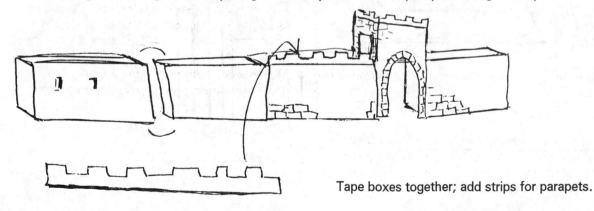

Tape boxes together; add strips for parapets.

DAY 341. Jeremiah 33-38
            Scroll
            33:1-9, 14-16; 34:8-9;
            35:12-19; 36;
            37:11-21; 38

Jeremiah 36:8. And Baruch the son of Neriah did according to all that Jeremiah the prophet commanded him, reading from the book the words of the Lord in the Lord's house.

Prayer: We love reading Your book.

COMMENTS: Although reading the Word was a powerful demonstration of faith, the king disregarded the message and shredded the scroll. He cast Jeremiah in a dungeon as punishment.

ACTIVITY: The people will be very small, so use wire for stick men and women, clothe with simple cutout robe and turban, tied with cord. Keep a record of the people to use for various stories, marking names on bottom of feet (attach each person to a cardboard stand to be moved about). Make heads of small styrofoam balls or cotton balls covered with cloth.

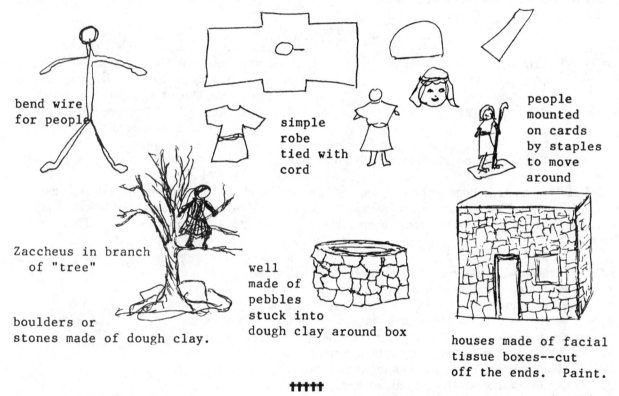

bend wire for people

simple robe tied with cord

people mounted on cards by staples to move around

Zaccheus in branch of "tree"

boulders or stones made of dough clay.

well made of pebbles stuck into dough clay around box

houses made of facial tissue boxes--cut off the ends. Paint.

DAY 342. Jeremiah 39:45
            Disaster
            39:1-14; 40;
            41:1-2, 10-18; 42:1-16;
            43:1-11; 44:11-14; 45

Jeremiah 44:23. Because you have burned incense and because you have sinned against the Lord, and have not obeyed the voice of the Lord or walked in His law, in His statutes or in His testimonies, therefore this calamity has happened to you, as at this day.

Prayer: Keep us true to You, Lord.

COMMENTS: Baruch was Jeremiah's scribe, a man of prominence. Jeremiah's last message was given in Chapter 44. His manner of death is unknown. The remaining chapters were inserted later but were his previous messages.

ACTIVITY: Construct the temple of cardboard to be moved on and off the scene. Use paper tubes for pillars, two on the front. See floor plan at Day 259. Make it about 12" high.

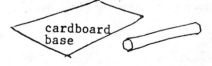

cardboard base

DAY 343. Jeremiah 46-52
Punishment
46:25-26; 47:1-2; 48:1-2;
49:1-2; 50:1-9; 51:15-16,
60-64; 52:15-20, 28

Jeremiah 46:28. "Do not fear, O Jacob My servant," says the Lord. "For I am with you; for I will make a complete end of all the nations to which I have driven you, but I will not make a complete end of you. I will rightly correct you, for I will not leave you wholly unpunished."

Prayer: Help us to keep the temple of our hearts beautiful.

COMMENTS: This prophecy was fulfilled in that age and also in this age.

ACTIVITY: Continue on the temple. Use boxes or cut cardboard the approximate sizes for main building and the rooms on each side. Paint it white. Have enough space on the cardboard stand for an outer wall and brazen altar in the courtyard.

add 2 sides

✝✝✝✝✝

DAY 344. Lamentations 1-5.
Starvation and Ruin
1:1-3; 2:17-19; 3:21-29;
4:1-2; 5:19-22

Lamentations 2:19. Arise, cry out in the night, at the beginning of the watches; pour out your heart like water before the face of the Lord. Lift your hands toward Him for the life of your children, who faint from hunger at the head of every street.

Prayer: We pray for our children; watch over them.

COMMENTS: Lamentations, or poems, were written by Jeremiah the weeping prophet, regarding the destruction of his country. Each chapter is a song of 22 verses, the number of letters in the Hebrew alphabet. In the third song, each verse is divided into 3 sentences, a form of Hebrew poetry.

ACTIVITY: Here is a quiz on unusual prayers of the Old Testament:
1.   Who prayed in the most unlikely place, where no one else has prayed?
2.   Who prayed for a wicked city if there were only ten righteous there?
3.   Whose servant traveled a long distance to pick a wife for his master's son, and God answered exactly as the servant asked Him to?
4.   Who prayed while wrestling with an angel?
5.   Who prayed 40 days and nights?
6.   Who was thought to be drunk while praying?
7.   Who prayed for the servant's eyes to be opened to see the army of angels?
8.   Who prayed for wisdom and received much more?
9.   Whose prayer was held up while an angel fought to bring the answer?
10.   Who told Mordecai and the Jews to fast and pray for three days?

✝✝✝✝✝

DAY 345. Ezekiel 1-6.
Vision
1; 2; 3; 4:1-5, 16-17;
5:1-8; 6:1-8

Ezekiel 1:28. Like the appearance of a rainbow in a cloud on a rainy day, so was the appearance of the brightness all around it. This was the appearance of the likeness of the glory of the Lord.

Prayer: Oh, such glories we are yet to see!

COMMENTS: Ezekiel was a contemporary of Jeremiah. Both were priests, writing about Israel's downfall. Ezekiel, however, was not in Jerusalem but with the captives in Babylon 597 to 570 B.C. He preached 22 years.

ACTIVITY: This is difficult but try anyway. In what books did these events occur--just in case someone asked you, and you had to find them?

1. Elijah's chariot of fire
2. Moses' miracles
3. Abraham's sacrifice
4. Peter walking on water
5. David and Goliath
6. Ten Commandments written
7. Creation
8. Crossing the Red Sea on dry ground
9. Peter's release from jail
10. Jacob's dream of the ladder
11. The flood and Noah's ark
12. Gideon's victory with 300 men
13. Naaman's healing
14. Paul's conversion
15. Mt. Carmel contest with Elijah
16. John's heavenly vision of the end.

✝✝✝✝✝

DAY 346. Ezekiel 7-11
New Heart
7:1-3; 8; 9:1-9;
10:1-19; 11:13-25

Ezekiel 11:19. Then I will give them one heart, and I will put a new spirit within them, and take the stony heart out of their flesh, and give them a heart of flesh.

Prayer: We want the new heart.

COMMENTS: This second vision seems to be a continuation of the first. He was in the presence of other people at the time and described it as it faded. The dazzling light of God's presence was awesome to Ezekiel. Paul was temporarily blinded by the light at his conversion.

ACTIVITY: Continue the scroll you started on Isaiah, adding Ezekiel's visions.

✝✝✝✝✝

DAY 347. Ezekiel 12-17
Dispersed
12:1-19, 27-28;
13:1-8, 17-18;
14:7-8, 13; 15:1-4;
16:60-63; 17:1-16, 22-24

Ezekiel 12:15. Then they shall know that I am the Lord, when I scatter them among the nations and disperse them throughout the countries.

COMMENTS: Considering the times Israel lived in other countries--in Egypt over 400 years, in Babylon and Assyria about 70 years--and since Jesus' resurrection almost 2,000 years ago, it is remarkable that they kept their nationality, their distinctive qualities, their religion, and their intelligence.

ACTIVITY: Learn the books of Minor Prophets as you put their names in the accompanying word block. Hosea, Joel, Amos, Obadiah, Jonah, Micah, Nahum, Habakkuk, Zephaniah, Haggai, Zecharian, Malachi.

✝✝✝✝✝

DAY 348. Ezekiel 18-24.
Covenant
18:4-9, 19-23; 19:1-9;
20:39-42; 21:19-23;
22:29-31; 23:46-48; 24:14

Ezekiel 16:60. Nevertheless I will remember My covenant with you in the days of your youth, and I will establish an everlasting covenant with you.

Prayer: Thank You for Your everlasting covenant to us, Your children.

MINOR PROPHETS

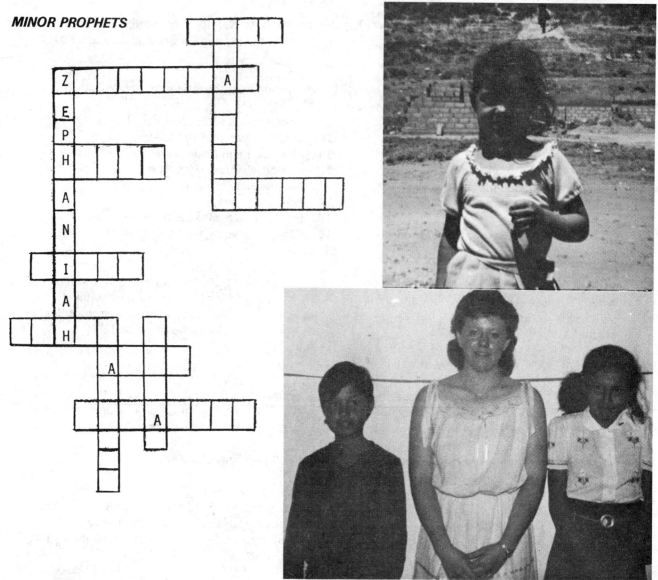

COMMENTS: Knowing God keeps His covenants, we want to keep ours, too.

ACTIVITY: My teen Sunday School class earned money for a teen mission trip to Tijuana, Mexico, by making things to sell. We flew from Calgary, Alberta, to San Francisco, rented a 15-passenger van and drove to San Diego, sightseeing on the way. Volunteer missionaries took us to Tijuana where they had built a church. We taught 60 little Mexican children to make the 25 scenes of the Life of Christ in the Easter holidays: Friday to Sunday. They didn't know each other's language, but "showing" was enough. I was so thrilled with my teens, ages 11-15, who sat down and taught those children, and with the Mexicans who so enthusiastically did the work. I continually praise God for His help. That class had put on 3 plays and made silhouette pictures and other projects, but the high point was the ability (in Christ) to do that mission work!

You might like to create music boxes to sell. Here's how:

1. Order music boxes (the instrument). Magic Music, Inc., 20 Van Cortlandt Place, Kearny, NJ 07032. From their catalog we selected many hymn tunes, plus Danny Boy, Chim Chim Cherie, Bless This House, You Are My Sunshine, etc. The keys to turn are regular, long stem, and turntable. We made about 100.

2. Gather all types of miniature objects to work with: small feather birds, nests, small animals, lichen, dried moss, straw flowers, cones, pebbles, sea shells, figurines, miniature furniture, bowls, dishes, scraps of braid, ribbons, scissors, pointed pliers, wire, sharp knife, paints, brushes, felt pens, plates, tiles, plastic trays, glue silicone, plastic flowers, leaves, etc.

3. Design or create your own music
box scene. For "Church in the Valley," use a turntable music box,
with an oval wallboard tray. Make
a miniature church, surround with
trees, path, tiny people. Or a small
nativity scene for "Away in a Manger."
One girl made an 8X10" tray scene
of cardboard Palestine village,
shepherd's field, stable, moss for
field area, and the music box hidden
under the hillside village.

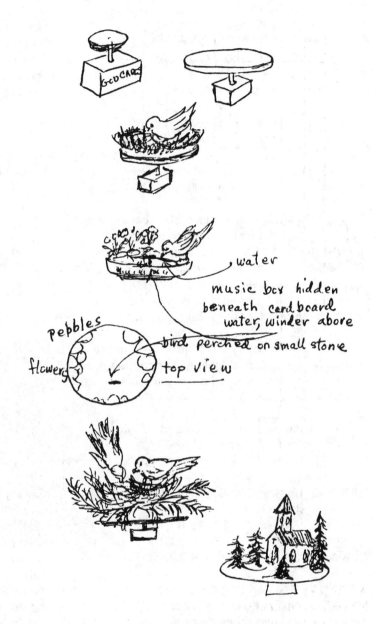

4. Birds sold quickly. One type
was a cereal bowl on a turntable music
box. The little bird was perched on a
small stone at the edge of the painted
water. Little flowers and leaves were
glued with silicone around the edge
of the bowl.
  Another was a nest in pine
branches, one bird in nest, the
other perched on branch.

5. One boy made a flour-salt-water
clay mound over the music box,
covered it with lichen and moss (from
florist shop), and a cave with two tiny
rabbits coming out; flowers were
around it.

6. A neat turntable idea was a boy
kneeling by the bed in prayer, with
window, braided rug on floor. Stars
and moon were glued on the blue
plastic window; the bed had a tiny
pillow and spread.

7. We printed a Bible verse for each
one, glued to the music box or turntable or side of bowl.

8. Another home scene was a hutch
made from small cardboard box,
added shelves, tiny cups, plates,
knick-knacks. A figurine stood near
it with a pot of flowers.
  Grandparents sitting in front of fireplace
(music box behind it) was a homey scene; dog
snoozing by the rocker, table with oil lamp,
all to the tune, "Bless This House."
  Some sets were bought, like Snow White
and the Seven Dwarfs, with "Whistle While
You Work."

DAY 349. Ezekiel 25:33.
Return
25:1-4; 26:2-3, 7; 27:27;
28:6-7, 20-22, 25-26; 29:2,
8-15; 30:20-23; 31:18;
32:18-20; 33:1-16

Prayer: Thanks for the mansions You
are preparing for us in heaven.

COMMENTS: Again the Lord prophesied the return of Israel to their land, which happened at
that time, and also in our own time (1948).

ACTIVITY: Most of the music box scenes were
made with the flour-salt-water clay, allowed to
dry overnight, then painted. The cornstarch
clay is more expensive but does a little better job.
All kinds of tools were used: punches,
toothpicks, dentist tweezers, sewing scissors,
kitchen scissors, plastic cutters, jigsaw.

Some music boxes were hidden in the scene
with only the winder showing. Others had the
music box out in the open so children could watch
the mechanics.

Whatever the setting, we used a Bible verse
to correlate the tune and scene.

✝✝✝✝✝

DAY 350. Ezekiel 34-39
Witness
34:1-6, 11-13, 26-31; 35:2-5;
36:6-11, 24-38; 37:1-14,
21-28; 38:2-4, 14-23;
39:1-7, 25-29.

Prayer: Oh, Father, help us to
witness to all You tell us to.

COMMENTS: This should make us tremble.
How much depends upon our witness.
When giving a program, we should give
an invitation--it may be the only one a
person gets. Follow up with a New
Testament, prayer, and other helps to be sure
they are born again and close to the Lord.
They will be eternally grateful, and the
angels in heaven will rejoice.

Ezekiel 28:25. Thus says the Lord God:
"When I have gathered the house of Israel
from the peoples among whom they are
scattered, and am hallowed in them in the
sight of the Gentiles, then they will dwell
in their own land which I gave to My
servant Jacob."

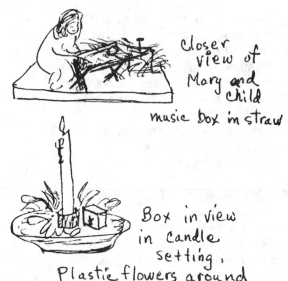

Closer view of Mary and child
music box in straw

Box in view in candle setting. Plastic flowers around

Ezekiel 33:8-9. When I say to the
wicked, "O wicked man, you shall surely
die!" and you do not speak to warn the
wicked from his way, that wicked man
shall die in his iniquity; but his blood I will
require at your hand. Nevertheless, if you
warn the wicked to turn from his way and
he does not turn from his way, he shall
die in his iniquity, but you have delivered
your soul.

music box among pebbles and flowers

music box among hillside stones
for nativity scene
and shepherds on hillside

ACTIVITY: Pre-schoolers will enjoy making a simple music box. See a 4" square tile, attach the music box at one side to "watch" using silicone. Attach one of their little figurines, or toys; or use a plastic cup, put clay in the bottom and let them stick in plastic flowers in a pretty way.

music box

One girl volunteered to make 15 jewelry boxes (we had bought some on sale) by putting the music box inside, covering it with velvet, and making a hole in the bottom so it would wind from beneath. We ran off a hundred Bible verses on a copy machine, cut them evenly and put them in the box for Promise verses.

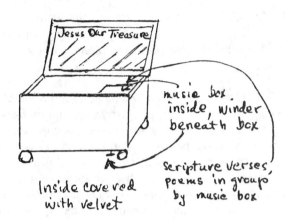

music box inside, winder beneath box

Inside covered with velvet

scripture verses, poems in group by music box

We bought a few small plush stuffed animals, removed some stuffing down the back and inserted the music box, "Jesus Loves Me," with the winder sticking out.

I did some oil-painted sceneries of mountains, lakes, etc., set them in box frames, added the music box, small plastic flowers and foliage in the ledge for "On Top of Old Smokey" and one of a mill for "The Old Mill Stream."

For "How Great Thou Art," I painted a Swiss scene (24X30") of the Matterhorn, Swiss church with steeple pointed to God, an autumn-colored tree with arms uplifted in praise, and on the ledge to the left had the music box surrounded with flowers, to right of center a Swiss boy (figurine) blowing his horn with his dog singing. I'm glad I kept it, for it's not only an inspiration to me but my guests.

"Jesus loves Me" music box inserted in back of bear.

frame-box oil-painting with dry flowers, pebbles and music box on bottom shelf. "OLD MILL STREAM"

There were other ideas. One girl arranged a tray for a sick person, with "O, What A Beautiful Morning" glued to the napkin holder, verses of thanksgiving on the holder, and "You are the salt of the earth" printed on the salt shaker.

Another was a turntable with an oval cut from scrap wallboard on it, mossy grass with little figurines dancing to "What A Friend We Have in Jesus."

music box turntable

There were many Christmas ideas for "Silent Night" and "Away in a Manger," for centerpieces and mobiles.

Several wedding gifts were made with arches covered with flowers and bell, the couple in the center, "You Light Up My Life" and "Laura's Theme," "Joint heirs together of the grace of life" (1 Pet.3:7).

music box behind fireplace wall

DAY 351. Ezekiel 40-48
            Vision
            40:1-5; 41:1-4,
            12-16; 42:1-3, 15; 43:1-12;
            44:1-4; 45:1-6; 46:1;
            47:1-12; 48:1, 30-35

Ezekiel 40:2. In the visions of God He took me into the land of Israel and set me on a very high mountain; on it toward the south was something like the structure of a city.

Prayer: Show us what You want us to do!

COMMENTS: The vision was of the future temple, the one rebuilt when the people returned to Jerusalem. All the details for rebuilding were carefully explained by God. If our Father gives us a job to do, He also gives the plans. Sometimes we have to seek diligently, but He points the way.

ACTIVITY: Your teens will have as many creative ideas as my group did. And I hope you will work out a mission trip. Many cities need workers in their poor areas. Take supplies along to do the Life of Christ scenes. We assigned two or three scenes to each teen, an envelope (you could use pizza boxes) and in it he or she put the number of popsickle sticks needed, cut the wires for arms and legs, cut out the clothes, took along the background boxes, newspaper strips, etc., and I carried the tempera paints, felt pens, brushes, boxes folded flat, etc. Plan ahead by writing to city missions or church leaders. Los Angeles is a marvelous place to visit, good weather, many immigrants looking for work, Disneyland, and other places to sightsee. There are also many inexpensive motels in the area for a group. Besides the ocean is great, and if at the right season, you can see the Rose Parade, or the dramas at Crystal Cathedral (a must!). I think Washington, D.C., is excellent, too--I grew up there--as it has many museums, national shrines, and places all free.

Back to the music boxes: We saved money because we used things we had on hand, and I am one to pick up many articles after Christmas and Easter on sale. Make the music boxes not only attractive, but durable and of good materials. And pray.

                                    ✝✝✝✝✝

DAY 352. Daniel 1-2
            Standards

Prayer: Help us dare to be like Daniel.

Daniel 1:17. As for these four young men, God gave them knowledge and skill in all literature and wisdom: And Daniel had understanding in all visions and dreams.

COMMENTS: Daniel is the great prophet concerning world empires. He was taken captive to Babylon by Nebuchadnezzar in 606 B.C. and became a prince in the royal house while still young. His 70 years of ministry exceeded any other Old Testament prophet. Because of his sterling character and personal charm, he rose from a young slave to become prime minister (like Joseph). At God's leading, he was a statesman during four of the world's greatest powers.

This short book is packed with fascinating events, miracles, prophecies. Every chapter is dramatic. Your notebook will have entries on angels, miracles, prophecies, how God communicates with us through dreams, events, angels, etc.

ACTIVITY: As there are 6 outstanding scenes in Daniel, a lazy-daisy will be used with 6 sections. The turntable should be about 18" in diameter. Divide by using triangles brought

together in the middle as shown, or taping six 6" sections in a hexagon shape. Each section will have a small scene, the characters made of wire about 4" tall. The scene for today is the four young men at a table. Use a block of wood or cardboard for the table; clay fruit and bread on table.

✝✝✝✝✝

DAY 353. Daniel 3-4
Fiery Furnace

Daniel 3:25. "Look!" he answered, "I see four men loose, walking in the midst of the fire; and they are not hurt, and the form of the fourth is like the Son of God."

Prayer: Oh, help us to be as brave as they.

COMMENTS: Daniel often spoke with angels, and in this instance an angel like the Son of God appeared with the three men in the fiery furnace. They were willing to die for God and He covered them with His presence so that they were not even singed. What a comfort it is to remember their experience when we go through trials. God is with us!

ACTIVITY: The six scenes for "Daniel Dial Display" are:

1.   Good eating: Daniel and three friends choose healthy food. (Chapter 1)
2.   Nebuchadnezzar's dream: King on left, Daniel on right. Dream is shown by a felt pen drawing on clear plastic showing figure of man. (Chapter 2)
3.   Fiery Furnace: Box with clear plastic front for furnace, red cellophane for fire, the four men in the fire. King outside. (Chapter 3)
4.   Tree dream: Dream in plastic with drawing of tree and stump. (Chapter 4)
5.   Writing on wall: King and nobles at table, Daniel on right, hand on wall with finger writing. (Chapter 5)
6.   Lion's Den: Daniel and quiet lions in den, king looking down from the wall into the den. (Chapter 6)

Work on the scenes each day and practice telling the stories as you make them.

✝✝✝✝✝

DAY 354. Daniel 5-6
Protection.

Daniel 6:22. My God sent His angel and shut the lion's mouths, so that they have not hurt me, because I was found innocent before Him; and also, O king, I have done no wrong before you.

Prayer: Thanks for Your miracles.

COMMENTS: The events in Chapter 5 took place about 23 years after King Nebuchadnezzar's death, when Daniel was about 80 years old. Daniel was blessed miraculously because he believed in God's protection.

ACTIVITY: The vessels on the banquet table in the 5th scene should be molded of clay and painted gold, for they were the Temple's vessels of gold.

✝✝✝✝✝

DAY 355. Daniel 7-9
Vision

Daniel 7:13. I was watching in the night visions, and behold, One like the Son of Man, coming with the clouds of heaven! He came to the Ancient of Days, and they brought Him near before Him.

Prayer: Thanks for Your visions.

COMMENTS: The visions God gave Daniel have been so accurately fulfilled that no one can deny that God knows the future. The head of gold was Babylon; arms and breast of silver, the Medes and Persians; bronze body, Greece; legs of iron, Rome; and the iron mixed with clay represents the democratic nations of today. Christ's return is the Rock that will crush the feet, and that is followed by the 1,000 year reign of Christ. That is the next big event to come.

The 70 weeks recorded in the last part of Chapter 9 are the times the Jews would be involved; first, 7 weeks or 49 years, which was the restoration of Jerusalem given in Ezra and Nehemiah; second, the 62 weeks or 434 years until Jesus came as Savior; and the last, one week or 7 years, the Tribulation foretold in Revelation.

ACTIVITY: Check your notebooks for the signs of the times we studied in Matthew 24, 2 Peter 1 and Revelation.

✝✝✝✝✝

DAY 356. Daniel 10-12.
Fearless

Prayer: We need to be patient for Your answers, Lord, for we know not the circumstances as You do.

Daniel 10:12-13. Then he said to me, "Do not fear, Daniel, for from the first day that you set your heart to understand, and to humble yourself before your God, your words were heard; and I have come because of your words. But the prince of the kingdom of Persia withstood me twenty-one days; and behold, Michael, one of the chief princes, came to help me, for I had been left alone there with the kings of Persia.

COMMENTS: It is surprising that God's answer to Daniel's prayer was held up 21 days as the angel of the Lord fought Satan's angel on the way. But God triumphed.

Listen to these words from Daniel 12:2-3:

"Many of those who have already died will live again: some will enjoy eternal life, and some will suffer eternal disgrace. The wise leaders will shine with all the brightness of the sky. And those who have taught many people to do what is right will shine like the stars forever." (GNB)

This is a challenge to keep on teaching God's ways.

ACTIVITY: Find an opportunity to tell of Daniel's experiences, perhaps at a rest home or church retreat. Each one in the family take part. People will inquire into the meanings, so be prepared to explain the signs of the times.

✝✝✝✝✝

DAY 357. Hosea 1-14
Live a Truth
1; 2:14-17; 3; 4:6, 11-13;
5:5-6; 6:1-3, 6; 7:13; 8:14;
9:8, 17; 10:12-13; 11:1, 8-9;
12:6; 13:2-4; 14.

Hosea 6:6. For I desire mercy and not sacrifice, and the knowledge of God more than burnt offerings.

Prayer: Help us to understand and forgive others, and learn Your lessons.

COMMENTS: God chose Israel symbolically to be His wife, but she proved unfaithful. He used Hosea to be a lesson to Israel, to live a lesson by marrying an unfaithful wife. Jesus uses the church as a symbolic wife. Are we faithful to Him, or are we more interested in other people or things or ourselves?

ACTIVITY: Identify the women in this quiz. Who was:

1.   the mother of Jesus?
2.   the wicked queen who killed prophets of God?
3.   the good queen who fasted and prayed for the people of Israel to be saved?
4.   one of the women, name beginning with S, who helped Jesus with possessions.
5.   hid the Israelite spies at Jericho?
6.   a Christian who was known for her good works?
7.   the wife of Abraham who had a child in her old age?
8.   Ruth's mother-in-law who helped her live in God's land?
9.   Jacob's only daughter?
10.   one of the women who helped Jesus and the disciples? (begins with J)
11.   the cast-away mother who was helped by an angel in the desert?
12.   the wife of David who was known as the one "who loved him" but later scoffed at him when he danced?
13.   the sister of Moses and Aaron?
14.   Timothy's grandmother, a godly woman?
15.   the girl who opened the door in the night for Peter while others prayed?
16.   the devout Christian who sold purple cloth and used her home for missionaries?
17.   the first woman?
18.   one of the women who took spices to Jesus' tomb with two Mary's?
19.   a prophetess who blessed the baby Jesus?
20.   the mother of John the Baptist?
21.   the wife of Herod?
22.   the beautiful woman David wanted to marry and sinned to get her?
23.   the sister of Lazarus and Mary?
24.   the woman who was found as a wife for Isaac?
25.   the wife of Esau?
26.   the barren Israelite woman who prayed in the temple for a son?
27.   Jacob's favorite wife?
28.   the woman who tricked Samson to tell the secret of his strength?
29.   the Christian who with her husband was a tentmaker and helped Paul?
30.   a prophetess and judge of Israel who sang to God?
31.   the woman who helped to feed David's army and whom he later married?
32.   the mother of Timothy?
33.   queen who did not come at the drunken king's request?
34.   the daughter-in-law of Naomi who remained in Moab?
35.   the other daughter-in-law who went with Naomi and later married Boaz?

✝✝✝✝✝

DAY 358. Joel 1-3
Spirit.
1:13-14; 2:14-32; 3

Prayer: Thank You for giving us
Your Spirit.

Joel 2:26 You shall eat in plenty and be satisfied, and praise the name of the Lord your God, who has dealt wondrously with you; and My people shall never be put to shame.

COMMENTS: God is pouring out His Spirit in our day as Joel prophesied. Joel 2:28: "And it shall come to pass afterward that I will pour out My Spirit on all flesh; your sons and your daughters shall prophesy, your old men shall dream dreams, your young men shall see visions."

ACTIVITY: Mother, it is your turn to say something: Prepare a talk on how Jesus lifted the role of women, how He honored so many (Mary, Elizabeth, the one who touched His garment, the one who poured ointment on His feet, etc.) and how He has given them special anointings in service through the years.

   Pre-schoolers: Tell why you like your mother. Others do the word block.

ACTIVITY: Fill in the names from the previous quiz on WOMEN OF THE BIBLE in the word block below. They read across or down, but the names do not always fill the spaces.

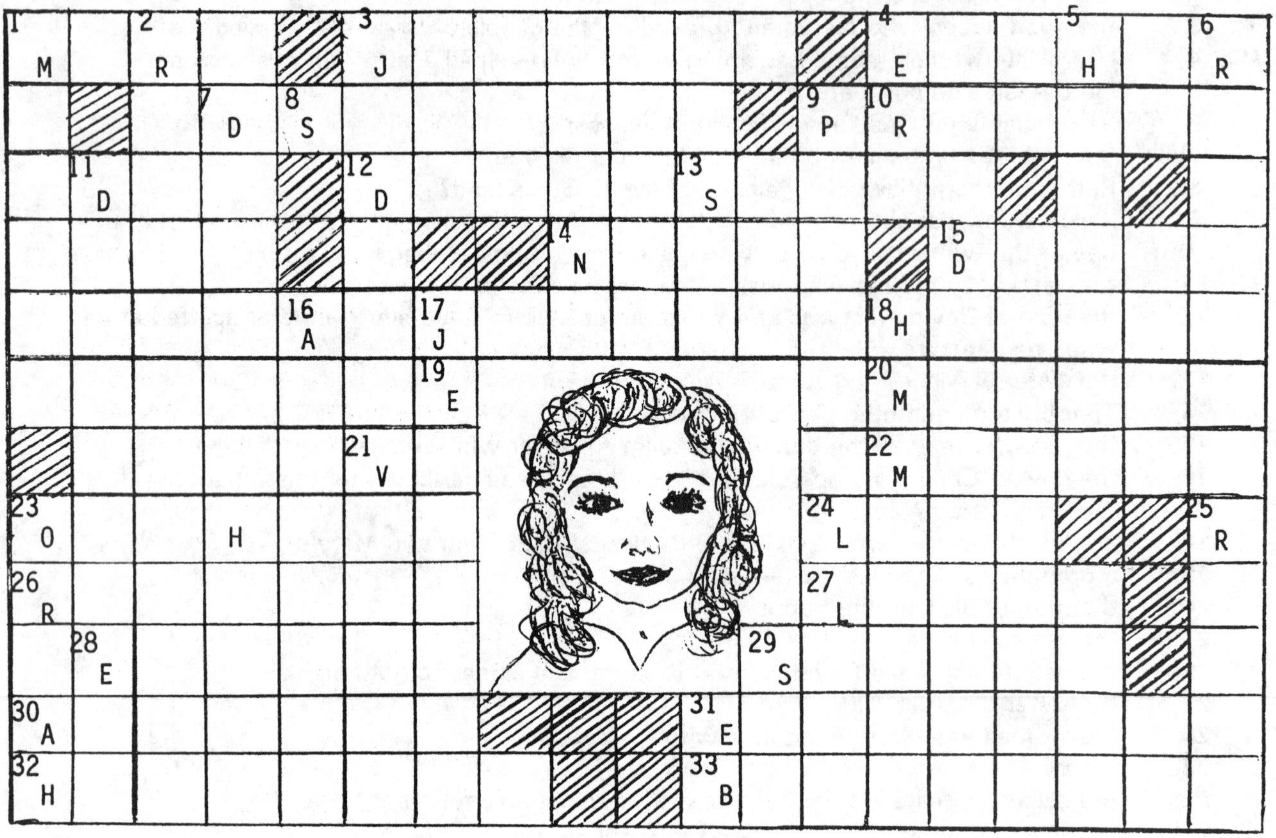

(crossword grid with numbered cells containing the following letters)

1 M   2 R   3 J   4 E   5 H   6 R
7 D   8 S   9 P   10 R
11 D   12 D   13 S
14 N   15 D
16 A   17 J   18 H
19 E   20 M
21 V   22 M
23 O   H   24 L   25 R
26 R   27 L
28 E   29 S
30 A   31 E
32 H   33 B

††††††

DAY 359. Amos 1-9
Together
1; 2:1-6; 3:1-7; 4:6-13;
5:6-9, 14-15; 6:8; 7:7-9;
8:11-12; 9:8-15

Amos 3:3 Can two walk together unless they are agreed?

Prayer: Thanks for making us One in You.

COMMENTS: God places a high priority on agreeing. In Matthew 18:19, He said, "Whenever two of you on earth agree about anything you pray for, it will be done for you by My Father in heaven." (GNB) It was when the 120 were praying in accord that the Holy Spirit was poured upon them.

ACTIVITY: A family in accord is most satisfying and positive. To keep reminding ourselves to keep in accord, make a wooden plaque with a heavy cord glued around a photo of the family. This will represent a "family in a cord."

Think of some things your family totally agrees on. Some that require discussion. Do you allow each one to follow the Lord as he or she feels led? Do you try to understand the other fellow's convictions?

DAY 360. Obadiah
Edom
1:1-4, 10-11, 17, 20-21

Obadiah 1:4 "Though you exalt yourself as high as the eagle, and though you set your nest among the stars, from there I will bring you down," says the Lord.

Prayer: Keep us from exalting ourselves.

COMMENTS: Edom's destruction foretold in the shortest book in the Old Testament was fulfilled and the ruins are seen today--Petra.

Jonah 1-4
Read as a drama

Jonah 4:4. Then the Lord said, "Is it right for you to be angry?"

COMMENTS: As you read the story as a drama, add tape-recorded background.

Jonah is a study in psychology--so human. He ran away from the task God assigned him, yet confessed his fault to the captain and was willing to be thrown overboard to save the ship. God provided the great fish to save him. He would rather die than face facts. When we see ourselves in Jonah, we laugh. Nevertheless, Jonah saved 120,000 or more people from destruction.

ACTIVITY; Everyone delights in the story of Jonah. Let's present it as a cube, gluing pictures or drawings on the four sides of a photographer's plastic cube.

1. Storm, sailors casting him overboard.
2. Big fish swallowing Jonah.
3. Jonah preaching, people wailing
4. Jonah, head bowed, sitting under a huge plant.
5. On top print, "God watches over all."

Study the pictures in the Good News Bible. They are so full of expression.

✝✝✝✝✝

DAY 361. Micah 1-7.
God's Requirements
1:1-9; 2:12-13; 3:1-7;
4:1-8; 5:2-5, 7-9; 6:8;
7:7-9, 16-20

Micah 6:8. He has shown you, O man, what is good; and what does the Lord require of you but to do justly, to love mercy, and to walk humbly with your God?

Prayer: Help us to keep those goals, Lord.

COMMENTS: Micah was written between 751-693 B.C., telling primarily the nature, kingdom and work of the Messiah.

ACTIVITY: Photographers, it's your turn again. Take pictures of the children at the institutions you visit. They will be delighted, especially if you have a video camera or movie camera and projector. If none of these but a regular camera, give each a copy on your next visit, mounted on a card with a cheery word, such as God Loves Me, God Made Me Special, I Can Smile for God.

✝✝✝✝✝

DAY 362. Nahum 1-3
Turn to God.
1:1-9; 2:1-2; 3:1-4.

Nahum 1:7 The Lord is good, a stronghold in the day of trouble; and He knows those who trust in Him.

Prayer: Thanks that You are strong.

COMMENTS: This was 100 years after Jonah's message; they had forgotten God and were one of the most evil cities of the Gentile world. Ninevah had a wall 100' high, wide enough for chariots to be driven six abreast. Nahum proclaimed the destruction of this city, which seemed impregnable, and 100 years later the Tigris River overflowed, carrying away large sections of the wall, and the enemy conquered the city.

Habakkuk 1-3 Predictions 1:1-4, 12-17; 2:1-6, 14, 18-20; 3	Habakkuk 2:3. For the vision is yet for an appointed time; but at the end, it will speak, and it will not lie. Though it tarries wait for it; because it will surely come, it will not tarry.

COMMENTS: Habakkuk foretold the overthrow of the Babylonian kingdom. It was soon after Ninevah's fall, 606 B.C. The message is a dialogue between God and Habakkuk. There are many verses to memorize: "The just shall live by faith." (2:4) "The earth will be filled with the knowledge of the glory of the Lord, as the waters cover the sea." (2:14) "The Lord is in His holy temple. Let all the earth keep silence before Him." (2:20)

ACTIVITY: Make a movie of your family, or a series of photographs to show the children or people in the institutions you visit. They will love seeing your family at fun times, picnic, sports, your home, garden, prayer room, Bible fun time, praying, crafts, Bible and Teen Clubs, pets, funny shots.

††††††

DAY 363. Zephaniah 1-3 Return to Land 1:14-16; 2:1-3, 7, 12-15; 3:14-20	Zephaniah 3:20. "At that time I will bring you back, even at the time I gather you; for I will give you fame and praise among all the peoples of the earth, when I return your captives before your eyes," says the Lord.

Prayer: Thanks for Your promises.

COMMENTS: Zephaniah's prophecies concern all nations, like a summary.

Haggai 1-2 Rebuild the Temple	Haggai 1:7-8. Thus says the Lord of hosts: "Consider your ways! Go up to the mountains and bring wood and build the temple that I may take pleasure in it and be glorified," says the Lord.

COMMENTS: Haggai was written in 520 B.C. after the people had returned to Jerusalem. The temple still needed to be rebuilt. He encouraged them to keep at it. He also referred to the Millennial Temple.

ACTIVITY: Take pictures of the church, Sunday School, special activities, pastor and family, teachers, choir. Sell copies for a mission project.

††††††

DAY 364. Zechariah 1-14 The Branch 1:1-3, 7-16; 2:4, 8, 10-11; 3:8-9; 4:6-7; 5:1-3; 6:12-15; 7:8-9; 8:1-8, 16-23; 9:9-10, 16-17; 10:1, 6, 9; 11:12-13; 12:8-10; 13:1, 7-9; 14:1-4, 6-9	Zechariah 6:12-13 Then speak to him, saying, "Thus says the Lord of hosts, saying: 'Behold, the Man whose name is the Branch! From His place He shall branch out, and He shall build the temple of the Lord; Yes, He shall build the temple of the Lord. He shall bear the glory, and shall sit and rule on His throne, so He shall be a priest on His throne, and the counsel of peace shall be between them both.'"

Prayer: Praise the Branch!

Activity: 66 Books of the Bible - Can you find them?

	1	2	3	4	5	6	7	8	9	10	11	12	13	14	15	16	17	18	19	20	21	
1	G	P	H	I	L	I	P	P	I	A	N	S	D	D	A	N	I	E	L	E	G	1
2	X	E	1	2	K	I	N	G	S	I	1	S	E	M	A	J	2	X	X	P	A	2
3	1	K	N	E	H	E	M	I	A	H	2	X	U	A	H	P	C	J	X	H	L	3
4	2	U	L	E	V	I	T	I	C	U	S	P	T	R	E	R	H	O	S	E	A	4
5	C	L	J	O	S	H	U	A	H	H	A	X	E	K	B	O	R	E	U	S	T	5
6	O	O	B	A	D	I	A	H	A	A	M	M	R	T	R	V	O	L	D	I	I	6
7	R	X	H	A	I	A	S	I	C	G	U	S	O	X	E	E	N	J	O	A	A	7
8	I	N	U	M	B	E	R	S	I	G	E	J	N	S	W	R	I	U	X	N	N	8
9	N	X	I	H	C	A	L	A	M	A	L	X	O	A	S	B	C	D	E	S	S	9
10	T	J	O	B	H	E	Z	E	K	I	A	L	M	C	I	S	L	E	N	E	R	10
11	H	A	X	C	1	2	T	I	M	O	T	H	Y	T	X	S	E	N	O	G	E	11
12	I	R	E	X	X	E	C	C	L	E	S	I	A	S	T	E	S	H	M	D	H	12
13	A	Z	E	P	H	A	N	I	A	H	A	I	M	E	R	E	J	O	E	U	T	13
14	N	E	L	A	M	E	N	T	A	T	I	O	N	S	U	T	O	J	L	J	S	14
15	S	O	N	G	O	F	S	O	L	O	M	O	N	A	T	I	N	3	I	O	E	15
16	M	A	T	T	H	E	W	K	U	K	K	A	B	A	H	T	A	2	H	H	C	16
17	1	2	T	H	E	S	S	A	L	O	N	I	A	N	S	U	H	I	P	N	X	17
18	S	N	A	M	O	R	E	V	E	L	A	T	I	O	N	S	M	L	A	S	P	18

| | 1 | 2 | 3 | 4 | 5 | 6 | 7 | 8 | 9 | 10 | 11 | 12 | 13 | 14 | 15 | 16 | 17 | 18 | 19 | 20 | 21 |

COMMENTS: Zechariah, the prophet of the Messianic Kingdom, was written between 520 and 518 B.C. Zechariah worked with Haggai, inspiring the Jews to rebuild the temple. God gave him visions: (1) the care God shows for Israel; (2) the four horns as world empires; (3) the measuring rod predicting a larger Jerusalem; (4) the restoration of the priesthood.

ACTIVITY: Pre-schoolers: Make a paper chain with 66 links, each representing one of the books of the Bible. Use various colors for the divisions. Everyone else can work on the Books of the Bible word block. Can you say all of them?

†††††

DAY 365. Malachi 1-4
Tithe
1:1-5, 11; 2:14-16;
3:1, 6-12, 16-18; 4

Malachi 3:10 "Bring all the tithes into the storehouse, that there may be food in My house, and prove Me now in this," says the Lord of hosts, "if I will not open for you the windows of heaven and pour out for you such a blessing that there will not be room enough to receive it."

Prayer: We want to give more than our tenth, Lord,
for it is all Yours.

COMMENTS: Malachi berates Israel's sins, tells of God's judgment and mercy, announces the coming of John the Baptist; predicts another like Elijah yet to come before the second coming of the Lord.

The blessings that God promises us if we tithe our income are like the multiplying of the boy's loaves and fishes--endless. He stretches our budgets to meet extra offerings to His work. He says to prove Him! You can't outgive God! After all, He has given His all for us!

ACTIVITY: CONGRATULATIONS! You have completed reading the entire Bible. Keep up the habit, making special studies as you go through the Bible. Read it one time from Genesis to Revelation to get the entire sweep of God's dealings with man from creation to heaven.

It is amazing how many new things you learn with every reading. God has so much to tell us. Let's listen to Him attentively. His Spirit is always instructing us anew.

You deserve a treat as a family. What about that trip to the Holy Land? Keep planning; it may work out some time. I hope so. God bless you! It has been fun going through this Bible study with you. These are things the Lord has given to me, and I pass them on to you, trusting they will bless you and your projects for the Lord as they have blessed me.

ONE LAST PROJECT: Sew a United Nations skirt for each of the girls, then when you travel, wear the skirts in the marketplaces. Also remark when witnessing that Jesus loves all the children of the world! Cut four panels, to applique or draw with fabric pens, two children on each panel. See directions in Appendix.

Appendix 1

Answers to puzzles, quizzes, word blocks and information are given by the <u>Day</u> of the year as they appear in the book.

<u>Holiday suggestions</u> are made following the answers section.

<u>INDEX of activities</u> are listed at the end by type of activity.

DAY 1.   A.   <u>Life of Christ Picture Booklets.</u>

You will notice that the pictures are not in the chronological order as the events took place, as each Gospel may not have the complete story. So it will be necessary to wait until all the pictures are completed, then put them in the order as given on Appendix pages 2-4.

To assemble them in your notebook, arrange pages 1 and 2 back to back, pages 3 and 4 back to back, etc. Staple 1 and 2 together or bind them with tape. Check to see that the moving parts do not conflict; if so, put a patch of paper over the moving parts before binding the pages together.

B. <u>Life of Christ Scenes.</u>

For paper mache rumple paper together and tape down with masking tape to make hills. Mix a cup of flour in 2 or 3 cups of water. Dip strips of newspaper into the pail of water, slip off excess with two fingers and place the strip over the crumpled hill as smoothly as possible. Keep on until it is entirely covered. It will dry overnight. Use washable latex paper with some tan mixed with it. Pat in some sand for a beach, or dirt for ground, add pebbles, lichen, small branches of bushes for trees, etc.

For flour-salt-water clay, use 1 cup of flour, 1 cup of water and 1/2 cup of salt. Mix to the consistency of pliable clay, adding flour to make it firm.

For a firmer (but more expensive) clay, use:

    1 cup cornstarch
    2 cups baking soda
    1-1/4 cups cold water

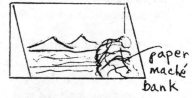

Mix cornstarch and baking soda in saucepan, add water, cook over medium heat stirring constantly until mixture reaches a consistency of mashed potatoes. Cool enough to knead like dough. Store in airtight container. Dry overnight after making or molding your objects.

<u>PRESENTATION:</u> When all scenes are completed, arrange to present them at a mall, library or fair, with leaflets explaining the scenes and giving Scripture references. A small card and number should be printed and placed in the corner of each scene corresponding to the leaflet. Our youth group of 15 children, ages 7-15, made 30 scenes in 1971 in Las Vegas, Nevada. They were presented in the large mall during Easter season, with thousands of leaflets given away. We also showed them at the church in a special program. The stories were recorded in the voice of the child who made the scene. They were shown one at a time on an elevated stage with curtain. While two children changed scenes, another worked the tape recorder, and a fourth turned on the light on the map showing where the scene took place. The rest sang in a choir outside. See photos and the map.

Appendix 2

FORTY SELECTED EVENTS I THE LIFE OF CHRIST

Title	*Map Location*	*Scripture References*
1. Angelic Annunciation to Mary	7 - Nazareth	Luke 1:26-38

(To Joseph: Mt. 1:18-25; Mary and Elizabeth, 12 Jerusalem, Lk. 1:39-56)

2. Birth of Jesus	15 Bethlehem	Luke 2:1-7
3. Angelic Annunciation to Shepherds	15 Bethlehem	Luke 2:8-20

(Visit to temple: Luke 2:21-38, 12 Jerusalem)

4. Visit of Wise Men	17 Far East	Matthew 2:1-12
	12 Jerusalem	
	15 Bethlehem	
	17 Far East	

(Flight to Egypt, 18 Egypt, Mt. 2:13-23)

5. Attends Passover, Age 12	12 Jerusalem	Luke 2:39-52
6. Baptism	9 Jordan River	Mt. 3:1-17; Mk. 1:4-11; Lk. 3:15-18, 21-22; John 1:14-34
7. Temptation	11 Mount	Mt. 4:1-11; Mk. 1:12-13; Luke 4:1-13
8. First Disciples	2 Sea of Galilee	Mt. 4:18-22; Mk. 1:16-20; Lk. 5:1-11; Jn. 1:35-51
	3 Capernaum	

(Other Disciples: Mt. 9:9; Mk. 3:13-19; Lk. 5:27-28; Mt. 10:2-4; Lk. 6:12-16)

9. First Miracle	6 Cana	John 2:1-11
10. Cleansing of Temple	12 Jerusalem	(I) John 2:13-22 (II) Mt. 21:12-14; Mk. 11:15-18; Luke 19:45-46
11. Jesus and Nicodemus	12 Jerusalem	John 3:1-21
12. Jesus and Woman at Well	10 Samaria	John 4:4-42
13. Healing of Paralyzed Man	3 Capernaum	Mt. 9:2-8; Mk. 2:1-12; Luke 5:17-26
14. Sermon on Mount	2 West of Sea of Galilee	Mt. 5:1-8:1; Lk. 6:20-49
15. Jesus Stills the Tempest	2 Galilee Sea Luke 8:22-25	Mt. 8:23-27; Mk. 4:35-41;
16. 5,000 Fed	4 So. of Bethsaida	Mt. 14:13-21; Mk. 6:30-44; Lk. 9:10-17; Jn. 6:1-14

(4,000 fed: Mt. 15:32-39; 16:6-12; Mk. 8:1-21)

Title	*Map Location*	*Scripture References*
17. Jesus Walks on Water	2 Galilee Sea	Mt. 14:22-34; Mk. 6:45-53; Jn. 6:15-21
18. The Transfiguration	1 Mt. Hermon	Mt. 17:1-13; Mk. 9:2-13; Luke 9:28-36
(Demoniac boy healed: Mt. 17:14-21; Mk. 9:14-29)		
19. Jesus Forgives	12 Jerusalem	John 8:2-11
20. Parable of Good Samaritan	12 Jerusalem, Story 10 Jericho	Luke 10:25-37
21. Parable of Lost Son	12 Jerusalem	Luke 15:11-32
22. Man Born Blind Healed	12 Jerusalem	John 9:1-41
(Other healings: Mt. 4:23, 24; Mt. 8:5-13; Mt. 9:18-34; Mk. 7:24-37; Mk. 8:22-26; Lk. 7:11-17; Lk. 13:10-13; Jn. 5:1-15)		
23. Jesus Visits Mary and Martha	14 Bethany	Luke 10:38-42
24. Raising of Lazarus	14 Bethany	John 11:1-44
25. Ten Lepers Healed	2 Sea of Galilee	Luke 17:11-19
26. Children Blessed	12 Jerusalem	Mt. 19:13015; Mk. 10:13-16; Luke 18:15-17
27. Zaccheus	10 Jericho	Luke 19:1-10
28. Triumphal Entry	12 Jerusalem	Mt. 21:1-11; Mk. 11:1-11; Luke 19:28-44
29. Passover Preparation	12 Jerusalem	Mt. 26:17-19; Mk. 14:12-16; Lk. 22:7-13; Jn. 13:1-20
(Judas: Mt. 26:14-16, 20-25; 27:3-10; Mk. 14:18-21; Lk. 22:21-23; Jn. 13:21-30)		
30. Lord's Supper and Farewell	12 Jerusalem	Mt. 26:26-30; Mk. 14:22-25; Luke 22:14-38; Discourses: Jn. Ch. 14-17
31. Agony in Gethsemane	12 Kidron Valley	Mt. 26:32-46; Mk. 14:26-42; Luke 22:39-46
32. Jesus Betrayed and Arrested	12 Jerusalem	Mt. 26:47-56; Mk. 14:43-52; Lk. 22:47-53; Jn. 18:1-12
33. Trials	12 Jerusalem	Jews: Mt. 26:57-27:1; Mk. 14:53-72; Lk. 22:54-71; Jn. 18:13-27 Pilate: Mt. 27:2, 11-14; Mk. 15:1-5; Lk. 23:1-5; Jn. 18:28-19:16 Herod: Luke 23:6-12 Pilate: Mt. 27:15-31; Mk. 15:6-20; Luke 23:13-25

Title	Map Location	Scripture References
34. Carrying Cross	12 Jerusalem	Mt. 27:32; Mk. 15:21-22; Luke 23:26-32
35. Crucifixion	12 Jerusalem Golgotha Hill	Mt. 27:33-56; Mk. 15:23-41; Lk. 23:33-49; Jn. 19:17-37

(Burial: Mt. 27:57-66; Mk. 15:42-47; Lk. 23:50-56; Jn. 19:38-42

36. Resurrection	12 Jerusalem To Women:	Mt. 28:1-8; Mk. 16:1-8; Lk. 24:1-11
	Jesus Appears:	Mt. 28:9-10; Lk. 24:9-11
	M. Magdalene:	Mk. 16:9-11; Jn. 20:1, 11-18
	Peter and John:	Lk. 24:10-12; Jn. 20:2-10
	Guards:	Mt. 28:11-15
37. Jesus Appears to Two Disciples	13 Emmaus	Mk. 16:12-13; Lk. 24:13-35
38. Jesus Appears to Disciples	12 Jerusalem	Mk. 16:14-18; Lk. 24:36-49; Jn. 20:19-31
39. Jesus in Galilee	2 Mountain 2 Sea of Galilee	Mt. 28:16-20 Jn. 21:1-25
40. Ascension	12 Mt. of Olives	Mk. 16:19-20; Lk. 24:50-53; Acts 1:1-11

Close-up of Joseph, Mary and Jesus in Bethlehem scene, Dec. 1987, Good News Club.

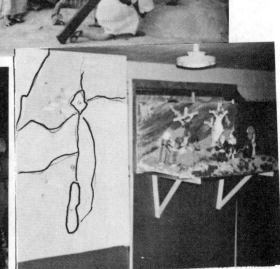

Las Vegas 1972 Church shown using map lights to locate each scene.

Appendix 5.

MAP OF THE HOLY LAND IN THE TIME OF CHRIST.

Use a 4X8 foot board. Draw the map on the board; paint the sections different colors. Drill holes for the cities and names of the seas, river, mountains. On the back also print the names of the locations, with corresponding numbers with those on the switchboard. ask someone in the church who has the expertise to put in the lights and switches so that one of the teens can operate it. As the story of Jesus is told, turn on the light for the place involved. For instance, the wise men came from the far East (17), traveled to Jerusalem (12), Bethlehem (15), then home (17).

1. Mt. Hermon, Mt. Transfiguration
2. Sea of Galilee
3. Capernaum
4. Bethsaida
5. Tiberias
6. Cana
7. Nazareth
8. Samaria
9. Jordan River
10. Jericho
11. Wilderness, Mt. Temptation
12. Jerusalem
13. Emmaus
14. Bethany
15. Bethlehem
16. Dead Sea
17. Far East
18. Egypt

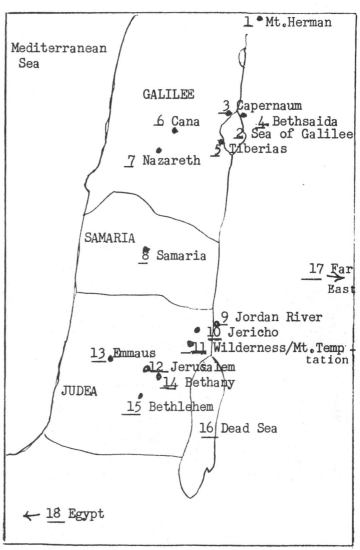

Appendix 6. 8' x 12' RELIEF MAP OF THE HOLY LAND WITH
EIGHTEEN SCENES OF THE LIFE OF CHRIST

Another way to show
the Life of Christ is
on a 8'X12' relief map.
Use 3 tables made of
4'X8' boards. Mark the
mountains, valleys, lakes,
river. With paper mache
fill in the landscape.

Locate the towns; drill
holes and insert a night
light for each scene.
Extend wires beneath
table to switch board.
Make tape recording of
the Life of Christ. As
the narration is told, the
lights go on at location
of the events.

This map was made by my Junior High Sunday School class, Rocky Mountain House,
and displayed in the Red Deer Mall, the local
church and library, 1983, Alberta, Canada.

Appendix 7.

DAY **4.** Word Block on 33 BIRDS, FOWL, INSECTS OF THE BIBLE. a = across;

b = backwards; u = up; d = down; su = slanting up; sd = slanting down.

	1	2	3	4	5	6	7	8	9	10	11	12	13
1	G	R	A	S	S	H	O	P	P	E	R	F	H
2	A	E	S	P	R	A	X	I	E	A	G	L	E
3	N	D	W	A	O	W	X	G	V	M	F	I	N
4	T	I	A	R	O	K	N	E	R	X	A	E	X
5	O	P	N	R	S	A	N	O	X	X	L	S	X
6	S	S	M	O	T	H	W	N	W	C	C	L	S
7	T	E	D	W	E	X	L	H	R	L	O	I	W
8	R	A	O	X	R	X	O	I	I	X	N	C	A
9	I	G	V	A	X	R	C	A	K	I	T	E	L
10	C	U	E	E	X	N	K	U	C	R	A	N	E
11	H	L	B	E	E	Q	S	T	O	R	K	X	O
12	F	L	T	T	B	A	T	H	E	R	O	N	W

raven 1-11sd Deuteronomy 14:14   owl 5-8sd Deut. 14:15   ant 2-1d Prov. 6:6

pigeon 1-8d Genesis 15:9   stork 11-7a Deut. 14:18   bee 11-3a Judges 14:8

dove 7-3d Genesis 15:9   heron 12-8a Deut. 14:18   hornet 7-8sd Ex. 23:28

sparrow 1-4d Matthew 10:29   bat 12-5a Deut. 14:18   flies 1-12d Ex. 8:21

ostrich 5-1d Deut. 14:15   crane 10-8a Isaiah 38:14   gnat 3-8sd Mt. 23:24

falcon 3-11d Deut. 14:13   quail 11-6su Numbers 11:32 moth 6-3a Mt. 6:19

eagle 2-9a Deut. 14:12   hen 1-13d Matthew 23:37   spider 6-2u Job 8:14

kite 9-9a Deut. 14:13   locust 7-7d Lev. 11:22   worm 6-7su Acts 12:23

seagull 6-2d Deut.14:15   cricket 6-10sd Lev.11:22   flea 12-1su 1 Sam. 24:14

hawk 1-6d Deut. 14:15   grasshopper 1-1a Lev. 11:22 lice 6-12d Ex. 8:16

swallow 6-13d Isaiah 38:14   rooster 2-5d Mt.26:34   swan 2-3d Lev.11:18 (KJ)

2.   Word block on 41 PLANTS AND TREES OF THE BIBLE

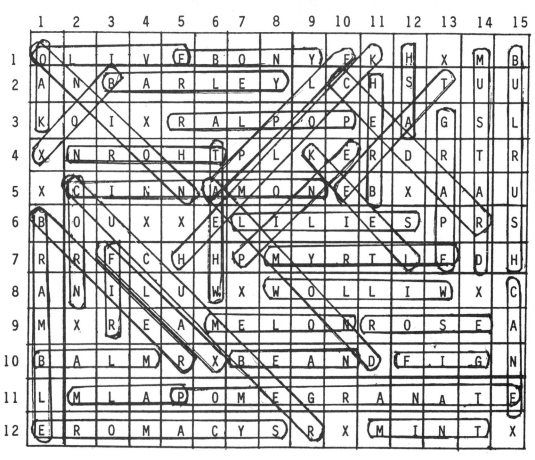

rose 9–11a Isa. 35:1

thorn 4–6b Mk. 15:17

almond 5–6sd Ex. 25:33

apple 5–6su Song.Sol. 2:3

oak 1–1d Isa. 44:14

balm 10–1a Ezek. 27:17

wheat 8–6u Ezek. 27:17

cedar 2–10sd Isa. 44:14

sycamore 12–8b Lk. 19:4

willow 8–13b Ps. 137:2

(in some versions)

fig 10–12a Lk. 21:29

pine 7–7su Isa. 44:14

ebony 1–5a Ezek. 27:15

fir 7–3d 2 Sam. 6:5

myrtle 7–8a Isa. 41:19

hemlock 7–5su Hosea 10:4

poplar 3–10b Hosea 4:13

flax 7–3sd Joshua 2:6

lilies 6–7a Lk. 12:27

barley 2–3a Ezek. 4:9

corn 5–2d Lk.6:1

bean 10–7a Ezek. 4:9

bramble 6–1d Judges 9:14

brier 6–1sd Ezek. 28:24

cinnamon 5–2a Ex. 30:23

olive 1–1a Judges 15:5

cucumber 5–2sd Num. 11:5

grape 3–13d Gen. 40:10

herb 2–11d Ex. 12:8

leek 7–12su Num. 11:5

melon 9–6a Num. 11:5

ash 3–12u Isa.44:14

onion 1–1sd Nm. 11:5

bulrush 1–15d Ex.2:3

mustard 1–14d Mt.13:31

palm 11–5b Ezek.41:18

pomegranate 11–5a
         1 Sam. 14:2

tare 2–13sd Mt.13:25

cane 8–15d Ex.30:23

mint 12–11a Lk.11:42

box 2–3sd Isa.41:19

Appendix 9.

16. Word Block on the Twelve Apostles

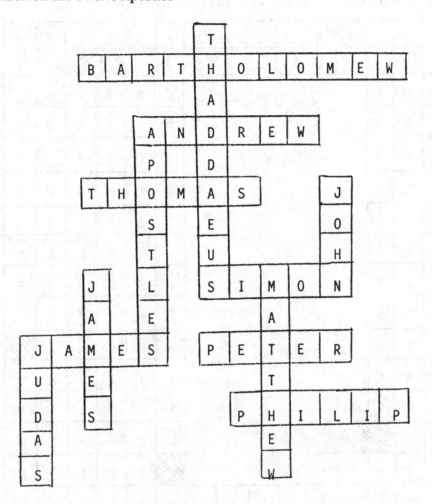

23. See Appendix page 10.

27. Keep Right; One Way

36. Scrambled words of Directions to Disciples:
    1. Preach the kingdom of God.   4. Take up cross daily.
    2. Heal the sick.   5. Follow Jesus.
    3. Deny self.   6. Don't look back.

39. Monument of organizations to help suffering:
    1. Hospitals   8. Travelers' Aid.   15. Bible translators
    2. Orphanages   9. Prison reforms   16. Blind institutions
    3. Eye donor   10. Army chaplains   17. Hospital chaplains
    4. Sanitariums   11. Halfway houses   18. Convalescent homes
    5. Blood donors   12. Prison chaplains   19. Veterans' hospitals
    6. City missions   13. Deaf institutions   20. Alcoholics anonymous
    7. Coffee houses   14. Homes for elderly   21. Rehabilitation centers

Appendix 10.

23. Word Block on the Parables and Sayings of Jesus

```
1S  O  2W  E  R  ██  3M  U  S  T  A  4R  5D  S  E  E  D
T   6G  I  7U  8T  W  O  S  O  N  S   I   E  ██ ██ ██  9L
E   R  S  N  10K              C   B  11B 12F  ██  O
W   E  E  J  I               H  13T  A   R   F   S
A   A  F  U  N               F   O   R   I  ██   T
R   T  O  S  G               O   R   R   E  14G   M
D   S  O  T  D               O   S   E   N   O    O
15W  U  L  S  O               L  16T   N   D   O    N
I   P  I  E  M               L   E   F   A   D    E
D   P  S  R  S               E   N   I   T   S    Y
O   E  H  V  E               A   G   G   M   A   ██
W   R  B  A  E               V   I   T   I   M  18V
19P  O  U  N  D  S            E   R   R   D   A    I
██ ██  I  T ██ ██            N   L   E   N   R    N
20T  A  L  E  N  T  S        ██  S   E   I   I    E
21H  I  D  D  E  N  T  R  E  A  S   U   R   E  G  T  Y
██22W  E  D  D  I  N  G  G  U  E  S   T   S   H  A  A
██23P  R  O  D  I  G  A  L  S  O  N  ██  ██   T  N  R
24L  O  S  T  S  H  E  E  25P  S  H  E   P   H   E  R  D
26R  I  C  H  M  A  N  A  N  D  L  A   Z   A   R  U  S
27P  H  A  R  I  S  E  E  /  P  U  B   L   I   C  A  N
```

Across 1 sower, 3 mustard seed, 8 two sons, 13 tares, 19 pounds, 20 talents,
21 hidden treasure, 22 wedding guests, 23 prodigal son, 24 lost sheep,
25 shepherd, 26 rich man and Lazarus, 27 Pharisee/publican
Down 1 steward, 2 wise, foolish builders, 4 rich fool, 5 debtors, 6 great
supper, 7 unjust servant, 9 lost money, 10 kingdom seed, 11 barren fig tree,
12 friend at midnight, 14 good Samaritan, 15 widow, 16 ten girls, 17 leaven,
18 vineyard

Appendix 11.

41. 26 Geographical Locations in the Time of Jesus

```
                    B               B
                    E         J  E  R  U  S  A  L  E  M
                    T            T                    G
                    H            H           G        Y
            S       A      G  A  L  I  L  E  E        P
         N  A  Z  A  R  E  T  H     E        T        T
            M       A            E           H     S
         C  A  N  A               M     D  E  A  D  S  E  A
            R                           M        I
            I        J                  A        O
         C  A  P  E  R  N  A  U  M      N        N
                     R           O      E  P  H  R  A  I  M
                     I           U
            G        C        T  N               J  U  D  E  A
         B  E  T  H  A  N  Y  Y  T                        M
            R        O        R  O                        M
            G                 E  F     J  O  R  D  A  N    A
            E                    O           N       A    U
            S  Y  C  H  A  R     L     T  I  B  E  R  I  U  S
            A                    I                   N
                                 V
                                 E
                        B  E  T  H  S  A  I  D  A
```

Appendix 12.

40. Answers to quiz on geographical places:
    1. Bethlehem
    2. Jerusalem
    3. Egypt
    4. Nazareth
    5. Jordan
    6. Sea of Galilee
    7. Dead Sea
    8. Judea
    9. Samaria
    10. Bethabara
    11. Cana
    12. Capernaum
    13. Tiberius
    14. Gergesa
    15. Bethany
    16. Sychar
    17. Gethsemane
    18. Jericho
    19. Nain
    20. Tyre and Sidon
    21. Bethsaida
    22. Emmaus
    23. Ephraim
    24. Mount of Olives

41. see Appendix 11.

53, 54. Answers to Quiz on the Names of Jesus:
    1. Jesus Christ our Lord
    2. Seed
    3. Man of Sorrows
    4. Redeemer
    5. Sun
    6. Prophet
    7. Emmanuel
    8. God with us
    9. Savior
    10. Christ the Lord.
    11. King of the Jews
    12. Master
    13. Man
    14. Physician
    15. Word
    16. Light
    17. Messiah
    18. Rabbi
    19. Teacher
    20. Bread
    21. I Am
    22. Door
    23. Shepherd
    24. Resurrection
    25. Way
    26. Truth
    27. Life
    28. Vine
    29. Friend
    30. Lord
    31. Son of god
    32. Prince
    33. Rock
    34. Unspeakable Gift
    35. head
    36. Heir
    37. First
    38. Priest
    39. Living Stone
    40. Rose of Sharon
    41. Lily of the Valley
    42. Lion
    43. Lamb
    44. Faithful and True
    45. Bright and Morning Star

55. Answers to Word Block of NAMES OF JESUS: (a-across; b-back; d-down; u-up; su-slanting up; sd-slanting down; first number is row down, second, across.)

1. 3-1a	2. 3-3d	3. 5-13d	4. 15-10b	5. 7-11a	6. 14-8b
7. 13-2a	8. 18-13a	9. 3-5d	10. 17-1a	11. 4-1d	12. 10-15u
13. 6-2u	14. 12-2a	15. 17-16b	16. 15-17a	17. 11-7b	18. 16-21b
19. 10-1a	20. 2-19d	21. 12-8u	22. 5-10sd	23. 16-1a	24. 18-1a
25. 17-16su	26. 17-17a	27. 12-15d	28. 13-12d	29. 14-21b	30. 4-9b
31. 2-20d	32. 12-14sd	33. 13-16a	34. 1-21d	35. 6-16a	36. 11-11d
37. 9-1a	38. 12-12sd	39. 4-9a	40. 3-17d	41. 2-9d	42. 12-15sd
43. 5-11a	45. 2-2a	45. 1-1a			

	1	2	3	4	5	6	7	8	9	10	11	12	13	14	15	16	17	18	19	20	21
1	B	R	I	G	H	T	A	N	D	M	O	R	N	I	N	G	S	T	A	R	U
2	X	F	A	I	T	H	F	U	L	A	N	D	T	R	U	E	X	X	B	S	N
3	J	E	S	U	S	C	H	R	I	S	T	O	U	R	L	O	R	D	R	O	S
4	K	N	E		A	D	R	O	L	I	V	I	N	G	S	T	O	N	E	N	P
5	I	A	E		V			Y	D	L	A	M	B	R	X	S	X	A	O	E	
6	N	M	D		I		X	X	O		A	X	E	H	E	A	D	F	A		
7	G		X		O			O	F	S	U	N	T	O	X	X	G	K			
8	O				R		R	X	T		O		S	A	F		X	A			
9	F	I	R	S	T				H	X	X	F	S	M	S	X	D	B			
10	T	E	A	C	H	E	R	M	E		S	M	H	L							
11	H	A	I	S	S	E	M	A	V	X	H	X	O	A	X	X	E	G			
12	E	P	H	Y	S	I	C	I	A	N	E	P	R	P	L	X	R	G			
13	J	E	M	M	A	N	U	E	L	X	I	V	R	I	I	R	O	C	K	X	I
14	E	T	E	H	P	O	R	P	L	X	R	I	O	I	F	D	N	E	I	R	F
15	W	X	R	E	M	E	E	D	E	R	N	N	W	Y	E	X	L	I	G	H	T
16	S	H	E	P	H	E	R	D	Y	C	X	E	S	X	A	S	I	B	B	A	R
17	C	H	R	I	S	T	T	H	E	L	O	R	D	R	O	W	T	R	U	T	H
18	R	E	S	U	R	R	E	C	T	I	O	N	G	O	D	W	I	T	H	U	S

55. Word Block on the Names or Titles of Jesus

Appendix 14.

60. WORD PUZZLE ON THE TEACHINGS OF JESUS:

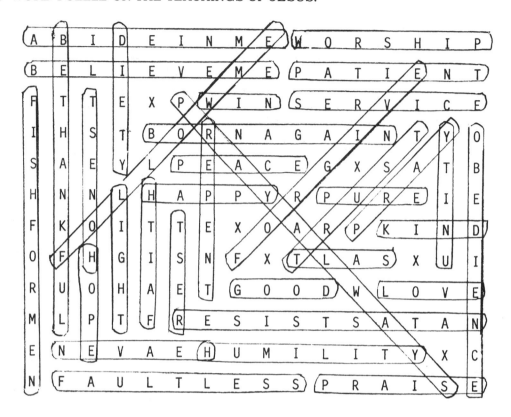

Horizontal:			Vertical:		Diagonal:
abide in Me	peace	love	fish for men	faith	follow Me
worship	happy	resist Satan	be thankful	rest	forgive
believe Me	pure	heaven	honest	repent	trust
patient	kind	faultless	hope	unity	pray
win	salt	praise	deity	obedience	pray always
service	good	humility	light		
born again					

71, 72. ANSWERS TO QUIZ ON THE HOLY SPIRIT.

1. Spirit of the Father
   Son
   Spirit of Holiness

2. a. Spirit of God
   b. inspired Scripture
Adoption
   c. Spirit of Prophecy
   d. Jesus
   e. dove
   f. raised Jesus

3. a. abide
   b. Truth
   c. teach
   d. testify
   e. convict
   f. guide

   g. brings to
      memory
   h. comfort
   i. walk
   j. fruit
   k. Sword
   l. empower
   m. gives gifts
   n. water

4. wind
   fire
   speak
   baptized
   fill

5. by faith
   a. rebirth
   b. indwell
   c. sanctifies
   d. spirit
   e. help
   f. pray

6. a. seal
   b. life
   c. witness
   d. searches
   e. strive
   f. Spirit of

73.   Word block on the Holy Spirit

	1	2	3	4	5	6	7	8	9	10	11	12	13	14	15	16	17	18	19	20	21
1	S	P	I	R	I	T	O	F	G	O	D	G	I	V	E	S	G	I	F	T	S
2	P				S	P	I	R	I	T	O	F	T	H	E	F	A	T	H	E	R
3	I	X	X	E				N	T	E	S	T	I	F	Y	B	E	F	S	A
4	R			A		X		D	E	M	P	O	W	E	R	A	I	E	I
5	I	X	X	R				W	P				B	X	I	C	L	A	S
6	T			C		X	I	E	R	X	Y	N	H	L	L	E
7	O	A	X	W	H	N	V	L	A	F	G	D
8	F	B	F	A	E	D	O	E	L	X	A	S	S	X	J
9	H	I	I	T	S	D	Z	S	O	N	G	X	I	T	P	X	E
10	O	D	R	E	B	I	R	T	H	H	T	U	R	T	O	E	E	S
11	L	E	E	R	T	T	X	W	I	T	N	E	S	S	H	X	M	A	U
12	I	N	S	P	I	R	E	D	S	C	R	I	P	T	U	R	E	K	X	I	S
13	N	X	A	U	H	F	E	X	T	C	I	V	N	O	C	O	M	F	O	R	T
14	E	B	R	E	I	S	A	N	C	T	I	F	I	E	S	W	O	R	D	T	X
15	S	F	L	L	Y	C	E	H	P	O	R	P	F	O	T	I	R	I	P	S	X
16	S	P	I	R	I	T	O	F	A	D	O	P	T	I	O	N	Y	W	A	L	K

2-5a Spirit of the Father	2-18d teach	2-9d indwell	16-1a spirit
9-8a Son	3-10a testify	14-6a sanctifies	7-4d water
1-1d Spirit of Holiness	13-15b convict	1-12a gives gifts	3-20d seal
1-1a Spirit of God	9-11sd guide	13-5sd help	15-4su life
12-1a inspired scripture	5-9sd wind	5-11d pray	11-8a witness
15-20b Spirit of Prophecy	8-3d fire	8-21d Jesus	2-5d searches
3-17d brings to memory	8-18d speak	13-15a comfort	15-20u strive
9-6su dove	14-2su baptize	16-18a walk	7-2d abide
2-21d raised Jesus	3-19d fill	15-2su fruit	14-15a Sword
16-1a Spirit of Adoption	5-15d by faith	10-15b truth	10-3a rebirth
4-11a empower			

78. EVENTS TOOK PLACE AT THE FOLLOWING LOCATIONS:

    1. Mount of Olives (1:12)

    2. Beautiful Gate to the Temple (3:1, 2)

    3. Damascus (9:3)

    4. Caesarea (10:24)

    5. Antioch (11:26)

    6. Macedonia (16:9)

    7. Philippi (16:12, 25-26)

    8. Athens (17:22-23)

    9. Ephesus (19:23-41)

    10. Jerusalem (20:22)

79. True and False Quiz:

    1. F - Luke accompanied Paul, not Peter.

    2. T

    3. F - The Holy Spirit came with a mighty wind and tongues of fire, not quietly.

    4. T

    5. F - Peter, not Paul, preached that day.

    6. F - Ananias and Sapphira cheated on land sale money which they promised to give to God; Priscilla and Aquila were the tentmakers.

    7. T.

    8. F - 3 Missionary journeys; the 4th trip was as a prisoner to Rome, starting from Jerusalem.

    9. T.

    10. F - God called him to preach to the Gentiles. However, he preached to the Jews also wherever he went.

88.   1. a and b are equal length.   2. Jars are equal height.

       3. 2nd and 5th lines are equal length.   4. FAITH.

112. Word block on   C H R I S T   I N   M E

```
       1  2  3  4  5  6  7  8  9 10 11 12 13 14 15 16 17 18 19 20 21 22 23 24 25 26
 1     C  H  R  I  S  T  I  N  Y  O  U  T  H  E  H  O  P  E  O  F  G  L  O  R  Y  I
 2     H  H  C  N  U  A  N  F  A  I  T  H  I  N  H  I  M  I  I  N  T  H  E  M  E
 3     R  E  O  N  P  C  H  I  F  C  H  R  I  S  T  I  S  I  N  Y  O  U  X  X  G  A
 4     I  C  N  P  P  C  H  I  X  C  R  E  A  T  E  D  I  N  C  H  R  I  S  T  X  A
 5     S  H  Q  E  P  E  M  I  N  I  S  T  E  R  X  T  H  R  O  U  G  H  H  I  M
 6     T  O  U  L  E  W  M  Y  W  O  R  D  S  A  B  I  D  E  I  N  Y  O  U  I
 7     L  S  E  I  C  T  E  C  O  M  P  L  E  T  E  I  N  T  H  E  S  P  I  R  I  T
 8     I  E  R  A  A  E  H  A  B  I  D  E  I  N  M  E  A  N  D  I  I  N  Y  O  U
 9     V  U  O  T  T  D  A  L  I  V  E  D  R  O  L  E  H  T  N  I  T  H  G  I  L
10     E  S  R  R  I  R  V  X  X  I  N  T  H  E  F  E  A  R  O  F  G  O  D  N  X  C
11     S  I  T  T  O  G  E  T  H  E  R  I  N  T  H  E  H  E  A  V  E  N  L  Y  X  E
12     I  N  S  O  N  D  R  O  W  S  G  N  I  H  T  L  L  A  N  I  P  U  W  O  R  G
13     N  H  D  B  E  R  E  N  E  W  E  D  I  N  T  H  E  S  P  I  R  I  T  U  O  Y
14     M  I  N  D  E  A  D  R  O  L  E  H  T  N  I  G  N  O  R  T  S  E  B  A  O  J
15     E  M  A  N  O  B  E  Y  Y  O  U  R  P  A  R  E  N  T  S  L  I  V  E  L  E  Y
16     H  O  L  Y  T  E  M  P  L  E  I  N  T  H  E  L  O  R  D  W  A  L  K  L  M
17     X  T  O  T  H  E  P  O  W  E  R  T  H  A  T  W  O  R  K  S  I  N  U  S  D  T
18     H  A  B  I  T  A  T  I  O  N  O  F  G  O  D  I  N  T  H  E  S  P  I  R  I  T
19     C  R  E  A  T  E  I  N  H  I  M  S  E  L  F  O  N  E  N  E  W  M  A  N  N  A
20     X  X  I  N  W  H  O  M  W  E  H  A  V  E  B  O  L  D  N  E  S  S  R  I  E  H
21     N  A  M  R  E  N  N  I  E  H  T  N  I  T  I  R  I  P  S  S  I  H  U  R  H  T
22     X  I  N  C  H  R  I  S  T  H  E  I  S  A  N  E  W  C  R  E  A  T  I  O  N  X
23     T  H  E  U  P  W  A  R  D  C  A  L  L  O  F  G  O  D  I  N  C  H  R  I  S  T
```

Answers: a - across, b - back, u - up, d - down, su - slant up

1. 1-1a	9. 19-1a	17. 9-24d	25. 5-7a	33. 2-18a	41. 12-3a
2. 1-1d	10. 5-16a	18. 12-26b	26. 1-5d	34. 14-1a	42. 13-3su
3. 2-2d	11. 16-1a	19. 13-4a	27. 7-16a	35. 16-20a	43. 6-25u
4. 2-6d	12. 18-1a	20. 9-25b	28. 3-8a	36. 12-25d	44. 20-26b
5. 1-7d	13. 20-3a	21. 10-10a	29. 2-3d	37. 7-8a	45. 22-2a
6. 1-26d	14. 2-8a	22. 15-5a	30. 21-26u	38. 12-9b	46. 23-1a
7. 11-1a	15. 21-26b	23. 14-23b	31. 8-8a	39. 9-7a	47. 15-4b
8. 4-9a	16. 17-2a	24. 1-4d	32. 6-8a	40. 15-20a	48. 14-4a
					49. 17-25d

Appendix 18.

126.   Word block on: <u>VICTORY IN JESUS!</u>

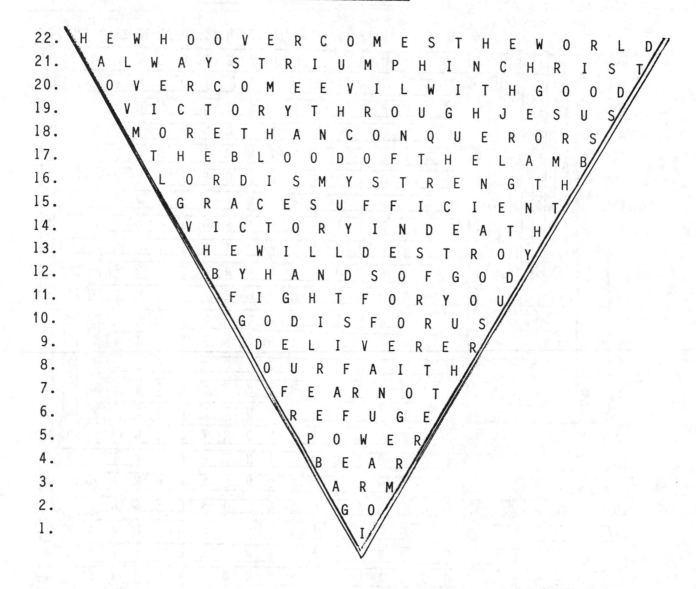

```
22.  H E W H O O V E R C O M E S T H E W O R L D
21.  A L W A Y S T R I U M P H I N C H R I S T
20.  O V E R C O M E E V I L W I T H G O O D
19.    V I C T O R Y T H R O U G H J E S U S
18.    M O R E T H A N C O N Q U E R O R S
17.      T H E B L O O D O F T H E L A M B
16.        L O R D I S M Y S T R E N G T H
15.        G R A C E S U F F I C I E N T
14.          V I C T O R Y I N D E A T H
13.          H E W I L L D E S T R O Y
12.          B Y H A N D S O F G O D
11.            F I G H T F O R Y O U
10.            G O D I S F O R U S
 9.            D E L I V E R E R
 8.            O U R F A I T H
 7.              F E A R N O T
 6.              R E F U G E
 5.              P O W E R
 4.              B E A R
 3.                A R M
 2.                G O
 1.                  I
```

1. Exodus 3:20	9. 2 Samuel 22:2	17. Rev. 12:11
2. Matthew 28:19	10. Romans 8:31	18. Rom. 8:37
3. Isaiah 51:5	11. Deuteronomy 1:30	19. 1 Cor. 15:57
4. Matthew 4:6	12. Genesis 49:24	20. Rom. 12:21
5. Matthew 9:6	13. Deuteronomy 9:3	21. 2 Cor. 2:14
6. Deuteronomy 33:27	14. 1 Corinthians 15:54	22. 1 Jn.5:5
7. Isaiah 41:13	15. 2 Corinthians 12:9	
8. 1 John 5:4	16. Exodus 15:2	

133, 134. ANSWERS TO QUIZ ON 56 PEOPLE OF GREAT FAITH:

1. Mary	20. Moses	39. Martha
2. Esther	21. Joshua	40. Mark
3. Mordecai	22. Rahab	41. boy (with lunch)
4. Simeon	23. Gideon	42. John
5. Aaron	24. Caleb	43. Peter
6. Ruth	25. woman (healed)	44. Paul
7. Isaiah	26. Barak	45. Silas
8. Jeremiah	27. Samson	46. Stephen
9. Ezekiel	28. David	47. jailor
10. Job	29. Samuel	48. Philip
11. Servant (of Isaac)	30. Elijah	49. Jonathan
12. Jairus	31. Elisha	50. Manoah's wife
13. Abel	32. Daniel	51. Zarephath widow
14. Noah	33. Ezra	52. Shadrach
15. Abraham	34. Nehemiah	53. Meshach
16. Isaac	35. Hannah	54. Abednego
17. Jacob	36. Hezekiah	55. Cornelius
18. Sarah	37. Barnabas	56. Centurion
19. Joseph	38. James	

135. ANSWERS TO WORD BLOCK ON FAITH:

6-10d Mary	11-15-su Abraham	1-2a Samuel	14-10sd Peter
8-2u Esther	7-5sd Isaac	15-20d Elijah	4-16d Paul
2-10a Mordecai	3-17d Jacob	10-5a Elisha	12-18d Silas
2-18d Simeon	11-1a Sarah	16-1a Daniel	21-21b Stephen
6-4d Aaron	6-19u Joseph	18-9a Ezra	5-12sd jailor
4-9d Ruth	1-4sd Moses	1-12a Nehemiah	4-10a Philip
3-10a Isaiah	2-4a Joshua	11-5a Hannah	14-15d Jonathan
15-12u Jeremiah	8-17a Rahab	12-1a Hezekiah	5-10sd Manoah's wife
12-16d Ezekiel	21-10su Gideon	5-11sd Barnabas	20-1a Zarephath widow
17-1a Job	1-10sd Caleb	3-21d James	1-1d Shadrach
11-19su servant	10-20d woman	20-16a Martha	9-1d Meshach
12-9d Jairus	5-20d Barak	8-11sd Mark	13-1a Abednego
13-13d Abel	11-16a Samson	8-3d boy	19-1a Cornelius
7-12b Noah	4-5d David	1-20d John	9-21d Centurion

Appendix 20.

13.5. Word block on <u>56</u> <u>PEOPLE OF GREAT FAITH IN THE BIBLE</u>

	1	2	3	4	5	6	7	8	9	10	11	12	13	14	15	16	17	18	19	20	21
1	S	S	A	M	U	E	L	X	X	C	X	N	E	H	E	M	I	A	H	J	X
2	H	X	X	J	O	S	H	U	A	M	O	R	D	E	C	A	I	S	P	O	X
3	A	R					S	X	L	C	I	S	A	I	A	H	X	J	I	E	H	J
4	D	E		X	D	X	E	A	R	X	P	H	I	L	I	P	P	A	M	S	N	A
5	R	H		A	B	A	S	U	M	B	J	T	X	X	A	C	E	O	B	M
6	A	T	A	V	S	X	T	M	A	A	N	X	U	O	O	J	A	E
7	C	S	A	I	H	A	O	N	R	I	A	L	B	N	H	R	S
8	H	E	B	R	D	X	R	M	H	O	N	L	V	R	A	H	A	B
9	M	X	O	O	Y	A	X	A	A	O	R	X	X	K	C
10	E	X	Y	N	E	L	I	S	H	A	I	R	X	H	B	R	E	X	W	E
11	S	A	R	A	H	A	N	N	A	H	M	X	K	A	S	A	M	S	O	N
12	H	E	Z	E	K	I	A	H	J	X	E	E	W	S	X	M	T
13	A	B	E	D	N	E	G	O	A	X	R	A	X	Z	X	I	X	A	U
14	C	W	I	T	H	O	U	T	I	P	X	E	B	J	E	X	L	F	N	R
15	H	X	F	A	I	T	H	X	R	X	E	J	E	O	K	A	E	I	O
16	D	A	N	I	E	L	I	T	U	I	S	T	L	N	I	S	L	O
17	J	O	B	I	M	P	O	S	S	I	B	L	E	O	A	E	I	N
18	T	O	X	P	L	E	A	S	E	Z	R	A	E	R	T	L	X	J	X
19	C	O	R	N	E	L	I	U	S	G	O	D	X	X	H	X	X	A	X
20	Z	A	R	E	P	H	A	T	H	W	I	D	O	W	A	M	A	R	T	H	A
21	X	X	H	E	B	R	E	W	S	G	11	:	6	N	E	H	P	E	T	S

148. Answers to Quiz on Love:
    1. Lazarus, Mary and Martha
    2. Love God and neighbor. Matthew 22:37-40.
    3. John 3:16.
    4. 1 Corinthians 13.
    5. a. love - fear
       b. love - commandments
       c. love - law
       d. giver
       e. those who love Him
    6. a. money
       b. world - world
    7. Peter
    8. Forgiven
    9. Jacob/Rachel, Isaac/Rebeccah, Boaz/Ruth.
   10. Jonathan/David, Ruth/Naomi, Paul/Luke.
   11. John 17:21: "that they all may be one in Me, as I am one in the Father."
   12. John 15:13: "to lay down his life for his friends."
   13. John
   14. They left their first love.

160. Answers to Quiz on Angels:
    1. Messengers (Hebrews 1:7)
    2. Jesus (Luke 1:31)
    3. Hagar (Genesis 16:7-12)
    4. host (Luke 2:13)
    5. chief (Jude 9)
    6. fight (2 Kings 19:35)
    7. Peter (Acts 12:6-11)
    8. holy (Matthew 25:31)
    9. fire (Exodus 3:2)
   10. eyes (2 Kings 6:14-17)
   11. Lot (Genesis 19:1-17)
   12. Abraham (Genesis 22:11-18)
   13. Jacob (Genesis 28:12)
   14. David (1 Chronicles 21:15-16)
   15. Daniel (Daniel 6:22)
   16. Satan (Revelation)
   17. Gideon (Judges 6:11-22)
   18. Philip (Acts 8:26-27)
   19. Herod (Acts 12:23)
   20. Balaam's (Numbers 22:22-35)
   21. ascension (Acts 1:10-11)
   22. never die (Luke 20:36)
   23. don't marry (Mark 12:25)
   24. praise (Psalm 148:2)
   25. rejoice (Luke 15:10)
   26. wicked (Matthew 13:49-50)
   27. Mary (Luke 1:26-38)
   28. Savior (John 4:42)
   29. Sons of God (Job 1:6 KJ)
   30. Gabriel (Luke 1:26)
   31. Zacharias (Luke 1:11-20)
   32. John (Luke 1:13)
   33. Elijah (1 Kings 19:5-7)
   34. Shepherds in field (Luke 2:8-15)
   35. keep (Psalm 91:11-12)
   36. tomb (Matthew 28:1-7)
   37. Paul (Acts 27:23)
   38. Manoah (Judges 13:6-24)
   39. Cornelius (Acts 10:3-7)
   40. Joseph (Matthew 1:20)

161. Word Block on Angels:

Across

1. messenger
6. Jesus
10. Hagar
11. hosts
15. chief
16. fight
17. Peter
19. holy
20. fire
22. eyes
23. Lot
24. Abraham
25. Jacob
26. David
27. Daniel
28. Satan
29. Gideon
30. Philip
31. Herod
32. Balaam
33. ascension
34. never die
35. don't marry
36. praise
37. rejoice
38. wicked

Down

1. Mary
2. Savior
3. sons
4. Gabriel
5. Zacharias
6. John
7. Elijah
8. shepherds
9. keep
12. tomb
13. Paul
14. Manoah
18. Cornelius
21. Joseph

Appendix 22

161. WORD BLOCK ON ANGELS

¹M	E	²S	³S	E	N	⁴G	E	R	S	⁵Z	⁶J	⁷E	⁸S	U	S			
A		A	O	⁹K	¹⁰H	A	G	A	R	A	O	L	¹¹H	O	S	T	S	
R	¹²T	V	N	E		B		¹³P	¹⁴M	¹⁵C	H	I	E	¹⁶F	I	G	H	T
Y	O	I	S	E		R		A	A	H	N	J	¹⁷P	E	T	E	R	¹⁸C
	M	O	O	P		I		U	N	A		A	H	¹⁹H	O	L	Y	O
	B	R	²⁰F	I	R	E	²¹J	L	O	R		H	²²E	Y	E	S		R
			G			²³L	O	T	A	I	²⁴A	B	R	A	H	A	M	N
²⁵J	A	C	O	B			S		H	A			²⁶D	A	V	I	D	E
			²⁷D	A	N	I	E	L		S			²⁸S	A	T	A	N	L
²⁹G	I	D	E	O	N		³⁰P	H	I	L	I	P	³¹H	E	R	o	d	i
³²B	A	L	A	A	M		H		³³A	S	C	E	N	S	I	O	N	U
³⁴N	E	V	E	R	D	I	E		³⁵D	O	N	T	M	A	R	R	Y	S
³⁶P	R	A	I	S	E	³⁷R	E	J	O	I	C	E	³⁸W	I	C	K	E	D

170. ANSWERS TO QUIZ ON CHART OF ANCESTORS OF JESUS:

1. Methuselah, 969
2. 1656
3. flood
4. 600
5. 930
6. 8
7. Seth, Enosh, Kenan, Mahalalel, Jared, Enoch, Methuselah, Lamech
8. 243 (930 - 687 when Methuselah was born = 243)
9. 56 (930 - 874 = 56)
10. 950
11. 10
12. Shem, Arphaxas, Shelah, Eber, Peleg, Reu, Serug, Nabor, Terah, Abraham
13. 1656
14. 2023
15. After the flood.

173. TRUE OR FALSE QUIZ ON ANGELS:

1. False - Genesis 19:1, 10.
2. True - Acts 5:19
3. True - Luke 1:28, 24:6
4. False - Psalm 148:2-5; Colossians 1:16
5. False - Luke 20:34-36; 1 Corinthians 6:3; Hebrews 1:14
6. True - Michael, Jude 9; Gabriel, Luke 1:26
7. False - 2 Peter 2:4; Jude 6
8. True - Revelation 5:11; Matthew 18:10; Hebrews 1:6
9. True - Genesis 19:11; Psalm 91:11; 34:7; Daniel 3:28; 6:22
10. True - Matthew 4:11; Luke 22:43

175. FANTASTIC CANDY VILLAGE.

For a Christmas display in a mall or other public place, start in November with two-hour sessions on a Saturday afteroon with your Bible Club. Contact the mall manager for permission to display. Decide on the organization you wish to submit donations to, request large pictures to attach to the skirt of the display. Later make a poster, "We have so much--let's give to the starving, homeless children." Prepare a solid, lock-proof donation box chained to the leg of the display table. For our display in the large mall in New York, we used a barrel, neatly covered, slit in top, chained to post, and sign, "Can you spare 50 cents for a starving child?" This simple request brought more response than any other display--but carry out the change in large strong boxes--it's heavy!

1. Have the children bring shoe boxes and other size boxes to make the buildings. See directions. Cut and shape them together, taping with masking tape. The frosting will cover the tape. You may have a special building in your community you wish to make, or make buildings in your small town. But generally, the most attractive is the Chritmas card picture with old-fashioned church, castle, little red schoolhouse, candy shop, train and train station, carolers around the town tree, Swiss chalet, barn with silo, ranch house, horse and sleigh. ice skaters on the stream near a low bridge, outside nativity scene by the church, and all the other heart-warmig touches that mean American Christmas love.

2. Use an old door, firm but not too heavy, for the base. Two card tables should hold it. Keep in mind that all this has to be moved through doorways and into a station wagon or van.

3. Plan your layout. We liked the castle on a hill on the left and a church on a hill on the right, with train track coming "round the mountain" on extreme right. town center was left of front center with stores around it; school to the left of plaza with children making snowman, seesawing (cookie people); carolers singing near the big cookie town tree; the skating area to the left below the castle and farm area, with a bridge across it.

4. Decide where the lighting box will be (behind the church or castle with opening at back for light cords to spread out to be used in buildings). Use separate night lightys in each building (for fire safety); or simply use Christmas tree miniature lights outside the landscape, just going from building to building, with small opening for the light in back of each building. This means some lights will be in the open, but this adds to the Christmasy effect, especially if some of the lights blink. Be sure to have lights in the castle, church and homes.

5. Make paper mache hills and valleys, leaving flat areas for the buildings to be added later. Smooth down with strips of newspaper dipped in flour-water. When dry, paint it with white latex paint, the ice skating area with a tint of blue. Spray with imitation sow. Be sure your light holes are left open with the night lights projecting firmly in place.

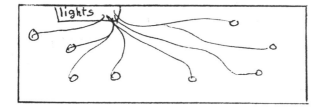
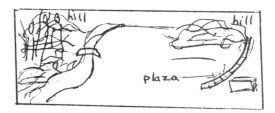

6. Make <u>cookie</u> patterns using pictures from coloring books, or design your own or use patterns shown in this book. Bake cookies ahead of decorating day. Teens will enjoy doing these together at one teen's home. Use this recipe or one you are familiar with:

1 cup butter or margarine.	1 cup sugar	2 egg yolks
1 teaspoon vanilla	2-1/2 cups flour	1/2 cups salt

Cream butter and sugar; add eggs and vanilla; beat well; add flour, salt. Roll. With cardboard patterns cut out figures; place on cookie sheet; bake 10 minutes at 400 degrees. Make them thick.

7. Prepare many bowls of icing of all colors. Bring varieties of candies, mints, raisins, cereals (for roof tile), gum drops like leaves and flowers, licorice for railroad tracks, caramels in wrappers for train load of goodies, round cookies (oreos) for train wheels, silver bell for train, marshmallows for snowman and mini- ones for around castle turrets, cones for castle spires, bells for church tower, chocolate chips, candy corn for barn. Decorate with instruments outlining and filling in the cookie people, signs "One Way" and "Keep Right" and name plates for "Home Sweet Home," "Castle in the Sky," "Food for the Hungry" on train car, "Come to Me" on church, gold cross on church, etc. Those who constructed and frosted the buildings or other designated people may have them after the display ends.

Simple Icing:	Royal Icing
1 lb. confectioner's sugar	1 lb. confectioner's sugar
1/2 teaspoon vanilla	1/2 teaspoon Cream of Tartar
coloring	3 egg whites
2 tablespoons margarine	
Hot water to mix	

Sift sugar with Cream of Tartar; add unbeaten egg whites; beat vigorously until it holds shape. Add coloring. Use decorator.

<u>Nativity Scene Sugar Molds</u> (if you have a set):

    2 cups granulated sugar
    4 teaspoons water
    1/2 teaspoon or more of egg white

Mix, knead 1 minute. When not using, keep covered with damp cloth. Dust molds with cornstarch. Press the sugar into each mold, scraping off excess with knife. Cover the mold with a stiff cardboard or plastic, turn upside down gently onto cookie tin, lift off the mold after carefully sliding the cardboard out. Bake 15 minutes in a 200 degree oven; or they will harden overnight without baking, by just leaving them in the molds. Use leftover sugar for more molds; remove any lumps.

8. It is simpler to transport the landscape and the buildings separately (in boxes) and assemble them at the display area. Use more frosting to stabilize each building and cookie in place. Add flowers around houses, castle, church; use suckers for edge rail on bridge; frost ice cream cones upside down for trees; make ranch fence with stick pretzels; and any other ideas you have.

9. If no one is attending the Candy Village at the display area, ask for chain and posts, if the mall has them to keep little ones away. On your poster state the names of the children who made the scene, their ages, and the group name. Explain that donations are being sent to World Vision (or whatever group) and give official envelopes for those who want to send checks.

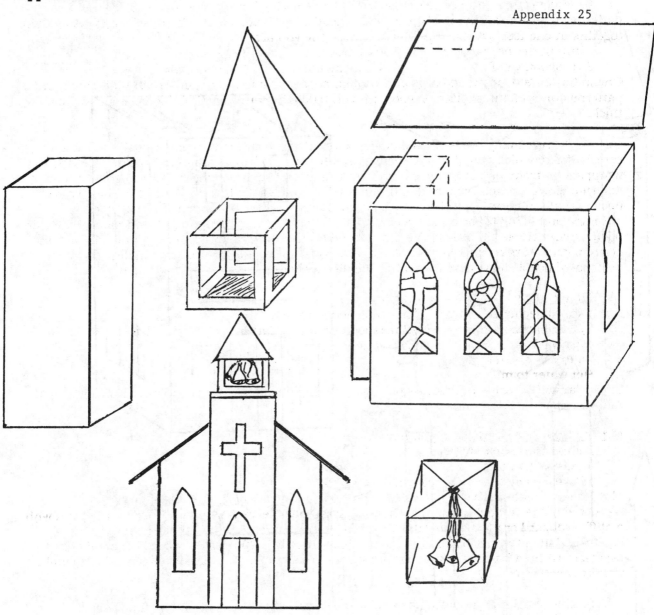

Fix boxes together to make the church and tower. String the bells from two wires, crossing the top of the bell section, before attaching that section to the tower. Pain a design on the church windows on clear plastic; tape the plastic from the inside of the box onto the backs of the windows, after the windows have been cut out. Pain a gold cross on the front.

Ice cream cones make novel turret tops.

Castle constructed with boxes and Christmas wrapper rolls and orange juice can. Cut into box at dots and fit the towers into place. Tape them on the outside. Frosting will cover the taping.

Use large marshmallows for the stone ballustrade around the roof, and miniature marshmallows around the turrets. Trim windows, door, etc., with candies and frosting. Tape a balcony on the front. Turret tops are made from the cone-shaped cardboard, taped together.

Appendix 27.

Buildings are made from boxes--cereal boxes, shoe boxes, others. Fit them together with tape. Cut out windows and attach clear plastic behind them. Miniature Christmas tree lights will brighten them from inside.

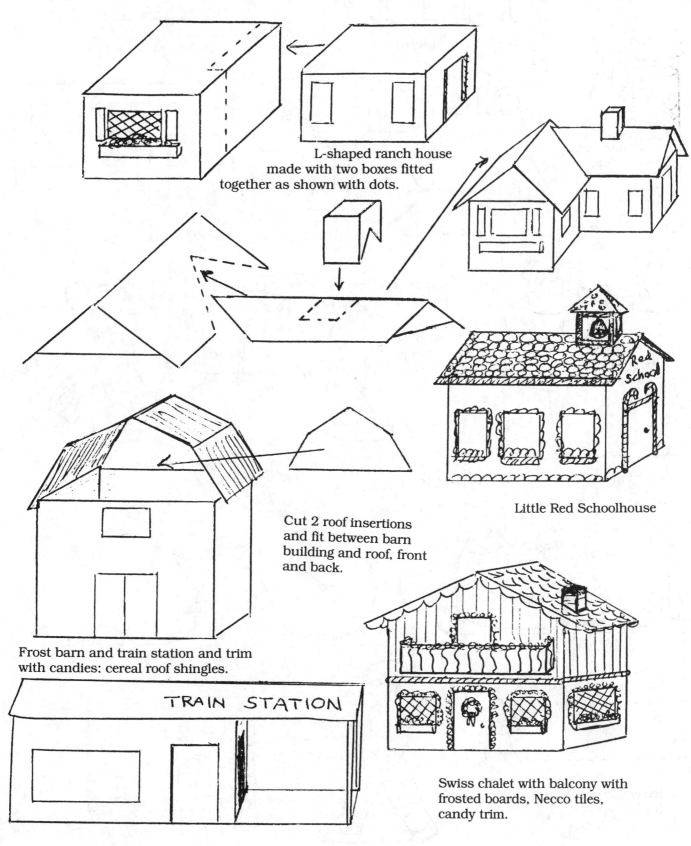

L-shaped ranch house made with two boxes fitted together as shown with dots.

Cut 2 roof insertions and fit between barn building and roof, front and back.

Little Red Schoolhouse

Frost barn and train station and trim with candies: cereal roof shingles.

TRAIN STATION

Swiss chalet with balcony with frosted boards, Necco tiles, candy trim.

Appendix 28.

suckers - side of bridge

frosted sign

ice-cream cone evergreens

cookie wheels

clear plastic windows

graham cracker train, raisin coal, goodies in car

marshmallow snowman

cookie people

carolers   cutout cookie people

bobsledding

bicycling

seesawing   ice-skater   Keep Right

Appendix 29.

Good News Club, Rocky Mountain House, Alberta, Canada, working on village, 1986. (Photograph by The Advocate, Red Deer, Alberta.)

Appendix 30.

177. Scrambled names: Isaac, Rebeccah, Bethuel, servant, Laban, Abraham.

181. Scrambled books of Law: Deuteronomy, Numbers, Genesis, Leviticus, Exodus.

182. Word block on sons of Jacob:

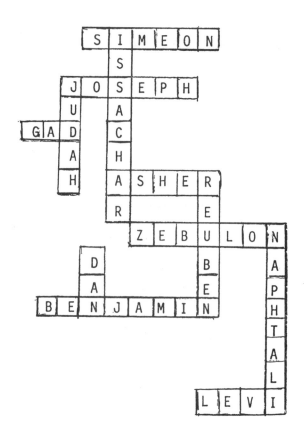

185. Similarities between Joseph and Jesus:
   1. Beloved son
   2. hated
   3. clothes taken
   4. sold for silver (Joseph 20, Jesus, 30)
   5. 2 friends in suffering, 1 saved; 1 lost.
   6. suffered without cause, the purpose to save others.
   7. Spirit of God in them.
   8. next to the throne
   9. Gentile bride (Jesus' bride, the Church)
   10. 30 years old then career began.

186. Word Block on 42 words from Genesis:

	1	2	3	4	5	6	7	8	9	10	11	12
1	G	E	N	E	S	I	S	J	U	D	A	H
2	A	V	G	O	D	C	A	I	N	X	D	O
3	R	E	U	B	E	N	T	A	E	S	A	U
4	D	A	Y	X	S	T	A	R	S	X	M	S
5	E	X	W	O	M	A	N	X	T	R	E	E
6	N	I	G	H	T	E	L	I	F	E	A	I
7	O	N	I	S	V	N	X	B	I	R	D	S
8	O	O	X	A	U	D	E	A	T	H	A	A
9	M	A	E	S	N	M	A	H	A	R	B	A
10	A	H	T	H	G	I	L	X	A	X	E	C
11	R	A	C	H	E	L	M	H	A	E	L	E
12	K	H	P	E	S	O	J	A	C	O	B	R
13	R	E	B	E	C	C	A	H	L	O	T	I
14	R	A	I	N	B	O	W	X	H	S	I	F

God 2-3a	death 8-6a
heaven 10-2su	Cain 2-6a
earth 5-12sd	Abel 8-11d
light 10-7b	life 6-7a
day 4-1a	ark 10-1d
night 6-1a	Noah 7-2d
sea 3-10b	rainbow 14-1a
sun 9-4su	Abraham 9-12b
moon 9-1u	Sarah 7-12sd
stars 4-5a	Lot 13-9a
fish 14-12b	Isaac 6-12d
birds 7-8a	Rebeccah 13-1a
animals 8-4sd	Jacob 12-7a
man 5-5a	Esau 3-9a
woman 5-3a	Rachel 11-1a
Adam 1-11d	Leah 11-11b
Eve 1-2d	Reuben 3-1a
garden 1-1d	Joseph 12-7b
tree 5-9a	fire 14-12u
Satan 1-7d	Judah 1-8a
sin 7-4b	Genesis 1-1a

Appendix 31.

187. BIBLE ARITHMETIC:
    1. $8 + 66 = 74$ divided by $2 = 37 \times 5 = 185$
    2. 12 divided by $3 = 4 \times 7 = 28 - 1 = 27$
    3. $7 \times 7 = 49 + 40 = 80 - 50 = 39$
    4. $2 + 3 = 5 \times 600 = 3{,}000$ divided by $2 = 1{,}500$

190.   10 squares in the circle.

194.   Scrambled sentences: Jesus walked on water. Jesus said, "Peace be still," to the storm at sea.

200.   Construction of the Tabernacle continued:

The fifth item was the <u>TABLE OF SHOWBREAD</u> representing the Bread of Life. Each week the priests ate the old bread and placed new loaves on the table each Sabbath. It was the "bread of His presence."

The sixth item was the <u>ARK,</u> in the Most Holy Place, representing God's law and mercy. It was a wooden ark or box which held the two pieces of stone on which God wrote the Ten Commandments. The mercy seat was a golden lid covering the "law," and at each end of it stood the figure of an angel bowing in adoration. The law and mercy are the character of God.

The ark was in the Most Holy Place, the back end of the tabernacle, and was entered only once a year on the Day of Atonement by the High Priest. this prefigured the work of Christ as He comes before the Father on the Day of Judgment, just before He returns to earth to be King.

The Holy Place is the room entered before the Most Holy Place. The daily services were here where the priest took some of the animal's blood, which the sinner had brought, and sprinkled it before the veil which hid the "law." This was the heavy veil which was torn from top to bottom (by God) when Jesus died on the cross, showing that now the Most Holy Place is open for all who confess Christ as Savior to come to the Father with boldness, to speak directly to Him. We might also refer to Adam and Eve, having sinned, there was a veil separating their previous friendship with God, the open fellowship broken by their unbelief and sin. Not until the "second Adam," Jesus, fulfilled the law was this veil removed, allowing redeemed sinners into the presence of God.

Paint the golden furnishings. Make the tabernacle (tent) using a wooden framework, covered with materials representing (1) goat skins, (2) red ram's skins, and (3) the top, leather.

As you present this scene, discuss the symbolism of the various furnishings, and lift the three curtains off the tent to disclose the two rooms.

The tent and all the furnishings, and the ark were carried by the Levites during the travels of the Israelites through the wilderness. the pattern of the tabernacle was also used in the building of the Temple during Solomon's reign, as directed by God.

Now, we as Christians are the Temple of the Holy Spirit (for God to work through us to win the lost). In heaven, God will be the Temple, and all His children (Christians) have full access to Him, and will join the angels in singing and worshipping Him.

Appendix 32.

207

Activity: 41 Words Found in Leviticus

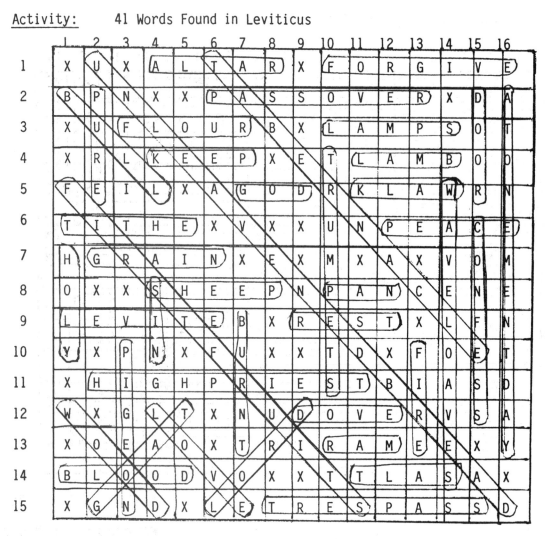

altar 1-4a 1:5
forgive 1-10 a 4:20
passover 2-6 a 23:5
flour 3-3a 2:1
lamb 4-11a 3:7
God 5-7a 11:44
tithe 6-1a 27:30
peace 6-12a 3:1
grain 7-2a 2:2
sheep 8-4a 1:10

pan 8-10a 2:7
Levite 9-1a 25:33
high priest 11-2a 21:10
dove 12-9a 1:14
ram 13-10a 5:15
blood 14-1a 1:5
trespass 15-8a 5:6
salt 14-14b 2:13
pure 2-2d 24:4
holy 7-1d 5:15

trumpets 4-10d 23:24
wave loaves 5-14d 23:20
confess 6-15d 26:40
atonement day 2-16d 23:27
sin 8-4d 4:3
pigeon 10-2d 1:14
burnt 9-7d 1:6
fire 10-13d 1:7
bull 2-1sd 1:5
unleavened bread 1-2sd 6:16

tabernacle 1-6sd 3:8
firstfruits 5-1sd 2:12
wood 12-1sd 1:8
love 12-4sd 19:18
goat 15-2su 3:12
Lord 15-6su 1:1
door 2-15d 1:5
walk 5-14b 18:4
keep 4-4a 20:8
lamps 3-10a 24:2
rest 9-9a 25:4

Appendix 33.

217.   Miracles in the Life of Moses

	1	2	3	4	5	6	7	8	9	10	11	12	13	14	15	16	17	18	19
1	X	M	O	S	E	S	S	H	I	N	I	N	G	F	A	C	E	Y	F
2	S	D	U	B	D	O	R	S	N	O	R	A	A	X	R	N	X	M	I
3	R	K	C	O	R	M	O	R	F	R	E	T	A	W	X	O	N	R	R
4	D	E	A	T	H	O	F	F	I	R	S	T	B	O	R	N	G	A	E
5	A	S	D	O	O	L	B	X	R	O	D	L	O	C	U	S	T	S	M
6	R	E	B	S	W	E	E	T	E	N	E	D	W	A	T	E	R	X	S
7	K	R	O	R	E	D	N	U	H	T	G	N	I	N	T	H	G	I	L
8	N	P	I	L	L	A	R	C	L	O	U	D	O	F	F	I	R	E	I
9	E	E	L	T	T	A	C	X	Y	S	O	R	P	E	L	I	A	H	A
10	S	N	S	F	L	A	M	I	N	G	B	U	S	H	I	I	X	X	U
11	S	T	K	E	L	A	M	A	F	O	T	A	E	F	E	D	C	X	Q
12	X	S	M	I	R	I	A	M	S	L	E	P	R	O	S	Y	X	E	X
13	M	O	S	E	S	E	Y	E	S	S	T	R	E	N	G	T	H	X	X

flaming bush 10-4a Ex. 3:2

rod 5-9a Ex. 4:2

leprosy 9-15b Ex. 4:6

blood 5-7b Ex. 7:19

frogs 1-14sd Ex. 8:3

lice 9-15sd Ex. 8:16

flies 8-15d Ex. 8:21

cattle 9-7b, Ex. 9:3

boils 6-3d Ex. 9:9

hail 9-18b Ex. 9:18

locusts 5-12a Ex.10:4

darkness 4-1d Ex.10:21

death of firstborn 4-1a 11:5

pillar, cloud of fire 8-2a 13:22

Red Sea 3-1sd Ex. 14:21

army 4-18u Ex. 14:24

sweetened water 6-4a Ex. 15:25

manna 5-19su Ex. 16:31

quails 11-19u Ex. 16:13

water from rock 3-14b Ex.17:6

defeat of Amalek 11-16b 17:13

lightning,thunder 7-19b 19:16

Moses shining face 1-2a 34:29

fire 1-19d Numbers 11:1

Miriams leprosy 12-3a 12:10

Aarons rod buds 2-13b 17:8

serpents 5-2d 21:8

Moses eyes,strength 13-1a
Deuteronomy 34:7

231. Answers to Quiz on Joint-Heirs with Christ:
    1. led, Spirit, sons, bondage, fear, adoption, witness, children, heirs, joint, suffer.
    2. Abraham's, heirs, promise.
    3. sons, Spirit, hearts, slave, son, heir, through Christ.
    4. inheritance, predestined, purpose, will, trusted, Christ, praise, glory, Him, truth, salvation, believed, sealed, Spirit, promise, guarantee, inheritance, redemption, purchased, possession.
    5. justified, grace, heirs, eternal
    6. ministering spirits, inherit salvation

Some of the things we share with Jesus:
Salvation, Eternal Life, Glory, Joy, Peace, Love, Faith, Riches, Abundant Life, Fruit, Ministry, Good Works, brothers/sisters in Christ, Father, sit with Jesus on His throne, Crown of Life, Tree of Life, etc.

237. See accompanying Word Block on Story of Samson.

238. Answers to Quiz on Judges:
    1. Samson - Judges 16:21
    2. Othniel - 3:10
    3. Gideon - 7:22
    4. Samson - 15:5
    5. Barak - 4:15
    6. Abimelech - 9:5
    7. Deborah and Barak - 5:1
    8. Manoah's wife - 13:5
    9. Gideon - 6:37
    10. Jephthah - 11:31

249. Answers on Quiz on Anger:
    1. Cain
    2. Saul
    3. Samson
    4. King Herod
    5. Jezebel
    6. Jonah
    7. Pharoah
    8. Moses
    9. Haman
    10. God

254. WORD BLOCK ON CROWNS:

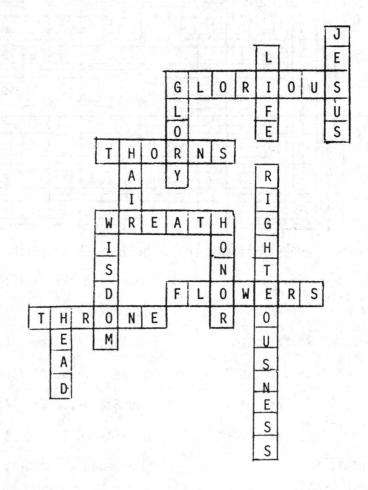

237. Story of Samson.

	1	2	3	4	5	6	7	8	9	10	11	12	13	14
1	P	J	P	X	B	L	I	N	D	X	B	P	C	N
2	H	A	I	R	I	D	D	L	E	X	U	O	O	A
3	I	W	S	O	I	M	O	T	H	E	R	W	L	Z
4	L	B	N	P	E	S	A	G	O	D	N	E	U	A
5	I	O	I	E	K	Y	O	N	F	X	E	R	M	R
6	S	N	A	T	N	N	E	N	O	I	D	Y	N	I
7	T	E	H	F	O	X	E	S	D	A	E	E	L	T
8	I	X	C	S	T	R	O	N	G	N	H	L	S	E
9	N	G	M	X	S	X	C	X	O	A	I	U	D	E
10	E	A	N	G	E	L	X	H	C	M	R	R	X	V
11	S	T	A	I	L	S	W	E	E	T	X	X	G	O
12	D	E	L	I	L	A	H	X	I	S	R	A	E	L

blind 1-5a	lion 1-6sd	rope 2-4d	strong 8-4a
burned 1-11d	Delilah 12-1a	mother 3-6a	foxes 7-4a
chains 8-3u	Israel 12-9a	God 4-8a	honey 10-8su
torches 6-4sd	power 1-12d	eyes 4-5sd	mill 10-10su
trust 11-10su	column 1-13d	Manoah 3-6sd	love 12-14u
Philistines 1-1d	Nazarite 1-14d	field 5-9sd	gate 9-2d
jawbone 1-2d	hair 2-1a	Samson 11-1su	angel 10-2a
prison 1-3sd	riddle 2-4a	grind 11-13su	tails 11-2a
knots 5-5d	sweet 11-6a		

255. Scrambled words from 2 Samuel:
Mephibosheth, David, Absalom, Joab, Abner, Sheba, Philistines, Bathsheba, Solomon, Nathan.

257. Numerical Quiz:
1. 5 + 12 = 17 X 40 = 680 - 2 = 678
2. 300 - 12 = 288 + 40 = 328 X 3 = 984
3. 5 + 2 = 7 X 20 = 140 divided by 2 = 70
4. 300 - 12 = 288 + 1 = 289 X 2 = 578

270. Scrambled words of good kings:

1. Saul	4. Asa	7. Amaziah	10. Hezekiah
2. David	5. Jehoshaphat	8. Uzziah	11. Josiah
3. Solomon	6. Joash	9. Jotham	

280. Answers to Quiz on GOD:

1. Almighty God	14. Lord of hosts	27. Word
2. omnipotent	15. Mighty God	28. right
3. omniscient	16. Creator	29. Mercy
4. omnipresent	17. Holy One of Israel	30. faithful
5. good	18. invisible	31. help
6. perfect	19. Father	32. Rock
7. holy	20. power, glory	33. sun, shield
8. Lord of lords	21. judge	34. temple
9. King of kings	22. upright	35. Father, Son, Holy Spirit
10. eternal	23. love	36. Most High God
11. righteous	24. refuge	37. wise
12. I AM	25. heavenly Father	38. just
13. Jehovah	26. everlasting	

281. Word Block on GOD:

Almighty God - 6-8a	Creator - 5-13a
omnipotent - 8-19d	Holy One of Israel - 2-2d
omniscient - 7-18d	invisible - 15-5a
omnipresent 7-13d	Father - 10-2a
good - 7-14a	help - 9-14a
perfect - 7-19u	sun - 16-15a
holy - 11-15d	temple - 17-1a
King of kings - 16-5a	judge - 3-3a
Lord of lords - 14-3a	upright - 17-7a
eternal - 13-13b	love - 8-10d
glory - 11-3a	refuge - 5-6a
power - 13-6b	heavenly Father 2-2a
Rock 2-15a	everlasting - 3-7a
righteous - 17-9a	right - 13-1d
I AM - 5-5d	word - 13-4d
Jehovah - 3-3d	mercy - 8-13a
Lord of hosts - 2-1d	faithful - 5-8d
Mighty God - 6-10a	shield - 12-2a
most high God - 4-8a	Father, Son, Holy Spirit - 1-1a
wise - 11-16d	just - 8-11d

281. WORD BLOCK ON GOD:

```
      1  2  3  4  5  6  7  8  9 10 11 12 13 14 15 16 17 18 19
 1    F  A  T  H  E  R  S  O  N  H  O  L  Y  S  P  I  R  I  T
 2    L  H  E  A  V  E  N  L  Y  F  A  T  H  E  R  O  C  K  C
 3    O  O  J  U  D  G  E  V  E  R  L  A  S  T  I  N  G  X  E
 4    R  L  E              M  O  S  T  H  I  G  H  G  O  D     F
 5    D  Y  H     I  R  E  F  U  G  E  X  C  R  E  A  T  O  R  R
 6    O  O  O        X  X  A  L  M  I  G  H  T  Y  G  O  D     E
 7    F  N  V     A        I              O  G  O  O  D  O     P
 8    H  E  A     M        T     L  J     M  E  R  C  Y  M     O
 9    O  O  H              H     O  U     N  H  E  L  P  N     M
10    S  F  A  T  H  E  R  F     V  S        I              I  N
11    T  I  G  L  O  R  Y  U     E  T     P     H  W        S  I
12    S  S  H  I  E  L  D  L              R     O  I        C  P
13    R  R  E  W  O  P  L  A  N  R  E  T  E     L  S        I  O
14    I  A  L  O  R  D  O  F  L  O  R  D  S     Y  E        E  T
15    G  E  X  R  I  N  V  I  S  I  B  L  E              N     E
16    H  L  X  D  K  I  N  G  O  F  K  I  N  G  S  U  N  T  N
17    T  E  M  P  L  E  U  P  R  I  G  H  T  E  O  U  S  X  T
```

Almighty God 6-8a	I AM 5-5d	judge 3-3a
omnipotent 8-19d	Jehovah 3-3d	upright 17-7a
omniscient 7-18d	Lord of hosts 2-1d	love 8-10d
omnipresent 7-13d	Mighty God 6-10a	refuge 5-6a
good 7-14a	most high God 4-8a	heavenly Father 2-2a
perfect 7-19a	wise 11-16d	everlasting 3-7a
holy 11-15d	Creator	right 13-1d
King of kings 16-5a	Holy One of Israel 2-2d	word 13-4d
Lord of lords 14-3a	invisible 15-5a	mercy 8-13a
eternal 13-13b	Father 10-2a	faithful 508d
glory 11-3a	help 9-14a	shield 12-2a
power 13-6b	sun 16-15a	Father, Son, Holy Spirit 1-1a
Rock 2-15a	temple 17-1a	just 8-11d
righteous 17-9a		

Appendix 38.

312. PSALMS OF PRAISE.

	1.		10.		19.		28.	
1.	23:1	2-1d	10. 93:5	20-16d	19. 100:5	3-21d	28. 147:6	6-18d
2.	23:1	11-5d	11. 98:1	23-1a	20. 100:5	4-6a	29. 147:7	6-9d
3.	23:2	6-15d	12. 98:4	1-17d	21. 146:1	1-1a	30. 147:7	6-16d
4.	23:3	7-2d	13. 98:8	5-5a	22. 146:2	5-3d	31. 148:2	6-20d
5.	23:4	20-14d	14. 100:3	3-5a	23. 146:5	6-8d	32. 148:3	6-19d
6.	23:5	20-15d	15. 100:3	5-4d	24. 146:6	6-10d	33. 150:1	14-8d
7.	23:5	19-20d	16. 100:3	9-6d	25. 146:6	4-20u	34. 150:3	6-11d
8.	93:1	6-12d	17. 100:4	2-5a	26. 146:8	6-14d	35. 150:4	14-10d
9.	93:4	17-12d	18. 100:4	11-7d	27. 147:1	6-13d	36. 150:5	13-9d

Appendix 39.

313-316. These are simple silhouetes I drew for my pictures and tables to be blacked in with India ink or paint. Print the verses on strips of plastic to be scotch-taped underneath, close to the border, but within the frame. Use permanent black pen for durable printing. The milkweed, butterflies, dried flowers are placed in the center before the glass (with silhouettes and printing) is lowered. Be sure to seal with adhesive tape all around the edges to prevent air, insects to penetrate the inside.

"Look at the birds--your Father feeds them. Consider the lilies-- He clothes them. Will he not much more clothe you?"

"Love one another as I have loved you." John 13:34.

Matthew 6:26-33. "Seek first the Kingdom of God, and these will be added to you."

"I am the Good Shepherd who gives His life for the sheep. John 10:11 "Follow Me, and I will make you fishers of men." Matthew 4:19

"Let your light so shine before men that they will see your good works and glorify God. " Matthew 5:16

"For we know that all things work together for good to those who love God and are called according to His purpose." Romans 8:28

"Whatever you do in word or deed, do all in the name of the Lord Jesus. " Colossians 3:17

"Abide in Me and I in you for without Me you can do nothing. " John 15:4, 5

"Study to show yourself approved unto God, rightly dividing the Word of truth." 2 Timothy 2:15

"Do to others as you would have them do to you." Matthew 7:12

"I press for the goal for the prize of the upward call of God in Christ Jesus." Philippians 3:14

"Rejoice always. Pray without ceasing. In everything give thanks; for this is the will of God in Christ Jesus for you." 1 Thess. 5:16-18

Appendix 42.

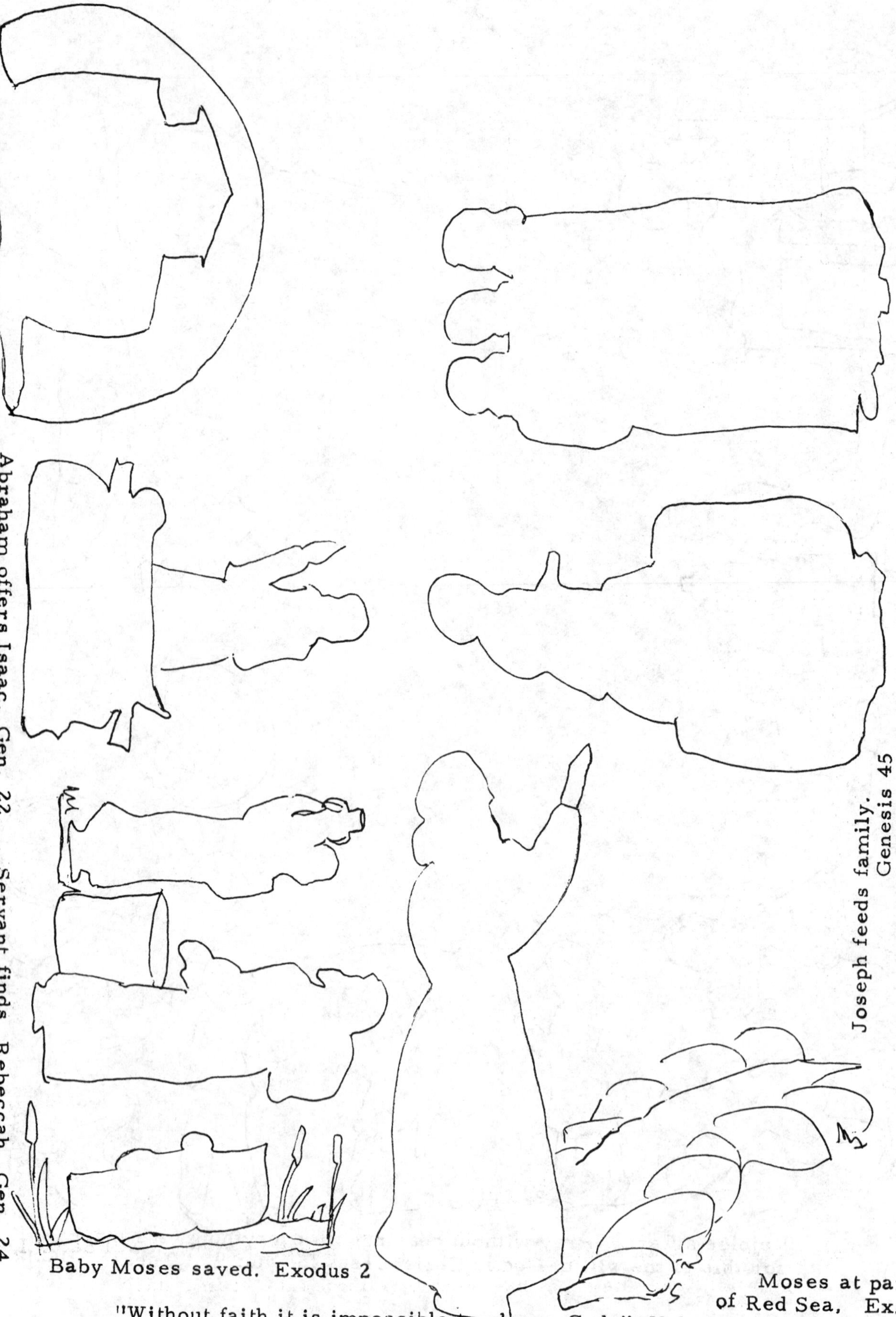

Noah and Ark. Gen. 6-9

Abraham offers Isaac. Gen. 22

Servant finds Rebeccah. Gen. 24

"Faith is the substance of things hoped for, the evidence of things not seen." Hebrews 11:1

Joseph feeds family. Genesis 45

"God sent me before you to preserve life." Genesis 45:7

Baby Moses saved. Exodus 2

Moses at parting of Red Sea, Ex. 14

"Without faith it is impossible to please God." Hebrews 11:6

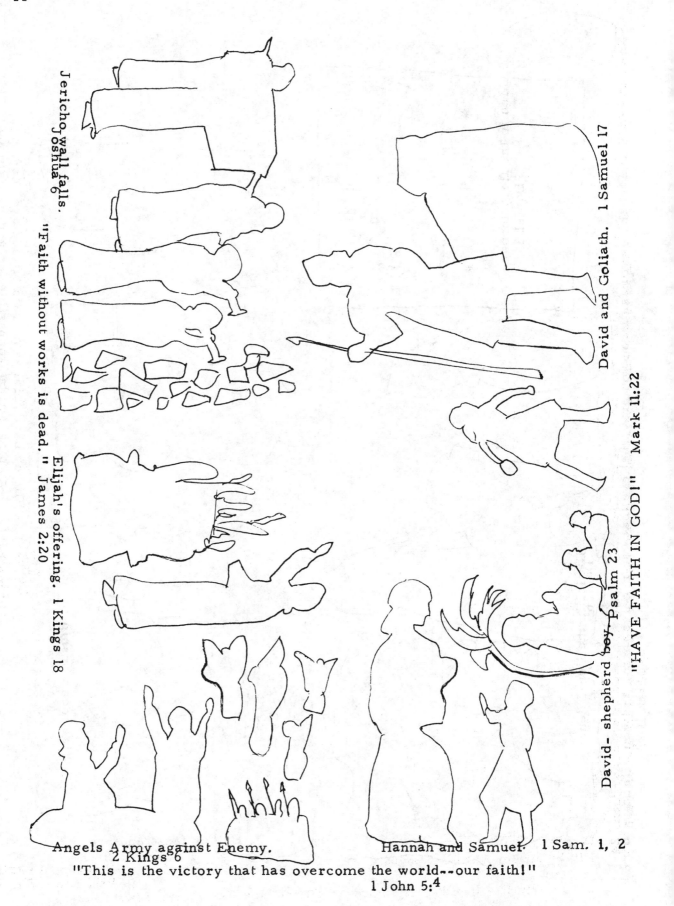

Jericho wall falls. Joshua 6.

"Faith without works is dead." James 2:20

Elijah's offering. 1 Kings 18

David and Goliath. 1 Samuel 17

"HAVE FAITH IN GOD!" Mark 11:22

David- shepherd boy. Psalm 23

Angels Army against Enemy. 2 Kings 6

Hannah and Samuel. 1 Sam. 1, 2

"This is the victory that has overcome the world--our faith!" 1 John 5:4

Appendix 44.

Men in the fiery furnace
Daniel 3

Boy's lunch multiplied.
John 6

"If you have faith as a grain of mustard seed.... nothing will be impossible for you." Matthew 17:20

"Whatever things you ask when you pray, believe that you receive them, and you will have them." Mark 11:24

Daniel in the lions' den
Dan. 6

Wise men worship Jesus.
Matthew 2

Esther fasts and prays.
Esther 4 - 9

Appendix 45.

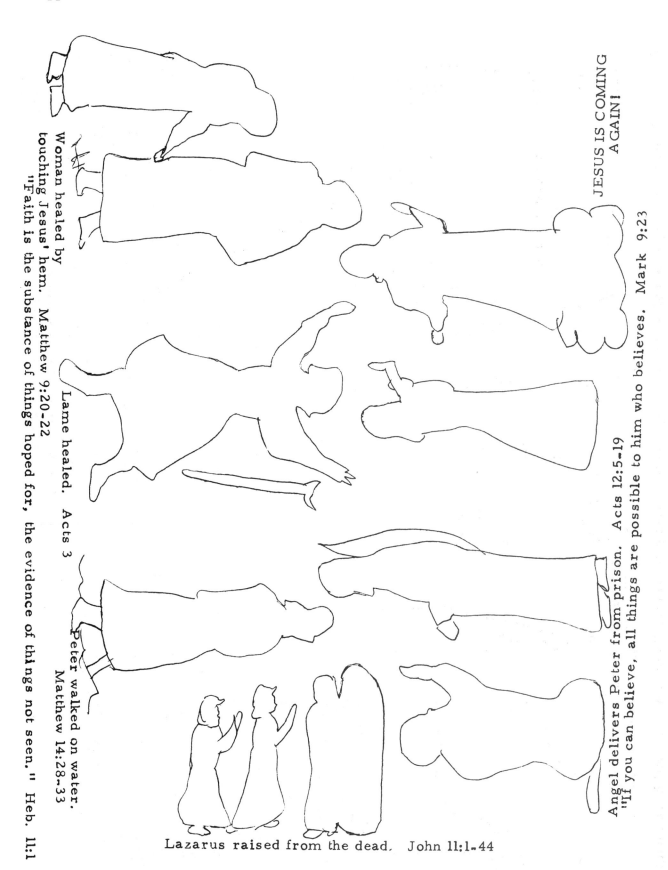

Woman healed by
touching Jesus' hem. Matthew 9:20-22
"Faith is the substance of things hoped for, the evidence of things not seen." Heb. 11:1

Lame healed. Acts 3

Peter walked on water.
Matthew 14:28-33

Lazarus raised from the dead. John 11:1-44

JESUS IS COMING AGAIN!

Mark 9:23

Angel delivers Peter from prison. Acts 12:5-19
"If you can believe, all things are possible to him who believes. Mark 9:23

329, 330. QUIZ ON MAN:

1. a. created perfect
2. c. in God's image
3. a. free will
4. b. named animals
5. b. Eve from Adam
6. a. Adam, Eve sinned
7. c. all sinned
8. b. death
9. a. God loved
10. c. grace, not works
11. b. saved
12. a. who
13. b. now
14. b. repent
15. c. no condemnation
16. c. open door
17. a. bread
18. a. light
19. c. shine
20. b. shepherd
21. a. feed my sheep
22. c. fruit
23. b. love
24. b. conquerors
25. c. works
26. a. abide in Me
27. b. run race
28. b. temptation
29. c. Christ/Me
30. c. temple
31. a. crown
32. b. bride
33. a. one
34. a. meet
35. c. able
36. b. all
37. c. rest

331. WORD BLOCK ON MAN.

1-1a created perfect
2-1a in God's image
2-12a free will
2-2d named animals
3-1d Eve from Adam
3-7a Adam, Eve sinned
4-7a all sinned
1-19b death
5-11a God loved
4-19d grace, not works

6-14a saved
12-16a who
4-16a now
14-19b repent
15-1 no condemnation
6-12d open door
10-18u bread
16-11su light
13-2su shine

14-1a feed My sheep
11-15sd fruit
16-10b conquerors
11-18d love
12-19d works
11-2a abide in Me
16-12a run race
12-4a temptation
13-17u Christ/Me

15-18b crown
6-8sd bride
6-10sd one
10-2su meet
11-2su able
6-5sd all
12-14u rest
10-6a temple
13-2a shepherd

332. Answers to QUIZ ON JERUSALEM:

1. 5
2. David, 2 Samuel 5:6-9

3. Jesus' life in that area; He will reign there 1,000 years; temple there.
4. Isaac offered by Abraham
5. Dome of the Rock

6. Jesus
7. David was man of war; 1 Chronicles 22:6-10
8. Solomon, 1 Kings 5:5-8
9. destruction, Matthew 24:1-2
10. Jesus in the Millennium

344. Answers to QUIZ ON UNUSUAL PRAYERS:

1. Jonah in the big fish; Jonah 2:1-9
2. Abraham - for Lot. Genesis 18:16-33
3. Abraham's servant for Isaac. Genesis 24.
4. Jacob. Genesis 32:24-32
5. Moses. Exodus 34:27-29; Deut. 9:25

6. Hannah, 1 Samuel 1
7. Elisha, 2 Kings 6:8-23
8. Solomon. 1 Kings 3:5-15
9. Daniel. Daniel 10
10. Esther. Esther 4:16-17

331. Word Block on M A N.

	1	2	3	4	5	6	7	8	9	10	11	12	13	14	15	16	17	18	19
1	C	R	E	A	T	E	D	P	E	R	F	E	C	T	H	T	A	E	D
2	I	N	G	O	D	S	I	M	A	G	E	F	R	E	E	W	I	L	L
3	E	A					A	D	A	M	E	V	E	S	I	N	N	E	D
4	V	M					A	L	L	S	I	N	N	E	D	N	O	W	G
5	E	E					X	X		X	G	O	D	L	O	V	E	D	R
6	F	D		X	A		X	B	O	X	O	X	S	A	V	E	D		A
7	R	A		L	T		R			N	P			X		M	A		C
8	O	N	L	E	E	I				E	E					T	E		E
9	M	I	E	L	D	E		X		N		T				S	R		N
10	A	M	B	E	N	T	E	M	P	L	E	D	D	S	X		I	B	O
11	D	A	B	I	D	E	I	N	M	E	X	O		E	F		R	L	T
12	A	L	H	T	E	M	P	T	A	T	I	O	N	R	T	W	H	O	W
13	M	S	H	E	P	H	E	R	D	X	X	R	U	H	X	X	C	V	O
14	F	E	E	D	M	Y	S	H	E	E	P	I	G	T	N	E	P	E	R
15	N	O	C	O	N	D	E	M	N	A	T	I	O	N	W	O	R	C	K
16	S	R	O	R	E	U	Q	N	O	C	L	R	U	N	R	A	C	E	S

Appendix 49.

358.   35 Women of the Bible

M	A	R	Y			J	E	Z	E	B	E	L			E	S	T	H	E	R
A		E	D	S	U	Z	A	N	N	A			P	R	A	H	A	B		A
R	D	B	E	D	O	R	C	A	S	A	R	A	H			N				C
T	E	E	L	I			N	A	O	M	I		D	I	N	A	H			H
H	B	C	I	A	T	J	O	A	N	N	A	S	H	A	G	A	R			E
A	O	C	L	B	H	E					C	M	I	C	H	A	L			L
	R	A	A	I	V	U					I	M	I	R	I	A	M			M
O	A	H	H	G	A	N				L	O	I	S				R
R	H	O	D	A	S	I				L	Y	D	I	A			U
P	E	V	E	I	H	C			S	A	L	O	M	E			T
A	N	N	A	L	T	E		E	L	I	Z	A	B	E	T	H
H	E	R	O	D	I	A	S	B	A	T	H	S	H	E	B	A

	Across				Down		
1	Mary	15	Dinah	27 Lydia	1	Martha	11 Deborah
3	Jezebel	17	Joanna	28 Eve	2	Rebeccah	16 Abigail
4	Esther	18	Hagar	29 Salome	3	Judith	19 Eunice
8	Suzanna	20	Michal	30 Anna	5	Hannah	21 Vashti
10	Rahab	22	Miriam	31 Elizabeth	6	Rachel	23 Orpah
12	Dorcas	24	Lois	32 Herodias	7	Delilah	25 Ruth
13	Sarah	26	Rhoda	33 Bathsheba	9	Priscilla	
14	Naomi						

345. Answers to QUIZ ON BOOKS IN WHICH NAMES OR EVENTS ARE FOUND:

1. 2 Kings 29-12
2. Exodus 7-12
3. Genesis 22:1-19
4. Matthew 14:23-33
5. 1 Samuel 17:17-58
6. Exodus 20
7. Genesis 1
8. Exodus 14:9-31
9. Acts 12:5-19
10. Genesis 28:10-22
11. Genesis 8
12. Judges 7
13. 2 Kings 5
14. Acts 9:1-19
15. 1 Kings 18:20-46
16. Revelation 1:1-2

347. WORD BLOCK ON MINOR PROPHETS:

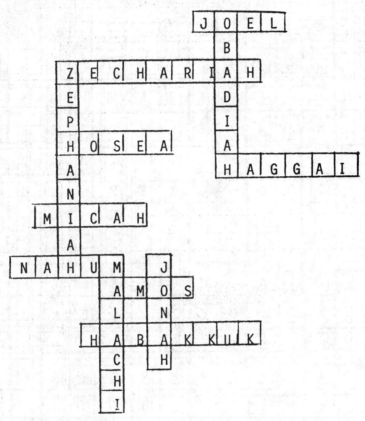

357. ANSWERS TO QUIZ ON WOMEN OF THE BIBLE:

1. Mary - Luke 1:26
2. Jezebel - 1 Kings 18:4
3. Esther - Esther 4:15-16
4. Susanna - Luke 8:3
5. Rahab - Joshua 6:25
6. Dorcas - Acts 9:36
7. Sarah - Genesis 17:15
8. Naomi - Ruth 1:2
9. Dinah - Genesis 30:21
10. Joanna - Luke 8:3
11. Hagar - Genesis 21:17
12. Michal - 1 Samuel 18:20
13. Miriam - Exodus 15:20
14. Lois - 2 Timothy 1:5
15. Rhoda - Acts 12:13
16. Lydia - Acts 16:14
17. Eve - Genesis 3:20
18. Salome - Mark 15:40
19. Anna - Luke 2:36
20. Elizabeth - Luke 1:5
21. Herodias - Matthew 14:3
22. Bathsheba - 2 Samuel 11:3
23. Martha - John 11:5
24. Rebeccah - Genesis 24:15
25. Judith - Genesis 26:34
26. Hannah - 1 Samuel 1:20
27. Rachel - Genesis 29:18
28. Delilah - Judges 16:4
29. Priscilla - Acts 18:2
30. Deborah - Judges 4:4
31. Abigail - 1 Samuel 25:39
32. Eunice - 2 Timothy 1:5
33. Vashti - Esther 1:9
34. Orpah - Ruth 1:4
35. Ruth - Ruth 4:13

364. Word block on the 66 Books of the Bible

	1	2	3	4	5	6	7	8	9	10	11	12	13	14	15	16	17	18	19	20	21
1	G	P	H	I	L	I	P	P	I	A	N	S	D	D	A	N	I	E	L	E	G
2	X	E	1	2	K	I	N	G	S	I	1	S	E	M	A	J	2	X	X	P	A
3	I	K	N	E	H	E	M	I	A	H	2	X	U	A	H	P	C	J	X	H	L
4	2	U	L	E	V	I	T	I	C	U	S	P	T	R	E	R	H	O	S	E	A
5	C	L	J	O	S	H	U	A	H	H	A	X	E	K	B	O	R	E	U	S	T
6	O	O	B	A	D	I	A	H	A	M	M	R	T	R	V	O	L	D	I	I	
7	R	X	H	A	I	A	S	I	C	G	U	S	O	X	E	E	N	J	O	A	A
8	I	N	U	M	B	E	R	S	I	G	E	X	N	S	W	R	I	U	X	N	N
9	N	X	I	H	C	A	L	A	M	A	L	X	O	A	S	B	C	D	E	S	S
10	T	J	O	B	H	E	Z	E	K	I	A	L	M	C	I	S	L	E	N	E	R
11	H	A	X	C	1	2	T	I	M	O	T	H	Y	T	X	S	E	N	O	G	E
12	I	R	E	X	X	E	C	C	L	E	S	I	A	S	T	E	S	H	M	D	H
13	A	Z	E	P	H	A	N	I	A	H	A	I	M	E	R	E	J	O	E	U	T
14	N	E	L	A	M	E	N	T	A	T	I	O	N	S	U	T	O	J	L	J	S
15	S	O	N	G	O	F	S	O	L	O	M	O	N	A	T	I	N	3	I	O	E
16	M	A	T	T	H	E	W	K	U	K	K	A	B	A	H	T	A	2	H	H	C
17	1	2	T	H	E	S	S	A	L	O	N	I	A	N	S	U	H	I	P	N	X
18	S	N	A	M	O	R	E	V	E	L	A	T	I	O	N	S	M	L	A	S	P

364. WORD BLOCK ON BOOKS OF THE BIBLE:

Genesis, 1-1sd	Isaiah, 7-8b	Luke, 5-2u
Exodus, 9-19u	Jeremiah, 13-17b	John, 14-20d
Leviticus, 4-3a	Lamentations, 14-3a	Acts, 9-14d
Numbers, 8-2a	Exekiel, 10-6a	Romans, 18-6b
Deuteronomy, 1-13d	Daniel, 1-14a	1, 2 Corinthians, 3-1d
Joshua, 5-3a	Hosea, 4-17a	Galatians, 1-21d
udges, 14-20u	Joel, 3-18d	Ephesians, 1-20d
Ruth, 13-15d	Amos, 5-11sd	Philippians, 1-2a
1,2 Samuel, 2-11d	Obadiah, 6-2a	Colossians, 16-21su
1,2 Kings, 2-3a	Jonah, 13-17d	1, 2 Thessalonians, 17-1a
1,2 Chronicles, 1-17d	Micah, 9-9u	1, 2 Timothy, 11-5a
Ezra, 14-2su	Nahum, 14-13sd	Titus, 14-16d
Nehemiah, 3-3a	Habakkuk, 16-15b	Philemon, 17-19su
Esther, 15-21u	Zephaniah, 13-2a	Hebrews, 3-15
Job, 10-2a	Haggai, 5-10d	James, 2-16b
Psalms, 18-21b	Zechariah, 13-2su	1, 2 Peter, 2-10sd
Proverbs, 3-16d	Malachi, 9-9b	1, 2, 3 John, 17-18u
Ecclesiastes, 12-6a	Matthew, 16-1a	Jude, 7-18d
Song of Solomon, 15-1a	Mark, 2-14d	Revelation, 18-6a

365.

Eskimo ice fishing

chinese girl with lantern

Hawaiian dancer

Dutch girl

Arab shepherd

Japanese tea girl

African drummer

Indian in canoe

All the children can be drawn and colored with fabric pens, but cloth appliqued children are more novel. Use yarn for hair, and let braids hang free. Let apron, turban, leis, fish, feather, etc., hang free, too. Copy children from library books.

PEEP-IN EASTER EGG SUGAR MOLDS

One of the most delightful memories I have of my childhood is looking into peep-in Easter eggs. There are tiny rabbits, chickens, flowers. I discovered I could make them myself for my children. Hee's how I have done it. You may find the professional way; if so, follow that, for this needs experimenting. This was another project my Junior High Sunday School class made for raising money.

Buy large (6") plastic Easter eggs, or as large as possible.

1. Knead a pound of granulated sugar with 1/2 teasp. egg white, 2 teasp. water.

2. Fill the plastic mold with the sugar, pat firmly, scrape off the top evenly. Do both halves of all your molds.

3. Place a stiff cardboard over the top of one mold, carefully flip over and place in corner of cookie tin upside down. Slip the cardboard out without breaking the mold. Put all the molds on the tin. Bake 20 minutes in 250 degree F. oven. Before baking, carefully slice off 1/2" from the pointed end for the peep-in opening.

Let cool a few minutes, then with teaspoon carefully scrape out the inside sugar (to be reused) leaving about 1/4" shell. If the shell breaks, use it as an open scene, placing it on a jar lid, fluting icing all around the lid to hold the egg in place. Match the tops and bottoms of the other shells.

4. Gather all kings of tiny scenery materials: pebbles, fiowers, seashells. Make little Easter scenes from Easter cards or pictures: Open tomb, angel saying, "He is Risen," or empty cross. Put icing in the bottom, stick the scenery in.

5. Check to see that the top will go on without touching the scene. Spread icing around the edge, put 2 molds together and flute around the seam and opening. Write child's name and "Happy Easter" on the top, with additional frosted flowers.

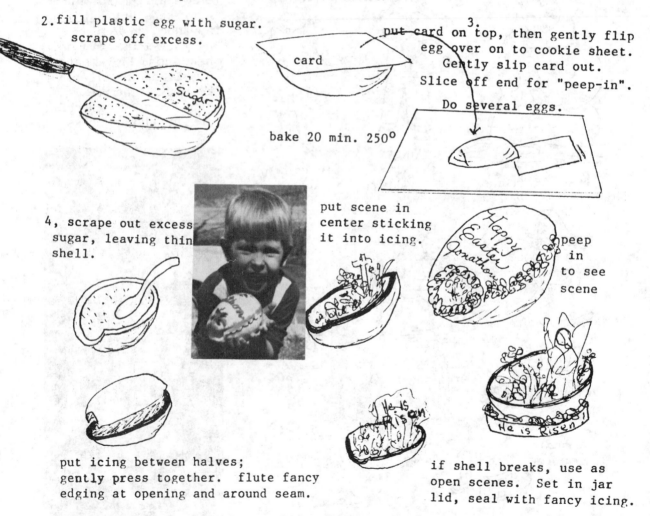

2. fill plastic egg with sugar. scrape off excess.

put card on top, then gently flip egg over on to cookie sheet. Gently slip card out. Slice off end for "peep-in". Do several eggs.

card

bake 20 min. 250°

4, scrape out excess sugar, leaving thin shell.

put scene in center sticking it into icing.

peep in to see scene

put icing between halves; gently press together. flute fancy edging at opening and around seam.

if shell breaks, use as open scenes. Set in jar lid, seal with fancy icing.

He is Risen

CHRISTMAS DECORATIONS

Follow the instructions for Peep-in Easter eggs, but use round molds; add Christmas scenes and Christmas decorations.

Since the candy molds are so fragile, use them only for centerpieces or on a mantel, not on a tree. For the Christmas tree, use styrofoam balls, decorating with braids, ribbons, sequins, beads, etc.

My grandchildren enjoy having a birthday celebration for Jesus, with a cake they decorate, then sing, "Happy Birthday, dear Jesus," and give "promise gifts" of help to others, service of various kinds.

Others save money to give to starving children at home or overseas.

It's memorable to go caroling in hospitals andrest homes; to attend a Christmas Eve candlelight service at a cathedral or large church--that feeling of adoring our Lord together is unforgettable.

I met a wonderful Christian when I was 1sixteen. Our Baptist youth group held services one Sunday afternoon each month at the Home of the Incurables in Washington, D.C. Our pastor prayed with the inmates in the wards while we put on our program in the large meeting room. A doctor had been crippled and blinded from an infection, but through her faith had received her sight. That Christmas Eve we carolled in the building, and she asked me if she could sing her praises to God. Of course, she did, and we were awestruck at her beautiful voice-- she had formerly been a concert singer. She wrote to me afterwards, and we became close friends. She had written a booklet of poetry when blind, "Rainbows through the Rain," and she eventually recovered from her crippled condition enough to leave the home and go to work. God does such miraculous things!

styrofoam balls or sugar molds with scenes

ball with inside scene

Scenes from cards pasted between braid, ribbon, or other trim

FROM OLD CHRISTMAS CARDS:

1. Cut out scenes from old Christmas cards. Make a stable scene from the end of facial tissue box, paint brown, cut out the people in the nativity scene and place in the box with bits of brown grass. Glue or staple the props in place.

2. Make mobiles using clothes hangers or wire circles. Hang assortments of cutout angels on one, bells on another, scenes or happy children's faces on others.

3. Cut cards to make the sides of a box and punch holes to sew together.

4. Make scrapbooks of carols, pictures, Scripture verses, story papers to take to children in hospitals or institutions.

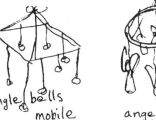

cards sewed together with yarn

Single bells mobile

angels from cards or cut out

Christmas Card cut

NEW CHRISTMAS CARDS:
1. Make a Christmas card with your own poem and drawing. The golding of the paper can be attractive. For example, here is one I made. Letter-size paper, folded down lengthwise one-third of the way, making the booklet 6" high. Fold into 4 sections as shown, giving 4 pages for poem and drawing with picture of Jesus at the end. The upper foldover part with first greeting will be upside down when you type or draw a picture on it.

The Real Meaning of Christmas

Christmas is not Santa,
  Tinsel and toys,
Candy and tres for
  Girls and for boys--
Blest thou these are
  Year after year
With memories fond as
  Families grow

What then is Christmas
  More than these things--
More than the fun that
  This season brings--
More than the shopping,
  Baking and frills--
More than the store crowds,
  Rushing and bills?

Here is the answer:
  JESUS HAS COME!
Sent from the Father with
  Love for each other;
Sent to bring faith and
  Purpose to life,
Joyous fulfillment,
  Freedom from strife!

Christmas means CHRIST--
  The time of His birth;
Glory to God and
  Good will on earth!
Healing from sickness,
  Drying of tears;
Cleansing from sin, and
  Freedom from fears!

"Come unto Me," His
  Arms open wide--
"My yoke is easy,
  In Me abide.
Open your heart's door,
  Let Me come in;
I'll take away your
  Burdens and sin."

Oh, what a Gift God
  Gave us that day!
Oh, what a Light to
  Show us the Way!
Oh, what a Friendship,
  Oh, what a Love,
Oh, what a Savior
  God sent from above!

2. Take close-up photos of each member (or use small school pictures of the children). Draw a large paper-size Christmas tree. The balls will be the pictures, with names, ages under each one. To do this, cut out circles. On the back of the tree tape the photo for the face to appear in the circle. Run off copies as offset printing. At the trunk add your greeting, poem, Scripture verse. Stick on colored stars and glitter or other trimming.

3. Make a booklet type card by writing your greeting in the form of a poem, showing pictures of the activities done through the year. The two upper pictures will be upside down; the paper after being run off as offset or photographed copies made will be folded twice to form book.

Place your photographs of family members' activitiesduring the year as a collage with strips of typing under each photo to tell the story, or center the message.

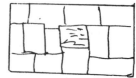

Appendix 55.

TOPICAL INDEX OF ACTIVITIES

(By DAY of Activity)

Appendix 56.

Day
FAMILY GROWTH
11 - Family deeds
26 - Musical
27 - Signs
42 - Prayer bouquet
67 - Rules
68 - Books to read
75 - Travel
95 - Write leaders
97 - Fast workers
105 - True Stories
129 - Training
131 - Judgments
140 - Be Happy
141 - Talents
152 - Type of church
178 - Heritage
191 - Miracles
198 - Directions
203 - Prayer room
205-206 - Prayer place
210 - Good spies
215 - Promises
218 - Speech-making
224 - Keep clean
225 - Patriotism
227 - Hymn stories
229 - Walls
231 - Miracles
236 - Emergencies
241 - Treasure box
243 - Prayer Bouquet
248 - Community support
251 - Jerusalem
253 - Stories re sins
263 - Neighbors outing
271 - King for a day
278 - Help our Country
283 - Singers
304 - Community stands
306 - Collecting
317 - Say No
323 - Work
324 - Marriage and Family
330 - Not Ruffled
334 - Hard Work
365 - Keep it up

FAMILY PLAYS
288-290 - Esther
214 - Balaam puppets
229 - Jericho
291-294 - Job
360 - Jonah

Day
FLANNELGRAPH LESSONS
20 - Parables
33 - Ruler
55 - Names of Jesus
66 - Stories in Acts
92 - Heart lesson
102 - Carol, Jesus
113 - Church
110 - Soldier
149 - Love - heart
179 - Jacob's ladder
285 - Prayer wall

GAMES
8 - Dart words
94 - Races
97 - Fast games
112 - Jar Lid race
114 - Recitations
120 - Memory Card Game
321 - extra verses
121 - Baseball Bible Drill
122 - Memory variations
151 - Toss - churches
180 - Jacob's Journey
187 - Bible Arithmetic
216 - Wandering
235 - Bean bags
250 - Miniature Golf
257 - Bible arithmetic
278 - Help our Country
300 - Balloons
320 - Peg Board
328 - Can You Remember?

GARDENS
9 - Sower
91 - Flower garden
166 - Terrariums

GENEALOGY
170 - Chart from Creation
225 - Addition to Chart

HELPING OTHERS
11 - Good deeds
24 - Handicapped picnic
91 - Flower gifts
101 Gifts to Missionaries
124 - Witness, Handicapped
145 - Surprise tree
146 - Macrame hanging
147 - Cards
157 - Bookmarks
182 - Food
184 - Tray
256 - Outing, Handicapped
303 - Scrapbook
334 - Hard work

Day
JIGSAW
110 - Soldier's Armor
142 - Signs of Times
162 - Verses
163 - Verses

MEMORIZE
5 - How to Memorize
82 - Tips
83 - Salvation Fingers
84 - Additional verses
90 - Special verses
96 - Love chapter
104 - Paulean Letters
107 - Galatians 5:22-23
112 - Game
114 - Recitations
120 - Memory Card Game
321 - Additional cards
121 - Baseball Bible drill
122 - Variation game
149 - Love verses
157 - Caring verses
182 - Books of Law
208 - Benediction
258 - Tic-Tac-Toe
284 - OT Books
309 - Alphabet
347 - Prophetic books

OBJECT LESSONS
3 - Light
9 - Sower
21 - Magnetic
29 - Walnut
33 - Ruler
85 - Paper circle
87 - Butterfly
88 - Optical illusions
93 - Stumblingblock
98 - Ball in water
99 - Mirror
103 - Glove
108 - Predestination
110 - Soldier's Armor
113 - Church building
172 - Timing
192 - Light
269 - Picture Character
335 - Potter and Clay

POSTERS
7 - Jesus Cares
15 - Current events
197 - Ten Commandments
233 - Idols
324 - Family

Appendix 57.

Day
PARTIES
24 - Handicapped picnic
56 - We Love Our Families
70 - Bible Club party
97 - Fast games
106 - Clay modeling
114 - Recitations
132 - World-wide party
162-163 - Sunday School
228 - Noah's ark
235 - Bean bags
250 - Miniature Golf
258 - Tic-Tac-Toe
262 - Neighbor Outing
298 - Cookie party
318-319 - Indian party

PHOTOGRAPHY
206 - Picture family altar
295 - Screen displays
298 - Psalm 23; angels
301 - Good photos
308 - Family photos
310 - Hands
311 - Albums, cards
361 - Children in institutions
362 - Family movies
363 - Church photos

PRE-SCHOOLERS
4 - Gather pictures
5. Ask
14 - Magazines
23 - Pictures
36 - Like Jesus
38 - Relief map
39 - Bank
40 - Draw
41 - Lost - game
51 - Obeying
52 - Biscuits
53 - Acting
54 - Blindfolded
55 - Titles of Jesus
57 - Lazarus
60 - What Jesus said
63 - Cube
67 - Rules
77 - Chains
78 - Blindfolded
79 - Almost
80 - Rowboat
83 - Finger memory
94 - Races
96 - Sew cards
97 - Fast games

Day
98 - Ball
99 - Mirror
111 - Act stories
112 - Jar lid race
120 - Memory game
125 - Blocks
126 - March
131 - Obedience
133 - Clothespins
134 - Chalk talk goal
135 - Faith chair
148 - Flower gifts
156 - Show books
158-159 - Potholders
160 - Angels
161 - Files
170 - Family tree
184-185 - Flower tray,
186 - Dress up/tag.
196 - Take a journey
204 - Pretend
208 - Town
217 - Tambourines
237 - Strong
254 - Crowns
258 - Sorting
280 - Draw
281 - Fans
292 - Pompons
306-307 - Collectors
310 - Mold hands
320 - Toss
364 - Bible chain

QUIZ, BIBLE STUDIES
40 - Geographical
51 - Miracles
53 - Titles of Jesus
60 - Lord's prayer
71-72 - Holy Spirit
78 - Geographical
79 - True or False
99 - Beholding Christ
109,111 - Christ in Me
113 - Church
116 - Outline of Future
123 - Divisions of Bible
126 - Victory
131 - Judgments
133-134 - Faith
138-139 - Prayer
142 - Signs of Times
148 - Love
152 - Churches
156 - Prophecy
160 - Angels

Day
170,226 - Genealogy
173, T or F, Angels
185 - Joseph vs. Jesus
227 - Moses vs. Jesus
231 - Heirs
238 - Judges
249 - Anger
280 - God
282 - Dates
285 - Prayer wall
327 - Prophecies
329-330 - Man
332 - Jerusalem
344 - Unusual prayers
357 - Women

MAPS
38 - NT Holy Land
73 - Paul's 1st Journey
74 - Second Journey
76 - Third Journey
171 - Abraham's Journey
196 - Israel's Wanderings
214 - Relief map, Israel
271 - Captivity lands

SCENES & BOOK PICTURES
1 - Wise men
2 - Baptism
6 - Healing
10 - Walk on water
12 - Transfiguration
17 - Trial
18 - Resurrection
19 - Paralytic
22 - 5,000 Fed
28 - Gethsemane
30 - Nativity
31 - Shepherds
32 - Temple
33 - Fishers
35 - Storm
37 - Good Samaritan
43 - Zaccheus
46 - Crucifixion
49 - Jesus, Nicodemus
50 - Woman at well
57 - Lazarus
58 - Triumphal entry
59 - Last Supper
62 - Appearance
64 - Ascension
167 - Ark
176 - Abraham, Isaac
189 - Moses, bush
199 - Tabernacle

Day
246 - David, Goliath
263-264 - Mt. Carmel
265 - Elijah
266 - Elisha
337-343 - Village
352-355 - Daniel

SEWING
69 - Moccasins
96 - Cards
183 - Smock
365 - UN skirt

SINGING
89 - Song books
283 - Jerusalem wall
286 - Action songs
287 - March, instruments

TEEN CLUB
69 - Start
74 - Trips
90 - Memorize
101 - Offering box
105 - True stories
106-107 - Clay modeling
115 - Balloons
120 - 1 Timothy 4:12
174 - Volunteer work
211 - Trip
348-351 - Music boxes

VALENTINE'S DAY
56 - Family party
92, 149 - Flannelgraph
148 - Quiz on Love

WITNESSING
86 - Books, Scenes
100 - Gifts
115 - Balloons
145 - Literature
156 - Jesus books
192 - Light
195 - 5-Day Club
266 - Elisha's Miracles

Day
WORD ACROSTICS, PUZZLES
5 - Acrostics
13 - Tricky verses
36 - Scrambled words
88 - Illusions - Faith
125 - Acrostics
144 - Acrostic L
177 - Scrambled words
181, 194, 255, 270, 278
190 - Squares in circle

WORD BLOCKS, CROSSWORDS
4 - Birds, Fowl, Insects
14 - Plants, Trees
16 - Apostles
23 - Parables of Jesus, stories
41 - Geographical
55 - Jesus
60 - Sayings, Teachings of Jesus
73 - Spirit
112 - Christ in Me
126 - Victory
135 - Faith
161 - Angels
182 - Sons of Jacob
186 - Genesis
207 - Leviticus
217 - Miracles, Moses
237 - Samson
254 - Crowns
281 - God
312 - Praise
331 - Man
347 - Minor Prophets
358 - Women
364 - Books of Bible

Appendix 59.

ALPHABETICAL INDEX OF ACTIVITIES - BY PAGE

Appendix 62.